The Victim as Hero

The Victim as Hero

Ideologies of Peace and National Identity
in Postwar Japan

JAMES J. ORR

UNIVERSITY OF HAWAI'I PRESS

Honolulu

Printed in the United States of America

06 05   6 5 4 3 2

Library of Congress Cataloging-in-Publication Data

Orr, James Joseph.
   The victim as hero : ideologies of peace and national identity in
postwar Japan / James J. Orr.
      p.   cm.
   Includes bibliographical references and index.
   ISBN 0–8248–2355–9 (cloth : alk. paper) —
ISBN 0–8248–2435–0 (pbk. : alk. paper)
   1. Atomic bomb victims—Japan—Hiroshima-shi.   2. Atomic bomb
victims—Japan—Nagasaki-shi.   3. Atomic bomb—Japan—Psychological
aspects.   4. Hiroshima-shi (Japan)—History—Bombardment, 1945.
5. Nagasaki-shi (Japan)—History—Bombardment, 1945.   6. Japan—
Intellectual life—1945–   I. Title.

D767.25.H6 O77 2001
940.54'25—dc21

                                        00–064897

Publication of this book has been assisted by a grant from the Kajiyama
Publications Fund for Japanese History, Culture, and Literature at the
University of Hawai'i at Mānoa.

University of Hawai'i Press books are printed on acid-free paper and
meet the guidelines for permanence and durability of the Council on
Library Resources.

Designed by Kenneth Miyamoto
Printed by The Maple-Vail Book Manufacturing Group

Contents

Acknowledgments

LIBRARIANS never receive their fair due. Among the many who have assisted in this project, it gives me great pleasure to acknowledge a few who have been particularly helpful: Emiko Moffitt of the East Asian Collection of the Hoover Institution; Naomi Kotake, also at the Hoover; Sekiko McDonald at Yale University's Sterling Library; Zoya Jenks of Bucknell's Bertrand Library; Nakamura Kikuji of the Textbook Research Center in Tokyo; Fujimura Megumi at Tokyo Shoseki's Textbook Museum; and last but not least, Koide Izumi of the International House of Japan.

I owe a deep debt of gratitude to mentors Susan B. Hanley, Kozo Yamamura, and Kenneth B. Pyle at the University of Washington and Peter Duus at Stanford University. I should also like to thank others who have stimulated my thinking on victim consciousness and Japanese remembrance of war, including James Ketelaar (formerly at Stanford, now at the University of Chicago), Kano Masanao of Waseda University, Muramatsu Michio of Kyoto University, Nakamura Masanori of Hitotsubashi University, Ronald P. Toby (at the University of Illinois and the University of Tokyo), David Titus of Wesleyan University, J. Victor Koschmann of Cornell University, Ray Moore of Amherst College, and Kevin Doak of the University of Illinois. I would also like to thank the anonymous reviewers at the University of Hawai'i Press for their astute and direct comments. Heartfelt thanks to Patricia Crosby and Masako Ikeda at the press for their efficiency and good humor and to Don Yoder for his professional copyediting. I would also like to thank Sharon Minichiello for her encouragement in bringing this manuscript to press. At Bucknell, I have benefited from the support of departmental colleagues Erik Lofgren, Paul Noguchi, James R. Pusey, and Mary Evelyn Tucker.

The following have provided financial and institutional support: University of Washington Committee for Japanese Studies; Stanford University Department of History; Japan Foundation; Bucknell University Office of the Dean, College of Arts and Sciences; Northeast Asia Council of the Association of Asian Studies; and the Center for Japanese Studies at the University of Michigan.

I would also like to thank Robert Eskildsen, Gregory Pflugfelder, Azumi Ann Takata, and Martha Tocco for collegial support in the early stages of the project. My parents, Raymond J. and Wilma B. Orr, fostered my curiosity and an ethic of constancy that have helped me see this project to completion. Finally, I wish to thank Margaret Wismer for her emotional support and for keeping things in perspective.

CHAPTER 1

Victims, Victimizers, and Mythology

Without planning it, we have for the moment been liberated politically. But if we push responsibility for the continuance of slavery conditions onto the military, police, and bureaucracy without seriously reflecting on our own guilt in permitting their dominance, then there will never come a time when the Japanese people will be redeemed.

—Itami Mansaku (1946)

There is a kind of indulgence *(amae)* that especially adheres to the victim experience. Label this indulgent psychology "victim consciousness" *(higai-sha ishiki)*. Indulgent reliance on it blurs the fact that we were, in principle at least, among the perpetrators in the war. We should have carefully gauged our own complicity in waging war and made a sharp distinction between it and our victim experience. . . . But it is an important fact that at some moment we conspicuously lost consciousness that we ourselves might have been perpetrators *(kagaisha)*. The only inevitable and outrageous conclusion from this is that everyone had been "fooled," that everyone was indiscriminately and unlimitedly a victim; but of course on the basis of this conclusion it was impossible to determine who had victimized whom and in what respect—who had "fooled" whom and how. It was easy to use the victim experience as a wedge to cut ourselves off from the state, assigning all blame to it, and leaving it as a mere abstraction, devoid of any constituent people who had subjective responsibility for having deceived.

—Oda Makoto (1966)

In Japan, every one from successive prime ministers to the Communist Party has repeatedly declared [us] "the only nation ever to have been atom-bombed" *(yuiitsu no hibakukoku)*. Putting aside for the moment the fact that they were forgetting the American soldiers who were exposed in the Nevada tests and the Pacific aboriginals of Bikini and Eniwetok, I feel that this declaration is replete with the single-minded assertion that Japanese were the victims of the atomic bomb. Why did the citizens of Hiroshima and Nagasaki become victims? Do the Japanese hold no responsibility whatsoever? Can you state simply that the citizens of Hiroshima were injured as if they one day suddenly met with some natural disaster? So long as we continue to avoid this issue, we will have to admit that there is cause, for example, for Chinese to make an issue of Japan's war of aggression or for Americans to call out loudly, "Remember Pearl Harbor!"

—Imahori Seiji (1985)

F ROM the end of World War II until Japan became an acknowledged mercantilist success in the 1960s, Japanese presented themselves as first and foremost a cultured, peace-loving nation. The prime axiom of their pacifist sentiment, a rejection of war institutionalized in Article 9 of the postwar constitution, was a resolve never again to experience a debacle on the order of their defeat in World War II. There were many permutations in the pacifist equation, but one central contested variable was war responsibility—though it was sometimes unclear whether it was the moral responsibility for waging a war of aggression or the strategic responsibility of losing it. If Japan were to avoid tragedy in the future, it was imperative that those responsible either learn from their mistakes or be removed from positions of authority. In either case, a thorough self-examination was regarded as necessary if Japan were to avoid another such destructive war.

Such self-examination was complicated by the fact—increasingly true after U.S. occupation policy shifted from reforming a vanquished enemy to nurturing a stable Cold War ally—that many within the ruling conservative leadership had played important roles in conducting Japan's last war. As a group they were naturally reticent in the public dialogue to address issues of personal and national responsibility for wartime actions, especially while the Shōwa emperor's own responsibility remained incompletely addressed. Not surprisingly, after the Yoshida Shigeru administration committed post-Occupation Japan to limited rearmament within a U.S. security arrangement, political progressives saw the conservative-led government as the inheritor of the prewar militarist state legacy. From their position as the perennial government opposition, Communists and Socialists consistently demanded that the conservative leadership acknowledge Japan's past as aggressor and attacked the postwar government on the grounds that its policies would only bring back the suffering caused by war. They tried to mobilize the masses against remilitarization by appealing to their moral revulsion at war suffering in general as well as their personal interest in avoiding becoming war victims again. For their part, conservatives found it easiest to deflect progressive accusations by proclaiming their own sincere regret over human suffering without granting the progressive case against them.

Progressive activists took the initiative in organizing a peace movement to lobby against what they perceived to be the government's relapse into the prewar sins of militarism and the police state. Although the peace movement was founded on the twin pillars of "the victim experience arising from wartime suffering and the victimizer experience as supporters of the war of aggression,"[1] by the 1960s it had come to rely increasingly on images of the Japanese people as war victims. The mythicizing of war victimhood within the peace movement manifested a tendency to privilege the facts of Japanese victimhood over considerations of what occasioned that victimhood. In its most common form this tendency appeared in the restricted contexts of discourse on personal Japanese war experiences in stories of the atomic and fire bombings, the repatriation of civilians from Manchuria and Korea, and general privations such as hunger on the home front. Memories of Japanese victimizing others were not always forgotten. But in many of the antiwar narratives that were asserted to represent the common war experience, issues of individual or collective responsibility for Japanese aggression were sidestepped. Where such aggression and attendant responsibility were articulated, their agency was typically divorced from "the people," whether this collectivity was understood as the proletarian masses *(minshū)*, a national citizenry *(kokumin)*, or an ethnic nation *(minzoku)*.[2] In the typical victim narrative, this transference of aggressive subjectivity usually involved placing the now innocent Japanese people on the high ground of victimhood; the role of victimizer was assigned to the military, to the militarist state, or to the vaguely defined entity called simply "the system." How Japanese pacifism and its supporting construction of the war experience came to rely on an image of self as victim, to the neglect of consciousness of self as victimizer, is the first subject of this study.

The most noted Japanese writer on the political consequences of victim consciousness is social critic and political activist Oda Makoto. Oda is perhaps best known for his prominent role in Beheiren, the grassroots citizens' movement that expressed solidarity with the Vietnamese people against the U.S. war in Vietnam in the 1960s. In a celebratory address in the late 1970s, one of Oda's contemporaries from the Beheiren years credited him with helping to expose the mechanisms of the victim consciousness:

Before Oda appeared on the stage, the discourse on peace in Japan
consisted mostly of talk about Japanese as victims. As a result of visiting Hanoi [under Oda's lead], we self-conscious victims realized that
we were victimizers *(kagaisha)* as well. In the peace movement
before Oda appeared, we were human beings who had been victimized by the atomic bomb. It was a peace movement that was against
anybody else ever being injured in the same way again. That changed
significantly after the 1960 Security Treaty. . . . We realized that the
nation of Japan was also a victimizer. We had victimized Korea in
the past and were victimizing Vietnam in the present. This victimizer
thesis was a major pillar of the [Beheiren] movement.[3]

Oda shared with other progressive peace activists a profound antagonism toward state authority. For him, as he claimed for other Japanese, it was the experience of being betrayed and thus effectively victimized by the Japanese state in the final years of the war that truly
liberated individual Japanese from the tyranny of state thought control. He saw this liberation as exceedingly beneficial, since it helped
establish the individual's autonomy from state authority. When people
understood the state to have been their oppressor, they adopted an
absolutist pacifism that denied the state the right ever to force its
people into war again. But there was a downside: the neglect of one's
own past as victimizer left one susceptible to future manipulation.
Projecting personal responsibility for victimizing onto the state, Oda
argued, "prevented us from totally separating ourselves from state
authority. By using the state as a scapegoat, we perpetuated our dependence upon it."[4] As Oda perceived it in 1966, the state had re-
asserted its hold on individuals through the co-option of the victim
mythology: "Our own victimization, now skillfully portrayed as the
ordeal of the Japanese people collectively, has become, willy-nilly, a
state experience. The state has adopted our victim experience as its
own; it is now viewed as only one element, or aspect, of the victimization of the state itself. In the course of that transformation, we have
again identified ourselves with the state, depended upon it, and fallen
into its grasp."[5] Without a critical understanding of their own past
as victimizer, according to Oda, the Japanese people were unable to
challenge the Japanese state's contemporary complicity in waging a
war of aggression in Vietnam. "Our immediate task, therefore, is to
unearth our own experiences as victimizer (or our potential for such
experiences) and indict them dispassionately and tenaciously."[6]

While Oda's analysis of the disempowering consequences of over-
indulgence in victim consciousness is astute, he was neither the first

nor the last to point out the danger of a myopic victimhood—to call for reclaiming the Japanese past as victimizer. His concern with establishing an autonomous self, capable of holding its own against the principle of ultimate state authority, is rooted in the same "community of contrition" discourse that includes the "subjectivity" (shutaisei) debates of the early Occupation.[7] Social commentators, mostly progressive intellectuals but also moderate conservatives (such as the banker Yoshida Mitsuru), had periodically warned of the need to remember Japan's past as perpetrator in World War II as well as one's personal participation in it. This group included such well-respected social commentators as Ōkuma Nobuyuki and Nanbara Shigeru during the Occupation, Kamei Katsuichirō and Maruyama Masao in the middle 1950s, and Shimizu Ikutarō and Sakamoto Yoshikazu in the years around renewal of the U.S. Security Treaty in 1960. These last two even framed their comments with the same terms Oda used: higaisha and kagaisha.

Shimizu Ikutarō's comments in a 1959 Sekai essay are particularly helpful in placing Oda's thoughts on victim consciousness in historical context. Referring to the Lucky Dragon Incident of March 1954, when a Japanese tuna trawler was caught in radioactive fallout from a U.S. hydrogen bomb test at Bikini Atoll, Shimizu reflected:

> It is natural and right that ever since Bikini, the ban-the-bomb movement has been at the center of the peace movement. But . . . the Bikini incident became an *opportunity* for victim consciousness to become widespread and strong among us. . . . Every time I recall those years—and I think it would have been hard to avoid this—I think that in the shadow of an enhanced victim consciousness, that bitter, vexing postwar awareness of having victimized (kagaisha ishiki) . . . gradually became weaker. Put rather simply, the subjectivity (shutaisei) that is [informed by] the victimizer's dark contrition . . . withdrew to the rear, and a passive victim consciousness came to the fore. . . . In order to regain our subjectivity, the first thing is to readdress . . . our pasts as victimizers and, accordingly, our ethical problem relating to the Chinese people. . . . Only after a thoroughgoing reflection on our past as victimizers will we have the subjectivity to face the increasing possibility of becoming victimizers again via a revival of imperialism or the American military alliance. So long as we remain merely victims and passive beneficiaries, we will easily become victimizers, and ultimately victimizers who die shameful deaths.[8]

Aside from the striking similarity regarding victim consciousness in Shimizu's 1959 essay and Oda's 1966 essay, one significant omission in Oda's essay is the sense that consciousness as victimizer ever played an essential role in Japanese pacifism. His Beheiren contemporary's statement in the late 1970s seems to corroborate this impression. The explanation is generational. Oda was thirteen years old in firebombed Osaka at the end of the war. He had no direct experience as a victimizer during the war, and with the revelations about Japan's aggressions he felt betrayed rather than contrite.[9] Furthermore, Oda ascribes his own earlier insensitivity toward victims of Japanese aggression to the fact that, in the two decades since the end of the war, the vast majority of personal recollections had been written from the vantage point of the victim—so much so that the war memories became in the public mind victim memories.[10] Oda's significance lay in the fact that he was the first of his postwar generation of peace activists to publicize his discovery that victim consciousness had blinded them to Japanese responsibility for past victimizing.

The mythologies of Japanese war victimhood, then, reached a critical period of common acceptance in the third decade of Shōwa (1955–1965), when the first postwar generation was coming into its own in adult society. Oda Makoto, the first of his generation to recognize the inadequacies of victim consciousness, began a reawakening in public discourse to the people's past as victimizer—an awakening at the very least for the postwar generations. For despite the very real tendencies noted by Oda, expressions of such awareness continued to occur in the decade after the Occupation. This awakening was long in coming. Even as confessions of victimizing experiences became more common in the 1970s and 1980s,[11] victim iconography had become entrenched in television dramas, movies, and other mass entertainment. The Shōwa emperor's death in 1989 unleashed a torrent of debate over personal war responsibility—forty-five years after the war's end—not only over the emperor's responsibility but that of individual Japanese as well.[12] The victim consciousness that Oda wrote about in the middle 1960s became a commonly discussed issue. *Higaisha* (victim) and *kagaisha* (victimizer) became part of the vocabulary of the day and figured prominently in the discourse on personal remorse for wartime actions long left unvoiced. Confessions of individual responsibility, sometimes with specifics of the regretted acts, flooded radio and television broadcasts, newspapers, journals, and other printed media. Even though peace activists in the 1960s were reminded of their indirect complicity in supporting Japan's war of aggression when they confronted their country's support for the American war in Vietnam, it took more time for mass consciousness to fully grasp the connection.[13]

Like any other ideological structure, the image of the Japanese people as war victims served multiple agendas, and this utility helps to explain its longevity in Japanese public discourse on war. Apart from its obvious effectiveness in creating visceral antiwar sentiment, war victim consciousness was promoted by Allied psychological warfare agents and Occupation authorities to encourage alienation from the wartime state and its military—and, after the conservative return to power, by left-wing activists to condemn in a coded way the postwar state and its Cold War U.S. security alliance. Conservative politicians appropriated the rhetoric of Japanese war victimhood in recognition of electoral pacifist sentiment, with the added benefit that in doing so they could position themselves apart from the militarist period and perhaps evade discussion of Japanese war responsibility. Once the war victim had become an icon of the nation's pacifist heritage, then interest groups such as the 3 million repatriates from Japan's overseas empire, and even landlords dispossessed of their tenanted land in the Occupation land reforms, tried to claim status as war victims in order to gain compensation from the state. How these groups used war victimhood to their own advantage is the second task of this study.

A critical step toward the privileging of victim consciousness lay in the sense of betrayal at the end of the war, when the ultimate sacrifice for the good of the state that was understood as "honorable death" *(gyokusai)* turned into what Oda called a "meaningless death" *(nanshi)*.[14] Chapter 2, "Leaders and Victims: Personal War Responsibility During the Occupation," describes how in the early years after defeat, during the U.S. occupation, people came to feel they had been wrongfully treated by their wartime leaders. In Japan there is a significant body of literature on how the Tokyo War Crimes Trials encouraged people to absolve themselves of personal war responsibility,[15] but most of these studies are focused on war responsibility itself, not the foundations of an emerging victim mythology. Chapter 2 discusses the interplay of American policies toward wartime leaders, the emperor, and "the people" who were to be democratized and the Japanese reaction to those policies.

The vision of the Japanese as innocent war victims reached its purest expression in the public dialogue over nuclear weapons. The Hiroshima and Nagasaki bombings privileged the Japanese nation with an exclusive claim to leadership in the global ban-the-bomb movement and provided the country with its first powerfully unifying national myth after defeat. Yet this "atomic victim exceptionalism" did not arise until the middle 1950s when the Bikini hydrogen bomb test created a third set of Japanese *hibakusha,* or atomic bomb victims. Chapter 3, "Hiroshima and *Yuiitsu no hibakukoku:* Atomic Victimhood in the Antinuclear Peace Movement," describes the political and cultural meanings that "Hiroshima" carried from 1945 to the early 1960s. As we shall see, the strongest impetus for victim consciousness can be found in scholar-activist Yasui Kaoru's efforts to expand the antinuclear peace movement from a Communist and Socialist project into a bona fide nonpartisan national movement after the Lucky Dragon Incident of 1954. Yasui, a former Tokyo University professor who found a local outlet for his peace activism as director of the Suginami Ward Community Center, led the nationwide antibomb petition movement that garnered over 30 million signatures and set the stage for annual ban-the-bomb world conventions, the first national medical aid program for *hibakusha,* and the establishment of an institutional base for the movement in the form of Gensuikyō (Japan Council Against Atomic and Hydrogen Bombs). By defining Hiroshima's meaning in ways accommodating to both left and right, Yasui helped recall pacifism to center stage at a time when conservative pressure to remilitarize was extreme. Although national identification with atomic victimhood quickly reached its limits in transcending conventional political disagreements over the military and economic accommodation with the United States, Hiroshima became a Cold War synecdoche of Japan's war victim experience that continues to inform Japan's pacifist identity, most concretely reflected in the three nonnuclear principles.

Chapter 4, "Educating a Peace-Loving People: Narratives of War in Postwar Textbooks," focuses on how the Asia-Pacific War in the 1930s and 1940s was presented in grammar and middle school social studies texts. Occupation-era texts established two perennial themes in postwar schoolbooks: the people were shown to have been forced or duped by their militarist leadership into cooperating with the war effort; and the proper means for Japan to contribute to the postwar international community was asserted to be in the realm of science and culture. In the middle 1950s, the ban-the-bomb movement that arose from the Lucky Dragon Incident and enthusiasm for Asian national independence surrounding the Bandung Conference led to a sudden assertion of Japan's special pacifist mission as the world's only people to have been atom-bombed, as well as a gradual tendency to portray the story of Asian peoples' liberation from Western and Japanese colonialism.

Immediately after the Ministry of Education implemented stricter textbook certification procedures in 1957, texts presented Japan's pre-war policies (apart from the military's predations) as understandable in the climate of 1930s international diplomacy. The Japanese people were portrayed as generally supportive of their government; but the military generally continued to be portrayed as the ultimate victimizer of both Asians and Japanese. At times the premilitarist civilian government is described in ways similar to the Japanese people, who shared with Asian peoples a heritage of suffering as victims either directly at the hands of the Japanese military or from war as an abstract force.

The apologist leanings diminish by the early 1970s, when the most widely used texts project an image of the Japanese people as a kind of "ethnic nation" (minzoku) set apart from the wartime Japanese state or the Japanese military as an international aggressor. Texts implicitly linked the Japanese "people" and Asian "peoples" together as common victims of the Japanese military, and war was to be rejected because of this victimization. In the middle 1970s, textbooks dramatically increase their treatment of Korean and Chinese suffering. And while the Japanese people are still portrayed as mutual victims of the Japanese army, their victim status does not entirely exempt them from responsibility for discriminating against Koreans or, for example, dispossessing Chinese farmers in Manchuria in the 1930s.

One of the main criticisms made of Japanese antiwar literature is that it is suffused with victim consciousness. In Chapter 5, " 'Sentimental Humanism': The Victim in Novels and Film," I analyze three popular antiwar novels and films to demonstrate how basic themes of war victimhood are reflected and reinforced. Tsuboi Sakae's novel *Nijūshi no hitomi* (Twenty-Four Eyes) and Kinoshita Keisuke's film version provide ideal examples of the victim genre in which Japanese civilians are innocent victims of the anonymous forces of war. Gomikawa Junpei and Kobayashi Masaki's *Ningen no jōken* (The Human Condition) are among the most soul-searching works in the antiwar genre. The protagonist serves as a test case in exploring how well a sincerely humanist intellectual could have maintained his autonomous subjectivity during the war. In many ways this work belies the idea that representations of Japanese as war victims clouded awareness of Japanese as victimizers. It is harsh in its condemnation of wartime state policies and the military; it describes in unflinching detail individual cases of Japanese brutality; yet themes of Japanese victimhood do form an essential part of the story's moral. Ibuse Masuji's *Kuroi ame* (Black Rain), the most popular artistic treatment of Hiroshima, received conservative accolades for making the atomic bomb experi-

ence more approachable for "normal" Japanese. Although it contains
antiestablishment rhetoric, the conservative audience interpreted it as
an affirmation of traditional Japanese values (which supported that
establishment). *Black Rain* helped conservatives embrace atomic
victim exceptionalism in a less threatening form than the progressive
ban-the-bomb movement, for "the people" were portrayed not as a
revolutionary force but as a wise folk.

Chapter 6, "Compensating Victims: The Politics of Victimhood,"
shows how in the 1960s the victim mythology had become political
capital that special interests could manipulate for their own benefit.
In a time of resurgent interest in nationalism as a positive force in the
country, the government instituted memorial services for war victims,
civilian as well as military. Veterans and bereaved families had been
awarded compensation since the end of the Occupation in 1952, and
hibakusha have slowly received medical care and other benefits since
1957. But in the 1960s other groups such as the repatriates and former
landholders laid claim to status as victims. The "consensus politics"
of the Ikeda and Satō administrations allowed for many ambiguities,
and in granting state compensation for private losses, the government
bordered on valorizing these victim experiences as service to the state.
This was an era in which the victim became the hero for Japan not
only metaphorically but in monetary terms as well.

A fascination with one's victimhood to the extent that it becomes
an integral part of a communal identity is not unique to the Japanese.
Centuries of routinized prejudice and periodic persecution, burned
into European and hence world consciousness with the Nazi holocaust, have made victimhood an integral part of Jewish identity.[16]
Depending on background and sensibility, one might cite numerous
other groups who have at one time or another invested what might
be called heritages of oppression, not all of which neatly fit the category of nation-state or even ethnic group. Examples that come immediately to mind are Armenians, the Irish, African-Americans, homo-
sexuals, and women. The closest example to the Japanese case is the
experience of the former West Germany, for that nation was in a similar situation of defeat, occupation, and reconstruction within a Cold
War alliance with its former enemies. In this regard, I have benefited
from Robert G. Moeller's essay on German victim consciousness in
which he notes how veterans and ethnic Germans expelled from
Eastern Europe by the Soviet Red Army at the end of World War II became symbolic of all Germans' war victimization.[17] As in the Federal
Republic of Germany, in Japan it continues to be widely lamented that

the Japanese are handicapped by not having fully addressed the issue of war responsibility immediately after the war. In Germany the themes of German victimhood are commonly thought to have been predominant in public memory in the first postwar decade, then supplanted in the 1960s and 1970s by a reawakening to German victimization of others, only to reemerge in the 1980s. In Japan, the timetable is delayed but similar. The narratives of Japanese war victimhood became more prominent in the second decade after the war, that is, from 1955 to 1965, until the anti–Vietnam War movement initiated a continuing rise in themes of Japanese victimizing others through the decades of the 1970s and 1980s. As Moeller shows in the German case, "remembering selectively was not the same as forgetting." In each period one encounters the expressions of the opposite side of the binary formulation of victim/victimizer consciousness.

Yet as others have shown, the German and Japanese cases differ significantly in their historical context, suggesting that the German *Vergangenheitsbewältigung* sense of responsibility for the Nazi past was more concrete than the Japanese *sensō sekinin* sense of responsibility for wartime aggression. While Germans were able to condemn the National Socialists for usurping state power, the Japanese condemned the militarists but had to confront the continuities between wartime and postwar in state personnel and civil bureaucracy. And while in Germany the occupying powers consisted mainly of Germany's victims, in Japan the major victims, various Asian peoples, found little representation in the occupying forces. One repercussion of this was a relative absence in Japan proper of forced confrontation with the worst excesses of Japanese aggression, such as the Unit 731 medical experiments in Manchuria, forced labor of Chinese, Koreans, and other Asian peoples, and wartime mobilization policies that disrupted local economies throughout Japanese-occupied Asia.[18]

Besides these historical differences, there are at least two culturally specific practices that help account for the ease with which war victim consciousness could thrive in Japan. The first is the literary genre of *hōganbiiki*, so ably illustrated by Ivan Morris in his classic *Nobility of Failure*. With its emphasis on the nobility of sacrifice to a losing cause, *hōganbiiki* evoked an aura of sentimentality around tales of futile suffering. With a traditional literary practice that gave aesthetic value to what otherwise might seem meaningless death, tales of Japanese war victimhood—whether the youthful suicides of the *tokkōtai* kamikaze corps or the travails and eventual forced suicide/murder of the *himeyuri butai* girl nurse corps in the battle of Okinawa—could be remembered with a kind of self-indulgent pathos. Couple this strong sentimentality with the heartfelt but easy conclusion that such suffering makes war unacceptable, and one ends up weakening the critical eye as well as the motivation to probe the causes of such war victimhood.

The mention of self-indulgence brings us to another idea in the pantheon of *Nihonjinron* (Japanese identity theory) themes of Japanese behavior: psychiatrist Takeo Doi's concept of *amae*. It should be stated from the first that Doi is very clear that the emotion and resultant behavior he describes as typically Japanese constitute a psychological pattern in all cultures. Doi simply claims that it is particularly well recognized in Japan. Briefly put, to *amaeru* means "to presume on familiarity to 'make up to' the other . . . in order to behave in a self-indulgent manner." Often the other is in a position of authority over oneself—as a parent to a child—and as in the parent/child relationship there is a prerequisite presumption of intimacy and an underlying desire to identify with the other. *Amae* is the emotion arising from the desire to deny the pain of separation from this other. In regard to war victim consciousness, on a superficial level this theory suggests a national proclivity to presume on other nations' indulgence in allowing Japan to avoid war responsibility—a line of argument that is itself a tempting but rather dangerous indulgence in national character study. Doi himself addresses victim consciousness among the New Left of the 1960s, a movement that included Beheiren as well as the more radical and violent student organizations such as the Zenkyōtō. Writing about the period of student unrest in the late 1960s, Doi observes: "What interested me was the odd way in which students of Zenkyōtō, though behaving as victimizers, frequently aroused in their victims a sense that they themselves were the victimizers. . . . The reason was, ultimately, because the students were putting themselves in the position of victims." At one point the students preached a strategy of self-negation designed to reject bourgeois privilege—to reject a latent bourgeois self-complacency, "a lurking desire to pretend not to see the victim . . . [that] is the same as arraying oneself with the guilty." Not denying that many left-wing activists took constructive action to aid past and present victims based on combined feelings of guilt and charity, Doi argues that a pathology arises when one adopts the victim position merely to avoid one's own feelings of guilt. Denial of one's privileges in these cases becomes denial in the psychological sense, involving transference of aggression, and in extreme cases develops into a paranoia about a "vast and repressive social organization, on which [New Left activists] launch a bold assault."[19]

In the course of research, I have encountered many who think of victim consciousness as a conservative tactic to avoid responsibility. This is an unsatisfactory conclusion. First, a victim mindset simply does not fit the style of proud, self-consciously virile conservatives such as Nakasone Yasuhiro. And second, the focus on war victimhood seems more characteristic of the liberal view of war as evil: as Doi's analysis indicates, even the most radical left indulges in it. In the pages that follow, I will show that victim consciousness has been used by groups from across the political spectrum and has led to conscientious civic activism and, as well, to avoidance of responsibility.

CHAPTER 2

Leaders and Victims
Personal War Responsibility During the Occupation

> Being deceived means that you have been injured at the hands of the unjust, but it is not necessarily written . . . that the deceived are in the right. Those who mistakenly think that just by saying they were deceived they are thereby relieved of all guilt, and can unconditionally join the just, must reconsider their position.
>
> —Itami Mansaku (1946)

O N the Shōwa emperor's forty-fifth birthday, the day after film director Itami Mansaku wrote these words, the Supreme Command for the Allied Powers (SCAP) announced its list of twenty-eight wartime leaders to be tried as A-class war criminals by the International Military Tribunal for the Far East. The trials were meant to be the instrument of "stern justice" that had been promised in the Potsdam Declaration, but they also served an educational purpose. SCAP operated under the assumption that because the Japanese people had been slaves to feudal habits of subservience to authority, their leadership had consequently been able to deceive them as to the real nature of the war. Through the agency of a public tribunal, they were to be taught about the atrocities committed by the Japanese army in their name and impressed with the necessity of exercising control over their leadership instead of obeying them blindly. In other words, the trials were meant to further the process of democratizing Japanese governance.

Although the public soon lost interest in the trials as they dragged on, other SCAP reeducation efforts were extremely effective. All but the most unrepentant chauvinists condemned the wartime state's actions, if only because they resulted in defeat and great suffering among the Japanese people. Most Japanese regretted their complicity in the nation's acts of aggression and found deliverance in the noble goal of rebuilding their country into a "peaceful and cultural state." But the Allied powers' construction of the war, which imagined a conspiracy of militarists and radical nationalists who were responsible for Japanese aggression, encouraged the attitude that Japanese, both as individuals and as a people, were somehow less accountable for their own wartime activities. In the passage just quoted, Itami criticized communists and newborn democrats who neglected to reflect on their own complicity even as they righteously worked to purge the establishment of people they deemed warmongers and fascist oppressors. But the mechanism against which he railed—the notion of innocence adhering to those who claimed victimhood—became integral to the postwar national mythology of victimhood. During the Occupation, the kernel of this mythology—the idea that the Japanese people had been in some sense innocent victims—became accepted as fact in public discourse.

The emperor's relation to war guilt was emblematic of the people's. Both SCAP and the Japanese government encouraged the view that he had been manipulated by the militarist clique; both refashioned his image as a kindly family man who well illustrated postwar Japan's peaceful and cultural ethos.[1] The emperor became a "symbol . . . of the unity of the people" in the new democracy, willingly leaving his prewar identity behind. But his symbolic existence was complicated by the fact that, under the new constitutional order, he remained the "symbol of the state" as well. As a public figure, he embodied the state both in its prewar militarist and in its postwar pacifist manifestations. For those who distrusted state authority and would neither forget nor forgive his prewar image, he was a constant reminder of that militarist past and the possibility that government repression might return in the form of the emperor system. He combined in a seeming paradox both remembrance and amnesia about the wartime past as victimizer. This paradoxical existence, protected by the evolving taboo on discussing the emperor's war responsibilities, was the reason his death in 1989 occasioned such widespread soul-searching over personal war guilt.

The Occupation affected the development of a victim mythology in postwar Japan in another less concrete way. One of the late Shōwa criticisms about the Tokyo Trials is that they gave crimes against Asian peoples short shrift.[2] Although this characterization can be contested, it is a fact that the Occupation was overwhelmingly an American affair and committed Japan to membership in the U.S. political and strategic alliance. Viewed through the American prism, the "Greater East Asia War" became the "Pacific War" and was remembered primarily to have been a conflict between Japan and the United States. National contrition for war actions came for a time to be directed mainly toward Americans. Contrition toward Asian peoples—by far the most numerous victims of the Japanese aggression that later liberal commentators such as Tsurumi Shunsuke labeled the "Fifteen-Year War" —could easily be neglected in popular remembrance of a war that began with Pearl Harbor in 1941.[3]

A People Misled

Once the war aims and the prewar social order came under general censure in the media and in SCAP announcements, people were humiliated for having cooperated—or for having permitted themselves to be manipulated into such cooperation—in domestic oppression and foreign exploitation. How did ordinary citizens come to believe in their innocence and think they had so little responsibility for their own suffering? How did the public memory of the war come to stress the Japanese people's experience as innocent victims of the system rather than accomplices to their own and other people's persecution? The first step was assigning guilt for the nation's crimes to the militarists in general and then to individuals among the leadership.

American policies set the framework in which the war was remembered in Japan. Even before the Occupation, Allied planners operated under the assumption that the typical Japanese was merely obeying the authority he or she had been raised to follow unquestioningly. As part of a strategy to encourage the overthrow of a purportedly incompetent and deceitful militarist leadership, perhaps by petition to the emperor, wartime propaganda depicted the people as victims of that leadership. A secret April 1945 report by the Psychological Warfare Branch of the U.S. Army explained the psychological "facts relating to the problem":

> The Japanese are honest, frugal, industrious, and patriotic. . . . They personally have contributed their full measure to the war effort and fulfilled their obligation to the Emperor. All their effort is to no avail because their military leaders have betrayed them. *The people are not to blame for their suffering.* . . . The military clique has practiced false indoctrination. The people have been denied unbiased information from the outside world.[4] [Emphasis added.]

This section of the report continued to assert: "All Japanese are a law-abiding people who posess [*sic*] a strong sense of responsibility." The U.S. wartime propagandists were not concerned with impressing the average Japanese with their own personal responsibilities for the war; rather, they proposed to relieve them of it:

> If people could be made to believe that they themselves are not to blame for disaster but rather that it is the fault of the military clique, it will ease their mental burden. As a scapegoat, the military clique is made to order.

The report concluded with three objectives for psychological warfare: undermine morale; charge the military clique with responsibility for the war; and encourage surrender to the mercy of the United States as the only means of saving self and country from total destruction. Significantly, one means of attaining these objectives was to "drive a wedge between the Emperor and the people on the one hand, and the military clique on the other."[5]

Other reports reflected this same basic strategy of dissociating the Japanese "people" from their government and military. A special intelligence report by the U.S. Foreign Morale Analysis Division recommended in June 1945 that propaganda give the average person hope in defeat:

> While making it perfectly clear to the Japanese that we are going to eliminate the militarists because they went to war with us, we may point out how the militarists have harmed the Japanese and we may make it clear that we have no intention of punishing the Japanese people once the militarists are overthrown. In this manner, *the militarists may be effectively used as a scapegoat*, with the double result of weakening their hold and leading other people to feel that there is something to hope for in surrender.[6] [Emphasis added.]

The propaganda leaflets dropped on Japanese military units in the Southwest Pacific and on the home islands encouraged conscripts to withdraw their loyalty from their leaders—with the added consequence that they could pretend they were not responsible for the war situation nor for their actions under such extenuating circumstances. For example, one leaflet absolved individual soldiers of the need to feel guilt for atrocities such as killing women and children. It condemned the officers who "cowardly killed defenseless civilians" and criticized their "cushy set-up" which allowed them, after placing their troops in desperate situations through poor strategy, to get away with simply telling soldiers the only way out was to die a divine death.[7]

The import of public Allied statements was no less clear, especially when promising vengeance and justice. The American attitude toward the people's responsibility for the war was well expressed in the Potsdam Declaration's intentions toward "those self-willed militaristic advisers whose unintelligent calculations have brought the Empire of Japan to the threshold of annihilation." Article 6 promised a purge of those responsible: "There must be eliminated for all time the authority and influence of those who have deceived and misled the people of Japan into embarking on world conquest, for we insist that a new order of peace, security and justice will be impossible until irresponsible militarism is driven from the world." Clearly the target of "stern justice," in the form of the trials and the purge, would not be the average Japanese.[8]

Although the Potsdam Declaration remained ambiguous about the emperor's status, Psychological Warfare Branch policy was to exempt him from war responsibility in its efforts to persuade the Japanese to surrender. The intelligence report of June 1945, for example, concluded with recognition of "the great strength and tenacity on the part of the Japanese beliefs, especially those symbolized by the Emperor. Support is therefore given to those Americans who feel that the duration of the war could be greatly reduced if we combined our attack on the Emperor's militarist advisors with a statement that we are not going to destroy the imperial system nor regard the Emperor as a war criminal."[9] American propaganda for Japan reflected this basic approach and encouraged the belief that he too was being fooled by his advisers. The leaflet titled "Emperor's Birthday," dropped over the home islands in 1945, for example, stated that the military leadership was responsible for the war and it ended with a question: "How much longer can these military leaders continue to deceive the Emperor?"[10]

After the defeat, the Supreme Commander for the Allied Powers, General Douglas MacArthur, adopted the same approach toward both the average Japanese and their emperor. To facilitate the Occupation's goals of demilitarization and democratization, SCAP continued to use the idea that the Japanese people had been misled by their leaders. In his message to the American people on the occasion of signing the documents of surrender, for example, MacArthur described as his task "to see the Japanese people liberated from this condition of slavery" in which they had been denied the freedom even to think for themselves.[11] The idea that defeat liberated the Japanese people from a condition of slavery under an oppressive, militarist government was a common theme in MacArthur's rhetoric. In his statement on the first anniversary of surrender, he declared that before the defeat "control was exercised by a feudalistic overlordship of a mere fraction of the population, while the remaining seventy million, with a few enlightened exceptions, were abject slaves to tradition, legend, mythology, and regimentation."[12] Use of such terms as "liberation" from "slavery" not only promoted America's image as savior; it also suggested that most Japanese need not feel responsible for their own past suffering since they had been victims of the militarists. Democracy was going to give them the responsibility for their future (which they implicitly lacked for their past). As MacArthur phrased it in his 1946 New Year's message to the Japanese: "The removal of this national enslavement [militarism, thought control, and the like] means freedom for the people, but at the same time it imposes upon them the individual duty to think and to act each on his own initiative. It is necessary for the masses of Japan to awaken to the fact that they now have the power to govern and what is done must be done by themselves."[13] The question of popular understanding of the emperor's war guilt will be addressed shortly. For the moment, one might note MacArthur's remembrance of his impression on first meeting with the emperor. After the emperor offered to bear sole responsibility for the actions of his people during the war, MacArthur was moved by this assumption of responsibility that was "clearly belied by facts of which I was fully aware."[14]

The two major instruments of SCAP policy that assigned blame were the Tokyo Trials and the purge. The trials lasted from May 1946 to April 1948 with sentencing and execution of seven wartime leaders at the end of the year.[15] The purge, aimed at removing potential opponents of Occupation reforms, affected over 200,000 people who had held influential positions during the war. The shift in SCAP priorities between 1947 and 1948—from reform to reconstruction—signaled the end of this purge.[16] The salient fact about the trials was that they placed responsibility for the nation's actions squarely on the shoulders of a select few individual leaders.[17] Ōnuma Yasuaki, probably the foremost scholar of the legal and moral implications of the trials, reflects the present consensus view of liberal Japanese academics:

The Tokyo Trials judged one part of the old leadership class categorically apart from the rest of the Japanese people; punished them for [waging] a war of aggression as bellicose militarists; and precisely for that reason the general Japanese public, who were never tried, observed the trials as a third party, so to speak, as people without guilt because they could not be punished.[18]

Ōnuma suggests that Tōjō Hideki became the object of secret resentment during the war, and his prosecution in the trials as the responsible agent enabled the Japanese people, as outsiders to the trials, to see themselves as his victims. He believes that most Japanese thought the sentences were just retribution for the suffering everyone underwent because of the leadership's poor prosecution of the war.[19]

On the whole, people seem to have at first reacted to the Tokyo Trials with an enthusiasm that some called "Tōjō-bashing." Then, as the trials dragged on over two years, general interest flagged. In a parade in Shimane prefecture in June 1946 at the beginning of the trials, a youth group's float titled "Jeep and War Criminals," which consisted of a Jeep with American MPs leading Tokyo Trial defendants, received cheers of approval from the crowds en route. Just a few months after the executions, though, the following poem appeared in the tanka magazine *Mizugame* (March 1949): "The news extra about the trial's decision / fluttering and tossing in the winter wind / No one looks back."[20] Public interest in the question of war responsibility was strongest in the first few years of the Occupation, that is, in the early stages of the trials and SCAP's purge.

During these early years of heightened interest, groups of predominantly communist intellectuals in literature, film, and academia conducted purges of their respective fields in what intellectual historians now call the "debate over war responsibility" *(sensō sekinin-ron)*.[21] These left-wing groups, generally consisting of younger artists below the age of forty, were criticized from the beginning for failing to recognize their own guilt even as they branded others. In this sense they serve as an archetype for the general one-sided consciousness that later proved fertile ground for victim consciousness. Although they did caution themselves that they should be careful to consider their own culpability while they attacked others,[22] their relative youth had prevented many of them from holding incriminating influential posts during the war. The Free Filmmakers Group (Jiyū Eigajin Shu-dan), for example, aimed to purge the industry of influential men who had shown themselves insufficiently repentant for their wartime collaboration. They recognized that "while we were living under a police order, we lacked the courage and knowledge to positively oppose the war."[23] Nevertheless they assiduously blacklisted the older generation of established industry figures.

Men like Itami Mansaku, who because of illness or some other coincidence never held positions of responsibility during the war, were generally left off these vigilante purge lists and were actually praised for their nonsupport of the war. Often these men felt uncomfortable about being accorded such privilege since, as they confessed in published essays, only circumstance had kept them from positions of influence in the war. Itami, for example, thought purge lists were inherently unfair and inappropriate because they indicated a lack of reflection on the fact that almost everyone shared some measure of responsibility for having allowed the system of domestic oppression to exist. Even those who had been deceived into cooperating were morally responsible for having allowed their deception in the first place. The primary task, Itami argued, was to understand one's own weaknesses that allowed such deception: one's "guilt in permitting [the militarists'] domination."[24]

In an essay published in the September 1947 *Bungei shunjū*, Ōkuma Nobuyuki expressed similar concerns about the people's passivity in the face of state authority and the long-term consequences of inadequacies he perceived in popular reflection on war responsibility. He worried that the fabric of the ethnic nation *(minzoku)* was in danger of disintegrating because Japanese were rejecting nationalism and its practices—flying the flag and pledging allegiance to the government—without reflecting deeply on that rejection. He spoke of a "darkness" *(kurasa)* that remained in postwar Japan precisely because people did not recognize the root cause of Japan's debacle in the nation's temperament: "If you think back for once on the character of the war, trying to remember the conditions behind defeat, then [you will see] in those conditions the heart of [that] darkness. . . . And if you look back even more earnestly *(shutaiteki ni)*, you can see that it is war itself and the temperament of the nation *(minzoku)* that caused that kind of war." Even if the individual had been powerless in the face of the oppressive state apparatus, Ōkuma rejected the Manichean assignment of war guilt to the leadership and innocence to the rest. The locus of moral responsibility—and accordingly the root of reform, Ōkuma argued—lay within the individual as a constituent member of the folk. And the lack of autonomous reflection by the individual augured a dark future for the ethnic nation.[25]

Japanese scholars frequently characterize these published self-analyses and self-recriminations as exceptional cases that were generally ignored by their peers.[26] But there are too many examples of such self-consciousness in print to condemn without qualification the artistic and intellectual communities or even society at large for neg-

lecting to examine their own guilt.[27] The preeminent China scholar
Takeuchi Yoshimi, to mention one influential conservative intellectual,
argued with notable passion for Japanese to acknowledge their prewar prejudices against the Chinese. In concluding a 1949 essay on
Chinese and Japanese consciousness of each other in the war, he
recognized the problem of a citizen's personal moral responsibility in
total war:

> It is true that the war of aggression confused the people's sense of
> values and gave rise to the type of moral frigidity of which Lin Yu-
> tang warned [in *Moment in Peking*]; but one can say at the same
> time that the meanness of the people's moral sense made the war of
> aggression possible. And people still have not realized this today.
> . . . Dissolving crimes against humanity into crimes against peace [as
> in the Tokyo Trials] may lighten the weight on one's shoulders but
> it does not solve the problem. Without pursuing crimes against
> humanity with that peculiar meaning, staring unflinchingly at one's
> own barbarity in the mirror, and grasping the chance to resuscitate
> ourselves from those depths by our own strength, without enduring
> that pain, our children and grandchildren cannot hope to be counted
> among the citizens of the world.[28]

On a more popular level, Aragaki Hideo reflected in his widely read
"Tensei jingo" column that everyone had made use of Japan's military
might:

> In China [before the defeat], the person who associated as a simple
> human being with Chinese was as rare as the morning star: everyone
> was a "subject of the great Japanese Empire." Every Tom, Dick, and
> Harry bad-mouths the military clique now; but up until just recently
> it wasn't only the fortune seekers who high-handedly did as they
> wished in a neighboring country, borrowing the authority of the mili-
> tary clique and using the sound of their sabers.[29]

In labor union and youth group publications from the Occupation
era, one finds numerous examples of self-aware essays regarding war
responsibility.[30] One extended passage, from a June 1947 essay by a
demobilized soldier who found work with the National Railways in
Niigata, should serve as an example of the profound understanding
that found expression at the height of the trials:

> We didn't know the rights or wrongs of the war. Doing just as our
> leaders ordered we went to war, our blood boiling with patriotic
> fervor. Be that as it may—now that we have been told and have
> opened our eyes, now that we have been shown this other [demo-

cratic] way of thinking about state and society, especially after learning about the way of living as a human being and the existence of a profound, expansive world—I feel a sense of guilt *(ushirometasa)*, that it isn't enough simply to say we weren't given the knowledge and opportunity at the time. Although we [cooperated] without any awareness of it as such, we are still war collaborators; and when I delve into my own self I sense that the problem is in the hearts and minds of each and every one of us. Can we stand to say without reservation that the leaders are responsible for our being led about, unaware due to our ignorance? Isn't it time for some serious self-reflection? War criminals are being tried in the Tokyo Trials and the purges are driving men out. But if we think that by this all responsibility for the war has been addressed, that we can all rejoice and proceed down the path of democracy . . . [sic]. We must realize that even though we were under compulsion [during the war], there was something Tōjō-like in every one of our hearts and we haven't gotten rid of it yet.[31]

Such warnings suggest, of course, that many who discussed war responsibility acted as if it were the exclusive burden of the former leadership. It may have been that, as Yoshida Mitsuru once complained, the absolute condemnation of everything remotely supportive of war stifled open reflection on the "dark" specifics of that "Tōjō-like something" in everyone's wartime thoughts and actions. Explaining why so few publicly admitted the flaws in their own personal wartime thinking, Yoshida remembered: "Soon after the end of that war, you would have been severely criticized if you honestly admitted your wartime feelings."[32]

This atmosphere of denial suggests one reason why many chose to take the safe course: denouncing the nation's war acts while maintaining a discreet silence on personal involvement. Ironically, SCAP censorship most likely contributed to this inhibition of deep self-analysis (as opposed to shallow condemnation) of wartime sentiment. When Yoshida made his own admissions in *Battleship Yamato* in order to grasp the means to reject his own wartime acts, for example, he was misunderstood and criticized for affirming them. Occupation censors, deciding his honest exploration of wartime thinking came too close to affirming militarist/ultranationalist thought, required him to revise his first draft.[33] The essays by Itami and others suggest a contemporary critical awareness of the common self-deception behind shallow condemnations of the war. When public energy and official priorities turned away from repentance and reform toward reconstruction

after the trials ended—exactly the period when SCAP censorship ended
—it was this incomplete recognition of war responsibility that remained
the safest and most common public position. Even as conscientious a
social commentator as Tokyo University president Nanbara Shigeru,
with a far wider audience than the exceptional intellectuals such as
Itami or Ōkuma, seemed implicitly to adopt this distinction between
the people and their leadership. Although in his commencement remarks at Tokyo University in March 1953 he reflected that the Japanese ethnic nation *(waga minzoku)* found "historical meaning" in disarmament as "national atonement as a people *(kokuminteki shokuzai)*
for the mistakes committed by our country *(waga kuni)* in the unlawful last war," he also quoted special envoy John Foster Dulles to
the effect that "mistaken leadership" was to blame for attempting to
achieve the people's great ambition through force. Peace and culture
were the new realms of Japanese ambition. "In our nation's history,"
Nanbara continued, "we have borne suffering and sacrifice. Let us
apply it in the cause of peace."[34]

In the summer of 1952, the prime minister's National Public Opinion Survey Institute conducted a series of polls to determine popular
reaction to SCAP's purge. The results suggest the extent to which only
the highest level of leadership was regarded as culpable. More than
half of those surveyed wanted the wartime leadership to take some
kind of responsibility—though the responsibility was more for defeat
and its domestic consequences than for actually waging war. People's
attitudes toward the purge depended on whether or not they thought
it had succeeded in selectively punishing wartime leadership. Of the
minority who thought that most of the targets had been leaders, 74
percent considered the purges proper. Yet a majority felt that most targets had simply been cooperating with national policy set by a culpable leadership. Some 72 percent of these respondents, who thought
the victims of the purge had typically not been among the leadership, regarded the purge as "inevitable" rather than "just." Apparently
"leaders" were to be held accountable. But in the minds of most
people, even those who held middle and upper-level leadership positions during the war were often not among the culpable leadership.[35]

An Emperor Betrayed

One of the central criticisms made of the Tokyo Trials is that they did
not include arraignment of the emperor. The story of the U.S. decision
to forgo prosecuting the emperor and use him instead to help effect

Occupation reforms is well known. But since the emperor was the central figure who spanned prewar and postwar Japan—and became the symbol of the people in the new democracy—any treatment of the origins of the Japanese victim ideology must explore how his participation in the war was mythologized.

Kazuo Kawai has written that the emperor's radio broadcast announcing surrender caused a comprehensive cathartic experience which released long-accumulating emotional tensions over the prosecution of the war. All Japanese realized the historical tragedy of their nation's defeat and shared the common sorrow over it. If some felt betrayed by the emperor as much as by the militarists, some reacted another way. Kawai wrote that after the broadcast people "felt as never before an intimate bond of understanding and sympathy" toward the emperor:

> The paradoxical significance of this event was prophetic. It revealed the unifying power of the imperial institution to be so strong that a crisis vitalized rather than weakened it. But it also indicated the emergence of a new attitude in which the people identified the Emperor with themselves so that he became a personification of the popular will instead of a manifestation of authority from on high. At the moment when the personal authority of the Emperor thus reached its height, he necessarily became less a remote deity and more a democratic symbol.

Kawai added that the emperor was not responsible for Japan's policy of militaristic aggression and should not, therefore, be personally punished.[36] There is little doubt that from Kawai's vantage point in 1960 the emperor's radio message seemed to have united him with his people in the face of an Occupation fraught with uncertainty. But the transformation of the emperor into a democratic "symbol of the unity of the people," as the new constitution phrased it, was effected over the first few years of the Occupation through a campaign to recreate him as a democratic, peace-loving man. Preliminary to this process was separating his person from responsibility for the state's acts of aggression.[37]

The first public action taken by the emperor's advisers to exempt him from personal guilt was Prime Minister Higashikuni's August 28 announcement that all Japanese should share responsibility and feel contrition for defeat *(sōzange)*. In his address to the Diet in early September, the first Diet to convene after the surrender, Higashikuni repeated his assertion that all Japanese needed to reflect on their unsuccessful efforts to win the war, this time stressing the emperor's early and continuing opposition to the war with the United States and Great Britain:

> His Majesty's sentiments did not change from the beginning to the end of the war. Many things will come of this defeat. All of us, on the front lines and the home front, the military, the civil servants, and the people, must especially now all repent and reflect on the past so that it may serve as a precept for the future. We must renew our spirit.[38]

The popular reaction to this *sōzange* theory of war responsibility was negative. Most seem to have regarded it as an attempt by the emperor's advisers to escape personal blame for the defeat, and most politicians rejected it as such. Ashida Hitoshi, for example, moderate conservative politician who helped found both the Liberal Party and the Democratic Party, questioned Higashikuni's *sōzange* statement:

> What do you think were the causes leading to the unfortunate end of the Greater East Asia War? In a certain sense, you cannot deny that the people as a whole should bear responsibility for that. But if you were to say that the nation's masses were responsible for defeat, you would definitely raise their ire. The question I think isn't being addressed is this: "What about those who are most responsible for defeat?"[39]

Higashikuni's strategy was more successful in diverting questions of the emperor's personal responsibility. In late September the prime minister told foreign journalists that the emperor had no responsibility for the war because, under Japanese political custom and as a constitutional monarch, he had no choice but to authorize the decisions of the government and the Imperial Headquarters (military staff).[40] Prime Minister Shidehara's cabinet passed a resolution to similar effect in early November, and in Diet interpellation in early December he said that state ministers bore total responsibility for actions taken on the emperor's authority.

Higashikuni reinforced the idea that the emperor's advisers bore the greatest responsibility when, in early November 1945, he renounced his own nobility in a public confession of "moral responsibility for defeat." In an interview that was printed on the front page of the *Asahi shinbun,* Higashikuni explained that he felt he had been irresponsible in not expressing his opinion on conditions to the emperor during the war, even though, he said, such contact was forbidden. "As a matter of form, I may not be held responsible since expressing one's opinion on events was forbidden. . . . But not [advising the emperor about the people's suffering] under such conditions was a cowardly thing and [results in] great moral responsibility." He continued that he had lived a life of ease, "thanks to His Majesty and the state," but the war ending as it did he resolved to give up the privileges of his class in order to "make clear his moral responsibility."[41] In this way, Higashikuni contributed to the theory that a small group of the emperor's advisers rather than the emperor himself should shoulder responsibility for leading the people to such grief.

Another comment in the same issue of the *Asahi* that addressed the emperor's responsibility was Sugiyama Heisuke's essay on the emperor system. In arguing for the continuance of the imperial institution, Sugiyama constructed an image of the emperor as a benign figurehead whose authority was abused by the military. He wrote that the emperor had "latent political power that appeared in ending the war . . . which surprised everyone . . . but even with this much power he could not prevent militarists from abusing it all, could not prevent . . . Japan's crises since the China Incident." Sugiyama admitted, in passing, that "of course the emperor must recognize his own responsibility" for the abuse of his power by the militarists, but he did not elaborate.[42]

In a newspaper column on the emperor's birthday in 1946—the day the list of defendants for the first A-class war crimes trial was announced—Nanbara Shigeru adopted the argument that the emperor bore no political or legal responsibility because he acted as best he could. As a constitutional monarch he was bound to support the will of the people as determined by government leaders. If the newspapers were any indication, the people were feverish for war in any case. Still, Nanbara thought the emperor bore moral responsibility as the leader of a people who waged war. Hinting at abdication, he argued that the emperor should make some explicit statement of his own personal responsibility in order to help the Japanese achieve a spiritual base for rebuilding the country.[43] In 1948, speaking to reporters, he was more direct: "The emperor should abdicate. This is not just my opinion alone but the common opinion of everyone from the nation's elementary schools to its university professors."[44]

Opinion polls conducted during the Occupation consistently showed that between 80 and 90 percent favored the continuance of the imperial institution, usually in a form without any formal political power. Opinion on the Shōwa emperor was generally favorable, but a significant minority felt he should take responsibility by abdicating. A poll conducted in June 1948 in Osaka, for example, found that 26.9 percent thought he should abdicate either immediately or at the earliest suitable time.[45] Such sentiment was articulated in the printed media by people from all walks of life—from the chief justice of the Supreme Court to housewives. One Buddhist cleric even suggested that the emperor abdicate and enter a cloister in order to expunge war guilt and pave the spiritual way for Japan to become accepted in international society as a peaceful and cultural nation.[46]

The interesting thing about the emperor's own contribution to these discussions is that he never made any explicit public statement reflecting on his war responsibility—neither from his new constitutional position as symbol of the state and the unity of the people nor as an individual. He was purported to have recognized his moral responsibilities privately (and he does seem to have considered abdication in 1948),[47] but his sense of contrition was infrequently reported, only on special occasions, and then only in ways which identified his burden with that of the people. On the occasion of the execution of Tōjō and his comrades in December 1948, for example, the *Asahi shinbun* reported what was purported to be the emperor's feelings on abdication. The headline read that he would "bear the cross of reconstruction" *(saiken no jūjika):*

> I deeply regret having led people into the abyss of today's misfortune. My abdication could be considered as one solution to accommodating my war responsibility. But I think that by remaining in my present post I am better able to console and encourage my people and would be acting in accordance with the wishes of my ancestors. This course of action is also in keeping with the aim of the Potsdam Declaration.[48]

With a suggestive allusion to Christ bearing the burden for humanity's sins, the text ended with the statement that the emperor was "determined to carry the cross of reconstruction."

In introducing these thoughts, the *Asahi* editorialized on comments made the previous month by Joseph Keenan, chief prosecutor of the Tokyo Trials. Keenan had told journalists on his departure from Japan that he

> considered that no satisfactory evidence existed to prosecute the Emperor as a war criminal. . . . I wanted to let the Emperor appear in court as a witness if only to explain his situation. However . . . according to what General MacArthur told me, if the Emperor were

to be asked to appear in court as a witness he was ready to take personal responsibility for all the actions committed by the Japanese government neglecting all evidence to the contrary.[49]

Although it was among the more liberal national dailies, the *Asahi* used the authority of Keenan's position to discount calls for the emperor's abdication. It praised Keenan's "frank evocation of the subtleties of the emperor's mental attitude toward war responsibility," arguing that it provided "a powerful answer" to most arguments for abdication based on the emperor's "moral" war responsibility.[50] Keenan's statement also reinforced the idea that the emperor, although theoretically the final authority, was in the end a victim because he lacked the assertiveness to challenge his militarist advisers: "According to all evidence, the Emperor was, from a Western point of view, a person with a weak will. However, it was proven clearly that the Emperor desired peace consistently. . . . The Emperor was a pacifist."[51] In essence, then, the emperor was portrayed as a pacifist who could not control the more assertive militarist advisers until conditions had patently discredited them.

There was speculation that the emperor might abdicate once Japan regained its independence, for then he could no longer be tried as a war criminal. By the end of the Occupation, though, war responsibility was no longer a burning issue in public discourse. In what has since been termed a "reverse course" in Occupation policy, SCAP became more concerned with building an ally in the Cold War than in purging otherwise capable conservative leaders. The Yoshida government, never enthusiastic about examining war guilt, was pushing economic recovery and attempting to roll back what they regarded as excesses of reform. On the fifth anniversary of the new constitution on May 3, 1952, a few days after Japan became formally independent, the emperor merely expressed his wish to work together with his people for the "reconstruction of the state." He mentioned the war only to express his "deep sympathy and condolences" to its countless victims.[52]

The program to humanize and democratize the emperor sidestepped the issue of war responsibility and, in the process, painted a picture of a monarch in many ways like his people. He was a pacifist at heart who could not control the militarists. Weary of war and the tensions contingent with the Occupation, he only wanted to get on with the task of reconstruction toward a truly bright and peaceful future. By the early 1960s, the campaign to humanize the imperial family had succeeded in transfiguring them into familiar and approachable personalities, icons of the Japanese masses "clothed in idealized middle-class respectability." In the weekly tabloids, the emperor's prewar activities were hardly discussed at all. His responsibility for prewar decisions was usually left unmentioned. Such issues were addressed only in accounts of his role in ending the war in order "to show the personal hardships he suffered" through his concern for his people and his sense of personal responsibility.[53]

Two commonly related episodes bridged prewar and postwar in a manner that recognized the emperor's personal moral responsibility and his willingness to shoulder it. The first episode established the received reality of militarist abuse of his authority: his intervention to break the deadlock of his ministers at the imperial conference in the early hours of August 10, 1945. In the August 1963 issue of a weekly magazine, Sakomizu Hisatsune, the chief cabinet secretary at war's end, recounted the emperor's decision to accept the Potsdam Declaration: "The Services say they are confident of winning but those words cannot be trusted. . . . For myself I cannot impose any further sacrifices on the people. If it will save Japan it matters not what becomes of me personally."[54]

The second episode, about his first meeting with General MacArthur, reinforced the impression of his willingness to shoulder complete responsibility personally. According to Grand Chamberlain Fujita Hisanori's recollection, the emperor told the general:

> Responsibility for the war which led to defeat is being sought, but the responsibility is completely mine. The military officers and civilian officials were appointed by me and they are not responsible. It does not matter what happens to me personally. I leave that to you. Beyond that, I should like to ask for the assistance of the Allied countries so that my people will not experience difficulty in their livelihood.[55]

The story ends with the strongly favorable impression the emperor made on MacArthur. Fortunately for the emperor, SCAP eventually decided to retain him in its service. Like the victorious sixteenth-century warrior generals who enlisted their former enemies for future campaigns, MacArthur graciously forgave the emperor, if not his advisers, in exchange for future cooperation.[56] In the narrative that proved convenient for both SCAP and the Imperial Household Agency, the emperor was portrayed as having met his war responsibilities with humility, compassion, and honor.

The emperor's ensuing reticence about his wartime responsibilities mocked the sensibilities of the quarter of his subjects who thought he owed them some explanation and expression of sincere apology. The mass media, however, came to avoid such issues. The belief that the emperor had been abused by the militarists, suffered, yet nevertheless emerged from the dark war years with his nobility intact encouraged a similar sentimentality among his newly liberated subjects who might identify with him in their postwar construction of themselves as innocent pacifists.

An American Perspective

American dominance during and after the Occupation encouraged a fixation on Japan's relation to its postwar sponsor and gives the impression that the war was remembered and indeed commemorated in most arenas as a conflict between Japan and the United States. One obvious way in which American policy structured Japanese remembrance of the war was SCAP's insistence that the war be called the "Pacific War" instead of the "Greater East Asia War," the term associated with Japan's ideological justification of its expansion in Asia to liberate it from Western colonialism.[57] The term "Pacific War" is still hotly contested by both the radical right and progressive historians and social critics. Progressives were more averse to it than ultraconservatives because, ironically, the new terminology reinforced a key element of that wartime ideology: Japan's real enemy had been the United States and not Asia. Kamei Katsuichirō, for example, one of the intellectuals involved in the "overcoming the modern" conference during the war, has reminisced that many felt relieved after the attack on Pearl Harbor because it clarified the various ambiguities about who the enemy was and how the fight was against (Western) cultural colonialism.[58] Not only progressives but conservatives like Takeuchi Yoshimi, who had a special interest in China, resisted this "Pacific War" construction because it downplayed Japanese militarist transgressions against non-Westerners. Japanese aggression against Asians—as in Unit 731's bacteriological warfare experiments, forced labor mobilization throughout Asia, and the countless violations of Asian civilian rights during the war—tended to be given less prominence than accounts of aggression against Europeans or Americans, such as mistreatment of Allied POWs.[59]

Progressives argued for a "Fifteen-Year War" construction that emphasized the war's beginnings with the Mukden Incident in 1931.

This history of the war elaborated Japanese military aggression against Asians and stressed militarist manipulation and suppression of the Japanese masses.[60] Owing to this construction of the war, the Japanese army's invasion of China was never really forgotten. Still, the public has never fully accepted this term—at least within the period under study—and "Pacific War" became the mainstream term for "the war."[61] The significant point is that the emphasis inherent in the terminology for "the war" lowered people's consciousness of Japanese aggression against Asians when discussing war in general.

While older Japanese certainly remembered that hardships in the home islands began with the China Incident in the late 1930s, the public memory as it evolved in the postwar often associated such hardships with the American conflict. Oda Makoto, who came of age after defeat, has written of the consequences for his own generation's understanding of the war:

> In my case, for example, the Sino-Japanese War and the invasion of China are hardly included in the intellectual experiences of my childhood. When I think about the Second World War, I am at first conscious of the Pacific War. The same is true of the Japanese people. The Japanese people don't have much consciousness of having invaded China and have a tendency to emphasize only the suffering they bore in the Pacific War. The reason, I think, is that for them the war was the Pacific War. The invasion of China isn't a part of it.[62]

Another consequence was that, as Kamei Katsuichirō explained, Japan substituted America for China as an object of war guilt. He thought the reason lay in the early Occupation perception of the United States, the predominant occupying power, as a comparatively just nation deserving apology: it had no colonies, had been faithful to its wartime ally Chiang Kai-shek, had fought fascism, and had given Japan an ethical and idealistic constitution.[63] In this context, SCAP's exemption of the Japanese people from personal responsibility—distinguished from the officially designated militarist leadership—helped assuage popular anxiety over their cooperation with Japan's war effort. Such a release from guilt consciousness was an important component of the more self-indulgent forms of victim consciousness.

The Evolution of Victimhood

The ideology of Japanese victimhood evolved from the idea that the people had been innocent of the nation's various transgressions dur-

ing the war. As most Japanese scholars argue, belief in this innocence was encouraged by the assignment of responsibility to the
militarists—either individually, as in the Tokyo Trials, or generically
as in textbooks and other reeducation media.

Placing all the blame on a few militarists was problematic because SCAP's American-style democracy (minshushugi) required an
assertive citizenry and introduced expectations that individuals accept
responsibility for their government's actions. Itami and Ōkuma argued
accordingly that the success of the democratic (and pacifist) reforms
depended on the people, both as morally responsible individuals
and as constituent members of the Japanese nation, owning up to
their past acquiescence to a system of oppression. Adopting a history
as passive victim would compromise the integrity of Japan's democratic future because it would debilitate the sense of "autonomous
self."[64] The American, "[democratic] way of thinking about state and
society" caused those like the Niigata railway worker to think seriously for the first time about their war responsibility as individuals;
but most of his fellows avoided such self-examination in public discourse. The consequence was an abandonment of the prewar awareness of self as active supporter of the state's war policies in exchange
for the postwar reconstruction of that same self as passive, unwilling
collaborator.[65]

Central to this redefinition of historical self was the people's
alienation from and condemnation of the wartime state—a natural
reaction when unquestioning allegiance to it had resulted in such
disaster. A strong emotional identification with the emperor complicated this alienation for many since, under the "family state" ideology, he embodied all facets of the polity, including state, ministers,
and people.[66] Since the United States had decided to retain the emperor, he too had to be distanced from the ignoble acts of the
wartime state. The divorce was achieved by implicit resort to a con-
glomeration of existing ideas on Japanese governance: Minobe
Tatsukichi's theory that the emperor was merely an "organ" of the
state, a glorified constitutional monarch; Yoshino Sakuzō's theory of
Japanese democracy as minponshugi, in which good governments
based their policies on the people's well-being and honored their
will (but need not involve their active participation) and in which the
interests of emperor and people are implicitly juxtaposed to those of
governing ministers;[67] and what might be termed the Japanese version
of the Confucian "Mandate of Heaven" philosophy of government
applied selectively to militarist advisers.[68] In this version, simply
put, the emperor and his people knew that peace was the best

policy, but the corrupt militarist government came between them, eventually bringing heaven's punishment when it failed to honor their united will.[69]

By placing blame for disastrous state policies on those who in traditional terms would be called "evil ministers," SCAP saved the emperor for use in constructing a democratic and pacifist postwar state. At the same time, however, SCAP inadvertently undermined its own program to give Japan a democracy in which the people ruled as well as reigned—that is, exercised citizenship rights of self-governance beyond merely holding symbolic sovereignty. By dissociating the emperor from the wartime state, SCAP effectively created a history that united him with his people as passive agents in the face of an aggressive and manipulative state (and unintentionally made both its victim). It is not surprising that doubts about the democratic potential of the Japanese people arose in postwar intellectual discourse on such subjects as war responsibility, subjectivity *(shutaisei)*, and modernity.

During the Occupation, personal guilt for war acts may have been deeply felt but it was inadequately expressed. Because the responsibility for such individual wartime acts was weakly asserted in public, it came to be weakly felt by postwar generations. There was no cathartic, galvanizing public confrontation with the issue of the average person's responsibility for the wartime state's acts of foreign aggression and domestic oppression. The emperor, as the preeminent and powerful symbol of both state and people, could have forced such a confrontation by publicly asserting his own sense of responsibility and facing the consequences. But by the end of the Occupation he and his government were no longer concerned with such issues. The debt had already been paid by the scapegoated militarists in the Tokyo War Crimes Trials, and government leaders remained circumspect about an imperial statement because they had themselves been the colleagues of those on trial. Had they admitted culpability, the opposition Socialists and Communists would have insisted they resign from government. It was only after the death of the Shōwa emperor and the arrival of the first prime minister of the postwar generation (Hosokawa Morihiro) in 1993 that a high official admitted Japan was responsible for starting the war. In any case, the emperor's reticence hindered open discussion of personal war guilt. Public memory of the people's past as victims was not well tempered by memories of their past as perpetrators.

The efforts of progressive historians and social critics assured that memories of a militarist Japan victimizing weak Asians never totally faded, and they complicated the growth of victim consciousness. Still, the "Pacific War" construction and Japan's subordinate postwar relationship to the United States helped to divert and decouple memories of Japanese aggression against Asians away from discussions of "the war." Undoubtedly they also reinforced memories of Japanese suffering inflicted by the overwhelmingly more powerful U.S. forces during the war. And no single act of the war expressed Japan's defeat and suffering at the hands of the Americans better than the atomic bombings of Hiroshima and Nagasaki. When in 1954 a small Japanese tuna boat crew was exposed to radioactive fallout from a U.S. hydrogen bomb experiment, the twin experiences as nuclear victim helped bridge wartime and postwar identities. In the Cold War era, the war victim became a formidably appealing mythohistorical hero for Japan.

CHAPTER 3

Hiroshima and *Yuiitsu no hibakukoku*
Atomic Victimhood in the Antinuclear Peace Movement

On rational reflection we take note that the Pacific War imposed incalculable suffering, especially on Asian peoples. We laid waste the countries of Asia with our muddy boots, robbed many people of their lives, and committed countless cruel sins. This is burned into our hearts as an unforgettable experience. But it was when for the first time we experienced for ourselves the series of fire-bombings, urban evacuation, defeat, and occupation . . . that [the reality of modern warfare] really hit home. . . . This is why most Japanese *(kokumin)* have come to hate war from the bottom of their hearts.
—Yasui Kaoru (1955)

T HE mythology of Japanese victimhood reached its purest and most universally accepted expression in the public dialogue over nuclear weapons. In the Cold War era, Hiroshima and Nagasaki came to represent an epochal shift in the technology of war engendering a conceptual disjunction between conventional and nuclear warfare. Accordingly, it was in the realm of antinuclear pacifism that Japanese war victimhood was most easily detached from Japanese wartime aggression.

Japan's unique experience of Hiroshima and Nagasaki gave the Japanese an exclusive and seductive claim to leadership of the world antinuclear weapon movement. Although Gensuikyō, the organizational center of Japan's ban-the-bomb movement, was divided by political factionalism, all parties spoke of nuclear weapons with a sense of mission based on a shared atomic victimhood. Cabinet ministers routinely declared Japan to be the "only country in the world to have suffered an atomic bombing" *(sekai yuiitsu no hibakukoku)*. Socialist Diet members had been using such rhetoric for years to protest Japan's reliance on the U.S. nuclear umbrella and to criticize what they felt was the ruling Liberal Democratic Party's halfhearted record on aid to the bomb's victims, the *hibakusha*. In 1966, atomic victimization was given formal sanction as a cultural ideal with the award of the Noma Prize and the Monbushō Order of Cultural Merit to Ibuse Masuji for *Kuroi ame* (Black Rain), a novel that dwells on the helplessness of the average Japanese in the face of war and stresses the postwar plight of the *hibakusha*.[1] In 1974 the Nobel Committee awarded former Prime Minister Satō Eisaku the Peace Prize in recognition of his respect for this vision, especially in the form of his formal declaration of Japan's three nonnuclear principles: Japan would not produce, possess, or permit the introduction of nuclear weapons onto Japanese soil.[2]

The Japanese nation did not adopt this victim's mission for nonnuclear peace soon after defeat. In the early years, SCAP censorship kept the scope and nature of A-bomb damage from being widely known. And when near the end of the Occupation the Japanese media finally brought forward the extraordinary destruction and lingering suffering caused by the bomb, it was often seen either as a regional story with no special significance for the nation as a whole or as a global event that transcended identification with any particular nation. Left-wing appropriation of the Hiroshima legacy in criticizing the American economic and security alliance alienated large portions of the nation. But fallout from the Bikini hydrogen bomb experiments and the exposure of the crew and catch of a Japanese tuna trawler, the Lucky Dragon 5, to its "ash of death" in 1954 attracted nationwide attention to Japan's continuing vulnerability to nuclear danger. Buoyed by the sense of national crisis, a ban-the-bomb movement attracted nonpartisan support based on a consensus about the inhumanity of nuclear weapons and a growing awareness of Japan as the only country to have been ravaged by them. As leader of this movement, scholar-activist Yasui Kaoru (1907–1980) played the central role in expanding the antinuclear peace movement from a Communist and Socialist project into a fully nonpartisan, ethnic nationalist movement in the middle 1950s. Hiroshima became both an icon of Japan's past as war victim and a beacon for its future as pacifist nation. A shared sense of responsibility for *hibakusha*—the unifying symbol of the Japanese community's atomic victimhood—helped form a consensus for better government-sponsored medical care, though the opposition Socialists continued to take the lead in pushing for such compensation.

Although conservative administrations came to respect this widespread antinuclear conviction by publicly prohibiting nuclear weapons on Japanese soil, they had to take care not to harm the U.S. security relationship, which afforded Japan a nuclear umbrella. Even Prime Minister Hatoyama, who came to power on a platform calling for an independent foreign policy and had privately promised cooperation to the movement's leaders, told foreign reporters in March 1955 that Japan would store nuclear warheads if asked.[3] In the new climate of raised sensitivity to nuclear weapons—Japan's "nuclear allergy"—such admissions became gaffes that government officials strove to avoid. His successor Kishi Nobusuke, arguably more concerned with protecting the U.S. alliance in the fight against communism, established the pattern of sending pro forma protests of U.S. nuclear testing in the Pacific. Although Kishi stated frequently that Japan would neither possess nuclear weapons nor permit their entry onto Japanese soil, Socialists continually challenged his sincerity because of his firm support of the U.S. alliance against communism.[4]

The ban-the-bomb petition movement of the middle 1950s helped make the idea of atomic victimhood a part of the Japanese cultural and political treasury. Yet it was an asset with contingent limitations. It could be tapped by Japanese of any political faction to push for *hibakusha* aid, by progressives to oppose Japanese remilitarization, by conservatives to exempt Japan from nuclear responsibility within the U.S. alliance, or even, in the Cold War era, to bolster national status in international arenas such as the United Nations. But the rhetoric of a shared heritage of atomic victimhood could not hold its parent movement together when progressive interests tried to direct it toward subverting the American alliance. Atomic victimhood also proved inadequate to convince many non-Japanese of the sincerity of Japanese pacifism since it held little awareness of the precursory Japanese aggression against Asians.[5] Yet the emergence of this sort of pacifist nationalism in a period when Japan was reestablishing a conventional army helped limit Japanese remilitarization.

Laying the Groundwork

At the very beginning of the postwar era, the Shōwa emperor laid the groundwork for atomic victimhood in his radio broadcast of August 15. Not only were the Japanese citizens injured in those bombings labeled "innocent" victims, but the emperor's implied mantle of responsibility for all human civilization foreshadowed the global scale of Japan's future antinuclear mission: "The enemy has begun to employ a new and most cruel bomb, the power of which to do damage is indeed incalculable, taking the toll of many innocent lives. Should we continue to fight, it would not only result in an ultimate collapse and disappearance of the Japanese nation, but it would also lead to the total extinction of human civilization."[6]

Still, the invidious nature of this "new and most cruel bomb" remained obscure to all but a few specialists and those who had come into direct contact with the bomb's destruction. For most urban Japanese it was the firebombings, rather than the atomic bombings, that they remembered from personal experience, and SCAP censorship ensured that most Japanese learned little about Hiroshima until the end of the decade.[7] During the early Occupation, censorship permitted public discussion of the destructive capacity of atomic bombs, but it inhibited public expression and awareness of the exceptional dimension of human suffering they caused. Outside of the two affected cities, the atomic bombings were simply not privileged in the emerging narratives of Japan as a pacifist nation, except indirectly as spurs to the national effort to develop Japanese scientific culture. In this complex field of censored discourse, the achievement of peace was linked to scientific mastery over natural and social forces. The atomic bomb was an example of the irrefutably superior technological potential of the American model of a rational, democratic, and therefore peace-loving society that had, significantly, defeated Japan through science.[8] In explicitly pacifist narratives of wartime suffering, the Hiroshima and Nagasaki victim, or *hibaku*, experiences were perceived as local issues—akin to the firebombings other Japanese cities had endured —or, when the global implications of this first use of nuclear weapons were understood, in universalistic terms that transcended national identities. The Tokyo-based literary circles, for example, tended to view the early "atomic-bomb literature" of Ōta Yōko and other well-known A-bomb writers as a regional phenomenon and discredited their work as too politicized to be considered literature. *Hiroshima*, John Hersey's sympathetic reportage on the experience of six victims of the bomb, earned a wide readership when it was first published in translation in April 1949, but the author implicitly denationalizes his six informants in the attempt to evoke a universal humanistic response.[9]

The "Tensei jingo" columns that Aragaki Hideo wrote for the *Asahi*

shinbun demonstrate how one major mirror of public opinion understood Hiroshima, nuclear weapons, and nuclear power. In his widely
read and influential daily front-page columns, Aragaki never presented
Hiroshima as an exceptionally Japanese event until after an August
1952 *Asahi gurafu* photo exposé on the city after the Occupation had
ended.[10] Perhaps reflecting a universal desire to move forward to a
brighter future, he first discussed Hiroshima in the context of potential
peaceful uses of nuclear energy. One early column about nuclear
energy (June 17, 1946) characterized it as a dangerous animal that
could either be tamed or let run wild: it could shatter modern civilization or help unite the world in peace. Aragaki praised the Baruch Plan
(for an international authority to control fissionable material and in-
spect atomic developments in all countries) and highlighted Einstein's
warning that only a global political institution could prevent nuclear
energy from being misused to bring about the destruction of humankind. The focus of the essay was on global cooperation. Falling back
on the issue of culture, the one acceptable area for Japanese assertiveness in the early postwar period,[11] the article ended with a comment about the potential for nuclear energy to transform world culture. A similar column two weeks later (July 2, 1946) expressed the
same concern over whether nuclear energy would be used for good
or evil. The essay began: "July 16, 1945, New Mexico; August 6, Hiroshima; August 9, Nagasaki; June 1, 1946, Bikini—these four dates
mark the path which nuclear energy has carved into the history of
world civilization." It was up to human wisdom whether it would be
used as in the tragedies of Hiroshima and Nagasaki or as in the experiments at Bikini (presented in this context as scientific efforts leading toward a new world civilization).

   In the progressive press, in a theoretical essay published in
November 1949 in the liberal journal *Sekai,* socialist advocate Kuno
Osamu made only an oblique reference to nuclear weapons in his
"Logic of Peace and Logic of War." When he did, he spoke from the
vantage point of a human being, not a Japanese. Kuno wrote that the
next world war threatened humankind with its own destruction:
"Our continued existence on this earth [is coming to] rely absolutely
on our ability to avoid this new war."[12] In a similar vein but to a wider
audience, Rev. Tanimoto Kiyoshi pled for all humanity to heed Hiroshima's lessons for their salvation in his afterword to the Japanese
translation of John Hersey's *Hiroshima,* published with special SCAP
permission in April 1949. After describing movements in the United
Kingdom and North America for aiding the city in recovery, he called
for a peace movement uniting compassionate people worldwide.[13]

After Occupation censorship eased and then ended in 1949, Cold War tensions began to heighten and Hiroshima slowly emerged as a broadly contested icon of the national war experience in political and cultural discourse over the character of postindependence Japan. Conservatives continued to prefer silence on the human suffering at Hiroshima and Nagasaki, for such questions raised troubling doubts about the government's commitment to a Cold War alliance with the United States. When pushed they tended to favor the earliest and most enduring narratives that treated the bombings as if they were natural calamities and were silent on who bombed Hiroshima and why, or else they advocated narratives that recognized respective responsibilities but preached reconciliation and, ultimately, forgetting. At the very beginning of the Occupation, Prime Minister Higashikuni expressed what became a typical conservative desire for reconciliation when he suggested to an Associated Press reporter that the former combatants might leave their wartime enmity behind: the Japanese might forget Hiroshima provided the American people forgot Pearl Harbor.[14] Of course, this easy equation of Hiroshima ending what Pearl Harbor began appealed to American sensibilities. But it was also emblematic of the preferred conservative government approach to Hiroshima—with its recognition that both sides injured each other in fighting the Pacific War, its silence about Asian victims of Japanese aggression, and its pragmatic willingness to let the past rest in the interest of working together to rehabilitate Japan as a contributing member of the international community.

This emphasis on reconciliation is evident in such cultural productions as *Never Forget the Song of Nagasaki*, a 1952 film described by noted critic Satō Tadao as a "saccharine *(amai)* romantic melodrama" in which the atomic bomb is reduced to a plot device to separate loved ones. This film's director, screenwriter, producer, and production company all had reputations for making films that supported the conservative agenda, and Satō suggests that their wartime experience making militarist vehicles explains their superficial treatment of the bombing in this film.[15] *Song of Nagasaki* stars Kyō Machiko (of *Rashōmon* fame) as a beautiful, comfortably wealthy woman who harbors extreme hatred toward Americans because she has been blinded by the atomic bomb. Her hatred is dissipated, however, by a kind young American soldier, apparently himself born in Nagasaki, who returns to the city in order to deliver an unfinished sonata that a dying Japanese POW had given him. The young man's sincere interest in the sufferings of *hibakusha* overwhelms her bitterness.[16]

During the Korean War the Japanese government earned independence in exchange for a commitment to U.S. Cold War diplomacy and partial remilitarization, even as public fear of nuclear weapons reached an early peak. President Truman raised anxiety when he was reported in November 1950 to be considering use of the atomic bomb in Korea, and the first post-Occupation publication of explicit photographs of Hiroshima *hibakusha,* appearing in the *Asahi gurafu* in August 1952, elicited sympathy for their plight. But with the Japanese economy experiencing a war procurement boom and—despite his shrewd resistance to American pressure for major rearming—with Prime Minister Yoshida's ultimate compliance to a forceful American security regime, peace activism, especially antinuclear peace activism, gradually became the purview of left-wing groups.[17]

Marxist groups typically situated Hiroshima and Nagasaki in narratives of class struggle that constructed the recent Asia-Pacific War as the inevitable result of competition among imperialist nation-states. The Red Purge and other efforts of conservative political parties to reverse liberal Occupation reforms exacerbated moderate and far-left activists' distrust of a conservative government they increasingly regarded as a reconfiguration of the wartime militarist state.[18] Accordingly, socialist and communist activists tried to use remembrance of Hiroshima to condemn the postwar alliance between the United States and Japan and mobilize the Japanese people to resist its fulfillment—which in their eyes included state infringements on civil liberties as well as remilitarization, expansion of American military bases on Japanese soil, and reliance on nuclear weapons for defense.

Quite often, progressive narratives of Hiroshima served the Soviet Union's Cold War interests in condemning U.S. nuclear policy. In 1952, the left-wing Japan Teachers Union (Nihon Kyōshokuin Kumiai) sponsored an egregious example of the anti-American approach in Yagi Yasutarō's *Hiroshima.* Based on war orphan stories, this radically anti-American film portrays the Japanese as guinea pigs in a racist American program of atomic bomb testing. Yagi denounces American imperialism by ending *Hiroshima* with the story of a delinquent orphan *hibakusha* who survives by selling to American tourists the skulls of war victims he has unearthed from an island in the Inland Sea.[19]

Soon after the *Asahi gurafu* published a graphic pictorial on the first atomic anniversary after independence in August 1952, "Tensei jingo" columnist Aragaki made his first explicit reference to Hiroshima as an exclusively Japanese experience. The focus of the column was another film the teacher's union had originally funded: Shindō Kaneto's *Children of Hiroshima (Genbaku no ko)*. The union ultimately rejected the film—which depicts a compassionate schoolteacher's efforts to ease the pain of former students who survived the bomb—because it failed to live up to the union's strident ideological requirements.[20] The film was thought by many to articulate an expressly Japanese understanding of the bombings. It is a good example of the most broadly embraced narratives of the time in which the bomb was treated more or less as an unexpected natural calamity with little (or at least suppressed) acknowledgment of either American or Japanese agency in causing it. To Aragaki, it showed that the victims of the bomb were all good citizens who were blameless *("Doremo koremo hito no yoi . . .")*. Indeed, the film depicts the people of Hiroshima as innocent victims of violence, fearful memories returning every time a plane flies overhead. Although the film in no instance mentions any specific country—Japan is not mentioned at all and no national symbols such as flags appear—and never suggests any national dimension to victimhood beyond one reference to firebombings in Tokyo and Osaka, Aragaki saw it as an experience that both privileged and obligated the Japanese, compelling them to aid global peace by proclaiming the suffering at Hiroshima: "This is a film only Japanese can make. Only Japanese have the right, more than that the greatest duty, to make it. . . . And it won't amount to anything if only Japanese cry [after seeing this film]. I'd like to show this film to all the people in the world; indeed, we must show it."[21]

Yet this emerging sense of an exceptional Japanese legacy of atomic victimhood was tempered by a feeling of impotence in the international community. Japan had been defeated in war, stripped of its imperial possessions, occupied and fundamentally reformed in a social and political experiment by its former enemy (creating a sensitivity against being used as experimental "guinea pigs" that resurfaced during the Lucky Dragon Incident), and excluded from the United Nations. Cold War tensions and increased knowledge of the destructive capacity of atomic weapons heightened concern over the dangers of atomic war, but Japan was more or less a bystander in these questions.

In a November 1951 *Sekai* essay remarkable for reasoning that foreshadowed the logic of the Japanese peace movement, Kuno Osamu recognized this powerlessness. But he argued that Japanese might, through asserting their neutrality in the Cold War, take some sort of initiative in helping a divided world attain peace. Beginning his essay with the dominant Occupation-era dichotomy, contrasting the peaceful potential for nuclear energy versus its dangers,[22] Kuno argued:

> The only role given to us can be nothing other than bearing witness in front of the world to our first experience as [the atomic bomb's] victim *(higaisha)*. It is the governments and peoples of the U.S. and the USSR that have atomic bombs, not us. It is necessary to solidify our resolve to produce no more victims *(giseisha)*, but there is no danger that we [Japanese] ourselves will become victimizers. The calls for "No More Hiroshimas" carry sorrowful echoes because of this reality of powerlessness behind them. . . . As for atomic bombs, we have no other option but to join with other peoples of the world and appeal to the governments and peoples of the U.S. and USSR.

Even as Kuno recognized the need to guard against the Japanese becoming victimizers again, he deflated his warning by denying that the Japanese were even able to victimize—presumably because in the Cold War what really mattered was the fact that they had no nuclear weapons themselves. While his recognition of the dangers of Japanese aggression was in line with the general leftist fear of any Japanese remilitarization, Kuno's facile rejection of this possibility presaged later tendencies in the ban-the-bomb movement to detach consideration of earlier Japanese aggressions of a conventional sort from nuclear issues. His argument also took advantage of the high moral ground of the victim who, by definition it seemed, could not be a victimizer. Victims, being disempowered, cannot be held accountable for the misuse of power; but they can empower themselves by bearing witness to their victimhood. Indeed, as members of the international community in the Cold War era, Kuno argued they had a responsibility to do so:

> The fate of world peace depends on the standoff between these two worlds, and so long as we ourselves bear partial responsibility for this standoff . . . our attitude cannot be too meticulous or too scrupulous. . . . [It] is not someone else's problem, but ours, one which our own will and strength will to some degree bring resolution. It is an issue that forces us to take responsibility.[23]

Furthermore, they could regain some control of their destiny by maintaining neutrality, by resisting "either great power's self-serving reasoning," and by voicing their views with other less-powerful peoples.

Organizing Grassroots Antinuclear Pacifism

Although by the early 1950s Hiroshima seems to have been widely embraced as a national icon of wartime Japanese suffering, left-wing peace activists failed to turn this sentiment to much account in organizing a broad grassroots opposition to nuclear weapons.[24] This failure was due partly to organizational difficulties within the Communist Party,[25] but also to an alienating insistence on subsuming the antibomb movement under other political positions of the left, less broadly shared, such as opposition to Japan's conventional rearmament and expansion of U.S. military bases.

Progressive Political Origins

The earliest peace movement did not address the nuclear issue, probably out of concern for SCAP's reaction. The January 1949 "Japanese Scientists' Declaration on War and Peace" made no mention of atomic weapons, even though the physicist in charge of Japan's wartime atomic weapons research, Nishina Yoshio, was among the fifty-two signers.[26] Several among this group were invited with other Japanese progressive activists and intellectuals to the communist-sponsored Committee for the World Convention for Peace to be held in Paris and Prague in April.[27] Since SCAP denied travel documents to the invited Japanese, they held their own convention in Tokyo: the Japan Convention for Peace (Heiwa Yōgo Nihon Taikai). But even though the European convention did adopt one clause for banning atomic weapons, the Japanese convention made no mention of atomic weapons in their idealistic eight-point "Outline for Peace."[28] The convention evolved into the Japan Association to Maintain Peace (JAMP; Nihon Heiwa o Mamoru Kai), which first organized nationwide mass peace rallies in August 1949.[29] Although the main thrust of these rallies was an idealistic plea for peace with no reference to atomic weapons, the Hiroshima rally called for a ban on atomic bombs.

The first widespread domestic political action against the atomic bomb came in 1950 with the "Stockholm Appeal," a petition that proposed a ban on nuclear weapons and declared first use a war crime. (See Appendix 1.) Although this petition, conducted in Japan by a JAMP subsidiary called the Japan Committee for Maintaining Peace (JCMP; Heiwa Yōgo Nihon Iinkai), eventually collected 6.45 million signatures, its impact was extremely limited.[30] During the period of the Red Purge, anything remotely associated with communism became suspect. Socialists and the Sōhyō, Shinsambetsu, and Sōdōmei labor unions all denounced the Stockholm Appeal as a "Red movement."[31]

With the Korean War and U.S. pressure for Japanese remilitarization, the focus of Japan's progressive-led peace movement shifted to more immediately relevant issues: to the fight over a comprehensive peace treaty, neutrality, and Japanese remilitarization.[32] Even with the gradual emergence of Japanese atomic victimhood sentiment, nuclear issues still took second place to opposition to conventional rearmament as the concern of Japanese leftist pacifists. In early 1954, activists were still busy protesting U.S. military base expansions and the Military Security Act (MSA) agreements with the United States. In the February 1954 issue of the left-leaning general-interest journal *Kaizō*, for example, chairman of the JCMP and recipient of the Stalin Peace Prize Ōyama Ikuo did not mention nuclear weapons once in his essay on making Japan a base for peace; he only argued against rearming Japan.[33]

The peace movement's efforts in the early 1950s, then, were directed against U.S. military bases on Japanese soil and protecting Japan's peace constitution.[34] Although the peace constitution held widespread support in principle, when it came to concrete policy issues opinions differed. In regard to nuclear issues, at this time Hiroshima's import as an antinuclear pacifist icon did not transcend other interests of the postwar state and society—especially those of wide sections of society benefiting from the U.S. military, diplomatic, and trade alliance. On the eve of the Lucky Dragon Incident, progressive pacifists were still troubled by their failure to attract mass participation. In early 1954, *Kaizō* assembled a panel of leftist intellectual activists to discuss the difficulties of getting the Japanese people to participate in peace activities. One participant related how his group was unsuccessful in attracting people to a peace meeting with reduced-price tickets to a Shinjuku showing of the movie *Hiroshima* on August 15 the previous year. Tsurumi Kazuko summed up the problem as it related to lack of extracommunity support for protests against military bases. The problem would never be solved until a sense of connectedness *(rentaikan)* caused people to feel that whatever happened to one Japanese would inevitably happen to themselves.[35]

The peace movement's stagnation was particularly vexing in this period of remilitarization. Although Prime Minister Yoshida Shigeru resisted U.S. demands for rapid remilitarization, he firmly supported Washington's nuclear diplomacy and committed his government to significant remilitarization when he signed the MSA assistance agreement in early March 1954. In fact, there was considerable pressure from the non-Yoshida conservative opposition to build an independent military capability. In September 1953, therefore, Yoshida felt compelled to agree to upgrade the National Safety Forces into a true military euphemistically named the Self-Defense Forces.[36] It was in this context that a grassroots ban-the-bomb movement arose in response to the Lucky Dragon Incident, an event that made exposure to radioactive fallout a reality for the whole nation.

Yasui Kaoru and the Ban-the-Bomb Movement

On March 1, 1954, a small Japanese tuna boat called the Lucky Dragon had the misfortune of being too close to a 15-megaton hydrogen bomb "Bravo" experiment that the United States was conducting at Bikini Atoll. At 3:45 in the morning the crew was awakened by a flash of light; then came a sound blast eight minutes later; then came a rain of radioactive ash for several hours. Although they were outside the danger zone the United States had announced, the bomb was more powerful than expected. On returning to their home port of Yaizu in Shizuoka prefecture, the crew complained of lethargy and began to lose their hair, early symptoms of radiation poisoning. Within a few days their story appeared in the nation's newspapers. Concern mounted when it was discovered that the Lucky Dragon's tuna catch was contaminated, resulting in the temporary closure of fish markets and a widespread examination of foodstuffs. Municipal, prefectural, and national assemblies, as well as social, religious, and professional groups, passed resolutions calling for the banning or limiting of nuclear testing.[37] Geiger counters became common stock in social commentary cartoons, and newspapers carried stories of radioactive air, radioactive snow, even radioactive cherry blossoms. Radio stations and newspapers provided updates on the condition of the crew, who were being cared for in special wards set up in two Tokyo hospitals. But it was the death of the boat's radio operator, Kuboyama Aikichi, from radiation sickness in September that whipped popular fears to a peak because it drove home the point that one could die from nuclear bombs without ever having actually been hit by the original blast.[38]

The city assembly of the Lucky Dragon's home port, Yaizu, was first to formally protest the crew's exposure to radioactive fallout, but it was quickly followed by the national Diet in early April and then by other assemblies.[39] The Suginami Ward Assembly in Tokyo passed its resolution against the hydrogen bomb in mid-April, and a meeting of ward residents in the community center on May 9 resulted in the formation of a special council, headed by Yasui Kaoru, which was charged with directing a petition campaign for banning the hydrogen bomb.[40] By the end of June their Suginami Appeal, as it came to be known, had gathered almost 270,000 signatures, or 69 percent of the ward's total population, suggesting that almost all the adult population of Suginami had signed.[41] With fear of radiation poisoning infecting the whole nation, the appeal's success received wide press coverage and spurred other petition efforts around the country. On August 8, various local movement leaders met in Tokyo to found a National Council for a Petition Movement to Ban Atomic and Hydrogen Bombs; Yamada Saburō, president of Japan's Academy of Arts and Sciences, and Nobel physicist Yūkawa Hideki would be codirectors. Yasui assumed organizational leadership as the general secretary at the council's headquarters in the Suginami Community Center.[42] Petition movements surged after the Lucky Dragon's radio operator died in September. The total number of signatures reached 10 million in October, surpassed 20 million in December, and eventually exceeded 30 million by August 1955.[43]

To maintain momentum, the National Council decided to inaugurate annual ban-the-bomb conventions beginning on the tenth anniversary of the Hiroshima bombing in 1955. This first World Conference invested a new organization—the Japan Council Against Atomic and Hydrogen Bombs (Gensuikyō), with Yasui as chair—with the tasks of continuing the petition movement and promoting assistance to the formerly neglected and newly elevated (and appropriated) symbols of Japan's antinuclear pacifist heritage: the *hibakusha* of Hiroshima and Nagasaki. By year's end every prefecture had organized an affiliate Gensuikyō. Starting in December with Hiroshima, municipalities around the country formed their own affiliates. These local organizations earned the active support of local conservative politicians. Indeed, by 1958 there were complaints from the left that the conservatives were merely using them as one more means to build electoral support.[44]

Although the quotidian reality of being exposed to radioactive fallout helps to account for the popular support for the ban-the-bomb movement, there is little doubt that Yasui Kaoru's style of consensus advocacy was essential to its success in accommodating disparate political camps and in its transcendence of the political divisions that had plagued Japanese pacifist activism. Yasui was uniquely qualified to bridge the rifts between the political left and right and their respective positions regarding the Hiroshima legacy. As professor of international law at Tokyo Imperial University during the war, Yasui had tried to find common ground between propeace liberal academics and the militarist establishment. Although by his own account he was personally opposed to Japan's imperialist ventures in Asia, he was also a patriot and persuaded himself to accept the propagandistic assertion that the eventual result of state policy would be the liberation of Asia from Western imperialism. In an effort to persuade ultranationalists of the patriotic integrity of the liberal academic position—that is, as an ideal basis for constructive and dispassionate social and political criticism—he compromised his own avowed liberal position during the war by writing apologist essays that justified Japanese military aggression in Asia. He also helped to develop strategy for handling indigenous peoples in occupied China.

Yasui was purged from his position in March 1948—ostensibly for his wartime collaboration, though there is some evidence that academic politics played a significant role. His dismissal caused him considerable spiritual and intellectual anguish, since he believed he was being punished not only for his honorable efforts to ameliorate wartime excesses but also for his courageous decision to pursue a politically charged research agenda. In the difficult years after his dismissal, Yasui came to recognize how exceedingly naive he had been in trusting state leadership to reform itself, though he never forswore the patriotic sincerity of his efforts. As he wrote in his memoir of the ban-the-bomb movement, *Minshū to heiwa* (The Masses and Peace), when one "makes political statements it isn't enough to act only with a subjective conscientiousness: it is necessary to have the clear expectation of the objective consequences of such action." Tapping into a dominant stream in postwar liberal thought, Yasui dedicated himself to the development of Japanese democracy and peace by promoting a grassroots spirit of civic-mindedness. To fulfill his newly discovered civic responsibilities as a social scientist, he resolved to work for peace through popular education at the local level by volunteering for his district's Parent-Teacher Association, teaching in night school, and agreeing to serve as director of the Suginami Community Center in 1952 and head of its library in 1953. In these positions he became involved in reading groups for housewives and in other community activities that he believed were the infrastructure on which a popular peace movement must rest.[45]

One of the first books his reading groups took up was E. H. Carr's *The New Society*—a book that was to influence Yasui's thinking on how to be effective in political activism and confirm his nationalist tendencies. Carr argued that in the new era of the postwar mass society, "individualist" democracies, in which a small number of elite individuals harmonized their interests through rational and peaceful negotiation, were increasingly becoming mass democracies in which interest groups relied on appeals to the emotions to persuade the mass electorate. Yasui—the elite who had failed in his attempt to alter national policy during the war—took to heart both Carr's pragmatic observation of the power of emotion in popular persuasion and his admonition that popular education was essential if mass democracy were to avoid degenerating into fascist dictatorship.[46]

When the Lucky Dragon Incident raised popular consciousness of Japan's exceptional nuclear history, Yasui was well positioned to help guide his own ward's residents in civic action. He understood that this was a historic moment: a singular opportunity to channel fear of nuclear weapons into a mass movement, first on the national level, then globally.[47] By understanding the threat of nuclear weapons, identifying opposition to it as a national cause, and taking action based on that identification, he thought that Japanese could regain some of their independence and sense of worth as individuals, as citizens, and as a nation. To him, as no doubt for other moderate progressives, the ban-the-bomb movement was nothing less than an exercise in democratic subjectivity, with all that implied for the maturation of the Japanese as a people and society.[48] Yasui's leadership gave the movement three of its characteristics that help account for its successes: its early purity of focus on opposition to nuclear weapons and the attending avoidance of divisive political issues that had hindered the peace movement's potential as a national movement; its reliance on a narrative of Hiroshima that emphasized witnessing of Japan's unique atomic victimhood, divorced from its origins, so to speak, in Japan's conventional wartime aggressions; and its celebration of women's special role in pacifist activism.

Yasui wanted the petition effort to be a "pure national people's movement" inclusive of all Japanese regardless of class or political leanings. In his memoir and elsewhere, Yasui discusses the special care that was taken in organizing the Suginami Council and National Council and drafting the Suginami Appeal in order to overcome the divisive structural and ideological limitations of the early peace movement. Membership on the Suginami Council included all groups and classes from the community: concerned resident academics, conservative Liberal Party and Socialist Party ward politicians, the chair of the PTA, and representatives from religious, women's, literary, and labor groups. The council purposely remained silent on Japanese remilitarization lest they alienate potential supporters—or, worse, lest the movement be sidetracked into a divisive anti-American crusade. In drafting the petition and lobbying for signatures, care was taken to avoid making any specific nation their target. They even refrained from using the Chinese characters for peace, *"heiwa,"* out of fear of giving the impression they were "of a particular [communist] persuasion." The text of the Suginami Appeal relied on the inclusive civic term for "the Japanese people" *(kokumin)* repeatedly, and it pointedly stated that it was directed not at a particular "state" *(kokka)* but at all states, governments, and peoples. (See Appendix 2.) Within the petition movement's organization, supraparty amity was maintained by an etiquette in which conservatives were referred to as *hoshu* or "conservative" instead of *handō* or "reactionary," and progressives were called *kakushin* or "reformist," not the colorful *urutora* or "ultra."[49]

Yasui had a deep appreciation for how wartime suffering alienated people from militarism. Quite consciously he promoted awareness of Japan's unique atomic victim experience as a means to motivate people to political action. In his memoir, he wrote that defeat in World War II had caused a "spiritual revolution" *(seishin kakumei)* for the Japanese people:

> On rational reflection we take note that the Pacific War imposed incalculable suffering, especially on Asian peoples. We laid waste the countries of Asia with our muddy boots, robbed many people of their lives, and committed countless cruel sins. This is burned into our hearts as an unforgettable experience. But it was when for the first time we experienced for ourselves the series of firebombings, urban evacuation, defeat, and occupation . . . that [the reality of modern warfare] really hit home. . . . This is why most Japanese *(kokumin)* have come to hate war from the bottom of their hearts.[50]

Although he took pains to recognize Japan's past militarist aggressions, Yasui understood that the ban-the-bomb movement's persuasive appeal and energy lay in such emotional appropriation of the atomic bomb as a domestic or home-front experience of being victimized by war. The Suginami Appeal reflected this victim sensibility: embracing the plight of the Lucky Dragon's crew, recalling the memory of "the tragedies of Hiroshima and Nagasaki," and asserting that "now we, the Japanese people *(watashitachi Nihon no kokumin)*, have suffered for the third time the egregious affliction of nuclear bombs." Having asserted nuclear victimhood to be a uniquely Japanese national experience, the appeal ended with the hope that the voice of the Japanese people would sway the consciences of all the world's peoples.

Yasui was less interested in dwelling on Japan's past sins than in promoting its future unity as a pacifist nation, and the focus on national witnessing of atomic victimhood in the Cold War era tended to divorce memory of Hiroshima from the conventional war that preceded it. Memories of the first two incidences of nuclear exposure in World War II gained contemporary salience as the relived reality of an explicitly recognized "third" exposure in the 1950s. Although the reemergence of the Japanese military in the form of the Self-Defense Forces drew vociferous progressive opposition—and military base expansion drew significant local opposition—conventional military issues alone lacked the proximate quotidian reality of nuclear fallout contamination of air, water, and foodstuffs for the whole nation. Hiroshima was to become an icon of Japan's past as innocent war victim and a beacon for its future as pacifist nation. Japan's past conventional war transgressions were relatively insignificant to this vision, and Yasui did not dwell on them.

The tendency to neglect Japan's conventional war aggression is evident in the first World Conference's deliberations and formal declarations. A representative from the Shiga Prefecture branch of the Japan Teachers Union argued, unsuccessfully to judge from the published record of the conference, that "the peace movement just won't fly . . . unless we apologize for the war atrocities the Japanese army committed in the Philippines, Burma, and the like." In his summation at the end of the conference, Yasui briefly noted the extreme importance of apologizing for war atrocities committed by Japan. But he laid considerably more emphasis on organizing for *hibakusha* aid and strengthening communication with the anti–military base movement. There was no mention of contrition for Japan's militarist past in the official conference declaration.[51]

Yasui consistently used the terms *"kokumin"* (the people, as in civic nation) and *"minshū"* (the people, as in popular masses) in order to emphasize the civic and popular nature of peace activism.

Yet he clearly understood the Japanese ban-the-bomb movement to be equally an ethnic nationalist *(minzoku)* movement. In trying to channel antinuclear sentiment toward the left-wing anti–military base agenda at the end of the first World Conference, for example, Yasui characterized the frequent discussion in subcommittees of remilitarization and U.S. military bases as "an expression of the Japanese people's *(Nihon kokumin)* earnest desire for the [Japanese] ethnic nation's *(minzoku no)* independence and Asia's freedom."[52] In Japanese leftist circles, the 1950s saw the reemergence of the Stalinist position on the ethnic nation as a force for liberation from capitalist imperialism and, in the midcentury Asian context, as a force for resistance against wartime Japanese militarist aggression.[53] The irony of this position for postwar Japanese progressives was that the ethnic nation had been glorified in the wartime ultranationalist, pan-Asianist rhetoric that justified the very same militarist state that had so recently oppressed the left during the war. In particular, the Japan Communist Party's unique record among Japanese political parties in clear-cut resistance to the wartime state and patriotic rhetoric was central to its postwar status, its amour propre, as leading defender against the state's reversion to militarism. The basis of its wartime resistance had been a commitment to supranational class struggle against the ultranationalism that the Japanese militarist state promoted and that seemed to lurk behind reverse-course efforts to promote patriotism. The success that a patriot internationalist such as Yasui attained in creating a leadership role for himself in the predominantly left-wing pacifist movement points to its nationalist character.[54]

The importance of Yasui's moderating influence in promoting a pacifist ethnic nationalist sentiment that was accommodating to the conservative mindset—one that preferred forgetting Japan's militarist past and avoided antagonizing the postwar American ally—can be appreciated by contrasting the representative views of one prominent anti-American, pro-Soviet, left-wing intellectual. Prizewinning antiwar novelist and Communist Party member Noma Hiroshi, whose novels of this period depicted the evils of the wartime establishment, offered a construction of the ban-the-bomb movement as a form of anti-imperialism that privileged both international class struggle and ethnic nationalism. Even before the Lucky Dragon Incident, Noma had appropriated the atomic victim experience for the Japanese ethnic nation. In March 1953, he asserted: "We Japanese are a nation *(minzoku)* that can attack the atomic bomb from our own experience, and more than anyone else based on this wretched sacrifice *(hisan na gisei ni yotte)* we must and will be able to grasp the evil of war."[55] Yet in a series of essays on nuclear weapons published in late 1954 and early 1955, Noma developed the idea that the threat of nuclear annihilation had created a new way for human beings to connect with one another across national and ethnic lines. This sort of idealism informed the antinuclear pacifism of Yasui and many others. Describing the potential for what Robert Jay Lifton was later to characterize as "species mentality,"[56] Noma wrote that the quotidian reality of radioactivity—radioactivity in children's milk, in tea, on the vegetables people ate—made "humanity" *(jinrui)* for the first time a concrete, shared feeling rather than an abstract concept. He reiterated philosopher Mutai Risaku's assertion that Japan needed to construct cultural as well as economic independence to accompany its political independence after the U.S. occupation. Turning the inherent tension between national and species consciousness on its head, Noma followed Mutai's theories on socialist humanism by contending that the basis for the Japanese ethnic nation's cultural independence *(minzoku jiritsu)* lay in just such a concrete consciousness of a common humanity as a basis for cultural creativity. But where Mutai perceived the beginnings of this concrete perception of a common fate in the crucible of the widely shared experience of modern warfare in World War I, Noma linked its emergence to the establishment of classless society in the Soviet Union in the same era. In such socialist societies, the sense of a common humanity was strong because the subjectivity *(shutaisei)* of humanism revealed itself in a self-actualized "people's masses" and the working class.

Moving to the 1950s, Noma asserted that the species consciousness arising from the common experience with radioactive fallout and the consciousness of common humanity arising from the classless Soviet society were one and the same. Altering the Occupation-era sensibility that linked peace with those who could master nuclear energy, Noma rejected the idea that American success in building nuclear weapons was emblematic of a superior model of a rational, peaceful society. Rather, the U.S. hydrogen bomb experiments at Bikini Atoll revealed the bankruptcy of such abstract arguments. Ignoring the Soviet nuclear weapons testing program, Noma counterpoised the danger of human extinction from nuclear weapons developed by the United States against the potential for humanity's salvation in the Soviets' success at harnessing nuclear energy for peaceful electrical power generation. In Noma's egregiously pro-Soviet view —a bias he shared with many progressive intellectuals of the day—

the Soviet leadership's tangible, living sense of a common humanity enabled them to immediately grasp the species consciousness engendered by the threat of nuclear weapons. Accordingly, left-wing critics such as Noma considered American nuclear policy duplicitous but praised as genuine the Soviet calls for the development of peaceful uses for nuclear energy and a ban on nuclear weapons.[57]

Yasui's vision of Japanese pacifism did not require such an ideological lens. At the height of nuclear fallout anxiety in the mid-1950s, he took steps to prevent his movement from narrowing its appeal by showing a Soviet bias. For example, Yasui argued forcefully to make the national petition coordinating council formed in the summer of 1954 a "clean organization unsullied by any factional or personal egoism."[58] In early 1955, he steered the movement away from the World Peace Council's "Vienna Appeal"—a communist-backed petition calling for a ban on nuclear weapons and opposition to any government preparing for nuclear war—because it would have weakened the Japanese movement's cohesiveness. And in his summation at the first World Conference in August 1955, he refrained from any anti-American references even when he suggested that the movement establish links with the left-wing campaign against expansion of U.S. military bases in Japan.[59]

Virtually all commentators on the Suginami petition movement mention the vital role of women in its success. Certainly the fallout from hydrogen bomb testing contaminated foodstuffs, which caused concern among housewives and mothers who were responsible for providing wholesome nutrition to their families. But Yasui's position in the Suginami community contributed also. Through his mass education efforts Yasui had much contact with the women of Suginami, most significantly the hundred women in his reading discussion group at the community center. When it came time to organize, his personal resolve to nurture a mass movement coincided with genuine concern among the Suginami women's groups. Yasui himself raised the women's profile with frequent references to their central contributions to the movement. The reason for Yasui's praise—besides the fact that Suginami women had collected over 200,000 of the 285,000 signatures on the ward's petition—lay in his belief in women's natural role in local movements. Speaking to the World Mother's Conference in 1955, for example, he said: "The greatest force for maintaining world peace is the immeasurable love of mothers who wish for their children's happiness. Even though the light shining from each individual mother is small, if you combine them the whole

world will brighten. Please believe that, and work for peace in the
neighborhoods and villages of the world."[60] Yasui believed that
women, as wives and mothers, played an essential and powerful role
in their local communities—an activity that formed the basis for true
mass movements.

The life-enhancing image of the healthy mother and child, so
often contrasted against a masculinized image of war, was especially
effective in attracting broad sympathy to the ban-the-bomb movement.[61] Instead of having workers gather signatures on street corners,
the Suginami Council relied on housewives canvassing door to door
in an effort to keep the message "bright," upbeat, and ostensibly
apolitical. The poster for the first World Conference Against Atomic
and Hydrogen Bombs (1955) featured a madonna and child motif
with children dancing around them. Of course, the violation of
this purity, as symbolized by women and children as representative
A-bomb victims, was all the more persuasive as an argument against
nuclear weapons. As one student of Japanese war memories has
observed, the "universal icon of love and life," the image of mother
and infant, was "transposed into a symbol of the broken life bond" in
photojournalistic and artistic images of *hibakusha* mothers trying to
nurse dead babies or babies trying to nurse from their mother's
corpse.[62] The first day of the 1955 World Conference ended with testimony from victims of the Hiroshima, Nagasaki, and Bikini bombs;
the last two speakers were women. The twenty-five-year-old chair of
the Nagasaki Atomic Bomb Maiden Association broke down in tears
several times during her speech as she related how she and others
often considered giving up on life because they had lost their mothers
or feared their mothers' sudden collapse from radiation sickness.[63]
Kuboyama Suzu, the widow of the Lucky Dragon crew member who
died from radiation poisoning, closed the day's formal meetings with
an impassioned plea for all to overcome their political differences in
a shared opposition to nuclear war. In her short speech, she referred
three times to Japan's triple exposure to atomic bombs as she called
for a ban on entry of nuclear weapons into Japan.[64]

Kamei Katsuichirō, who participated in the wartime "overcoming
the modern" conferences and initiated the "Shōwa History" debates
with his criticism of the Marxist study of that name, represents a
member of the conservative intelligentsia who embraced this privileging of women as witnesses to a uniquely Japanese atomic victimhood. In one of his social commentary columns at this time, "On the
Nuclear Bomb from Japan's Viewpoint," Kamei reflected on the pathos
of children being exposed to radioactive fallout: "It is precisely be-

cause of this, I think, that mothers are particularly sensitive to opposing nuclear bombs." After emphasizing the moral legitimacy of the maternal position against nuclear weapons, what he called the "power of mothers," Kamei expanded this moral high ground to encompass the Japanese nation, arguing that nuclear victimhood actually strengthened Japan's international position: "The country is weak internationally. But in the fact that we actually realize the damage and suffering of nuclear weapons, we stand on the bodies of its victims and openly witness the danger to the world. In that sense I think it is appropriate to see ourselves as internationally strong."[65]

The iconograph of Japanese *hibakusha* motherhood accommodated identities of the left as well as the right. Members of the Gensuikin Mothers Association (Gensuibaku Kinshi Hiroshima Haha no Kai) and other women writers in the 1960s and 1970s took anti-American and anti-imperialist positions while they expressed a consciousness of themselves "as Japanese mothers and as Hiroshima *hibakusha* mothers."[66] Yet John Treat, perhaps the most incisive interpreter of atom-bomb literature, notes that in fiction "America remains relatively absent from the pages of a-bomb literature" because of the inescapable difficulty in isolating and assigning total guilt, and because of the transcendent horror of the A-bomb experience.[67] In the middle 1950s, Yasui relied on the plentiful narratives, artistic and otherwise, of women as symbolic (nuclear) war victims that were silent on America's agency in Japan's victimization. It was Yasui's pragmatic insight to recognize that the appeal of a film like *Children of Hiroshima* lay in its ostensibly apolitical plot. To illustrate the quintessential experience of atomic victimhood in his memoir of the ban-the-bomb movement, published to coincide with the first World Conference in August 1955, Yasui chose to quote a woman's poem characteristically lacking in anti-American, anti-imperialist sentiment. Yashima Fujiko's poem, "I Will Testify About Hiroshima," is about a mother's anger over the atomic bomb and her resolution to oppose war by giving testimony of her experience:

> I who have survived
> more than anything want to be human
> more than anything else as a mother. . . .
> A mother rejects her child's death . . .
> as a surviving witness of Hiroshima I will
> go anywhere and testify
> and plead with all my life
> "let us renounce war."[68]

This poem and Yasui's project were of course rooted in the reigning conservative ideology of gender relations in that they relied on and sustained the dominant, inherently conservative assignation of women's purview to the domestic sphere. In her nuanced study of the politics of Hiroshima remembrance, Lisa Yoneyama suggests: "The deployment of womanliness, a quality that was believed to introduce critical differences into the [usually masculinized] political process, in fact rearticulates the communal and distinct space of women within the language of patriarchy and consumer capitalism."[69] And on the international level Yoneyama notes that the case of the "Hiroshima Maidens"—disfigured *hibakusha* women who were brought to the United States for reconstructive cosmetic surgery in the middle 1950s —"loyally figured the [Japanese] nation in its relation to the paternalized America."[70] In this respect, the prominence given to women as symbolic victims of nuclear weapons provided a normative social framework for those of diverse political views to espouse antinuclear pacifism.[71]

The First World Conference and Beyond

The most eminent chronicler of the antinuclear pacifist movement in Japan was Imahori Seiji, professor of Chinese history at Hiroshima University and activist within the movement. Writing in 1974, Imahori argued that the Suginami petition movement was flawed in several respects. Pointing out that the Suginami Appeal neglected aid for the *hibakusha,* Imahori contended that the movement was "spiritually shallow" because it had failed *hibakusha* in its own midst.[72] He recognized that the movement's immediate aim was limited to effecting a national change in attitude. But making the movement apolitical— especially on the inherently political issue of banning nuclear weapons —left it a "ship without a compass" the moment it ventured beyond mere education. Finally, he thought the movement had lost a valuable legacy of scientist and artist opposition when it cut itself off from the pre-Bikini pacifist movement.[73]

Imahori's criticisms of the movement's political and spiritual weaknesses are well founded, but he failed to suggest any better way of attaining and maintaining widespread Japanese consciousness against nuclear weapons. Yasui was aware of the pragmatic limitations of the movement—which is why he tried to keep the message simple and avoid the contentious issues at that stage of the mass movement. In early 1955 he opposed mobilizing for the Vienna Appeal, even after

20 million Japanese had signed the petition, because it would have weakened the movement's cohesiveness and had no chance of getting as many signatures.[74] And on the eve of the Hiroshima Conference in August 1955, he wrote: "Under the concrete conditions in Japan at present, I have determined there is no other kind of peace movement in which the people can cooperate from the heart on the scale of tens of millions."[75]

The widespread identification with atomic victimhood, as articulated and promoted by the ban-the-bomb movement in the middle 1950s, compelled Japan's successive conservative administrations to make antinuclear pacifism an unchallengeable component of national policy. As part of its commitment to the U.S. security alliance, the Yoshida government had long supported Washington's nuclear policy. Despite the popular sentiment against nuclear weapons reflected in the increasing numbers of petition signatures, Yoshida did not change this position in the last year of his administration. His successor, Hatoyama Ichirō, wanted to regain a measure of Japanese independence by strengthening Japan's own military; but he was also committed to continuing the alliance with the United States against communism and supporting U.S. nuclear policy.[76] Hatoyama recognized antinuclear sentiment, and on becoming prime minister in December 1954 he privately promised the National Council leadership he would cooperate with their movement.[77] Hatoyama did not touch on nuclear issues in explaining his policy of "autonomous peace diplomacy" (*jishu heiwa gaikō*) in his administrative policy speech to the Twenty-first Diet in January 1955. But his foreign minister, Shigemitsu Mamoru, did:

> Due to the development of weapons of mass destruction, humankind is at the crossroads of mutual existence or mutual destruction. As the only state (*yuiitsu no kokka*) to have fully tasted the horrors of the atomic bomb, Japan, one should say, carries the mission of freeing the world from the nightmare of atomic war. For this reason, Japan has taken the initiative in supporting the U.N.'s proposals for peaceful use of nuclear energy. I fervently pray that the world lose no time escaping confusion and realizing true coexistence.[78]

Hatoyama's government, then, co-opted atomic exceptionalist rhetoric for the state at an early stage—including the popular notion of an exceptional Japanese mission. In light of this mass sentiment, Shigemitsu was able to arrange an informal promise from the United States in May not to station nuclear weapons in Japan without consulting the Japanese government first.[79] But at this point the administration would—perhaps could—only pursue that mission by promoting peaceful uses of nuclear energy, not by advocating the elimination of nuclear weapons.

That Hatoyama did not wholeheartedly share in the ban-the-bomb petition sentiments became apparent the next month when he told a foreign press conference that he might have to permit storage of American nuclear weapons if asked.[80] Then, at the end of July, he said that in an emergency Japan might want nuclear armed missiles for its defense, but at that time there was no need for them.[81] At the World Conference Against Atomic and Hydrogen Bombs that August, he limited his message to a mere greeting to foreign participants and an earnest hope that nuclear energy be used for the welfare of humankind. Since the convention was first and foremost planned as a celebration of the antibomb petition movement, his obvious reticence on banning nuclear weapons revealed the limits to his cooperation.

Hatoyama's reticence was just one symptom of the limited conservative leadership support for Yasui's Suginami Appeal ideals, for even at this stage the movement was strongly influenced by leftist activism. Despite Yasui's efforts to keep the movement free of the divisiveness of political factions, the first World Conference Against Atomic and Hydrogen Bombs itself showed signs of being co-opted to a progressive political program.[82] Standard treatments of the antinuclear movement hold that this first World Conference achieved consensus on adding *hibakusha* relief to its goal of banning nuclear weapons and that it was only in the late 1950s that leftist agitation against Kishi's renegotiation of the U.S. Security Treaty politicized the movement.[83] While it is true that aid for *hibakusha* became the next focus of the movement and gained multiparty support, leftist insistence on criticizing U.S. military base expansion at the first conference was already repoliticizing the movement. Although the conference retained its focus on the victim's message and continued to give prominence to women in the movement, the unity that Yasui had tried so persistently to maintain was threatened.

The tensions between conservative and progressive were evident in the speeches delivered the very first day of the conference. In the keynote speech, Yasui began by recognizing the plight of the *hibakusha* and asserting that the petition movement was based on the "onrush of the nation's feelings" *(kokumin kanjō no honryū)* caused by their third exposure to nuclear injury. He expressed guarded hope that Hatoyama would abandon the Yoshida administration's cooperation with atomic bomb testing.[84] Then he described the conference as the summation of the national petition movement and an assembly to determine the movement's future. At this point Yasui made no mention of any contentious issue such as U.S. base expansions in Japan; rather he stressed the conference's unity in opposing nuclear weapons. After Prime Minister Hatoyama's sparing message, all the representatives of political parties and civic groups gave their greetings; but as neither the Liberal Party nor the Democratic Party sent representatives, his was the only conservative speech that day.[85] Matsumoto Ji'ichirō, Left JSP peace activist, famous proponent of *burakumin* outcast class rights, and the Japanese representative from the Asian Peace Convention that had been held in Delhi earlier that year, was most vocal in denouncing the Hatoyama cabinet for preventing the Chinese and Soviet delegates from attending. Matsumoto then complained of "a certain country at the Four Great Power Conference" that seemed to have wanted to distance Japan from the Soviet Union and China. Even if Hatoyama pledged to support the movement against the hydrogen bomb, it is little wonder that he and the conservative mainstream were slow to give uncritical support to this kind of leftist agitation within it. Ideological divisions between conservatives and progressives threatened to surface the moment the movement entertained the notion of changing government policy.

The second day was taken up with six subcommittee meetings held simultaneously around the city. There was quick consensus on aid for Hiroshima and Nagasaki *hibakusha*. All six subcommittees separately discussed the need to call on the Japanese government to aid *hibakusha*. The second subcommittee included the justification that "the tragedy of Hiroshima victims is all Japan's tragedy," so the government should fund facilities, medical care, and studies for them. There was also uncontested agreement that the movement should not disband but should expand operations and broaden its goals. Four of the six subcommittees discussed joining forces with the movement opposing military base expansion. The third subcommittee could not agree, as Shimane prefecture's representative stated that the movement would lose support if they opposed military bases.[86] These concerns were overridden on the final day of the conference. In his summation of the conference, Yasui advocated that the government be made responsible for the *hibakusha*. He then came out with an explicit statement on military bases:

> This is an expression of Japan's condition today, an expression of the Japanese people's earnest desire for the [Japanese] ethnic nation's

independence and Asia's freedom. We think we should develop a broad peace movement based on strengthening close communication among the antibase movement, the ban-the-bomb movement, and all peace organizations.[87]

The conference's closing declaration began with a reference to the hundreds of millions of people who signaled their opposition to nuclear war and a call for nuclear energy to be used for humanity's happiness and prosperity.[88] It then said that the basis for the movement lay in the world knowing the plight of nuclear victims and taking quick action for their aid through a global relief movement. There followed a call for the people of the world to overcome differences in political party, religion, and social system to further advance the movement. These were all nonpartisan issues on which everyone was sympathetic. But after referring to the general relaxation of international tensions accompanying the Geneva Four-Power Meeting—popular opinion is credited with bringing the meeting about—the declaration stated that the movement's goal had not yet been realized. What was needed to prevent nuclear war was opposition to stockpiling of nuclear weapons and expansion of military bases, not just in Japan and Okinawa but around the world. Accordingly, the struggle against military bases (in Japan) had to be joined with the movement to ban the bomb.[89] Thus at the culmination of the early ban-the-bomb movement, leftists were succeeding in directing its momentum to serve the ends of the anti-U.S., antibase movement. Even in 1955, the movement was heading into more controversial areas.

In his preface to the pamphlet containing the official report on the conference, Yasui noted that it was successful "to a certain extent" in bringing together Japanese from around the country regardless of political affiliation or social position. The conference provided a forum for reflection on the petition movement, he wrote, and the delegates resolved to change concrete political policies, not just attitudes. Opposition to bases was part of this shift. But for the time being aid for *hibakusha* became the primary project for the revamped movement.[90]

Gensuikyō continued to organize world conferences against nuclear weapons, but multiparty support gradually weakened as popular enthusiasm waned and professional activists took control of the national organization. The first new issue taken up was procuring aid for *hibakusha*. The conservatives were piecemeal in their support to begin with. And when the progressives forced the conference's platform into opposing renewal of the U.S. Security Treaty in 1959, the conservatives withdrew their financial support and caused local conservative politicians to leave Gensuikyō affiliates. These are the facts behind conventional narratives of the movement's fragmentation in the late 1950s. In 1961, they formed their own organization with moderate socialists, the National Council for Peace and Against Nuclear Weapons (Kakuheiki Kinshi Heiwa Kensetsu Kokumin Kaigi, or Kakkin Kaigi), holding separate conventions. Left Socialists and Communists bickered over the Soviet resumption of nuclear bomb testing and split at the 1963 conference. The Socialists formed their own organization: the Japan Conference Against Atomic and Hydrogen Bombs (Gensuibaku Kinshi Nihon Kokumin Kaigi, or Gensuikin).

Although politicization of Gensuikyō's national office led to loss of nonpartisan support, the idea of a uniquely privileging Japanese atomic victimhood remained a part of national culture, occasionally reinforced by event and policy, and always available to serve any political interest. One event that helped reinforce the pacifist Hiroshima legacy of atomic victimhood was Sasaki Sadako's death due to leukemia on October 25, 1955. This seemingly healthy twelve-year-old girl suddenly became ill with the disease in sixth grade because she had been exposed to radiation at the Hiroshima bombing. While in the hospital, she heard that if she folded a thousand cranes her wish to get well would come true, but she died before she could fold one thousand. Her friends too had folded strings of cranes for her benefit. When her story became widely known, elementary school children from around the nation collected donations for a children's monument in the Hiroshima Peace Park. The monument was completed on May 5, 1958, and has ever since worn a continually replenished mantle of strings of a thousand paper cranes made by schoolchildren visiting the park.[91]

Atomic victimhood was reinforced as it found expression in novels, movies, and school curricula. Besides the well-known *Godzilla* series featuring the innumerable replications of Tokyo being stomped and burned to destruction, Japanese being victimized by nuclear weapons, directly or indirectly, became the theme of films ranging from Kurosawa Akira's *I Live in Fear* (1955), the story of an old man driven mad by his paranoia over nuclear fallout, to Shindō Kaneto's plodding documentary *Lucky Dragon Number 5* (1959). There was, of course, an ebb and flow of interest and contemporary relevance about the Hiroshima legacy. In the middle to late 1950s, for example, social studies and history textbooks showed a sudden emphasis on Japan's unique role as atomic victim in calling for global peace. Atomic victimhood lost its prominence in later editions —during the years of détente and the first flush of Japanese economic success in the 1960s and 1970s (reflecting a shift in contemporary concerns from antinuclear pacifism to economic nationalism)— but regained importance in the early 1980s when Cold War tensions rose again. Still, Hiroshima retained its prominence in several realms of national life. The city and its peace park have become a central destination of what might be termed "peace tourism." Except in years of economic recession, or renovation to its physical plant, the park's Peace Museum has received ever increasing numbers of visitors since it opened in August 1955. By the middle 1980s, over a million and a half people had visited the museum; a third of these were members of school groups, especially from the Kansai (Osaka–Kyoto) and Kantō (Tokyo) regions. National news organizations reinforce Hiroshima's iconographic presence when they report on annual memorial ceremonies on August 6, including scenes from across the city as the minute of silence is observed at 8:15 A.M.[92]

Some Japanese thought the ban-the-bomb movement was so intrinsically a Japanese mission, based on their exceptional atomic experience, that they came to believe it had actually begun in Japan and then spread throughout the world. Nishimoto Atsushi, a Nichiren priest who made a name for himself by getting clubbed and bloodied by police in a protest against the American base at Sunakawa, boasted during a "peace march" from Hiroshima to Tokyo in 1958 that "the ban-the-bomb movement that started in Japan has had influence throughout the world." The journalists who reported Nishimoto's boast felt it necessary to remind readers that the antinuclear movement had not existed continuously since the Hiroshima bombings: it became a national movement with the mass media reporting after the Bikini Incident. It was only then that the Japanese "remembered" Hiroshima and Nagasaki. By 1958, then, there was a tendency to believe that the antinuclear peace movement had Japanese origins.[93] The mythic import of the movement had grown so strong that memory of its origins could be altered, the narrative embellished, to meet the requirements of pride in Japanese victimhood.

The Ideology of Victimhood

The Japanese knew that they were victims of war before they understood "Hiroshima" as a symbol of their nation's atomic victimhood.

The war crimes trials and other Occupation policies had convinced them that their militarist leadership had victimized them as well as other peoples: their loyalty to the state had been betrayed. The Mac-Arthur Constitution was accepted, not just because of its guarantees of civil liberties, but because its peace article articulated this rejection of the state's right to victimize its own in war. The Japanese as a people would rely on the consciences of other peoples to protect them from war in the future.

Early antibomb sentiment in Hiroshima was based on a similar psychology but transcended the realm of nations to lay claim to the consciences of all fellow human beings. Literary, artistic, and religious commemorators of Hiroshima and Nagasaki rejected war because they simply refused to allow human beings ever again to become the victims of nuclear weapons. Japanese were as sympathetic as any to this claim when they were finally allowed to hear it. While it remained a frightening warning to humanity of the dangers of the nuclear age, by the end of the Occupation many, like "Tensei jingo" columnist Aragaki, began to integrate the Hiroshima experience into their own identity as Japanese. But the left's appropriation of nuclear victim-hood failed to mobilize this identification into an effective political movement. Radioactive fallout from the Bikini tests helped all Japanese to experience the Hiroshima A-bomb victimhood as their own, and Yasui Kaoru's ban-the-bomb petition movement involved them in making atomic victimhood a peculiarly transcendent national experience.

Nationalist mythologization of the Hiroshima and Nagasaki bombings appealed to Japanese in many ways. The atomic bombings lent themselves to myth building because they ushered in the new nuclear era—one that resonated with the Japanese and American desire to construct the end of the war as a watershed in Japanese history. Defeat marked a new beginning: postwar Japan was giving up military options, adopting peace as a foreign policy, and relying on the consciences of other nations for its defense.[94] Nuclear weapons raised the stakes of war to encompass the possible annihilation of all human civilization, creating for many a new compelling reason to oppose war absolutely. Just as Japan had renounced conventional warfare, so should all nations forgo nuclear weapons. National history and world history intersected at Hiroshima. Internationally recognized as the birthplace of a new epoch, Hiroshima validated both Japan's absolute rejection of war and its national rebirth as a cultural nation.

Atomic victimhood also assured the Japanese nation a special status in a Cold War era preoccupied with nuclear war. Hiroshima and Nagasaki became the symbols of the worldwide antinuclear movement precisely because they were the only instances of the use of nuclear weapons. The international community was inclined to recognize as natural the Japanese adoption of the *hibaku* nuclear victim experience as its own *minzoku*'s (ethnic nation's) special history, since ethnonationalism was especially pervasive in the middle years of the twentieth century.[95] In 1961, political scientist Sakamoto Yoshikazu described the atomic experience as the "singular national principle" *(yuiitsu nashonaru (kokuminteki) na genri)* that made the peace movement in Japan peculiarly Japanese:

> The spiritual support for postwar Japan's peace movement can be found more than anywhere else in the Hiroshima and Nagasaki atomic bombings. Of course there is no doubt that the victim experience arising from wartime suffering and the victimizer experience as supporters of the war of aggression carry great significance as the source of the peace movement.[96] But while it is unavoidable that memories of war damage and awareness of war responsibility tend with the passage of time to be seen as past issues, the issue of nuclear bombs forces itself on us, on the young generations especially, as a future problem.[97]

In other words: memories of atomic victimhood were continually reinforced in the Cold War atmosphere, when nuclear war seemed all too likely. The younger generations never experienced the hardships of defeat, but they understood the nuclear threat. Their pacifism naturally grew with consciousness of themselves as Japanese, a people with a special mission in the nuclear era.

Although Imahori, Yasui, and other leaders in the movement occasionally cautioned Japanese to remember their past aggressions against Asians, Japanese consciousness as victimizer played little role in antinuclear pacifism. The movement was based on the idea of righteous innocence. To some extent this was true of the Japanese peace movement at large, whose left-wing leadership in the 1950s and early 1960s was not vigilant in maintaining memories of the Japanese people's, as opposed to the state's, aggressions against Asians.[98] One might consider this oversight a consequence of the left's exclusive tradition of wartime opposition to the Japanese *state's* policies of aggression. To leftists it was significant that it was the United States that had thrice been the agent of Japanese atomic victimization. This sense of being victimized by the United States was continually reinforced by Japan's client state status—and resentment quite often surfaced in progressive complaints that Japan was being "forced to remilitarize" by the U.S. imperialists. Leftist activists no doubt felt somewhat victimized by the postwar conservative establishment and their "American imperialist" sponsors and easily identified the United States with Japan's wartime leadership and militarist past. Rejecting U.S. nuclear bombs coincided with their rejection of Japan's wartime aggressions. For leftists, Asian solidarity meant uniting against the U.S. imperialist nuclear threat. They continued to condemn their wartime state for victimizing Asians, but the leftists themselves belonged to a tradition of opposition to that militarist/conservative state. Implicitly, then, they were not responsible for its wartime crimes.[99]

As careful and self-reflective as Yasui Kaoru was, he too found a common cause with Asians through a shared sense of oppression. Perhaps unconsciously revisiting his predefeat advocacy of Japan's liberation ideology—the propagandistic idea that Japan was liberating Asia from the shackles of Western imperialism—or following the left-wing fascination with the revolutionary potential of ethnic nationalist movements, Yasui spoke of the psychic benefit of atomic victimhood as a sort of self-actualization. He envisioned the petition movement as one of the many national independence drives in Asia after World War II. Yasui claimed that the underlying force impelling the "flow of this great river" of history was recognition of human beings' right to life and happiness: "In Japan, too, the people have begun to realize this right. You can probably say that the petition movement trying to protect lives and happiness from the threat of atomic and hydrogen bombs is one branch leading into the flow of this great river."[100] Yasui wanted to foster grassroots activism—to assist people in asserting their right to life and happiness to help build a democratic Japan. By understanding the threat of nuclear weapons, identifying opposition to it as a national cause, and taking action based on that identification, he argued, the Japanese had regained some of their independence and sense of worth as a nation. He was no doubt correct. But in this context Asian fellowship became merely a symbol of the Japanese people's liberation from their own state. Few seem to have noted the irony that Japan had once been the oppressor of Asia.

Left-wing pacifists were alienated from the state. But as Fukuda Tsuneari argued in a *Chūō kōron* essay in December 1954, they may have preferred it that way. Fukuda shocked the progressive pacifist community when he called them irresponsible precisely because they maintained ideological distance from their government.[101] He criticized the "united front" (tōitsu sensen) for complicating local issues by diverting energies into a national cause that often became an obstacle to local resolution. In language startlingly similar to psychiatrist Takeo Doi's later analysis of radical student activists, Fukuda diagnosed this behavior pattern as the "disease of self-denial" (jiko massatsu byō) because it "cuts you off from subjectivity which is the self" (jiko to iu shutai kara kirihanashi). The benefits of the illness were clear: because the individual had no direct connection with the problem, his burden was lighter and he was released from responsibility for taking action since the problem was unsolvable.[102] Herein lay a paradox of antinuclear pacifism based on atomic victimhood: absolute rejection of nuclear weapons not only prevented compromise and hindered resolution of security concerns and complicated diplomatic relations with the United States; it also effectively relieved the ideologically pure activist of responsibility for solving them. Progressives suffered for their dogged insistence on the victim mindset. By the early 1960s even the liberal Asahi shinbun criticized them for opposing everything "in delusions of victimhood."[103]

Yet it is important to recognize the successes of Yasui's brand of leadership in the movement's post–Lucky Dragon emphasis on nuclear victimhood and willingness to avoid anticapitalist, antistatist rhetoric. The state, after all, faced the reality of continuing subordination to the United States.[104] The electorate recognized this reality— or at least was resigned to accept it—after the flush of grassroots petition activism faded and professionals began to run Gensuikyō. Popular sentiment against nuclear weapons had, after all, forced Prime Minister Kishi to develop a means for placating it. Hiroshima had become an icon of Japan's past as a nuclear victim that no astute politician could ignore. Kishi protested all nuclear testing and repeatedly went on record that Japan would neither possess nor permit the entry of nuclear weapons into Japan proper, even as he continued to cooperate in the U.S. alliance. An Asahi shinbun poll in mid-July 1957 suggests that he succeeded in mollifying public opinion. Some 87 percent of those polled agreed that nuclear tests should be banned, yet 91 percent of men and 87 percent of women polled also supported government policies.[105]

In an April 1958 essay in the intellectual journal Shisō, social commentator Arase Yutaka concluded from these poll results that the Japanese people were naive. He also concluded that the Kishi administration had succeeded in pulling the wool over the people's eyes with its pattern of posing to protest nuclear weapons and their testing while continuing to support the U.S. alliance.[106] Arase also argued that in its concern for maintaining supraparty unity at all costs and in its rush to appeal to world trends, the antibomb movement neglected an examination of Japan's own state policy. Thus when the government adopted its Janus-faced position on nuclear issues, it gained popular support without having to change its basic security policy.[107]

It is difficult to say whether Arase was right regarding the naïvete of the Japanese public. People might have recognized the difficulties of implementing an idealistic and absolute opposition to nuclear weapons at the same time they insisted their government voice that idealism. Or they may have felt that, as atomic victims, the most they were able to do was voice a protest in the self-indulgent *(amai)* hope that other more powerful peoples and their governments might change their policies. The pre-Bikini sense of impotence appears often in the *Asahi shinbun* newspaper in the late 1950s and early 1960s.[108] This does not mean that the ban-the-bomb petition movement had no impact, however, for it prevented the United States from openly stationing nuclear weapons on Japanese soil.

A common sense of stewardship over antinuclear pacifism was expressed in the "Tensei jingo" column of August 4, 1962, when it praised the growing antibomb movements abroad in the same phrase it lamented the fragmentation of the movement's main house *(honke)* —which, the essay asserted, preceded and encouraged these foreign movements. The Yasui-sanctioned narrative of innocent Japanese atomic victimhood—denatured of the troubling and divisive question of why Hiroshima had ever become a nuclear target and somewhat obscure about the fact that Japan's postwar ally had dropped it— held continuing popular appeal and remained a prominent part of national culture.

Yasui's efforts to include Japanese from across the political spectrum, as well as his faith in the practice of witnessing victimhood, led him by default to sanction the type of Hiroshima narrative that was least explicit about responsibility for the bombing. This approach was effective in the short run, for it permitted everyone to unite as a nation, righteously indignant over their undeserved suffering. But in the long run this domestication of Hiroshima was problematic since it was self-indulgently silent on Japan's agency in the war. Because it obscured Japan's agency—both that of the state and that of the people as a nation—in waging conventional war before Hiroshima, it ultimately discredited Japan's witnessing of its atomic victimhood as an international pacifist praxis.[109] It also probably delayed the wide-spread emergence in the 1970s and 1980s of what historian John Dower has called the "complex perception that innocence, guilt, and responsibility may coexist at both individual and collective levels."[110] Nevertheless, this sentimentalized narrative's weakness accounted for its strength as heritage. The creation of a middle ground on which Japanese of all political persuasions could gather—in other words, a space for Hiroshima in the nation's heritage—may have ameliorated the rigidly oppositional stances in Japanese political life in the 1950s. It obviated the antagonistic narratives of class struggle that still informed political activism of the left; it permitted those on the right to join hands with those who would otherwise condemn them. This accommodation came at a critical moment in Japan's post-war history: the post-Yoshida conservative administrations were poised to remilitarize in a significant way. Yasui's flexible strategies for building national antinuclear consensus succeeded in making anti-nuclear pacifism—indeed, pacifism itself—into a viable conservative, even patriotic, position.

It is easy to see why Yasui's populist vision of the Hiroshima heritage held such appeal. It permitted Japanese, regardless of their class identities or how they felt individually about their state and its military alliance with the United States, to share the unifying idea that they as an ethnic nation had a mission of considerable importance in the Cold War era. This vision—to witness their shared national experience of atomic bomb victimhood in a way that accommodated conservative sensibilities—was ritualized in school trips to Hiroshima and Nagasaki, in minutes of silence on August 6, and in the three non-nuclear principles that later governments professed with easy disingenuity whenever suspect U.S. naval vessels came to port. Hiroshima remained important to Japanese identity as a compassionate, pacifist nation, even as nationalist sentiment found another focus in Japan's increasingly successful economic enterprise in the 1960s. Ibuse's *Black Rain* capped the hegemonic cultural construction of Hiroshima in the 1960s. But it was Yasui's political domestication of antinuclear pacifism in the 1950s that laid the foundation for Hiroshima to become the premier enduring icon of Japanese war victimhood in the nation's pacifist heritage.

CHAPTER 4

Educating a Peace-Loving People
Narratives of War in Postwar Textbooks

Our country lost. The people suffered greatly during the long war. This misfortune was caused by the militarists oppressing the people and waging a reckless war.
—*Kuni no ayumi* (Footsteps of the Nation; 1947)

There is no more dramatic indication of the change from democratic politics, which had developed gradually since the Meiji period, to the dark, gloomy reactionary politics, than the phrase reportedly uttered by Premier Inukai as a pistol was pressed against his breast—"Let us discuss it," the blunt reply of the naval officer, "No discussion needed," and the following report of the pistol. Parliamentary government is politics based on "discussion"; dictatorial government is the politics of "No discussion needed." When we reflect on it, the report of the pistol at the time of the May 15 Incident was the funeral knell for democratic party politics, which had begun to progress. It was an ominous sign of things to come, driving toward the outrage of the Pacific War from which there was no turning back.
—*Minshushugi* (Democracy; 1949)

E DUCATION was an integral part of the Occupation's efforts to reconstruct Japan and rehabilitate the Japanese as a democratic, peace-loving people. The strategy was straightforward: SCAP's Civil Information and Education (CIE) Section eliminated courses in history, geography, and morals that inculcated ultranationalist thought; it then directed the Ministry of Education to produce new textbooks for social studies courses that condemned militarism and ultranationalism and encouraged democratic habits of thought. From the prosaic *Kuni no ayumi* (Footsteps of the Nation) to the dramatic *Minshushugi* (Democracy), these texts built the basis for pacifism and democracy by condemning the militarist leadership for forcing the Japanese people into a reckless war and causing misery to the Japanese and other peoples.[1] Occupation-era texts established two perennial themes in what came to be called "peace education" *(heiwa kyōiku):* the people had been forced or duped by their militarist leaders into cooperating with the war effort; science and culture were the proper realms in which Japan could contribute to the postwar international community.

After independence, history narratives in social studies textbooks became the object of contention between politically progressive forces —often allied with the Japan Teachers Union (JTU), which championed the UNESCO credo that education is the surest safeguard for peace— and conservative forces that viewed Occupation reforms to have been as excessively destructive of the national fabric in education as in other areas. Between these two camps in the struggle over the content of peace education lay a chasm between progressives' alienation from state authority and conservatives' faith in it. Progressives feared any revision that encouraged patriotism without unconditionally condemning Japan's militarist past, for they felt this threatened a return to wartime militarism and its intolerance of pacifist and liberal thought.[2] Conservatives argued that textbooks had become so thorough in condemning ultranationalism and so radical in promoting liberal thought that younger generations were becoming deficient in patriotic sentiment and bereft of any moral foundation as Japanese. Yoshida Shigeru complained near the end of the Occupation: "Since the termination of the Pacific conflict, the individual had become everything and the state nothing."[3]

In the half century since the Occupation's end, conservative groups have made repeated attempts to regain a measure of control over history and social studies textbook narratives.[4] The first and most successful effort took the form of the Democratic Party's commitment to revise what were termed "lamentable" *(ureubeki)* texts in the middle 1950s.[5] Conservative political and administrative pressure brought several changes to the textbook authorization procedures in the late 1950s and early 1960s, generally making publishers more sensitive to Ministry of Education guidance. In 1956, local boards of education were made appointive rather than elective, and these boards were given final authority to choose textbooks the next year. In 1957, Education Minister Kiyose Ichirō brought examination and approval of texts more directly under ministry control by adding and expanding ministerial representation in the evaluative and review stages of certification. The 1963 Textbook Law required publishers to register as qualified textbook providers and limited them to two resubmissions of texts. There were two primary consequences of these developments: smaller publishers were driven out of the textbook business, and the remaining textbooks became generic. Ever since this formalization of strict Ministry of Education procedures, progressive forces have complained that the ministry has moderated references to Japanese imperialist aggression in Asia. Although conservative administrations did achieve some success in correcting what they regarded as excessively self-recriminatory histories, they were not as successful as progressive critics complained (nor as is commonly presented in mass media).[6]

Professor Ienaga Saburō's widely reported civil and administrative suits against the Ministry of Education assured that questions about textbook certification as a form of revisionist censorship remained prominent in popular discourse.[7] Yet as Lawrence Beer observes in his incisive and wide-ranging study, *Freedom of Expression in Japan,* the controversy surrounding textbook certification procedures in Japan continues to be part of a larger social and political process: the struggle over "which substantive values shall become the eventual basis of ideological consensus." Whatever revisionist pressures the Ministry of Education certification officers brought to bear on authors and publishers, in 1965 the Japan Teachers Union began issuing critiques of current textbooks that provided countervailing pressure against reactionary militarist texts.[8] Furthermore, the focus on the certification review process has obscured another factor that affects the content of history textbooks—namely, the considerable marketing incentive for publishers to revise their textbooks so that they will be regarded as unbiased, educationally sound, and pertinent to concerns of the day.[9] In the middle 1950s, for example, popular opposition to nuclear weapons came to be reflected in textbook narratives through a full assertion of Japan's special pacifist mission as the world's only people to have been atom-bombed. Enthusiasm for Asian national independence movements surrounding the Bandung Conference (1955) at this time also encouraged the beginnings of a tendency, especially marked in texts by JTU authors, to portray the story of Asian national liberation from Western and Japanese colonialism. The Ministry of Education has itself changed in response to shifting political pressures—most notably in the early 1970s after the diplomatic rapprochement with the People's Republic of China; in the early 1980s after the 1982 controversy over whether to characterize Japan's military occupation of the Asian continent as an invasion *(shinryaku)* or an advance *(shinshutsu);* and in the early 1990s when LDP rule seemed to be ending. In these years the ministry encouraged expanded treatment of Asian national liberation movements, eventually allowing more candor in treatment of Japanese aggression against Asians.[10]

A thorough survey of the elementary and junior high school social studies and history textbooks used in the postwar era reveals greater nuance and frankness about Japan's militarist past than is commonly assumed in media discussions of Japanese textbook histories. Immediately after the implementation of strict textbook certification procedures in 1957, texts presented the state's prewar policies (apart from the military's predations) as somewhat unavoidable and therefore understandable in the climate of 1930s international relations. The national history in textbooks in the late 1950s and early 1960s did make it easier for young Japanese to see their country in a positive light. Some of the contemporary rationale for waging war in China and the Pacific in the late 1930s and 1940s—most notably the idea of a Great Power encirclement that threatened Japan's national interest —did creep into textbook narratives so that prewar expansionist policies seemed less indefensible and the nation's record less despicable. Except for a few extreme cases, however, texts continued to portray Japanese (and to some extent Asian) civilian suffering at the hands of the Japanese military. In some texts the revisionist pressure resulted in the civilian Japanese government itself being portrayed at the mercy of the militarist clique—thereby uniting people and government as mutual victims of the military.

Contrary to common assumptions about whitewashed treatments of Japan's war past, apologist leanings diminish by the early 1970s. In the middle 1970s, texts expanded narratives of oppressed peoples, including victimization of the lower classes in Japan's industrialization at home and victimization of Japanese and Asians in Japan's militarist expansion abroad. Texts projected an image of the Japanese people as a kind of "ethnic nation" *(minzoku)* set apart from wartime Japanese state and military as an international aggressor. The most widely used texts implicitly linked the Japanese "people" (usually referred to as *kokumin*) and Asian "peoples" *(minshū, minzoku,* or *kokumin)* together as common victims of the Japanese military, and war was to be rejected because of this victimization. The early 1970s rapprochement with the People's Republic of China was reflected in even more extensive coverage of Asian national liberation movements. In the late 1970s, textbooks dramatically increased treatments of

Korean and Chinese suffering. And while the Japanese people continued to be included as common victims of the Japanese army, their victim status did not so clearly exempt them from responsibility for discriminating against Koreans or, for example, dispossessing Chinese farmers in Manchuria in the 1930s. In short, while victim consciousness in textbooks blunted awareness of a Japanese people's war responsibility, it sharpened awareness of Japanese aggression overall and, eventually, a people's complicity in those aggressions.

Education Under the Occupation

Transforming the Japanese into a democratic and pacifist people was a paramount task of the Occupation. SCAP punished Japan's militarist leadership through purges and war crimes trials, but it merely condemned as misguided the enthusiastic support that the average person gave to militarist expansionist policies. It inherited the U.S. war intelligence bureau's psychological warfare approach that, argued as part of a strategy to undermine the authority of the war leadership, ordinary Japanese had been manipulated into fighting the war.[11] The underlying assumption of the American efforts in education was clear: the root of Japanese aggression lay in the people's servile habits of thought that made them so susceptible to such manipulation. SCAP hoped to raise people's awareness that this submissive habit of mind had led to their own victimization—thereby motivating them to become a new, "peaceful and responsible citizenry" that could avoid future manipulation.[12] Self-abnegation was condemned. And although in other arenas (as suggested in Chapter 2) SCAP's attitude abetted an avoidance of personal responsibility among the general population, in education the new civic subjectivity required that all who had not actively opposed the war effort ought to recognize their responsibility for it. To assure proper instruction, the teaching ranks were purged of militarists and a comprehensive program of reeducation and training was introduced. In the words of the main directive on education: "Students, teachers, educational officials, and public will be informed of . . . the part played by militaristic leaders, their active collaborators, and those who by passive acquiescence committed the nation to war with the inevitable result of defeat, distress, and the present deplorable state of the Japanese people."[13]

Japanese education experts expressed similar sentiments—at least in their communications with SCAP and in early statements on the role of education in creating a new pacifist Japan. On becoming director of the Ministry of Education's School Education Bureau in May 1946, Hidaka Daishirō submitted to SCAP an essay on education which began with a frank admission that the Japanese had only themselves to blame for the war and its consequences:

> All of us must, each according to our own position, reflect upon and repent for the fact that such a miserable condition has been brought about so as to let the people suffer from the lack of daily necessities, be resolved to bear honestly the painful responsibility for it, and deeply acknowledge our own faults not only towards our fellow countrymen who were led to death through this war but also towards the peoples of neighboring countries.[14]

The same sense of contrition for wronging others was evident to some extent in the "Guide to New Education in Japan," issued by the Ministry of Education in May 1946 as a teacher's guide, though personal responsibility was mitigated by a hodgepodge of *sōzange* apologies —everyone is responsible, therefore no one is—and structural theories that assigned blame to militarist and ultranationalist factions. According to this first specific guide to teaching in the postwar era, "the leaders who plunged the nation into [war] must be held responsible," but they erred "because there were defects in the various systems of Japan and its social setup, and in the wrong way of thinking of the people themselves."[15] The guide continued:

> Although the direct cause of Japan being in the condition she is today is due to the wrong leadership of those in power lately, i.e., people who are now being cross-examined by their own people and the Allied Powers as those responsible for the war [in the Tokyo Trials], it was because the Japanese nation as a whole possessed this weakness. In this sense, the responsibility of the war should be borne by the Japanese nation and they must apologize most humbly to the world for the sins they have committed.[16]

Despite this apparent admission that all Japanese were responsible, the guide suggested that the people should not really be held accountable because:

> The government cheated the people [by] concealing the facts and oppressed those who gave criticisms and warnings. . . . It was the militarists and ultranationalists composed of the military clique, rightist reactionaries, fascist thinkers, bureaucrats, *zaibatsu,* etc., who led Japan since about the time of the Manchurian Incident, that drove Japan into desperate war and put its people into the distresses of defeat.[17]

These passages reveal ambivalent feelings of contrition and anger that recur in later texts. The Japanese nation should be contrite for wartime aggression, but the individual people themselves should not be held too strictly accountable because they were deceived by the government and misled by militarists. Yet anger toward these leaders may also be misdirected. As the preceding passage concluded: "These people meant [well] . . . but their thoughts were narrow . . . and deaf to the true voice of the people." The real diseases were militarism and ultranationalism, which corrupted the honorable efforts of both the leaders and the people and led the state to rely on war as an instrument of foreign policy. The guide concluded with an assertion that Japanese "love peace [not] because we were defeated in war. . . . Rather . . . we love peace in order to satisfy the real desire of man." Then comes a bitter comment on meaningless wartime sacrifices, a comment that reflects the victim psychology:

> We have fought for our country, offering our husbands, losing our sons, having our homes burnt, and bearing many other calamities, but we have all been secretly thinking that it would be best if we could do without this wretched war. . . . It is because they make us act against this true will of man that militarism and ultranationalism are wrong.

Facilely the guide concludes that the solution is to eliminate these ideologies, "produce peace-loving, culture-seeking people," and "build up Japan as a peaceful cultural state."[18]

What sort of textbooks did this approach produce? Under CIE guidance, the Ministry of Education developed a complete series of stopgap texts. When social studies classes replaced history, geography, and morals instruction at the end of 1946, there were three major history textbooks: *Kuni no ayumi* (Footsteps of the Nation) for use in upper elementary and lower junior high schools; *Nihon rekishi* (Japanese History) for high school; and *Minshushugi* (Democracy) for use in high school and adult education. These texts assigned responsibility for the war and the people's suffering to the militarist clique and the prewar governing system. The civilian government, *zaibatsu* financial combines, and prewar political parties were generally also culpable, while the liberal and progressive intelligentsia, a generally agentless "people," and their emperor were held less strictly accountable.

Written for elementary school children, *Kuni no ayumi* was sparse and factual. But the message was clear: responsibility for the war lay with the militarists, who also made the Japanese people victims of war. It was the "Japanese militarists" who established the government of Manchukuo, an act condemned by the League of Nations as "not right." Although the Japanese government strove to settle the Marco Polo Bridge Incident, the military hindered it by aggressively extending the lines of battle so that the fighting became uncontrollable. It was in those circumstances, the text stated, that the government declared the object of the war to be the creation of a new order in the Far East. Eventually the civilian prime minister, Konoe Fumimaro, had to resign in the face of conflict with the militarist party. After a narrative of the battles in the Pacific War, readers were told how the emperor ended the war by accepting the Potsdam Declaration. The idea that the people were shackled by the militarists was reinforced with the statement that one of the Occupation's goals was "uprooting the idea of militarism to give our people freedom."[19]

Minshushugi—called the "Primer of Democracy" by CIE staff as it was intended for general adult education as well as secondary school—began with the historical context, which helped explain how democracy, in the form of party politics, failed to keep Japan from waging war. First, corrupt political parties became the target of popular criticism for ignoring the people's interests in pandering to *zaibatsu*. Second, fear of the left led the government to suppress free speech, which strengthened the right. The rise of militarist influence over government was seen as the natural outgrowth of militarist expansion on the continent, presaging later textbook portrayals of a community of Asian and Japanese war victims. After describing the various army intrigues of the early 1930s, the text maintained: "Although this [Manchurian] incident was the beginning of direct action by the military men to gain control of the Asian continent through armed force, their atrocious sword was also wielded in the arena of domestic politics."[20] As in SCAP's broad reorientation efforts, the official textbooks produced under its authority constructed narratives of militarists victimizing an oppressed Japanese people.

Privately Produced Textbooks: The Early Years

By 1948 the paper shortage had abated enough for private companies to begin publishing their own social studies texts—subject to review by the Ministry of Education and SCAP. The new review process set up by the Ministry of Education consisted of having an independent panel pass judgment. These panels of five (two scholars and three teachers) independently rated the quality of the texts on a numerical scale totaling 1,000, each panelist assigning a score up to 200. If the sum of scores exceeded the cutoff point of 800, the ministry passed the text. If the total was insufficient, the ministry returned the panel's comments to the publisher, who could resubmit a revised textbook as often as it wished. This system lasted until 1956 when the ministry instituted a new protocol.[21]

The standard curriculum for compulsory education directed that the history of Japanese involvement in war, and its international relations in general, be treated in the social studies courses of the sixth grade and junior high school. Accordingly, the findings in this chapter are based on a survey of these texts—especially the question of how textbooks reified the relationships among the Japanese state, government, people, political parties, and military from the 1930s to the end of the war. Among the historical incidents considered here are the Russo-Japanese War, the Manchurian and China incidents of the 1930s, World War II's end, the Lucky Dragon Incident and ensuing anti-nuclear movement, and Japan's role in the contemporary world.[22]

Changes in the certification process in the late 1950s and early 1960s had a flattening effect on textbook content, as the new process favored large publishers and gave authors and editors common incentives to produce what would be acceptable to the Ministry of Education's reviewers. The number of texts fell by half from the dozen or so available in the early to middle 1950s. Statistics show that after 1959, Tōkyō Shoseki's text has consistently accounted for 30 to 50 percent of all elementary social studies texts used and Kyōiku Shuppan's text has risen to about 25 percent of market share from 1963. Among junior high social studies texts, Chūkyō Shuppan and Tōkyō Shoseki together accounted for 50 to 60 percent of market share up to 1981, after which Tōkyō Shoseki rose to 30 to 40 percent—more than double any of its competitors.[23] Before the introduction of stricter procedures—and to a discernible but lesser extent afterwards—a distinction in textbooks can be made that generally corresponds to the political leanings of their authors and editors. Of the three main publishers whose social studies textbooks came to be most widely used in the 1960s, that is, after institution of certification procedures, Kyōiku Shuppan and Chūkyō Shuppan authors and editors included scholars affiliated with the left-wing Japan Teachers Union.[24] For the most part, we will look at these progressive texts and Tōkyō Shoseki's texts, using other texts to substantiate general trends across publishers.

Elementary School Texts

Regardless of ideological coloring, the early texts all followed the SCAP-authorized narratives that presented the Japanese people as victims of their own military—and, regardless of the degree of national contrition they assumed for the war and Japan's imperialist past, laid most of the opprobrium on the military. Kyōiku Shuppan's sixth-grade text, *Nihon to sekai* (1952), was the most explicit in condemning Japan's past wars as aggression. It carried a damning description of Japan's annexation of Korea—the assassination of Itō Hirobumi, former prime minister and then chief Japanese official in Korea, seems almost justified in this presentation—and a description of how Japan waged war in China and started the Pacific War. As in most texts, the Japanese military was blamed for willfully pursuing war and it was suggested that Japan could serve the Asian countries it overran by using science and technology for their benefit. This text was unique in asserting that Japanese needed to relearn Eastern culture, develop the correct attitude of respect for their neighbors, and learn not to look down on other ethnic nations *(minzoku)*.[25]

Chūkyō Shuppan's *Akarui shakai* (1953) was the most vehement in laying blame on the military and state abuse of power. Not only were they responsible for attacking China and setting up Manchukuo as an "independent country that was really like a Japanese colony," in Japan the "reckless military men" killed politicians who did not fall in step, took over important cabinet seats, and restructured the country for war. The government suppressed the antiwar voices of many academics, intellectuals, and artists. At one point the text intimated that the people *(kokumin)* might bear some responsibility for the war's prosecution, holding that they became complaisant when the economy improved because of the boom in military industries. But the more insistent message was that they had been duped by the government. In the nine-page coverage of the war, the reader is told three separate times that people believed it a just war because newspapers could not report the real facts of the Japanese army's atrocities in China and the government did not report the truth when it became clear that Japan was losing the war.[26]

This text, *Akarui shakai,* was especially criticized by conservatives as a communist-inspired tract that disparaged Japan. A sensitive reading does reveal postwar progressive political themes: a championing of the Chinese and Japanese peoples (referred to variously as *minzoku, kokumin,* or *hitobito*) against an aggressive and oppressive Japanese "state" *(kokka)* and an imputation that the postwar conservative government was repeating prewar mistakes in support-ing the U.S. military alliance in the Cold War. The opposition of "the people" to "the state" is a motif sustained in the account of the war on both the domestic and foreign fronts. The China Incident defied solution because "even applying the power of the state *(kokka no chikara)* [with military force], the [Chinese] nation *(minzoku)* united as one and resisted."[27] After extensively quoting the sections of the Potsdam Declaration that blamed the militarists for duping the Japa-nese ethnic nation *(minzoku),* the textbook spelled out the moral of the Japanese people's wartime experiences:

> A peaceful and just world will not be born until militarism is elimi-nated. The force *(chikara)* that duped the Japanese people *(Nihon kokumin)* and tried to conquer the world must be removed forever. We do not want to enslave or bring ruin to the Japanese nation *(Nihon minzoku);* but we must severely punish the war criminals. All those who would obstruct the democratization of Japan must be removed.[28]

While *Akarui shakai* sang the praises of the people in the face of militarist state force and other texts carried similar though less ex-plicit messages about the righteousness of oppressed peoples, the most conservative of the texts surveyed, Teikoku Shoin's *Sekai to musubu Nihon* (1954), plainly encouraged a more conventional na-tionalism with a closer relationship between people and state. The frontispiece was bordered by national flags: the Japanese *Hi no maru* was at the top left, the U.N. flag on the top right. After the usual de-scriptions of international organizations in which contemporary Japan should participate (the U.N., the Red Cross, and the Olympics), the history of Japan was presented as a series of imperialist successes. Japan "won" the Russo-Japanese War, and then "our country annexed Korea whose political situation was unsettled." The military over-whelmed the politicians and "made Manchuria independent of China," suggesting that this puppet state was a preexisting national entity. The text ended with an explicitly patriotic message reminiscent of the prewar mentality as it stressed one's duties to the state rather than one's rights: "The nation's economic base will not stabilize with so many people [living] in a smaller territory. Whether or not democracy will really lay down roots is the responsibility of the people *(koku-min).* . . . Japan is our country. To make Japan a good country, should we not all try to become good Japanese?"[29]

Junior High Texts

Junior high school texts, of course, carried much more detailed narratives of Japan's war history, but they shared with the elementary school texts the basic approach toward war and peace. All textbooks surveyed here depicted the Japanese military's oppression of civilians at home and peoples abroad. The early texts, such as Tōkyō Shoseki's *Atarashii shakaika: Chūgaku 3-nen,* approved in 1951, presented the military as responsible for causing the war, taking away the people's freedom and hence their ability to stop the militarists from waging war, advancing on the continent, and leading the nation into the unjust Pacific War. Regarding the Manchurian Incident of 1931, the

> military declared that [Japan's economic problems] were due to a population too large for its restricted territory and that the advance onto the continent was the only means to solve them. The army advanced its troops into China's northeast, and before anyone knew it [the conflict] had turned into the Pacific War. Of course in this era too there were individuals who worked earnestly for peace but the militarist clique had taken away these people's freedom before war began, so they could not raise their voices for peace.
>
> But today we have been given the freedom of speech through the constitution and have the right to oppose a wrong war. We must not under any circumstances throw away this precious right.[30]

Tōkyō Shoseki's *Atarashii Nihonshi* (1953) suggested that the political parties were negligent in representing the people's interest. They had lost the people's faith by ignoring their condition and catering to *zaibatsu* interests:

> The militarist clique used this [disaffection] skillfully, trying to implement a militarist dictatorship, and eventually developed the ambition to rule the world through forceful aggression against foreign countries. After the February 26 incident, military men occupied most of the important political positions, and the bureaucracy joined the militarist clique. The backbone of course was taken out of the Diet, newspaper and radio's journalistic freedom was taken away, and academic freedom disappeared. It goes without saying for socialists, but even democrats and liberals were attacked as traitors *(kokuzoku)*. In this way, the people *(kokumin)* were forced to war step by step.

At the end of the war, "the military wouldn't lend an ear to this wish of the people [to end the war and their suffering], merely preparing forcefully for the final mainland battle."[31]

Nihon Shoseki's junior high text, *Chūgakusei no shakai: Jidai to seikatsu* (1954), also depicted a people at the mercy of the military and the ultranationalists: "The Japanese people *(kokumin)* were against the military and the right's methods, but from around 1930 . . . speech was suppressed. . . . There was no means for the people to express their feelings against the war." The text made their plight explicitly clear a few pages later: "Even before the beginning of the Pacific War, political parties, labor unions, and peasant unions had completely disappeared, and all the people were forced to cooperate with the war in industrial service associations and neighborhood associations."[32] Chūkyō Shuppan's junior high text, *Kindai no sekai to Nihon* (1954), offered a substantially similar view although, as in its sixth-grade text, there was mild recognition of a people's complicity in the war effort. The military suppressed free speech through intimidation, assassination, and control of the cabinet, but at the beginning of the Pacific War the people *(kokumin)* were "delirious" *(uchōten ni natta)* from news of early victories. Moreover, the Chūkyō text was more explicit about the people's hardships near the end of the war, mentioning the mobilization of middle school students as labor in munitions production, the evacuation of the lower elementary school children, and labor shortages in farming villages.[33]

A-Bomb Victimhood and Asian National Liberation: 1955–1957

Starting around 1955, elementary and junior high school texts underwent three discernible changes regarding war victimhood. First, reflecting the rise in atomic victim consciousness after the Lucky Dragon Incident, many textbooks began to depict the Hiroshima and Nagasaki bombings as unique experiences that invested the Japanese with an exclusive pacifist mission. Such textbooks tended to dwell on Japanese victimhood in conventional war as well. Second, expositions of Asian national independence movements *(minzoku dokuritsu undō)* set the foundations for the inclusion in later texts of tales of Asian suffering at the hands of Japanese as well as Western imperialists. This extended coverage of Asian people's movements was undoubtedly a reflection of the existence of newly independent countries in Asia and Africa and, as well, the appeal of the nonaligned movement to Japanese who wanted a measure of freedom from the U.S. alliance.[34] And third, perhaps reinforcing this fascination with Asian and African countries was a general awakening of interest in people's history and greater emphasis on the sufferings of explicitly innocent noncombatants in general due to war.[35]

Elementary School Texts

Before the ban-the-bomb movement galvanized Japan in 1954 and 1955, sixth-grade texts usually took up the issue of nuclear weapons in describing how weapons developed to a dangerous level of destructive power[36] or how the atomic attacks helped bring an end to the Pacific War. Kyōiku Shuppan's *Nihon to sekai* (1952), compiled during the first post-Occupation exposés on Hiroshima, was unusual in describing Japan as the "first country to receive the tragic damage of atomic bombs." The text also allotted four pages to a letter from an "atomic bomb child" recounting her story,[37] but these passages were omitted from the publisher's 1954 text. Of the seven surveyed sixth-grade texts authorized in 1954, only one expressed undue consciousness of Japan's unique status as the first country to be A-bombed. Most made no mention of the bombing beyond connecting the atomic bombing with the end of the war.[38]

The first textbook to reflect the impact of the Lucky Dragon Incident was Tōkyō Shoseki's *Atarashii shakai* (1954), a totally new sixth-grade text developed under the general editorship of a prominent educator, Tokyo University professor of education Kaigo Tokiomi.[39] The 1954 edition was remarkable: it was the first to extend major coverage to both the atomic bomb damage and the civilian suffering in war, with heightened sensitivity to Japanese suffering in this "horrible war" *(osoroshii sensō),* as the section reflecting on World War II was titled. The military continued to be presented as the culpable party in starting the conflict on the continent and oppressing the people by keeping "a tight rein on [them], labeling those who did not agree with their way of thinking as individuals who were not good for the country." In the long section on world peace, which followed the narrative on Japan's political history, the message was that everybody wanted peace now because of the damage modern weapons caused. The first subsection began with a one-third-page photo of Hiroshima rebuilding. With pointed historicity the caption read: "The peace tower: Directly above this tower the world's first atomic bomb exploded at 8:15 A.M., August 6, 1945 (Shōwa 20)." The next subsection recounted the recent war as eight years of Japanese suffering:

For the Japanese people *(Nihon kokumin)* it was a succession of the most tormented and mournful days. . . . Fathers and older brothers were being mobilized and great numbers died or were wounded in battle. The families left behind had sent their important [breadwinners] to the battlefields and had to live restricted *(fujiyū)* lives. On top of that, after the war's end came near, due to bombing night and day, they lost their homes. Factories were destroyed and trains made useless. And the people were never sure of that day's meal.

Losing the war was a sad thing, but the war's ending was a greater joy than anything. In the sky above Nagasaki, the bells of peace rang and people came out of their air raid shelters and barracks to listen.[40]

Before ending with the standard praise of international organizations and the goodwill they create, the text described how Japan lost 120 cities and 2.36 million homes and 600,000 people died in the firebombings. In an ironic assertion of national corporeal unity, the authors told their sixth-grade readers who were born the year the war ended: "We have felt with our own flesh and bones how great that damage was." The final section on peace was even clearer about the connection between Japanese atomic bomb victimhood and postwar Japan's pacifist mission:

As the first people *(kokumin)* to be afflicted with the atomic bomb, we are able to address all the countries in the world and call loudly for peace so that this kind of evil might never happen again. The postwar Japanese constitution . . . was made in the spirit of building world peace. This spirit of seeking peace at all costs is something we can be proud of in this world.[41]

Kyōiku Shuppan's revisions to its sixth-grade *Hyōjun shōgaku shakai* social studies text in 1955 also developed the theme of an exceptional Japanese atomic victimhood. And in giving more consideration to Asian national liberation struggles the text suggested a connection between Japanese and Asians as sharing a mutual resistance to war because of the general human suffering it causes. There is a subtle shift in this text: earlier versions had been conscientious in expressing regret over the Japanese people's aggressions against Asians; now the Japanese people, along with other Asians, were portrayed as righteously innocent victims of the Japanese military. To the account of the Russo-Japanese War a sentence was added to the effect that many Japanese *(ōku no hitobito)* opposed the war because of the lives lost. Moreover, the section on the Manchurian Incident (1931) and Marco Polo Bridge Incident (1937) was edited to include Chinese people's *(Chūgoku no hitobito no)* opposition to the Japanese army's aggression. In the previous edition it had only mentioned Chiang Kai-shek's role in leading a boycott of Japanese goods and his commitment to a long struggle. Changes to the passage on the Japanese people's reaction to developments after the Marco Polo Bridge Incident are suggestive as well. While the previous edition merely noted that the military expanded hostilities, effectively ignoring those among the people *(kokumin)* who wanted the emerging war with China resolved quickly, the 1955 edition added a clear statement of military oppression of the Japanese: "The militarist clique labeled these people traitors *(hikokumin)* and severely suppressed speech. Moreover, elementary schools were renamed people's schools *(kokumin gakkō)*, and a curriculum of irrational dedication to the emperor and the state was implemented." Immediately preceding this statement, the 1955 text also inserted a one-sentence paragraph noting that many Chinese children suffered greatly in this war, losing their parents and homes.[42]

A new subsection on the Korean annexation explained that it not only resulted in making Korea a platform for "extending onto the continent" but also caused many Koreans to hope for Korean national independence *(Chōsen minzoku no dokuritsu)* since their language was being replaced by Japanese.[43] Just before the final section on international organizations, a new section titled "New Asia and Japan" was added that described the newly independent Asian nations and explained how Japan could work with them to contribute to world peace. The authors chose this section to insert a statement of Japanese atomic exceptionalist rhetoric: "Especially we, who were the first in the world to be atom-bombed and therefore learned how horrible future war will be, must work hard for peace."[44]

Junior High Texts

Junior high school textbooks were slower to place such increased emphasis on atomic bomb victim consciousness and Asian national liberation movements. Tōkyō Shoseki's middle school texts, unlike its sixth-grade social studies textbooks, did not immediately exhibit an explicit Japanese mission for peace based on a sense of atomic victim exceptionalism as distinct from war victimhood in general. The text approved in the early fall of 1954 reflected the rising awareness of nuclear issues by mentioning the bomb's role in ending the war, adding a footnote outlining the number of Japanese casualties in Hiroshima and Nagasaki, and noting the new danger of human extinction by nuclear war. The 1955 text added a section on anti-nuclear movements, as well, including a photo of closed fish markets and a reference to Lucky Dragon radio operator Kuboyama Aikichi as a Japanese fisherman whose death made him the first sacrificial victim *(giseisha)* of the hydrogen bomb.[45] Tōkyō Shoseki's texts followed the shift toward more extensive descriptions of Asian national liberation movements, but only slowly and indirectly. When such narratives did begin to appear in the early 1960s they inevitably highlighted Japan's imperialist role in victimizing these peoples—though generally the Japanese people's responsibility for their state's policies was mitigated or made ambiguous by their own suffering and impotence in the face of militarist cliques. This ambiguity, of course, was present even in the SCAP-authorized texts from the very beginning of postwar education. In the 1955 text, on the one hand, militarist cliques and ultrastatists rose to prominence by "skillfully grasping the people's *(kokumin no)* discontent" with the political parties who failed to concern themselves with stabilizing people's livelihoods in the face of the Great Depression. The "militarist dictatorship" gained control of society in the first place by suppressing pacifists and other critics and censoring newspapers and radio to create hatred for foreign countries and "urge [the people] on to war."[46] On the other hand, the military's rising influence at home is related in a way that implicitly identifies the Japanese and Asian peoples as fellow victims of the Japanese military: "The invasion *(shinryaku)* of China became tougher and tougher, and at home military influence grew. Not only did thought control become more strict, but even clothing, the *kokuminfuku*, was legislated. In this way the people's freedom was taken away, and sentiments for war were gradually raised."[47] In other words, the Japanese people are presented as somewhat lacking in agency to resist the militarists' proactive policies. Their true innocence as impotent victim is clear when, in recounting the suffering in the final years of the Pacific War, the text repeats the common refrain, by now familiar to the reader, that the people wanted the war to end "but the military would not lend an ear to this wish of the people, merely preparing forcefully for the final mainland battle."[48]

Nihon Shoseki's 1956 text only added that Hiroshima was the first incidence of an atomic bombing in history. The book did not reveal any exceptional Japanese sense of atomic victimhood, though it did suggest a common Japanese civilian and Asian people's suppression at the hands of the Japanese military authorities. In new sections on China's May Fourth and Korea's March First movements, for example, the text linked the three people's experiences by noting: "In 1919 when the Chinese national movement (*minzoku undō*) became furiously active, in Korea too students, workers, and peasants initiated a Korean independence movement in Seoul and every other region. But this was suppressed by the Japanese military and police, and in the previous year the Rice Riots occurred in Japan proper (*Nihon naichi*)." The following passage usefully encapsulates this text's representation of the Japanese people's position regarding Japan's prosecution of the Asia-Pacific War.

> At that time [in the late 1930s], the idea that "Japan is the leader of Asia" was spread while freedom of academic research was no longer permitted. It came to be that only those plays, poems, and movies that exhorted the people [to war] were made. Newspapers and radio argued for cooperation with the war. In this context the people gradually came to cooperate with the war. Everyone heartily sent off those who were called up [for military conscription] and cooperated by buying public bonds and paying taxes. The people's war cooperation eventually rose with the beginning of the Pacific War.[49]

In Chūkyō Shuppan's junior high school texts, the heightened sense of Japan's unique atomic-bomb experience led to a more self-assured sense of mission for peace at the same time it directed attention away from Japan's provocation of war toward Japan's victimization in war. The 1954 edition, for example, began its chapter on World War II without even mentioning Hiroshima in the summary of the war's end—even though an unidentified photograph from Shindō Kaneto's documentary, *Children of Hiroshima,* was placed above the text. The preface stressed that Tokyo and other major cities were laid in ruins and asked: "Why did our country begin such a war?" The final section of this text rather timidly expressed doubts about Japan's postwar direction and the postindependence military alliance with the United States.[50] The 1956 version, however, began its section on World War II with the same photograph and the following assertion of the atomic bomb as a defining Japanese experience of international significance. The passage exudes hope for Japan's future as a peaceful community, with the city and people of Hiroshima symbolic of that rebirth:

> On August 6, 1945, we Japanese confronted something horrible which humanity had never before experienced. The atomic bomb

was dropped on Hiroshima and many innocent people were thrown into the depths of hell in the blink of an eye. . . . But as you can see in the photograph above [a photo of boys jumping off a bridge and swimming in the river], children are happily playing among the ruins. By now these children are no doubt fine young men and women. And Hiroshima has been reborn a city of peace, and the ringing bells there echo with calls for peace to the people of the world.[51]

In the section on postwar Japan's future path, the text shows a resolve and confidence not apparent in the earlier edition:

> Our country lost the war. But it wasn't a total loss *(makeppanashi de wa nai)*, for we are getting back up on our own feet and finding a new path for us to follow. . . . There may be many more difficult problems in the future. [The question is:] what should we do to resolve each and every one of these problems?[52]

The Apologist Interlude: 1957–Early 1970s

In response to the conservative Democratic Party's campaign to rein in the more progressive texts, two successive ministers of education, Matsumura Kenzō and Kiyose Ichirō, moved to stiffen the certification process in late 1955 and 1956. Under the system in place since 1950, each textbook had been evaluated by an independent panel of five textbook investigators *(kyōkasho chōsain)*—three teachers and two academics—who each reported comments and assigned a numerical ranking on a scale of 200. A sixteen-member Textbook Certification Investigations Council (Kyōkayō Tosho Kentei Chōsa Shingikai, usually referred to as Kentei Shingikai), composed of academics appointed by the education minister, reviewed the evaluation and advised the minister on certification. If the total points for all five panelists reached or exceeded 800, the text was generally approved. If not, then the publisher could make revisions and resubmit the text.

In September 1955, Matsumura took a preliminary step toward stiffening the process by changing the personnel in the Kentei Shingikai. In what the media called the "F-Purge," he replaced Kentei Shingikai members such as Nakajima Kenzō, who was thought to hold liberal views, with men such as Takayama Iwao, a retired Kyoto University philosophy professor known to have conservative leanings. When the texts to be used in 1957 were reviewed, eight were ultimately rejected despite having over 800 total points from the five-member panel. All of these texts were disqualified for "slanted" *(henkō)* treatments as determined by Takayama (known only as "F" in the original media reports to distinguish his opinions from those of the original five textbook investigators who were designated by the letters A to E).[53]

In October 1956, Kiyose made more substantive changes to the process by introducing Ministry of Education officers to a new Kentei Shingikai, with membership expanded from sixteen to eighty, and restructuring the five-member examination panel. The original evaluation was now conducted by a five-person panel including two Ministry of Education textbook examiners *(kyōkasho chōsakan)* along with one academic and two teachers. Their exact role was not widely understood, but the appointment of officers with known conservative leanings—such as Murao Jirō, a disciple of Hiraizumi Kiyoshi, a wartime proponent of emperor-centered historiography—made authors wary of how they wrote their history texts. Publishers were also limited to only two resubmissions should their texts fail the first round of review. In the spring of 1957, some 33 percent of all texts submitted in the first round of these new procedures failed—the highest failure rate since screening procedures were begun in 1950.[54] Such pressure led both Chūkyō Shuppan and Kyōiku Shuppan to produce alternative textbook series authored by scholars less likely to draw conservative ire. When the Ministry of Education indicated that beginning in 1961 it would only accept one textbook series in a subject per publisher, Chūkyō Shuppan terminated *Akarui shakai,* the sixth-grade social studies text that revisionists of the middle 1950s had labeled the most "shameful textbook."[55] Kyōiku Shuppan merged its texts.

Elementary School Texts

The revisionist impact of the new certification process is most noticeable in Kyōiku Shuppan's sixth-grade text described earlier for its narratives of Japanese and Asian people's victimization at the hands of the Japanese military. *Hyōjun shōgaku shakai* (hereafter called *Hyōjun shakai*) failed certification on its first submission and only passed after major revisions and distancing of the title from the original JTU-affiliated author, Munakata Seiya, a Tokyo University professor of education who later played an important role in the Ienaga suit. Although the new text, approved in 1960, retained mention of the Chinese boycott of Japanese goods, it otherwise presented what can only be characterized as a patriotic narrative of Japanese continental aggression. Quite contrary to the progressive viewpoint of its previous editions, in this text the government and people were portrayed as coming together to overcome the unfair commercial treaties of the pre-Meiji era. In its apologist recounting of the Russo-Japanese War, the text omitted mention of popular opposition and anti-Japanese Korean sentiment for independence from Japanese colonization. The animosity toward the emperor system was eliminated. And in an unusually uncritical presentation of the militarist clique's subversion of domestic politics, the text merely noted that politicians in the opposition were "shunted aside" *(nokemono ni)* without mentioning the political assassinations. The textbook continued its praise of postwar Asian and African national independence movements, though it dropped atomic bomb exceptionalist rhetoric and added a comment on Japan having regained national strength.[56]

Like Chūkyō Shuppan, Kyōiku Shuppan produced an alternative social studies textbook series under a different editorial team when it encountered certification difficulties. This text, *Shakai,* was authored by a group under Tokyo University education professor Hosoya Toshiyo and encountered no problem with certification. It shared with the certified revision of *Hyōjun shakai* the patriotic sense of a nation overcoming difficulties—whether obtaining equal treaties in late Meiji after fifty years of effort or dealing with antagonists in the Pacific War. For the beginning of the Pacific War, the text relied on the war-era explanation: "The United States, England, Holland, and China showed signs of encircling our country from the South. . . . Our country tried to resolve this through negotiations with the United States but things didn't go well, and in 1941 started the Pacific War against the United States and England." In the prewar narrative in this text, the Japanese government and people were silent components of "our country," only appearing as agents in the postwar era when "the government and the people *(kokumin)* joined forces in working for economic recovery." Accordingly, there is little sense of people as victims of war—the text only mentions that the major cities were firebombed—and while Hiroshima is mentioned in the text there is no assertion of any special Japanese mission for peace connected with it. The text ends with a statement on the importance of balancing love of country and flag with working with other countries for peace. Given the limitation of one text per publisher, Kyōiku Shuppan combined its two teams to continue *Hyōjun shakai,* without Munakata, beginning with the 1964 text.[57]

This 1964 edition drops the wartime apologist history narrative of encirclement and reemphasizes the people as occasional agents in history, though as patriotic citizens rather than as pacifists. For example: "The *kokumin* overcame difficulties in fighting the Russo-Japanese War . . . so that Japan achieved victory."[58] The plight of "farmers and the people" under low depression-era rice prices and unemployment is explained in detail, but there is still little sense of the people as victims of the war and no mention of Asian suffering. Although the text reintroduces the idea of a special mission against nuclear weapons, it is quick to note that Japan was not the only country to have incurred war damage.[59] In any case, this atomic bomb victim exceptionalist rhetoric is dropped in the 1967 edition and replaced with the earlier text's patriotic message about flag and country and pride in postwar economic success. The 1967 text reintroduces the emphasis on state power. The military's intervention in politics in 1930s seems understandable as the text relates how the political parties ignored the people's *(kokumin)* suffering during the depression and some soldiers, seeing this, came to think that by reforming politics through military force and placing Manchuria under Japan's influence they could stabilize the people's livelihoods.[60]

Tōkyō Shoseki's *Atarashii shakai* sixth-grade texts from this era present a prewar people who are less distanced from their government. In the text that emerged from the "F-Purge" round of certification, for example, the political parties continue to be portrayed as selfish, but students no longer read that this caused people to lose faith in the parties or the Diet. The militarists still clamp down on the people, as in earlier texts, but now they take away nearly all of the people's freedom. In the 1960 text the prewar state is presented in a better light—though perhaps this was more a reflection of the fuller picture that texts were presenting than ideological pressure applied by Ministry of Education bureaucrats. In 1960 the sixth-grade text was quite similar to Kyōiku Shuppan's text from the same year: it had greatly expanded its coverage of Japanese international history in a narrative of national struggle to succeed in a hostile international imperialist environment. In addition to expanding the section on Japanese civilian suffering during the Asia-Pacific War, the 1960 text tripled coverage of international relations in the preceding imperialist era. Japan's continental "advances" are presented in maps and texts in the context of European and American entrenchment in Asia and represent Japan's efforts to "raise its status" in the effort to catch up with the advanced (imperialist) countries. Japan fought China and Russia around the turn of the century in order to "protect Korean independence" and, after "victory" in the Russo-Japanese War, worked to "prevent Korea from being threatened by foreign countries," eventually annexing it.

Beginning in the 1960 text, the Japanese people *(kokumin)* are portrayed as working hard in concert with the government to raise "national strength" *(kokuryoku)*, the goal being revision of the unequal treaties imposed on Japan earlier in the era. People and state are more closely linked in the narrative of 1930s imperialist activity as well. Instead of reading in the 1957 text that "some soldiers" *(ichibu no gunjin)* found a way out of economic depression and political stagnation by "starting a war on the continent" and clamping down on those who disagreed, after 1960 students learned once again that the *kokumin* had lost faith in the parties—the Diet is not mentioned —so "some people" *(ichibu no hitobito)* advanced the solution of reforming politics through military force and "extending Japanese influence on the Asian continent." Once the Pacific War began, however, the people lost their freedom of speech and were not told the truth about the war so they continued to sacrifice their livelihoods in the war effort.[61] In other words, the people are described as having worked for national strength and success in the era in which imperialist expansion was the norm; when the militarists' influence over government increased during the Pacific War, the people continued to sacrifice for the country as they never learned the truth about the fighting and their freedom of speech had been taken away.

Junior High Texts

In the early 1960s a group of Waseda historians reviewed changes in junior high school history texts in order to assess the impact of these new procedures and curricula revisions on the textbook treatments of war. The group concluded that versions written after the new guidelines went into effect, although more specific in describing the progress of events, obscured Japan's provocation and impropriety in waging aggressive war. The group also concluded that the misery of the people's wartime livelihood was less clear.

The Waseda group pointed out, for example, that the Nihon Shoseki treatment of the origins of the Pacific War changed in a manner which obscured how it developed out of the China War. It thus weakened the notion that it was another aggressive war—as well as the notion of Japan's provocation and impropriety. The 1954 version had explained that "even if Japan defeated China in war, it could not

control China" because the government that Japan set up was "powerless and could not gain the hearts of the Chinese people *(kokumin)*."
The newer version, by contrast, was less direct and implied Western
meddling as the cause of Japan's failure:

> Japan attributed the difficulty in resolving the China Incident to the
> United States, United Kingdom, and France sending them supplies,
> and so tried to block them. Thinking to liberate Southeast Asia from
> Western colonial control, it built a "Greater East Asia Coprosperity
> Sphere" encompassing all of East Asia, with Japan as its leader who
> could freely use the region's resources.

The change between the two texts is also evident in the description
of Japan's attack on Pearl Harbor. Instead of the 1954 text's "Japan
unexpectedly attacked Hawai'i and began the Pacific War," the new
version merely left it that Japan "declared war on the United States
and the United Kingdom."[62]

The newer versions also gave the impression that the people did
not oppose war so much and their suffering was not so extreme or
meaningless. Where Nihon Shoseki's 1954 text told students that during the Russo-Japanese War Uchimura Kanzō, Kotoku Shunsui, and
others "passionately conducted an antiwar movement," the new version related that some outside of government *(minkan de)* actually
argued loudly for attacking Russia, and although Uchimura and
Kotoku protested they "did not gain much influence."[63] Similarly, the
new version of the China Incident failed to touch on domestic points
such as the people's mild antiwar sentiments, suppression of academic
freedom, and the attitude of social democrats.[64] Where the 1954 version held, as quoted earlier, that the people were "forced to cooperate
in the war" and farmers were "forced to sell crops at low prices to
government," leading to many children and old people dying from
undernourishment and lack of medical care, the new version lessened
the sense of useless hardship. It presented a populace fighting and
persevering willingly for victory:

> When war began, the people who had been unsure before were en-
> couraged one after another by news of victory. They went to war in
> the southern regions or worked for production on the home front.
> Accordingly, production of nonmilitary goods fell, shops could no
> longer stay open, and farm families did not have enough tools or
> fertilizer, on top of being short-handed. . . . One after another youths
> were sent off to the battlefield, and as there were not enough
> laborers, middle school students and even girl students worked in
> military factories.[65]

One can conclude from the Waseda group's evidence, then, that the newer junior high text presentations implied that the war was not so despicable, the government's policies were not so evil, and the people were more or less behind them. It was clear that the people still suffered, but students were less likely to get the sense that they had been victimized by their own government. To the extent that Japanese foreign policy was presented in a favorable manner and government and military positions were parallel, texts reduced the overall sense of useless suffering (and victimization).

The Waseda group implied that the Ministry of Education was putting revisionist pressure on publishers in order to establish the ruling conservative administration's ideology and thereby build support for the Self-Defense Forces (SDF) and revision of the constitution. These were indeed two conservative aims. But as noted earlier there were countervailing pressures that limited the degree to which war could be devilified—and in any case the basic conservative aim was to instill patriotism in the minds of youth. To the extent that the government and more generally the nation itself were less culpable for the evil of war, there was less condemnation of patriotism in its conventional manifestation as service to the state. But patriotism did not necessarily result in support for constitutional revision or remilitarization. Nor did it necessitate texts that justified war itself in the abstract.

The effect of the Ministry of Education tightening control of the certification process is difficult to assess in its entirety because of variations among publishers. Nevertheless, one can discern important characteristics beyond the softer condemnation of prewar policies as found by the Waseda group and the occasional adoption of an overtly patriotic tone. For example, the one major text that the Waseda group did not survey, Tōkyō Shoseki's junior high text, does not really show much change from 1955 to 1961 regarding the degree to which the military and militarists forced the politicians and government leaders to submit through assassination and intimidation. In fact, in some instances military subversion of the state is even more egregious. Nor is there much change in how the militarists were portrayed as having duped the people into believing in "fascist" or "totalitarian" doctrines that promised release from domestic problems through foreign expansion and military force. The 1961 Tōkyō Shoseki text does present Japan's prewar diplomacy in a better light by expanding, for example, its presentation of European imperialist expansion into Africa and Asia in order to provide the generally exculpatory context for Japanese expansion. But where the 1958 edition merely relates the details of the military's expansion of hostilities arising from the Marco Polo Bridge Incident, the 1961 text adds that the military failed to comply with the government's policy to contain them. And where in the 1955 and 1958 texts it is Prime Minister Konoe who imitates German fascists in consolidating political parties into the Imperial Rule Assistance Association, in 1961 it is implied that the government does so because of the needs of the military. In these cases the civilian prewar government was being portrayed as less responsible than the military for warmongering.[66]

One useful way of describing what was happening to the narrative in Tōkyō Shoseki's top-selling junior high text is that the victim group was being redefined to include the Japanese government along with the people as victims of the Japanese military. In textbooks that relied on narratives of Japanese victimhood, this strategy allowed a closer identification of people and government without necessarily validating war or militarization of the state. One sees this approach in Nihon Shoseki's junior high texts as well. The texts approved under the stricter certification procedures dropped mention of the government as an agent of the people's oppression in the 1919 rice riots, for example, where the 1956 text had it dispatching the military to quell the riots. In a general softening of the sense of class conflict that was characteristic of the newer texts, the 1961 and 1965 editions also dropped mention of government suppression of labor and tenant strife in the early years of the Great Depression. Furthermore, the newer editions added favorable information about instances when the civilian Japanese government took an antiwar stance—noting its original opposition to the expansion of hostilities in Manchuria in 1931 and Prime Minister Konoe's early opposition to expansion of the Marco Polo Bridge Incident. This special exemption for the government did not continue to the end of the Pacific War in this 1961 narrative, which implied that the Japanese government should be thought partly responsible for the Allied forces resorting to atomic bombs after it ignored the Potsdam Declaration and decided to continue fighting.[67] To the extent that the Japanese people supported their government's position (if not necessarily the competing military position), as in most texts in the late 1950s and early 1960s, text narratives reduced the overall sense of alienation from the (nonmilitarized) state and hence permitted greater accommodation of patriotic sentiment.[68]

Yet this enlarged victimhood did not always divert war responsibility from the Japanese nation. In the 1961 Tōkyō Shoseki junior high text, for example, the victim narrative was expanded with the addition of a full page dedicated to a reminiscence of shortages and mobilization during the war. An additional new subsection on the people's wartime lives told of more hardships—in this regard different in tone from the Nihon Shoseki text passages that the Waseda group noted—and added that "the military didn't tell the people (kokumin) about the real conditions [of the war effort]." Despite the increased treatment of the victim experience, the book ends with a statement invoking Japan's special pacifist mission, not only because of its unique atomic bomb victim past, but also because of the country's responsibility for causing war:

> Japan is the first A-bombed country in the world, and, considering our position of responsibility for World War II, we must work with firm resolve for the achievement of peace. To do this, first it is important to develop much further democracy, which values our mutual human rights and respects others' positions, and build a peace-loving country from the heart.[69]

In 1961, there was a definite sense of civic national responsibility for starting World War II. But it is clear from the presentation that the people's responsibility was for what the militarized state did and for what it forced or duped them into doing. Even as later Tōkyō Shoseki editions expanded their coverage of civilian suffering and condemnation of the military and the militarists, people's complicity is never totally papered over.[70]

Asian Victimhood and National Liberation

Even at its peak revisionism did not foreclose coverage of Asian liberation struggles, for such narratives could as easily emphasize a common Asian struggle against Western as against Japanese imperialism. Consider, for example, the treatment of the Russo-Japanese War. From the early 1960s Tōkyō Shoseki and Chūkyō Shuppan's junior high texts noted that Japan's victory over Russian imperialism in Korea proved inspirational to Asian liberation movements—the first instance of a non-European people overcoming Western imperialism. From the early 1970s, however, texts dropped this favorable comment on Japanese imperialism in favor of increased treatment of indigenous popular opposition to Japan's colonization of Korea.[71]

In junior high texts, the trend was toward greater treatment of the wartime suffering of Japanese civilians (more often the nonelite)

and its association with Asian people's suffering. The military was
still the main responsible agent for war. In Tōkyō Shoseki's 1961
junior high text, a drawing of Lu Xun and photos of Gandhi and the
May Fourth movement drew attention to the fact that national self-
determination was an ideal that the post–World War I powers did not
apply to Asia. In fact, the publisher's company history indicates that,
beginning in 1965, a conscious effort was made to "strengthen the
connection between Japan's history and Asia, especially China."[72] In
1965, the year Japan normalized relations with the Republic of Korea,
this text introduced descriptions of Korean opposition to the Japanese
protectorate, along with a photo of Itō Hirobumi and the Korean
prince, and cited the May Fourth movement in discussing the failure
to apply the principle of national self-determination to Asia. The
1965 text also noted for the first time that during the Asia-Pacific War
the Japanese military was unable to get the support of the various
Asian peoples in mobilizing natural resources in the regions they
occupied. In earlier texts students read simply that Japan made, or
helped create, native governments.[73]

Even Nihon Shoseki's junior high text's patriotic narrative of
Japan's international adventures—a text that in 1961 substituted ABCD
encirclement for Chinese people's resistance to explain Japan's inability to defeat the Chinese government in the late 1930s and omitted
mention of indigenous people's resistance to Japanese occupation of
southern regions later in the war—retained its large section on Asian
liberation movements with a photo of Gandhi and discussion of the
May Fourth and March First movements. In 1965 the text noted for
the first time that an anti-Japanese movement arose among the Chinese people (kokumin) in response to the Twenty-One Demands,
added that several thousand Koreans were killed (in vigilante violence) after the Great Kantō Earthquake of 1923, and reintroduced
the Chinese people's role in resisting Japanese aggression in the
1930s. In the gradually expanding narrative of Japanese civilian home
front victim experiences, this 1965 edition also introduced information on wartime Korean suffering with the mention of late war
mobilization of Korean workers.[74]

Chūkyō Shuppan's Nihon no ayumi to sekai (1961) was more explicit than earlier editions about Japan's imperialist interlude: its
chapter on the two world wars began with maps showing the gradual
expansion of Japanese territory up to 1945 and noted Chinese and
Korean anti-Japanese movements. The 1968 text included an earlier
map showing Japan's participation among "great power inroads"

(shinshutsu) into China, as well as a graphic contemporary depiction of the Twenty-One Demands as chains imprisoning a map of China. The section on the Manchurian Incident added a photograph of Chinese female students putting up anti-Japanese posters protesting the "Japanese military invasion" *(Nihon no buryoku shinryaku hantai)*. The description of China's League of Nations' protest against Japan's "military movements" was changed to characterize them as a "Japanese invasion." The military remained the evil agent in oppressing both Asians and Japanese. This section ended with a photograph of the children's monument in Hiroshima's Peace Park.[75]

Narratives on Chinese and Korean liberation struggles became much more prominent in texts from the 1970s—probably reflecting the growing interest in Asian history that followed the official policy of rapprochement with mainland China. Tōkyō Shoseki's 1974 junior high text, for example, introduced a paragraph-long passage on the content and consequences of Japanese colonization of Korea:

> Japan conducted a land survey when it made Korea a colony, and as a result most Korean peasants lost rights to the land. They became tenant farmers, vagrants, and the like, and the increasing numbers inevitably emigrated to Japan. Moreover, [Japan] tried to force the Koreans to assimilate by teaching the Japanese language and forbidding the teaching of Korean history. Nevertheless, Japanese prejudice against Koreans grew.

In the section on Gandhi and the May Fourth movement, the 1974 text added a map and paragraph explaining Korea's March First movement that spread because the goals of independence found sympathy from the "masses *(minshū)* suffering under Japanese colonial rule." That Japanese imperialism drew Chinese antagonism was highlighted by a photograph of a "Down with Japanese Imperialism!" graffito on a Chinese wall, and the section on the China Incident was now labeled the "Sino-Japanese War." Furthermore, the passage on people's lives during the Pacific War *("Sensō to kokumin seikatsu")* now mentioned the forced labor of Koreans and Chinese under harsh conditions in mines.[76]

At the same time that texts increased their treatment of Asian suffering, they also increased detailed information about Japanese civilian suffering, including the plight of the proletariat classes within Japan. In the section on social movements and progress toward universal male suffrage in its 1974 text, for example, Tōkyō Shoseki added a short description of the *"burakumin"* outcasts forming the Suiheisha to overcome discrimination. A new "documentary" page on life during the war described government promotion of pumpkin patches to alleviate food shortages and school munitions factories and carried a reminiscence by an Okinawan woman. An expanded description of the elimination of freedoms of speech furthered the impression of distress during the war, and a new paragraph and chart explained the material and human impact of the atomic bombs. A paragraph and chart detailing *hibakusha* suffering were added to the postwar section as well.[77]

The trend toward greater exposition of people's victim experiences continued in the 1977 edition and beyond—and with such extensive coverage of Asian victimization at the hands of Japanese that the complex issue of the Japanese people's complicity inevitably arose. In brief, vigilante persecution of Koreans after the 1923 Kantō earthquake was introduced, as was a note on the Nanjing atrocity that made clear the inhumane actions of the Japanese army while explaining the Japanese people's ignorance of same: "On entering the city walls of Nanjing, the Japanese army killed a huge *(obitadashii)* number of Chinese women, children, soldiers who had thrown away their arms, and nonuniformed soldiers. This incident was called the "Nanjing Massacre" and was criticized by foreign countries, but most common Japanese *(ippan kokumin)* were not told of it." This section on World War II concluded with a newly added comment that the end of the war meant not only the end of fifteen years of wartime hardship but also the liberation of Korea from thirty-five years of Japanese rule.[78] The 1986 text noted that public opinion *(seron)* in the 1930s favored the militarist solution to economic and political impasses, moving the government to plan such policies.[79]

The increased coverage of Asian liberation movements was not so overwhelming in Chūkyō Shuppan's junior high text, though it is discernible. In the 1971 text, the Chinese masses *(minshū)* were given a little more subjectivity in discussion of Chinese opposition to the Twenty-One Demands and the Japanese military's expansion of hostilities after the Marco Polo Bridge Incident. The 1971 edition revised its map of Asian national liberation movements (which included Western colonies) to show Chinese and Korean movements as well as Japanese colonies. And the section on the war ended with the added explanation that "national mobilization" enabled coordination of the people and matériel (instead of simply remarking that it focused national strength) and noting that freedom of speech and assembly were curtailed. The Potsdam article stating that the Japanese people were duped by their leaders was added to the sidebar listing of significant points.[80]

Asian liberation movements and Asian war suffering do not appear in the two major elementary school social studies texts until 1976, when both Tōkyō Shoseki and Kyōiku Shuppan reassembled their editorial teams.[81] In Tōkyō Shoseki's text, a renewed emphasis on the personal side of history brought more description of personal suffering by Japanese and by Asians and less emphasis on Great Power politics. Korean opposition to annexation and assimilation policies was mentioned for the first time, as was the killing of innocent Koreans in the confused aftermath of the 1923 Kantō earthquake. Narratives of civilian hardship during the Pacific War now included the forced mobilization of Korean and Chinese laborers, as well as students having to work in field and factory and young men being taken off to war, in addition to the stories of hunger and homelessness in earlier editions. Later texts gradually expanded such tales of human suffering, making it clearer that Japanese and Asian peoples alike suffered as victims of war. Moreover, the government was no longer granted victim status in the beginning stages of the war, and its prewar suppression of civil liberties was no longer presented in such a good light. Beginning in 1976, for example, the narrative of increasing political representation culminating in the 1925 universal male suffrage was followed by the warning that the government established a law for controlling people's political activities that same year. Beginning in the 1979 text, the Japanese government was no longer presented as the military's victim—in fact, it was presented as the propagandist for Japan's war effort that fooled the Japanese people (kokumin) into "cooperating with the war."[82] And yet the overwhelming increase in Asian victim narratives brought recognition in the 1985 text that Japanese had displaced Korean farmers in the first decade after the annexation of Korea.[83]

Kyōiku Shuppan's 1976 text retained its focus on national strength in Japan's revision of the unequal treaties of the Meiji era. But for the first time since the initiation of stricter certification procedures, the text noted the existence of popular opposition to the Russo-Japanese War. Korean hardships due to annexation—such as loss of land, being forced to learn in Japanese at school, and having to emigrate to Japan and Manchuria for work—joined mention of forced Korean and Chinese labor during World War II. The text fully describes the plight of common people: Ainu impoverishment, the development of tenant and labor unions in the face of harsh working conditions during

Japan's modernization, and lower-class efforts for social betterment such as the Suiheisha. A special sidebar highlighted labor conditions at the Ashio mines, and the text noted that Japanese products could be exported to Asia because low wages (one suspects in comparison to European rather than Asian wage scales) kept products cheaply priced. While during the apologist interlude Kyōiku Shuppan's texts implied noble aims behind the militarist rejection of political party rule, this text reemphasized the military's role as evil oppressor and the government's complicity in suppressing liberal culture and democratic political potential. Although universal suffrage was celebrated, as in Tōkyō Shoseki's text, students also read that the government strengthened its ability to control the political activities of workers. Militarist assassinations of party politicians were reintroduced, and attacks on scholars were mentioned to show how difficult it had become to express one's opinion. The people's plight during the war was highlighted with descriptions of shortages impinging on livelihoods and school life.[84]

If the 1979 edition extended its privileging of victim narratives, it also brought attention to Japanese people's responsibility for the victimization of others. The section on the Russo-Japanese War begins with a depiction of the tombstone of one Natsuemon who died on Hill 203 at the age of thirty-four and continues with portrayals of the difficulties people encountered. Yosano Akiko's famous antiwar poem was introduced in the context of why Japan went to war in Asia. The text recognized that "while antiwar sentiment existed, most of the people welcomed news of victory at Port Arthur and the Japan Sea and cooperated in [prosecuting] the war." A map of Korean uprisings of the March First movement was added, as well as a paragraph on Korean victims of vigilantes after the 1923 earthquake. The section on the war was refocused to become a victim's history, beginning with the story of a woman carrying her child as she attempts to flee the Tokyo firebombing. The text was much clearer about the Japanese army causing the war—from blowing up the railroad tracks outside Mukden to attacking Pearl Harbor. Progressive distrust of the state reveals itself in the statement that at the end of the war, "the government (seifu) announced that [we] were winning the war and didn't tell the people the truth. And then it called for the people to fight the determining battle on the main islands." This statement was followed by a full-page description of schoolboy recruits and the "Lily Corps" (Himeyuri Butai), the group of Okinawan schoolgirls who were killed while serving as nurses during the Okinawa invasion.

Yet the potential for civic pacifist agency among the people as war victim is celebrated in a description of how Japan's ban-the-bomb movement arose from "among the people" *(kokumin no aida),* and the Lucky Dragon Incident is described as the third time Japan had suffered from atomic bombs. In the second volume of this social studies text, the responsibilities attendant on victim and victimizer are clear: "Our country *(Waga kuni wa)* is the only country in the world to have experienced the horrors of the atomic bomb. Our country must put this experience to good use through proactive engagement in the prevention of war and banishment of nuclear weapons, activities that the U.N promotes." Although this text emphasizes the Japanese people's history as victims of government and militarist oppression, it also takes pains to recognize Japanese responsibilities to Asia and at least some civic responsibility for Japan's postwar actions. In this regard, the text mentions pointedly that China, "which Japan damaged seriously during the war, was not invited to the [San Francisco] peace conference" and that U.S. combat planes in the Korean War were based in Japan. In other words, this text is a good exemplar of the conscientious progressive position that stresses the wrongs done to people, both Asian and Japanese, by governments and states, in war and in peace, and implicitly calls for political activism in order to shoulder war responsibility and assure that such wrongs would not occur again.[85]

Writing and Rewriting History

Peace education originated in the belief, shared by SCAP reformers and most of the intellectuals who constituted Japan's early postwar "community of contrition,"[86] that the Japanese people had followed their leaders in waging a self-destructive war of aggression because they had not fully developed modern, democratic, autonomous habits of mind. To raise future generations of peace-loving citizens in a liberal democratic state, SCAP reformers instructed, the citizenry would have to be educated not only about the horrors of war but also about their own civic right to insist that their government adopt policies that would avoid future wars.

In this chapter we have seen that in educating children to reject war, Japanese textbooks focused on the Japanese people's experience as victims in an unjust war. The problem with the victim orientation in peace education is that it did not always spell out the lesson of the victim's own subjective responsibility for his fate and explain how owning up to that war responsibility—accepting it and acting on it—was an important step toward building a pacifist citizenry. After the implementation of stricter procedures, textbooks that linked a collective, national sense of responsibility for Japan's wartime predations to postwar citizenship either ceased publication or altered their narratives in ways that obfuscated the issue. Progressive texts, despite their insistence on recording Japan's past aggressions and rejecting war, encountered a problem in their construction of the Japanese people as an ethnic nation alienated from as well as victimized by the state: how was the people's struggle against their state to be transformed into the people's sovereignty within it? Peace education based on victim consciousness, then, while effective in fostering pacifist sentiment, evinced problematic implications for the construction of a liberal postwar democratic nation-state.

The revisionist movement of the middle 1950s certainly drew to itself those who rejected a pacifist postwar national identity, as well as those who desired a return to the wartime intimate identification of the ethnic nation with the state. But it could also gain support from those whose goal was the reclamation of peace education to a less revolutionary, more conventionally patriotic vision of the Japanese people and their postwar state. Under the generally conservative pressure of the newly stringent certification procedures, textbooks from the years of the apologist interlude tended to justify certain aspects of the Japanese state's wartime position. They also lessened the impression that the civilian government had been responsible for the suffering of innocent people. But opposition to war because of such suffering remained the central moral. The patriotic merging of citizen and state involved two strategies that in some texts overlapped: the text conveyed a conventionally patriotic plot in which citizen and government work together to overcome a hostile Western imperialist order; or it constructed a history in which government and people were both overwhelmed and oppressed by the military, which remained discredited. This second strategy freed the postwar government and state from inheriting the legacy of a militarist wartime Japan and encouraged a pacifist direction for postwar Japan.

By the early 1960s, when passages on the war were rewritten so that the state's actions seemed less indefensible in diplomatic terms, the agency of victimization had been distilled into a defunct prewar military or a vaguely defined entity called "war." This kind of victim narrative accommodated the gradual expansion of sections on Asian nationalist movements and their successful struggles against Japanese and Western imperialism and colonialism, for the Japanese people could now share war victimhood with other Asians. This accommodation was more easily made in texts that neglected war responsibility in the enthusiastic embrace of Japan's unique heritage of atomic victimhood.[87] Students might have readily identified with Asian peoples, not as their victimizers, but as fellow victims of militarism and war. Yet the apologist interlude ended in the early 1970s. And in any case conscientious teachers would have made sure their students understood the postwar implications of the wartime past to the extent the curriculum allowed.[88] As this chapter shows, not just the Japanese military but the Japanese people's complicity in victimization of Asians eventually accompanied the dramatic expansion of Asian treatment in the late 1970s. As maligned as Japanese textbooks may be, it can be said that the focus on victimization ultimately brought about greater awareness of a national people's responsibility for Japan's past as aggressor.

CHAPTER 5

"Sentimental Humanism"
The Victim in Novels and Film

There was a pool at the First Hiroshima Prefectural Middle School, and lined up around it, heaped on top of one another, lay dead hundreds of middle school students and volunteer workers. . . . From a distance they looked like beds of tulips, but on close inspection they lay atop one another like the petals of a chrysanthemum.

—Ibuse Masuji, *Black Rain* (1966)

W HILE education curricula reflect the consciously sanctioned national heritage, it is in popular culture that one typically encounters less self-consciously propagated mythologies. The psychology of war victimhood is ubiquitous in postwar antiwar literature. Since my purpose in this chapter is to illustrate victim literature, not survey it, I focus on three novels and their film versions that have earned wide audiences.[1]

Tsuboi Sakae published her *Nijūshi no hitomi* (Twenty-Four Eyes) in late 1952, when Japan was responding to American pressure to rearm during the Korean War. In her epilogue the author wrote: "I was halfway through this novel when one day, sitting in front of my desk, I happened to remember something which made me nervous and distressed. It was a newspaper account of the Prime Minister making a speech before the main division of the Security Force on Etchū-jima. The caption below his photograph, taken from his speech, read: 'You are the foundation of the national army!' "[2] Tsuboi's straightforward antiwar novel sold moderately well and became a bestseller after Shochiku Studios released Kinoshita Keisuke's film version in 1954.[3] The story revolves around a young pacifist schoolteacher and her twelve first-grade students. Isolated both geographically and politically from the mainstream of Japanese life at the beginning of the

Shōwa era, the children and their teacher are relentlessly torn from their idyllic Inland Sea setting as Japan mobilizes for total war. After they advance to the main school in town, the children are indoctrinated by the militarist curriculum. Miss Ōishi, the teacher, becomes so dispirited by the oppressive state control of education and its poisonous effect on both teachers and students that she quits teaching. Quitting, however, does not spare her from the oppressive society in which it is dangerous to express one's pacifist thoughts too frankly. As the children mature, they seem to realize the oppressiveness of the militarist system but are unable to avoid their fate. Only two of the five boys survive the war (and one has been blinded), and the girls suffer from illness, missing husbands, and other hardships. Ōishi loses her own husband and a child to the war, and the story ends in profound sadness for the loss of life. Both the book and the film versions contextualize the story with reference to political events, and there is a clear correlation between the gradual loss of joy among the children and the teacher as Japan moves from the late 1920s' remnants of Taishō democracy into the late 1930s' total mobilization for war. *Twenty-Four Eyes* offers a prime example of Japanese innocents victimized by the vast anonymous forces of war and serves as a model for the artistic foundations for victim mythologies.

Ningen no jōken (The Human Condition) by Gomikawa Junpei was published in six best-selling volumes from 1956 to 1958 and made into three lengthy films by Kobayashi Masaki from 1959 to 1961.[4] Where *Twenty-Four Eyes* remains silent on Japanese aggression abroad and avoids describing actual acts of oppression in Japanese society, *Human Condition* breaks new ground with its grim descriptions of Japanese atrocities perpetrated on Asians and on fellow Japanese. The plot follows the travails of an idealistic, talented, young Japanese named Kaji who is forced by circumstances to compromise his pacifist-humanist principles and then, inevitably, suffer for them. The story is divided into three sections, each ending in a crisis in which Kaji makes a critical choice to act in favor of justice—propelling himself into a lower level in what might be called a hierarchy of oppression. In the first stage he is an idealistic humanist who nevertheless owes his good life to his position at the top of the hierarchical colonial system of exploitation. As an army private in the second stage, the imperative for survival makes him an efficient agent of war despite his tempered humanism. Finally, he falls to the level of a POW whose labor is being exploited by Russians just as he once exploited the labor of Chinese POWs. At each stage his talent and his sympathy for the oppressed—what his more cynical and pragmatic friends call his "sentimental humanism"—place him in charge of a group of down-trodden: Chinese civilians unjustly seized as POWs; a motley group of young, old, and infirm army inductees; and his own labor camp work group. In each case he manages to improve his wards' lot for a while. But eventually the forces of war, the army, the system, and ultimately the "human condition" prove insurmountable.

Of all the postwar artistic treatments of war responsibility, this is the most soul-searching investigation of personal responsibility for Japanese wartime aggression. No one is totally innocent in this sad tale; yet the ultimate lesson is that conditions for Kaji and other Japanese in the 1940s did not permit innocence. All were caught in the hierarchy of oppression in which even those of goodwill on higher levels inevitably exploited those below. On occasion even the perpetrators of violence are shown to be the product of an evil system or war itself. Anti-Japanese sentiment among Chinese and Koreans is rendered with the same compassion. Readers and viewers alike are encouraged to forgive average Japanese their complicity in Japanese aggression since they too were victims caught in the vortex of larger forces.

Ibuse Masuji's *Kuroi ame* (Black Rain), serialized in the literary magazine *Shinchō* from January 1965 until September 1966, is the most popular novelization of the Hiroshima bomb experience in Japan. Ibuse was awarded the Noma Prize for it in 1966, and the Ministry of Education awarded him its Order of Merit in partial consideration of his success in capturing the Hiroshima experience in a manner so accessible to the general populace. The story revolves around a small rural landowner and former white-collar worker named Shigematsu and his efforts to find a husband for his ward and niece Yasuko. Yasuko's marriage prospects are repeatedly stymied by rumors that she was, like her uncle, in Hiroshima at the time of the explosion. In an effort to disprove these rumors to a particularly promising match, Shigematsu decides to transcribe his diary and Yasuko's from August 6 until the end of the war. In the process, however, he discovers that Yasuko was splashed by the radioactive "black rain" that fell soon after the bombing. Before long, Yasuko begins to show signs of radiation illness and the prospective groom's family withdraws from the talks.

Generally praised for its success at making Hiroshima comprehensible within the context of the ordinary lives of one *hibakusha* family, *Black Rain* has achieved a status in Japanese educational circles similar to that of John Hersey's *Hiroshima* in the United States.

Although contemporary reviewers generally agreed that Ibuse succeeded in breaking through the mold of ideologically slanted treatments of the bombing, in fact *Black Rain* contributed to two contemporary trends of ideological import. First, it helped to integrate Hiroshima into the ideology of Japanese war victimhood: Shigematsu and Yasuko were average people with whom average Japanese could identify, and their problems, though uniquely complicated by their *hibaku* status, were fundamentally variations on the domestic and social problems all Japanese faced during and after the war. Second, it gained widespread approval among conservatives because it affirmed traditional Japanese culture, which they increasingly appreciated as the basis for prosperity in the 1960s. Accordingly, *Black Rain* helped make atomic victim mythology more acceptable to political and social conservatives who were unhappy with the stridently antiestablishment rhetoric of progressive antibomb activists. In these two ways it brought a measure of closure to Japanese victim ideology even as Japan's indirect involvement in the Vietnam War was beginning to undercut the Japanese pacifist position as righteous war victim.

Choosing three out of the thousands of antiwar works of the era cannot, of course, represent the totality of that literature. I have chosen these three because the written and cinematic versions received wide audiences and have not faded from the popular mind. Indeed, they are recognized as classics because they have continued to be read and viewed over the postwar years.[5] Those familiar with postwar popular culture can easily draw up their own lists of other works of equal stature,[6] but they will find the same themes in those works as in *Twenty-Four Eyes, Human Condition,* and *Black Rain.* Short of conducting a comprehensive study of postwar literature and cinema, one cannot prove the general impression that all antiwar literature employed victim themes. My purpose here is simply to illustrate how the basic themes of Japanese war victimhood are reflected and reinforced ("resonate") in a few works that are acknowledged as important. In analyzing these works, I have tried to give particular consideration to the authors' motivations, to the obvious and not so obvious messages embedded in the texts, and, finally, to the impression these texts made on contemporaries.[7]

Twenty-Four Eyes

Nijūshi no hitomi (Twenty-Four Eyes) is widely regarded as one of the most successful antiwar works in postwar Japan. Odagiri Hideo places Tsuboi's book in the canon of representative modern Japanese literature's classics,[8] and Kinoshita's film was a critical as well as a box office success. Eminent film critic Satō Tadao regards Kinoshita's film as "the greatest Japanese antiwar film" in the sense that it extols a kind of sentimental patriotism, "the ultimate expression of the theme of lovable and loving people suffering together in adverse circumstances." Satō writes that it "has probably wrung more tears out of Japanese audiences than any other postwar film."[9] *Twenty-Four Eyes* presents a people at the mercy of an increasingly militarist social/political system that offers no respite from poverty and war. Under the pressures of war, this system forces everyone into a seemingly inescapable victimhood.

Children play an indispensable role in this story as the archetype of pure victimhood. Readers and viewers are drawn to identify with the children's evolving relationship to the war effort: from innocent detachment, through ignorant and therefore willing cooperation, to silent and begrudging acquiescence. While still very young, these children have a special dispensation in the face of the oppressive educational system and society. They are free to express their joy and sadness without fear of censure. The first parts of the novel and film portray Miss Ōishi enjoying their innocence, singing simple children's songs in an idyllic child's world, symbolically isolated from political change as their village sits at the tip of a peninsula on an island in the Inland Sea. The children's gradual entry into adult society is unambiguously contextualized with references to contemporary events.[10] In the first of the four periods into which the story is divided, the children enter their village's branch school in 1928—the first year that elections were held under universal male suffrage, although later the same year a strengthened Peace Preservation Law was used to clamp down on left-wing political activity. By the time the students enter the main school in 1933, "many fellow Japanese who demanded freedom for people and planned reforms had been put into jail by the government, which suppressed new ideas. The cape children, however, knew nothing of this."[11] For the children, economic hardship is the only reality that impinges on their lives. They do not feel oppressed, however. Depression and the stirrings of war are treated almost as if they were natural calamities, equated with famine in northeastern Japan, which simply have to be endured since nothing can avert them. The children make play out of economic necessity and take simple joy in the straw sandals they make for themselves every week.

In this childlike innocence there is a simple pacifist wisdom that reveals itself from episode to episode. A good example is their reaction to their male teacher's attempt to teach them patriotic songs. Miss Ōishi has injured her ankle and can no longer teach at the isolated school, so the only other teacher at the small village school, an older man, takes charge of her lessons. We read that the old man thinks the songs Ōishi taught are silly—possibly acceptable for girls but inadequate for boys because they do not instill the Japanese spirit *(yamato damashii)*. He tries to teach them a song that exhorts boys to dream of sacrificing themselves in battle; but the children end up ignoring the lyrics and singing the melody with the quaint *hi-fu-mi* note scale the old man used.[12] In playfully mocking this teacher's old-fashioned teaching technique, the children seem to reject the militarism in the song instinctively.

As the children mature, their lives and thoughts are unavoidably touched by the world of adults. The girls' options seem especially limited by the country's economic problems. One girl must leave school to be indentured after her mother and baby sister die. Another is made to feel guilty for being born a girl since her family has no sons and her mother must work on a fishing boat alongside her husband. This girl's shame at not being a boy is particularly poignant. As the boys reach the last year of elementary school in 1934, they come under the influence of a militarist education and the general trend in Japanese society toward a militarist patriotism. The two brightest and most articulate boys, for example, Takeichi and Tadashi, announce that they want to be soldiers after finishing their higher schooling. When Miss Ōishi demurs and tells them that she much prefers fishermen and rice dealers to soldiers, the boys tell her she's a scaredy-cat *(yowamushi)*, and befitting her straightforward character she agrees. Two other boys whose families cannot afford further schooling, Kichiji and Isokichi, listen enviously. But Tsuboi notes that regardless of family circumstance and personal preference they would all one day be drafted in any case.[13]

Even as these children's aspirations are formed by prewar Japan's misplaced values and social mores, they remain unaware of the limitations being put on them. Bluntly Tsuboi tells the reader that the children could not have understood the connections between political suppression in Japan (represented by the jailing of a progressive teacher) and Japan's isolation from the international community (represented by Japan's leaving the League of Nations). So all-encompassing was the militarist spirit of the times,[14] they did not even know they had been deprived of the freedom to understand these things. In other words, they were innocent of any personal choice in the matter.

Even though their teachers are aware of these limitations, they too are trapped in the oppressive system even as they play central roles in sustaining it by teaching a militarist curriculum. One day Miss Ōishi comes to school to find the police interviewing the principal about a fellow teacher arrested on suspicion of being a communist.[15] The sole reason for suspicion was that he had been a college class-mate of a Mr. Inagawa who had been arrested for teaching pacifism to his sixth-grade students at a nearby school. Inagawa had collected his students' compositions into a booklet, "Seeds of Grass," which was being used as evidence of his communism. Although there seemed to be no real evidence that Inagawa was a communist, beyond his actively teaching pacifism, he was labeled one, thrown into jail, and on his release prohibited from resuming his job as a teacher. Miss Ōishi admired his collection—presumably for the students' pure and sincere pacifist sentiment—and in fact had read some of the essays to her own class. When her superior learns of this he immediately has her bring the collection to his office where, still scared and bewildered from his interview with the police, he burns the incriminating evidence. He then cautions Ōishi to take care lest she too be labeled a Red.[16]

Like all adults in *Twenty-Four Eyes,* the teachers too are at the mercy of state sanction and thought control. As an experienced male teacher and Ōishi's superior wryly say at moments of relative safety among peers, as if it were a mantra of common sense among school-teachers of the era, "You're a fool to teach with honest sincerity."[17] Trying to teach your students with too much honesty and sincerity, they clearly feel, only brings trouble with the authorities. The impli-cation, of course, is that all teachers know that the state-sponsored and sanctioned militarist education is dishonest—that it is manipulat-ing the students into serving the needs of the state. The only safe course is to adopt a "patriotic and loyal" attitude.[18] Although news-paper headlines about Inagawa's case read "Red Teacher Corrupts Pure Spirits" *(Jun'i naru tamashii wo mushibamu akai kyōshi),*[19] the reader understands that ironically it is the government—embodied in the militarist curriculum and the police who enforce the teachers' conformity to the curriculum—which is corrupting innocent minds. Teachers like Ōishi, who had resolved "never to deceive those [bright and trusting children's] eyes,"[20] are pressured into avoiding genuine intimacy and honest exchange of information and ideas. As these conditions inevitably lead to a false and empty *(sorazorashii)* teacher/pupil relationship, Ōishi decides her only escape from this twisted, topsy-turvy reality of prewar Japanese education is to resign.[21]

The oppressive atmosphere in the schools eventually permeates all society. The next time we see Ōishi, in 1940, now married with children, we are told that national spiritual mobilization has "forced people to follow its dictate so that they see only the war, believe only in the war, and throw body and soul into the war."[22] One cannot survive without hiding one's disaffection and discontent, "even in one's sleep." Paranoia runs so deep that even the naturally forthright Ōishi is half-suspicious of an old friend of her long-deceased father she meets at a lonely bus stop.[23] She is particularly circumspect when the old man expresses regret that her smiling former students, who have passed by on their way to conscription physicals, will be made the target of bullets. Even though Ōishi completely agrees with him, she refrains from voicing her views lest she be arrested. Perhaps the old man feels free to express these heretical pacifist sentiments because of his age and the unexpected meeting. Certainly he recognizes the danger. He whispers to Ōishi that perhaps he should be quiet lest he be handcuffed and taken away under the provisions of the Peace Preservation Law.[24]

After this encounter she returns home to find her children marching to a children's war song, and this leads her to muse on the pain that all mothers in Japan of the time had to bear. Her pain is compounded by the fact that her own son yearns to sacrifice himself for the nation—to make her a "Yasukuni mother" *(Yasukuni no haha)*.[25] He is ashamed of his mother's passive resistance to the war effort, especially when she chooses not to display the medal of honor for her husband's death. Eventually Daikichi takes the medal out of his mother's drawer and nails it to the gate in front of their home, as was the custom. After the war's end all these medals were taken down, Tsuboi editorializes, "as though their families thought that would take their guilt away." Implicitly Ōishi's family is guilty of supporting the war as well; but the irony is that Tsuboi's story expunges guilt through victimhood. The characters in her book are either duped or coerced into conforming to the state's expectations and supporting the war effort. Although as boys Ōishi's students dreamed of becoming soldiers and sailors, by the time they are old enough to be drafted some of them, perhaps all, have gained the wisdom to know that war is wrong. As adults they simply join everyone else and resign themselves to being trapped by the demands of their oppressive society. Like all adults, they can do nothing about their fates.

The war kills Ōishi's husband and three of her five male former students. When her youngest child, starving, dies from eating unripe persimmons soon after the war ends, Ōishi blames her death on war too. In Ōishi's mind, all the war's victims were as innocent as her daughter. The reader is encouraged to feel the same way: to connect her death with the deaths of Ōishi's husband and four former pupils.[26] Kinoshita's film shares with Tsuboi's novel this lachrymose message: We were all victims of forces beyond our control during the prewar era. Both film and novel discount any possibility of active resistance, stress people's immobilization through fear, and omit direct portrayal of explicit intimidation.[27] In criticizing the film for its avoidance of the issue of war guilt, Satō Tadao noted:

> Miss Ōishi is an idealization, and as such her appeal is strong throughout the film. However, as the main character she is weak because she drops out of the picture at the most important time, when she should be questioning the responsibility of teachers for indoctrinating their pupils with wartime ideology. Conversely, by reducing her responsibility to nil, the director is able to describe the war from the passive point of view of an innocent victim and to turn *Twenty-Four Eyes* into a tear-jerker.[28]

Keiko McDonald interprets this sense of resignation as simply a presentation of *mujō:* the Buddhist and purportedly typical Japanese attitude toward life, the "acceptance of the flux of time in recognizing the mutability of human affairs." After visits to her pupils' graves, after the final tearful reunion party in which we learn that boy-turned-man Isokichi is blind, the movie soundtrack ends with "Aogeba Tōtoshi," the traditional farewell song for graduation ceremonies. McDonald writes:

> Now we are brought strongly face to face with the feelings of *mujō,* which keeps the traditional Japanese in accord with the passage of time, never resenting or trying to fight against fate. We really do not feel any indignation against the injustice done by war to these survivors—Ōishi, her fatherless children, and the blind [Isokichi]. Instead, we encounter the feelings of quiescence, which lead the individual characters to accept things as they are. It is in *mujō* that we spectators, Ōishi, and her ex-pupils are finally united together.[29]

Without getting sidetracked into discussing the validity of McDonald's cultural assertions, we must admit that *mujō* does capture the attitude of the disempowered, agentless self portrayed in *Twenty-Four Eyes*. It is precisely this sentimentalized lack of subjectivity which leads Satō Tadao to argue that, of all postwar Japanese films, Kinoshita Keisuke's 1954 production "most succeeds as a thoroughly self-deceptive portrait of the people's war experience."[30]

Part of the deception is that the only active proponents of war are boys who have been educated to think that manhood requires a warlike Japanese spirit. As Ōishi broods over her former students going to their conscription physicals, she realizes that they would all be sent to remote places as soldiers: "This was a road that men could not avoid."[31] Although both film and novel introduce the dilemma of manhood in wartime Japan—to be a man meant one had to die for the state—neither treated the actual reality of men. As Satō describes it:

> Ōishi remembers one [former student] who perished in the battlefield as an innocent, smiling schoolboy, a particularly moving image to a Japanese audience, as if the boy had been killed in all his purity. However, it does not take much imagination to suppose that these innocent schoolboys went to their deaths fighting. One wonders how many enemy soldiers they might have killed, whether they committed any atrocities or engaged in rape or pillage. . . . In *Twenty-Four Eyes* we are only filled with the emotion that our peaceful lives were disrupted by the war and that we lost so many pure and sincere young men. The question of how much damage we did to the enemy is neglected entirely. We only feel that we, the Japanese people, were as innocent as those adorable children and that we suffered grievously.[32]

Men of soldiering age are conspicuous in their absence in *Twenty-Four Eyes*. They appear in the early scenes as teachers; Ōishi's husband makes a few appearances; but they remain secondary and Ōishi's male students are sent off to war as soon as they become men. The appearance of men in the final scenes offers little more. While her female students more or less return to normal lives after the war, only two of the boys survive, one blinded. One was Kichiji, the boy who was always unsure of himself, quiet and unwilling to take independent action. The other, Isokichi, was an active enough boy, but he survived the war at the cost of his sight, and it is clear from the discussion at a postwar reunion of Ōishi and her students that his future livelihood is far from certain.

A student of women and war in Japanese film has explained the relevant gender norms: "Women do not *belong* in the realm of politics. Women may object to the war and to the pointless destruction it brought to Japan, but their opposition should be social and cultural, not political."³³ As a woman's and children's story, then, *Twenty-Four Eyes* is a useful vehicle for a depoliticized image of wartime Japanese. But pacifism, as viewers like Satō readily perceive, is a highly political moral. Satō's criticism points up a gendered compartmentalization of memory in the antiwar genre. If they are masculine traits that must form the modus vivendi of the political realm, then one important task for pacifist activism in postwar Japan would seem to be to construct a pacifist masculinity as well as debunk the militarist one. Satō considered *Twenty-Four Eyes* inadequate because Tsuboi addressed only half of this task.

Presumably Tsuboi thought her readers were quite aware of what men were compelled to do in the army. Perhaps she implicitly understood what Yasui Kaoru, the contemporary organizer of the antibomb movement, articulated in his journal: it is the experience of being victimized rather than that of victimizing that really motivates for peace.³⁴ For his part, Kinoshita aimed from the beginning for a lyrical antiwar film:

> In any case it's a sad story. I was aiming for that sentimental beauty from the beginning, so criticizing [it] as a sentimental film misses the mark. . . . I wanted to capture people's fate as they followed it *(ningen no tadotte iku unmei o)* in the beautiful scenery of the Inland Sea, and I believe there was no better [way] to forcefully pitch an antiwar [message] to the audience.³⁵

The Human Condition

If *Twenty-Four Eyes* limits our vision of the Japanese experience to the archetypically innocent women, children, and devirilized men, *The Human Condition* represents an explicit attempt to explore the complexities of politically responsible behavior during the war.³⁶ Kaji, a young man struggling to develop a humane yet assertive persona under conditions that compel acquiescence to brutal exploitation, represents a positive model for those seeking a pacifist alternative to the militarist caricature of wartime masculinity.

The story begins in Manchuria in the early winter of 1943. Kaji feels he cannot marry his sweetheart because he may be drafted any day. In a scene with many metaphorical layers, the novel opens with Kaji and Michiko walking together in the snow late at night, neither wanting to end the evening. Kaji's eyes catch a porcelain rendition of Rodin's *The Kiss*—two lovers in passionate embrace oblivious to the world around them—but as Michiko notices he averts his eyes. She challenges him by saying it's not like him to be running away from the issue at hand—yet that is precisely Kaji's personal problem at this stage of his life. The immediate question of whether they would spend the night together, the larger question of whether Kaji would have the courage to marry Michiko in the face of an uncertain future, and the ultimate question of Kaji running away from his own responsibility as a humanist Japanese in a system where Japanese are exploiting others—all these are issues he has been dodging.[37]

Kaji is unexpectedly given an opportunity to resolve these issues when company management offers him a draft exemption in exchange for implementing a proposal he had made—to increase production at his company's mine by improving working conditions for the Chinese laborers. His idea—"to treat human beings as human beings"— is his small way of trying to maintain humanistic principles in the face of an inhumane war. Yet as he explains to his friend and fellow humanist draft-evader Kageyama, he hesitates to accept because it would make him an accomplice to their exploitation. Kageyama scoffs at this: he and Kaji are already complicitous, he points out. Although they oppose the war, neither has the courage to face jail—the certain consequence of rejecting all complicity with the war effort and maintaining a pure humanist position without compromising their principles.[38] So they choose an expedient if hypocritical method of avoiding the draft: they emigrate to Manchuria, the "leading bastion of Japanese imperialism." It is odd for him to worry about selling out now, notes Kageyama, having already transformed himself from a "young antiwar champion to a henchman of the merchants of death." Kageyama, the first of several friends who share Kaji's humanistic impulses but are reconciled to their inability to change conditions, borrows Kaji's own metaphor and tells him to make the most of his exemption—to become the "good sheepdog who leads the sheep to green pastures." Kaji, nodding his assent, worries whether such a pasture even exists.[39]

Hoping to mitigate the worst excesses of Japanese imperialism from within the system while realizing his desire for personal happiness, Kaji accepts the draft exemption. He marries Michiko and tries to implement his ideas at the mine. There his immediate colleague is Okishima, an experienced labor manager and, like Kageyama, a pragmatic humanist who understands his limited power to change things.[40] Though he sympathizes with Kaji's ideas and tries to work with him, he doubts their ultimate workability. In a passage typical of both Okishima's self-awareness and the novel's explicitness about good people's complicity in victimizing others, Okishima tells Kaji about his own past. Years earlier, serving as a translator for the army, he helped hunt down, interrogate, kill, and bury "anti-Japanese resisters" in front of their wives and children, whom he then forced to walk over the graves. It made no difference whether he did it of his own volition or was forced to do it, Okishima continues. "Those children are certain to still remember the sound of [their fathers'] bellies bursting open under the earth, and they haven't forgotten my face." If he had tried to help these Chinese, he implies, he would have been buried along with them. In other words, the only path for survival lay in compromise. Kaji simply hadn't been forced into the final recognition of this fact yet. The only difference between the two of them, he tells Kaji, is that, "at this stage of the war, you're the lucky bastard who can still say things like 'treat human beings as human beings.' "[41]

Although he succeeds in improving living conditions for the laborers and production does increase, Kaji is drawn even more directly into the war machine when the *kenpeitai* (military police) force him to introduce six hundred POW laborers into the mine's workforce. Aware that he has in effect become an army prison guard, Kaji tries to justify himself with the idea that the prisoners are lucky to have a humanist like him in charge. Yet he is repeatedly hindered by a panoply of characters including gung-ho foremen and *kenpeitai* sergeants, subversive Japanese and Korean malcontents, and Chinese laborers and prostitutes. He is, for example, unable to change the foremen's brutal treatment of the workers, especially the behavior of one Okazaki, a macho ultrapatriot who taunts Kaji with aspersions on his manhood.

In his efforts to establish a humane relationship with his wards, even as he exploits their labor, Kaji gets to know two of the POWs. Gao is a recalcitrant prisoner. Unyielding in his hatred toward all Japanese and in his rejection of what he regards as Kaji's duplicitous kindness, he despises Kaji for his ulterior motives in improving living conditions and distrusts his sincerity. Self-righteous and proud, he condemns Kaji for his seeming disregard of basic human dignity— especially when three dozen or so prostitutes are brought in to service hundreds of imprisoned workers.[42] Despite his haughty attitude, or perhaps because of it, he falls in love with one of these prostitutes. Their relationship forces Kaji to recognize that his own comfortable life with Michiko is supported by the same system of exploitation that causes Gao and his lover's unhappy separation. Kaji comes to feel his own marriage was attained at the expense of Gao's. When Kaji considers gaining Gao's cooperation by permitting him to marry and live outside the barbed-wire compound, it pains him to know that he is trying to manipulate Gao just as the Japanese war establishment had manipulated him.[43]

The central Chinese character in Kaji's life story is Wang Heng-li, a natural leader of the POWs and a former university professor. Wang's strength of personality, intelligence, eloquence, and integrity make him both Kaji's conscience and mentor. In a forceful letter that one Kyoto University reviewer has called a "masterpiece,"[44] Wang tries to explain why the POWs keep trying to escape. He describes how his village's women were raped and forced into prostitution in army brothels, the men indiscriminately murdered, the survivors rounded up as "anti-Japanese" elements and organized into work gangs, and a few used as "guinea pigs" (morumotto) for medical experiments.[45] Noting that conquerors themselves are inevitably conquered, Wang predicts that Japanese, Kaji included, "have already taken on the fate of witnessing your own wives, lovers, and sisters suffer humiliating violation, your comrades killed for no reason, and your property plundered."[46]

It is a measure of Gomikawa's rigor that he explores these ideas in a manner that is almost a fictionalized critique of the emergent Japanese victim mythology of the 1950s. Kaji objects to Wang's condemnation of all Japanese: "But the problem, Professor Wang, is that certain kinds of Japanese have already been encroached on before you Chinese, and by Japanese themselves. In other words, the fire that is killing us has spread and is now scorching your skins." Wang makes a pointed rejoinder: "Everyone wants to see himself as a tragic figure, to become drunk on the tragic beauty he makes through manipulation of his ideals. But you cannot twist facts. For example, a human being outside the barbed-wire fence cannot tell a human being inside that he is the more fortunate. And you cannot force me to believe it, because it is contrary to fact."[47] If Kaji is to overcome his hypocrisy and maintain the purity of his humanist principles, he must embrace the victimized POWs' position as his own. Kaji faces his most difficult and consequential test when Gao and six other POWs, wrongly accused of attempting escape, are summarily sentenced to beheading by a visiting kenpeitai sergeant. The issues at stake are further clarified in a discussion between Kaji and Wang dramatically positioned on either side of the POW compound's barbed-wire fence. In the film, director Kobayashi brings the audience into the conversation gradu-

ally with a long shot followed by progressively closer views of the
two men as the viewpoint switches back and forth across the barbed
wire. The cropping is such that it becomes unclear who is on the
inside and who is on the outside. Wang is clearly the noble figure,
the teacher with whom the audience is encouraged to identify through
Kaji. One is left with the feeling that we are all encumbered by that
fence—that our nobler selves lie inside the fence on the side of the
victim, as indeed Kaji comes to discover.

When Wang learns that the chances of getting a reprieve are slim,
he encourages Kaji to embrace his nobler self and assert this common humanity. He knows that the only hope for his compatriots lies
in getting Kaji to act without concern for his personal safety: "This is
not just our problem. Just as seven of my companions stand at the
brink of life and death, so do you now stand at an important cross-
road. . . . If you fail at this moment, no one will ever trust you as a
human being again. You will also lose faith in yourself." When the
unnerved Kaji replies simply that Wang is right, Wang asks: "You
understand, yet you would do nothing?" The immobilized Kaji merely
asks what he should do, to which Wang retorts: "Is one who walks
freely outside this barbed wire asking me? Not all the Japanese on
this mountain are murderous devils. If you combined their wills together in opposition to the executioners, you would be more effective than just acting alone." Kaji points out that if he acts as Wang
suggests he would no longer even be on the mountain let alone in a
position to help—a clear echo of Okishima's reasoning—but Wang
advances to the essential moral issue at stake:

> You and I will both make minor mistakes (*chiisa na kashitsu*). We
> can be forgiven if we correct them. But an error made at the crucial
> moment becomes an unforgivable crime. So far as I can see, your life
> has been a long series of errors stemming from the conflict between
> your work and yourself, though you've probably tried to correct
> them. But for this coming crucial moment . . . that moment will sepa-
> rate the murderers who wear the mask of humanism from those
> worthy of the beautiful name "human being."

Kaji says he knows that—though he is unsure of his own courage to
claim the privilege of being called a "human being." Wang tries to
reassure him: "You don't have as much faith in human beings as you
think. Regardless of what you think, human beings will always find
fellow human beings . . . somewhere."[48]

After trying desperately to get the upper-level management to intervene, Kaji spends a long night in anguish.[49] Sitting by the office phone he waits for Okishima to call from company headquarters to report on his fruitless efforts there. Gao's lover, the prostitute Yang, visits to plead with Kaji but all he can do is tell her to go home. He feels powerless. In the novel, he notices a scrap of newspaper headline proclaiming the new Sino-Japanese pact of alliance (October 1943): "Establishment of Permanent Basic Relationship of Harmony, Stability, and Mutual Equality—Empire Advances Liberation of Asia!" In fact, this headline symbolizes an actual shift in Japanese army policy toward China—toward a less harsh, less obviously exploitative relationship with the puppet Wang Ching-wei regime. For Kaji, however, the headline highlights his own role in this exploitation:

> Tomorrow, in order to liberate Asia, Japanese Asians are going to decapitate seven Chinese Asians. This is the permanent basic relationship, the testimony of harmony, stability, and mutual equality. . . . In a few days the Greater East Asia Conference will be held in Tokyo and the six nations of Japan, China, Thailand, Manchuria, the Philippines, and Burma will probably announce a joint declaration for Greater East Asia. And in every region where there are Japanese, the pale ghosts of humanism, such as Kaji, are merely serving as a camouflage of mutual equality.[50]

In accepting the draft exemption and the job as mine labor supervisor, Kaji knew that he was compromising his principles of political justice in exchange for a safe and comfortable life with Michiko. He hoped he could at least serve as a buffer against the worst of Japanese cruelty and exploitation, but Wang has forced him to confront his failure to save his fellow Chinese human beings and his failure, as well, to limit any further compromise of his humanism. The emotional strain is simply too much for him: at one point he envies Wang's place inside the barbed-wire fence.

In this state of mind he returns home. Michiko senses his dilemma and pleads with him not to endanger their chance for a normal married life, but Kaji answers that she need not worry: he will fulfill his implicit obligation to her. Michiko is not just acting selfishly in this scene. She is trying to protect her family from the disruption of war, which is her privilege and duty in wartime Japan.[51] Kaji, by contrast, is torn between two conflicting imperatives. As husband and future family patriarch, he must assure the survival of his family. But as a responsible humanist, especially as Wang uncompromisingly defines it, he must act to save his fellow human beings. At one point his conscience becomes too much for him and he gets out of bed determined to set the condemned men free. As Michiko tries to stop him, he cries out that he must set them free or else he will no longer be human *(ningen ja naku naru)*. Ultimately he breaks down—partly out of fear for his own safety, partly out of concern for Michiko.

At the execution ground, Kaji remains immobilized as *kenpeitai* Sergeant Watarai coldly and cleanly beheads the first two prisoners.[52] He realizes that the prisoners will no longer take his humanism seriously. Indeed, he can no longer convince himself of his own purity of heart, since he has so clearly failed at this crucial moment. But at the same time he justifies his inaction by asking what anyone else would have done standing next to the bloodthirsty *kenpeitai* sergeant with his blade ready for the kill. Without a doubt it would be Kaji's own head that would roll. But then Gao is brought forward. Gao demands to know why he is being executed, eventually calling all Japanese devils as he is led to his execution.[53] When the inexperienced adjutant fumbles Gao's beheading, Kaji can no longer stand himself and intervenes. The sergeant threatens Kaji with the sword, but when Kaji holds his ground, daring him to kill him as well, the prisoners rise up in his support. In one of the most moving scenes of the film, Wang shouts out a demand to "stop this slaughter of our comrades" and the prisoners begin to chant "Murderer!" as they rhythmically advance on the soldiers and policemen. In order to bring the prisoners under control, the noticeably shaken Sergeant Watarai calls off the execution.

Kaji was forced to make a choice between consenting to unjust punishment of the Chinese or protesting at his own peril. Choosing justice, he also chose humanity over brutality and to some extent regained his purity of heart despite the three dead prisoners. Yet he was only able to do so by making himself a victim as well. This too has its advantages, especially in the Manichean moral universe constructed by Wang. There is less emotional strain in one respect, for he is much more unambiguously on the side of right, and he earns the fellowship of other human beings, which Wang sanctioned in calling him a comrade. But victimhood has its price. Kaji is arrested, tortured, and interrogated by the *kenpeitai,* stripped of his exemption, and ultimately sent off to the army. And his personal decision to bear these burdens leaves his wife Michiko in an uncertain state. Kaji has achieved purity of action at the cost of betraying his private obligations.

So ends the first section of the story. The last two sections follow the same basic outline as the first. Kaji recommits himself to Michiko. To live up to his private obligation to her, he simply tries to survive without compromising his principles too much, without making too many "minor mistakes." Yet in each section, his superior intelligence, talent, and physical stamina place him in positions of authority. And when conditions reach critically inhuman dimensions, he inevitably sacrifices himself in favor of principle. To fail to make such a sacrifice, he feels, would be cowardly and leave him living merely a false humanism.

In the second section, although he is held in suspicion of communist tendencies, Kaji's resolution to survive the war and return to Michiko, as well as his strong constitution, lead him to become an excellent soldier. Just as Wang insisted, even in the army he meets fellow human beings. At one point he has the good fortune to be put under the command of his old friend Kageyama, who has become a lieutenant since we last saw him at the very beginning of the story. Despite his reluctance to be placed in a compromising position of authority, Kaji allows himself to be put in charge of a new group of young, old, and infirm recruits—provided he has control over their training. A survivor of extreme hazing himself, he wishes to blunt the brutalizing influence of the military training system. Yet his insistence on treating his men fairly leads the veteran soldiers to beat both Kaji and his men. Through force of courage and intelligence Kaji survives the fierce first battle with the Soviet Red Army as the war draws to a close. Unwilling to surrender, Kaji finds himself leading two soldiers —Aihara is a noncommissioned officer who later rapes and kills an eighteen-year-old Japanese refugee; Terada is the patriotic son of an army colonel who gradually learns from Kaji the foolishness of sacrificing oneself for the state—and other Japanese they encounter as they try to return to their loved ones. Along the way Kaji finds himself killing both Russian soldiers and Chinese militia and realizes that he has adopted the morality of war in order to survive. Finally he surrenders for the sake of a group of isolated Japanese women who reawaken him to the pointlessness of bloodshed.

In the final section, Kaji becomes the leader of his small work group in a Soviet POW labor camp. Once again he confronts brutality by Japanese noncommissioned officers. (The Soviets follow international agreements respecting military hierarchy.) At the mercy of unscrupulous Japanese superiors and hindered by an incompetent and unsympathetic interpreter, Kaji is mistaken for a "fascist samurai" war criminal. He seems destined for hard labor in a Siberian concentration camp; but Kaji has come to accept his prison term as both punishment for his past misdeeds and an opportunity to rebuild himself spiritually. He resolves to survive long years in Siberia in order to return, eventually, to the woman whose love has sustained him through his suffering—and then abruptly abandons these plans when Aihara cruelly and unjustly causes Terada's death. In a state of righteous vengeance, Kaji brutally kills Aihara, escapes from the camp, and wanders the north Manchurian plain, driven by cold and hunger to hallucinations of Michiko. He eventually dies believing that he will reach Michiko after a short nap, during which the snow gradually blankets his cold body.

In his introduction to the novel, Gomikawa states: "Since today's history was made by the majority of us who, after all, even if indirectly, spent those war years in collaboration, I felt that I couldn't move forward *(mae e susumenai)* unless I delved into the past once more from my own particular point of view."[54] Like his alter ego Wang, for whom writing was a way to assert subjectivity as a human being, Gomikawa feels that writing about the war experience will help him get a better grip on his life. Contemporary reviewers recognized the sincerity of his effort, and most praised his success. The *Tokyo shinbun* labeled *Human Condition* a brilliant work that "artistically raised the issue of war responsibility from the most thoroughgoing position."[55] The Kyoto University campus newspaper praised the protagonist's force of intellect and courage in analyzing his humanism. The paper also praised Wang's letter detailing the Japanese military's barbarous acts against the Chinese.[56] Gomikawa and Kobayashi both portray in brutal detail the dehumanizing daily occurrences inside the Japanese community—the *kenpeitai*'s abuse of the average Japanese as well as the systematic cruelty within the Japanese army—and the relentlessly inhumane treatment Japanese heaped on Chinese. And it is not simply brutal army types who victimize Chinese. Characters with whom the reader and viewer become sympathetic, namely Kaji and his admirable friends such as Okishima, also vent their rage on innocent Chinese.

Yet ultimately the story carries a message of the individual's inability to change things in the face of war and institutions such as the military. The Communist Party newspaper *Akahata* noted with typical skepticism that "Kaji's sincerity does not change the fact that it was a war of aggression, nor the fate of the people one bit. There is a great deal of personal . . . growth, but one must note the inevitable process in which he [conforms to] the system. The correct way to see/understand the author and the work is to reflect [on the fact that Gomikawa] isolated him and could have him offer at most only conscientious resistance."[57]

In other words, *Human Condition* is a complex morality play that permits a great deal of sentimentality while asserting rigorous standards of humane conduct. One can indulge in a sentimental reading in which the all-pervasive "system" is the ultimate scapegoat, even for the sins of especially cruel characters. In the army, for example, Kaji tells his men and his superior officers that the blame for the beatings inflicted by the veteran soldiers lay not with them but with the "military" *(guntai)* itself. Even *kenpeitai* Sergeant Watarai is shown in the book to have been a disadvantaged tenant farmer whose only road out of poverty lay in the army. It was in the army, then, that he learned to be callous and brutal.[58] At the end of Wang's letter, he thanks Kaji for lending him the paper and pencil because "as long as I have paper and pencil in my hands, I and others will recognize that I am still a human being. Even so, as I write this there is no more space to write in. This shows, in short, the meaningless limits on the human condition."[59] *Human Condition* is a sincere artistic effort to deal directly with issues of responsibility for individual Japanese as victimizers—Gomikawa's attempt to regain something ineffably essential to human dignity—but it recognizes with a great deal of sympathy the limitations that conditions sometimes impose on people.

Human Condition found its earliest readership among university-age youth,[60] for whom the story of Kaji's attempt to maintain purity of heart in the face of pressures to conform—to remain true to his principles of justice—undoubtedly served as a parable for their own personal development as they made the transition to adult society with all its compromising demands.[61] This is not simply because they stood on the threshold of adulthood, evaluating principles, deciding how much compromise is acceptable, and facing the task of consolidating an identity out of competing career and social options.[62] They were coming of age in the 1950s, a period of violent political struggle between conservative patriots and progressive liberals. As in other societies experiencing open political contention, Japanese university students of that era represented the conscience of the nation's public life. Politics was an important part of life, for many of them, so the dilemma Kaji confronted at the interface of public and private spheres during the war was no doubt exceedingly relevant. Just as important, they had been educated in the liberal pacifist curriculum that condemned traditional masculine achievements in war and privileged women and children over men as noble protagonists. For such a generation, Kaji became, as newspapers called him, a "new hero for modern times."[63]

One notes in this context that both the film and the novel establish a tension between two types of male adulthood distinguished by the terms *"otoko"* (man) and *"ningen"* (human being). One is left with the distinct impression that Kaji's story is a parable for defining a new kind of masculinity—one that would indeed make Kaji a new "hero" for the modern man. Although *"otoko"* is commonly used in everyday language, in this novel and film the term is repeatedly connected to the crudest and cruelest of wartime excesses. The first significant *otoko* character is Okazaki, Kaji's macho nemesis in the mine. Okazaki is convinced the only way to get the *chankoro* ("Chinks") to work is to compel them by force. He is especially willing to use corporal punishment to increase production for the war.[64] He seems to take joy in inflicting pain. Inevitably snapping his whipping rod on his leggings to punctuate his point and to vent his aggression, he repeatedly challenges Kaji's humanistic labor principles. He is proud of his own manhood and uses *otoko* phrases again and again to assert it. When the mine is ordered to increase production 20 percent to meet growing war requirements, he "stakes his manhood" *(otoko o kakete hikiuketa)* on meeting his quota. He rallies his subforemen to make a "man's promise" *(otoko no yakusoku)* with him to step up their brutal methods. He tells them: "If the Chinks try to slack off, it don't matter. Just knock 'em down." He will take responsibility for any consequences and share the incentive money with them if they meet the quota.[65] All this *otoko* brutality is justified in the name of increasing war production. Even when Okazaki beats a worker to death, the mine director accepts it as a "minor mistake" *(chiisa na kashitsu)* that can be overlooked in considering the demand for increased production for the war effort.[66]

Okazaki's incessant use of *"otoko"* could be overlooked except that both novel and film are suffused with gendered allusions. Kaji's humanistic treatment of his men in the army, for example, is regarded as "femininely weak" *(memeshii)*. The sword-brandishing *kenpeitai* Sergeant Watarai compliments Kaji on his calm appearance after the first beheading by telling him men usually "turn pale and their balls shrink up."[67] When Watarai tortures Kaji in the *kenpeitai* cell, he says he will make him weep "like a woman." The ultimate punishment that the hardened veterans inflict on an older recruit is to force him to pretend he is a prostitute and make him solicit customers. Much of this, of course, is not untypical of armies at war. But in *Human Condition* this male bonding through rejection and persecution of the female other is especially linked with the worst evils of war and military life. Rifles, whipping rods, and swords appear repeatedly as appendages to mean-spirited ultrapatriotic or militaristic Japanese men.

Despite his bouts with moral uncertainty, Kaji leaves no doubt that he can endure anything these male archetypes of cruelty dish out. In fact, his military superiors recognize his stamina, skill, and grit, which make him a most resilient soldier. They also recognize a potential threat in Kaji's kind of manhood.[68] Kaji struggles to maintain his dignity as a human being *(ningen)*—a more profound achievement than maintaining the cruel, insensitive manliness demanded by the morally corrupt militarist system of wartime Japan. For Kaji, the task of maintaining his manhood is bound up in maintaining his purity of heart and action in humanism, as well as his courage to face the consequences of his beliefs. It is the only way he can be a man worthy of what his mentor Wang called the "beautiful name 'human being.'" Gomikawa seems to have been searching for an assertive and appealing wartime masculine identity that was worthy of postwar sensibilities, which condemned war and militaristic bravado.

In this regard, Kobayashi's *Human Condition* provides a counterpoint to the postwar film genre called *hahamono* ("mother") films, which depict fatherless families as metaphors for the "demasculinized" family state.[69] *Human Condition* belongs to another genre of films that attempted to integrate two traditional male theatrical roles, the *tateyaku* and the *nimaime*. As described by the film critic Satō Tadao, the *tateyaku* type was a "noble, idealized samurai . . . sagacious, with a strong will and determination to persevere," who nonetheless placed no value on romantic love. "Such a character," he wrote, "was never permitted to place his love for his wife or sweetheart above loyalty to his lord." The *nimaime* type was handsome, pure of heart, though often weak in moral character, and was "always kind and gentle toward the heroine." Kobayashi's film with Nakadai Tatsuya as Kaji was an effort to combine the best qualities of both role types: a strong but loving, handsome, and moral hero.[70]

Hori Hidehiko argues in a contemporary literary review that Kaji became a popular hero because he embodies so many admirable masculine qualities: a man who has a pure and strong sense of justice, who loves only one woman his whole life, who always takes the side of the underdog, who always acts according to his own will, who masters the skills of soldiering and maintains control over his fears—

in short, a "man's man" *(otokorashii otoko)*. Yet Hori cannot bring himself to admire Kaji because, as a fictional character, he is not "consistent, he's a patchwork person," a "mosaic." He is introduced as an intellectual, for example, but he fails as an intellectual because he lets his emotions rule. While this is noble in its purity of principle, Kaji's righteous resistance to injustice inevitably leads the authorities to crush his righteousness and further restrict his ability to change things. Hori thinks that Gomikawa's *Human Condition* was popular with the masses for its shocking description of brutality, its exciting battle scenes, its explicit language regarding sex, and, ultimately, its romanticization of Kaji's exploits: "Anger and personal resistance against tyrannic authority and the system and vexation with yourself for your ultimate powerlessness—these human feelings are woven into scenes of war and the military in this popular novel."[71] Kaji is able to survive when he permits himself to cooperate with the system and make Wang's "minor mistakes." These are the only mistakes Japanese are likely to feel they made during the war. So while the story ostensibly glamorizes Kaji's purity of character, it also implicitly validates Kageyama and Okishima's compromised position as the only pragmatically viable option. Such was the human condition in wartime.

Ultimately Kaji becomes a kind of *hōganbiiki* hero—a tragic figure whose weakness and inevitable failure elicit sympathy—since he dies a cold, lonely death.[72] This "sentimental humanism," which suffuses book and film, allows Kaji to be both a man's man and a victim's victim. The aim, of course, was for Kaji to be both at the same time: to regain his masculinity by taking responsibility for his actions but also to ennoble him with a humanist pacifism. The irony is that he was required to become a victim in order to achieve the purity of manhood as a "human being." It is this trade-off that turns this project to examine war responsibility into support for the ideology of Japanese war victimhood. The lesson seems clear enough. As Kobayashi himself noted:

> We [Gomikawa and Kobayashi] have many regrets from our youth. Scars. We wish we could have done things this way or that way. In our hearts we wanted so much to resist the army, that inhuman institution; but we couldn't do a thing about that either. Gomikawa couldn't either, no doubt. After the war, we were able to get that all off our chests for the first time in *Human Condition*. That's why I think of it as a dream we couldn't realize, a romanticization of resistance during our youth.[73]

Human Condition shares this combination of resignation and romanticization with the less rigorously self-reflective forms of victim literature and film.

Black Rain

Ibuse Masuji's *Kuroi ame* (Black Rain) is a montage of diary narratives —of small rural landowner and *hibakusha* victim Shigematsu, his family, and others' encounters with the atomic bomb; of his difficulties in ensuring his niece Yasuko's prospective marriage five years later; and of daily life in wartime urban Japan and postwar village Japan. By embedding the *hibakusha* experience within the context of more commonly experienced war suffering, Ibuse makes it easier for non-*hibakusha* to relate to Hiroshima and incorporate it into their own mythologies of war victimhood. *Black Rain* is a more complex variant of the *Twenty-Four Eyes* model of victim literature: although it portrays people as victims of larger systemic forces of war, its protagonist recognizes that in some ways the people were behind the war effort. The atomic bombing is a shock that opens their eyes to the misguidedness of war.

The novel restricts our view of the war to its impact on the relatively innocent civilian population on the home islands. Although Hiroshima was a significant military center, soldiers do not appear in the story except as arrogant officers whom the civilians fear and resent, as victims themselves of the bombing, or as work crews collecting the scorched corpses for mass cremation. Young men from Shigematsu's village appear only in work crews building firebreaks in Hiroshima or as volunteers in search of the injured after the bombing.[74] The main characters are civilians—men too old for military service, women, children—whose travails are all attributed in vague terms to war, to the state *(kokka)* or the "system," and, of course, to the atomic bomb.

Children are idealized as innocents. A passage about middle-school pupils mobilized for war work reminds one of the militarist-educated students in *Twenty-Four Eyes*. Certainly it must strike a chord in the memories of a whole generation of Japanese:

> One can usually tell the way things are going by watching the children, who are more simple in their reactions than adults. . . . Almost without exception wiped out by the bomb, [they] were helping to pull down houses to make firebreaks almost every day right up to August 5. Not one of their faces betrayed the slightest desire to play truant or to hide away. The schoolgirls in the voluntary labor units

wore white cloths round their foreheads and bore armbands proudly
labeled "School Volunteer Unit." On their way to the steel factory,
and on their way home again, they marched together, singing in
chorus as they went:

> A rifle in your hand, a hammer in mine—
> But the road into battle is one, and no more.
> To die for our country's a mission divine
> For the boys and the girls of the volunteer corps![75]

As in *Twenty-Four Eyes,* people had to be careful what they said
during the war. Shigematsu's wife, Shigeko, notes in her account of
the wartime diet an incident that illustrates the need for circumspec-
tion. Sometime before the bombing a Mrs. Miyaji happened to complain to the person next to her on the train about a change in her
son's schoolbook that she regarded as "an insult to learning." The
food shortage was so severe that the rice ration had been lowered
from four to three *go,* and a verse in a famous Miyazawa Kenji poem
about rural hardship had been altered to match. These remarks came
to the attention of "the authorities" who regarded them as "imper-
tinent," "irresponsible talk . . . [and suggested] it was a breach of
the National General Mobilization Law, which was a capital offense.
By that time, everybody was taking care what they said in front of
others."[76]

Although clearly someone had reported Mrs. Miyaji to the authorities, the emphasis is on the danger of expressing dissent—a danger
that compelled people to acquiesce. Still, they generally harbored resentment toward the system that oppressed them. And they managed
to express their anger in surreptitious ways. As Shigematsu and his
family are escaping from the city after the bombing, for example, they
overhear a man relate an incident that occurred several days earlier.
After complaining about the ineptness of bureaucrats at the municipal
defense office—interestingly, a complaint that Ibuse discounts with
supplementary information—the man describes how some people in
a jammed train played a practical joke on an arrogant army lieutenant
who had kicked off his boots and sprawled across an entire seat.[77]
No one dared complain to him. But after he fell asleep, one of the
passengers stuffed two halves of a rice ball down each boot before
getting off the train. Before he got off, another passenger shook each
boot to "make sure that a sacrifice so noble—considering the scarcity
of food—should have the very maximum effect." Others nearby
"looked at [the officer's] sleeping form with grins on their faces, though

several of them moved along to other coaches for fear of getting embroiled."[78] After describing the lieutenant's rude surprise, the storyteller's travel companion elbows him to stop before he gets himself into trouble.

After the bombing, Ibuse's characters are less circumspect in expressing their resentment of their oppression by the state and the military, though they still are careful. This release of the dissenting voice is Ibuse's tribute to the cataclysmic power of the atomic bombing to lift the normal rules of social and political decorum, at least in its immediate aftermath.[79] At certain moments it has the capacity to jolt Shigematsu out of his habitual cooperation with Japan's war effort. Despite his own injuries and debilitation, he reenters the city a few days after the bombing on an errand to procure the coal necessary to get his factory back into production. When he sees the eyes of one of the bloated corpses twitching, he thinks the person might still be alive or even possessed by some supernatural spirit. On closer inspection he is horrified to see that the twitching is the simple result of maggots squirming under the eyelids. For a moment he "felt like flinging my bundle [with his papers and survival gear] in the river. I hate war. Who cared, after all, which side won? The only important thing was to end it all as soon as possible: rather an unjust peace than a 'just' war!"[80] On regaining his composure, he realizes his own survival depends on persevering, so he resumes his mission. Even when they continue to perform their duties, as Shigematsu does, the hibakusha's eyes are opened to the folly of war as a policy of state. One of the soldiers at work cremating the endless piles of corpses, for example, blames the nation-state system for bringing such devastation. He expresses his disgust by sighing that he wishes he had been born in "a country without a state."[81]

Remembering his admiration for an unusual newspaper article critical of Hitler at the time of the Tripartite Pact, Shigematsu writes in his diary that after he went to work in a factory producing military supplies, he "slipped into the habit of hoping, for our sake, that Hitler would win. But from the time the bomb was dropped, my ideas had suffered an abrupt about-face, and I began to feel that what I had been believing was a lot of nonsense." In an anecdote that he says epitomizes the feelings of factory workers during the war—and presumably a measure of the perversely liberating impact of the bombing—he describes how an official notice was defaced in the final weeks of the war. One sentence in this notice, which exhorted the Hiroshima survivors to go back to work, stated that the "army is already providing us with incalculable aid." Soon someone had emphasized the irony inherent in the statement by circling the characters for "already providing"—the army provided precious little aid—and by the next day someone had torn the message off the bulletin board. In the vacant space someone else had written: "You can't wage war on an empty stomach." This bold graffito remained until after the emperor's radio address announcing surrender on August 15.[82]

Still, the state "system" managed to keep the average Japanese under control. Indeed, we read that it debilitated him. Near the end of the work Shigematsu notes:

> Ever since the Hiroshima bomb, no one knew just when the enemy might land, or the whole nation be called on to lay down its life, and at heart the factory workers must have been just as frightened as I was. The trouble was that all of us, spiritually, were bound hand and foot, and fiercely suppressed every urge to express anxiety, let alone dissatisfaction. Such was the power of the system.[83]

Despite these persistent antiestablishment statements condemning the state, the military, and the system, the novel was praised by mainstream conservative critics for *not* being political. Etō Jun, for example, wrote that *Black Rain* was "really the first novel I have read that has looked directly at the atomic bombing with eyes unclouded by ideology."[84] And Yamamoto Kenkichi juxtaposed it against the politically progressive works of Hara Tamiki, Ōta Yōko, and Ōe Kenzaburō, which he characterized as "too strenuously serious . . . too sullied by politics. Or too full of simplistic catchphrases. Had Ibuse not written this novel, I would never have been able to feel better about myself as a Japanese. . . . Sartre came to Japan and stirred up our intellectuals; but it was Ibuse who, with the calm and unperturbable attitude of a common, ordinary Japanese, wrote this book."[85]

Black Rain gained such acceptance because it tapped into at least two wells of sentiment in the 1960s. First, it fits easily into the sentimental war victim literature. Unlike the earlier atomic bomb literature, which it far outstrips in popularity, *Black Rain* does not dwell on the eerie unreality of the *hibaku* experience. In fact, since survivors of the immediate blast had to escape a firestorm, many of the episodes of their escape could easily have happened in the many other cities that were firebombed.[86] Second, *Black Rain* also appealed to conservatives—and enabled Yamamoto to feel better about himself as a Japanese—because it tapped into a resurgent conservative pride in Japanese traditions. Ibuse embedded the *hibakusha* experience in a social context that conformed to deeply held idealized conceptions of traditional Japan. With no real work to sustain him, Shigematsu finds spiritual sustenance in the rhythms of the rural village. He frequently mentions village festivals and folklore, and his efforts to get along with his village neighbors and Yasuko's potential suitors inevitably involve the reader in various rural social customs. Children's rhymes and the flora and fauna of rural areas are lovingly described to give a nostalgic picture of the *furusato* culture: the Japanese equivalent of the American hometown. In August 1966, conservative literary critic Etō Jun openly explained the appeal of Ibuse's *Black Rain* in comparison to the strident atomic bomb literature favored by political progressives:[87] "The protagonist appears to be a small landowner who leaves the farm to work in the city during the war, not some lonely intellectual, and our sympathy is raised because he always acts responsibly in the context of the concrete, living human relations of family, work, and village."[88] Shigematsu is taken to be the epitome of the common man acting with simple, inherently Japanese, "common sense."

Social conservatives in particular appreciated the presentation of rural village Japan as the wholesome norm. But Shigematsu's rural wisdom held appeal for contemporary progressive critics too.[89] In the progressive journal *Nihon bungaku*, Isogai Hideo even praised the book for its reliance on "common sense" rather than a vaguely Christian "God," and he noted with approval that of all modern Japanese literature, it was the "least tinged with westernisms" *(mottomo batakusaku nai)*. For progressive critics like Isogai, however, the praiseworthy quality of the common sense of the common man lay, not in his conformity to an idealized rural Japan, but in his ability to see through militarist ideology: "Ibuse really sees the fallacy of the various militarist ideas from the standpoint of the healthiest part of the Japanese common man *(Nihon shomin)*. Shigematsu and others, who never lose their common sense in the middle of this devastation, certainly [embody] Ibuse's image of the ideal common people."[90] Aihara Kazuo took a more sober view. "In today's age when rural communities *(nōson kyōdōtai jitai)* are rapidly disappearing," he noted, "you can see elements of a kind of 'New Agrarianism' *(shin nōhonshugi)* in this work."[91]

Although the novel ends with images that especially stress the innocent victimhood of the Japanese people, it leaves a degree of ambiguity over the identity of their oppressors. On learning that the war is over, Shigematsu cries tears of relief that he no longer has to endure the hardships of the war the militarists had forced on him and all Japanese:

> I suspect they had not been tears genuinely shed for that moment—that moment, shortly after noon, on a particular day of a particular month—but for something quite different. They reminded me of the time when I was very small and used to go out to play around our house. At those times I was often tormented by a tall village lout, almost a half-wit *(sei no takai manaba hakuchi no muhōsha)*, called Yōichi, but I would never let myself weep in front of him. No—I would run home instead, and badger my mother into baring her breast for me; and it was only then, at the sight of that familiar haven, that I burst into tears at last. Even now, I can still remember the salty taste of her milk. The tears I shed were tears of relief, and I believe that my tears this day were of the same kind.[92]

Although the bully here is clearly the militarist system, there is enough ambiguity in the description that a die-hard patriot might envision him as the tall Americans with their inhumane and therefore, under international agreements, unlawful weapon.[93] In the last few pages, the emperor's August 15 radio address is quoted as if to give the ultimate conservative sanction to Japanese victimhood. The new and savage bomb inflicted injury on "innocent victims," and unless the war was ended soon the "final result would be to bring about not only the annihilation of the Japanese race but the destruction of human civilization as a whole."

Besides bringing closure to the book, these final passages afford a multiple kind of closure to postwar Japanese victimhood. Giving the emperor pride of place in asserting Japanese victimhood and innocence identifies him yet again with the "common man" and his "common sense" that the book celebrates. He and his people are redeemed from the debacle into which they were bullied by the militarists. The cause of their redemption is the atomic bombing—which perversely frees them from the shackles of the militarist system even as it inflicts extreme suffering. Surrender brings a chance for recovery, and the nurturing force for their regeneration lies in their traditional Japanese culture.

Black Rain proved inspirational for Japan of the 1960s—a nation in the midst of its conservative-led regeneration as an aggressive mercantilist state. This economic success would slowly lead to a new pride in what came to be perceived as its basis in Japanese cultural traits. This was culture not just in the sense advocated in the early postwar textbooks—the broad cultures of science, economic development, the arts, and sports—but in the sense of the traditional relational values, the *ningen kankei* that Etō Jun praised in his 1966 review. As adopted by the conservative mainstream, it was nothing less than a reassertion of a self-consciously traditional Japanese subjectivity. *Black Rain* constituted an artistic link between the 1950s pacifist national identity based on atomic bomb victimhood and the 1960s economic nationalism.

Romanticizing the Past

Film critic Satō Tadao has described how early postwar Italian and French filmmakers presented images of their people as ardent antifascists and resistance fighters when in fact most were good fascists or collaborators.[94] Japanese authors and directors had no such models for active wartime resistance—too few communists survived imprisonment without betraying the cause. Accordingly, passive resistance had to be romanticized.[95] In *Twenty-Four Eyes,* Ōishi disengages from the system as best she can; but she and her children survive only at the cost of life and severe disability. In *Human Condition,* it is only Kaji's perseverance in passive collaboration that seems to offer hope of survival; his moments of active resistance earn only death in the end. In *Black Rain,* it is only through the crucible of the atomic bombing that ordinary Japanese are liberated from bullying by the militarist system; although Ibuse seems to avoid the conventional Christian imagery, the eye-opening effect of the Japanese nuclear "baptism" does afford them a new chance. The metaphor of the return to childhood signifies a return to purity and innocence. It is not without reason that General MacArthur relied on the same imagery in describing the task of reeducating the Japanese as peace-loving democrats.

Purity is a continuing theme in all the works. Ōishi's children and Shigematsu's niece Yasuko are pure in their innocence as victims; Kaji strives toward purity of principle. Oppression by the military and the vague "system" or "state" is another continuity.[96] Juxtaposed against this demonization of a shadowy oppressor is a faith in the ultimate wisdom of the common people to reject such oppression if just given the opportunity. This faith in the people, or the masses, is a profoundly democratic notion, but their political potential is stymied by their passivity.

In *Human Condition,* Wang ends his letter to Kaji with thanks for his loan of paper and pencil and the comment that "so long as I have paper and pencil in my hands, I and others will recognize that

I am still a human being." As Wang regains respect through the subjective act of writing, so too do these postwar authors and directors reclaim their humanity from Japan's debacle in the Asia-Pacific War. Reading, viewing, and reviewing these works is also an act of creation. In other words, the impact of these works depends on what the audience makes of them. Popular culture is "a language of argument, not a chorus of harmony,"[97] and it behooves us to recognize that there are many voices contesting the victim iconography as it reveals itself in each of the foregoing works. Still, this analysis suggests an overarching harmony of sorts in those works granted hegemonic status as part of a canon of antiwar literature and film. Their construction of inescapable if admirable victimhood had serious implications for the public's understanding of their political selves, especially in regard to the state and its organs of government.[98]

CHAPTER 6

Compensating Victims
The Politics of Victimhood

This memorial service [for the war dead] signifies the entire nation's sober desire to offer its sincere tribute to the more than 3 million whose sacrifice has given us today's peace and development.
  —Kurogane Yasumi, Chief Cabinet Secretary (August 1963)

A t noon on August 15, 1963, people in public places across Japan observed a moment of silence for the war dead. At Hibiya Hall in Tokyo, for only the third time since independence from the U.S. Occupation eleven years earlier, the government sponsored a memorial ceremony.[1] With the empress at his side, the emperor read a message of regret, condolence for bereaved families, and appreciation to the dead. After one year at Yasukuni Shrine in 1964, the annual ceremony has been held every year since in the Nippon Budōkan.

The Japan Bereaved Family Association, an organization of families of military who died in the war, had been pressuring the government for years to institute a ceremony to publicly recognize their dead relatives' wartime service to the state. The wholesale condemnation of Japan's wartime aggression and the general pacifist sentiment in postwar Japan had prevented the government from sanctioning such ceremonies, but now the constraints on official expressions of patriotic sentiment were easing. Emerging pride in Japan's economic recovery in the 1950s and 1960s—a period of high economic growth now enshrined as the defining experience of contemporary Japan— was slowly evolving into a kind of economic nationalism, especially among government bureaucrats and the business managerial class. This pride differed from the earlier pride in atomic victimhood precisely because it was based on accomplishment. Kano Masanao has described two forms of this new consciousness. First, Japan's history was reevaluated in the positive light of modernization theory, most clearly evident and known to American scholars from the Hakone Conference and its subsequent publications. Second, the 1960s witnessed a bureaucratic emphasis on a "national essence" theory *(kokutairon)* that revealed itself in government actions commemorating the Meiji centennial, reintroducing an ethics curriculum from 1958, and institutionalizing components of that theory as holidays in the official calendar—setting a "National Founding Day" on the traditional date of the founding of the imperial dynasty (proposed 1957, adopted 1967), for example, and reintroducing the imperial reign name calendar (proposed 1970, implemented 1979).[2] The birth of new nations in Asia and Africa, as well as intellectual soul-searching after the security treaty riots of 1960, contributed to a new discourse over nationalism in which most agreed on its desirability, if not its character, as a basis for national independence and democratic development.[3] As the *Asahi shinbun* noted in its August 15, 1963, editorial, there was a new consciousness of self as Japanese: a new awareness of the country as Japan.[4] It was now publicly acceptable for the government to establish an annual memorial service for compatriots who had died in the war.

The conservative government tried to encourage pride in Japanese accomplishment and raise awareness of nationhood through subtle manipulation of textbook histories—as discussed in an earlier chapter—and by decorating individuals for exceptional service to the nation beginning in 1963, conducting state ceremonies like the August 15 memorial to the war dead, sponsoring the Olympic pageant in 1964, and celebrating the Meiji centennial in 1968. These actions were received by many with not a little suspicion. For while pride in Japan was growing, distrust of state power remained strong, especially among political progressives. The press questioned conservative motivations in reinstituting decorations for national service and warned that reintroducing status distinctions via the eight-tiered system of state honors would undermine the democratic fiber of postwar Japan.[5] There was strong resistance to the government's celebration of the centennial in 1968, especially among progressive historians who complained that it glossed over the class antagonisms and aggressive foreign policies they regarded as Meiji's legacy. At the time of the memorial service in August 1963 this deep ambivalence over the character of the prewar polity—and over the state's role in supporting it—prevented any official statement on whether the war dead had died for their country's sins or for its honor. But there was no disagreement over revering the memory of war victims as victims. In the announcements and interviews in the days preceding the ceremony in 1963, government officials took care to emphasize that all Japanese victims of the war, military and civilian, were to be memorialized. As the chief cabinet secretary, Kurogane Yasumi, told the press on August 14, the service reflected "the entire nation's sober desire to offer its sincere tribute to the more than 3 million whose sacrifice has given us today's peace and development *(heiwa to hatten)*."[6]

But which war victims were to be honored and why? These questions involved not only the dead but the living. Due to the extreme destruction the war had wrought, as well as the pervasive ideology of war victimhood, most Japanese felt themselves more or less to be victims of the war. But in addition to the conventional recipients of state aid such as veterans, bereaved families, and other associated groups that received pensions and condolence payments, there were a few groups who thought their situation entitled them to special compensation or at least special treatment. From the high ground of atomic victimhood, *hibakusha* and their supporters argued that their symbolic position and the special nature of their radiation-induced illness entitled them to better assistance than provided for in the 1957 Medical Care Law—the legislation that emerged from the consensus on Japan's special A-bomb victim heritage after the Lucky Dragon Incident. Former landlords who had been forced to sell their land cheap in the U.S-directed land reform had been trying to gain fair compensation—or "recompensation" as their opponents would have it—ever since the end of the Occupation in 1952. Repatriates who had lost their overseas assets in the turmoil at the war's end had received token payments disguised as welfare in 1957 but now wanted better compensation.

Hibakusha, landlords, and repatriates had several basic obstacles to overcome. First, even sympathetic government leaders resisted payments because they feared the impact on government finances. Although this impediment was never a problem for the small number of *hibakusha,* for the other two groups it was a serious issue but one they were able to negotiate around as continuing prosperity raised government revenues in the 1960s. The ruling conservative Liberal Democratic Party (LDP) had begun using the pork barrel and expanded welfare expenditures to build constituency support. Landlords and repatriates, who were well organized and claimed influence over 3 million votes each, gained special consideration by exercising their electoral clout on rank-and-file LDP Diet members and by accepting levels of compensation lower than they had originally sought.

But there was a second, more formidable, obstacle to obtaining government payments: the need to argue a special state obligation that transcended the principle of equity in social welfare services. As part of the larger program of demilitarization and democratization during the Occupation, SCAP established an impartial social security system that no longer accorded special consideration to veterans and others who had served the nation in war. The idea was that a peaceful and democratic society did not distinguish between the general citizenry and a privileged class of military professionals.[7] Soon after independence in 1952, however, Yoshida's conservative government was able to reinstate veterans' pensions, aid for disabled veterans, and assistance to bereaved families "based on the spirit of state compensation" *(kokka hoshō no seishin ni motozuki),* as stated in the 1952 Wounded Veteran and Bereaved Family Assistance Act.[8] *Kōjien* (third edition) defines *kokka hoshō* as "special compensation by the state to people who have suffered losses caused by the implementation of state policy." Clearly the vast majority of Japanese suffered due to state policy. The salient and ultimately political question was which war service and attendant suffering the postwar state would valorize as deserving of compensation. Through legislation and bureaucratic policy, the privilege of state compensation was extended over the succeeding two decades to include civilians employed by the military, members of the girls volunteer corps, and mobilized students.

All three victim groups discussed in this chapter laid claim to state compensation for losses incurred because of defeat in war— and all three encountered resistance to consideration beyond the principle of welfare equity. Landlords and repatriates failed to convince the courts, the government, and the print media that there was such an obligation; the *hibakusha* were able to win the argument only in stages. Still, all the groups eventually did receive payment. The hard money question was how their situation qualified them for exceptional treatment in the welfare system—or, put differently, how it transcended normal welfare needs. One means was suggested by the War Widows Special Payments Law of 1963. Although the first clause of the law stated that these payments were based on the "spirit of state compensation," government officials recognized that they were also compensating for more than material loss. As Welfare Minister Nishimura Eiichi told the Lower House Social Labor Committee on March 26, 1963, government grants to war widows "were an effort by the state to give special consolation for the emotional pain they bear because of their extremely unique position in society."[9] In addition to the benefits widows were already receiving under the 1952 law, the 1963 law provided for consolation payments of 200,000 yen for the "special emotional anguish" (seishinteki tsūku) they had to experience in the years without their husbands since the end of the war.

For hibakusha, their iconic status in Japan's nonnuclear peace heritage and the unusually debilitating nature of radiation illnesses—called "atomic bomb sickness" (genbakubyō)—earned them minimal but gradually improving medical benefits soon after they became symbols of Japanese atomic victimhood. Slowly and with the help of the courts and the opposition Socialist Party, they were able to gain recognition that the state had a moral responsibility to compensate them for their suffering since it had been responsible for the war that occasioned the bombings.

Both landlords and repatriates used their considerable electoral strength with great calculation to force the LDP leadership into committing to government grants. They also argued that their particular victim experience was exceptionally traumatic. But even more suggestive was their ultimate argument that their victim experience embodied a special service to the nation that elevated their claims on the government from an issue of welfare or even compensation to one of national honor. Stretching the limits of credibility, landlords and repatriates reconstructed their private losses and suffering into public sacrifice which, because it had benefited the nation's development, deserved recognition in the form of honoraria and solatia. This chapter explores how these special interests manipulated the mythology surrounding war victimhood and the emerging pride in postwar national prosperity in order to construct their experiences as heroic victimhood.

The late 1950s was a period of divisive ideological clashes between conservatives and progressives—clashes over such issues as constitutional revision, remilitarization, and educational and electoral reform. After the explosion of protest over Prime Minister Kishi Nobusuke's decision to force ratification of the renewed U.S. Security Treaty in 1960, his successor Ikeda Hayato introduced a more consensus-oriented political style. His "political pact to foster economic growth and enhance industrial productivity" was achieved by dropping Kishi's confrontational posture on divisive issues and including the opposition in the policymaking process.[10] In coming to a consensus on legislation, conservatives and progressives agreed on a mutually acceptable vocabulary that helped to express and consolidate national understanding of issues. This "inclusive strategy" involved more muted but equally passionate struggles—especially when the legislation concerned compensation for war victims. On the surface the political issue was whether to grant *hibakusha,* dispossessed landlords, and repatriates honor and privilege via state assistance. But this question devolved into a question of whether to recognize their respective sufferings as worthy sacrifice for the "peace and development" *(heiwa to hatten)* that defined the economically prosperous and peaceful Japan of the 1960s. The Socialists championed the *hibakusha;* the conservatives worked hardest for the landlords and repatriates. Underlying this political exercise—in contemporary parlance, an effort to "bring resolution to the postwar"—was a rhetorical struggle over which values would define the new post-postwar Japan.[11] Progressives strove to protect the postwar civil liberty guarantees, preserve the antinuclear pacifist national image, and disconnect Japan from the American-dominated capitalist alliance system. Conservatives tried to reintroduce patriotic values that would bind the individual citizen in loyalty to the mercantilist state and recapture a national past that one could be proud of. As the ambiguities of the compensation legislation showed, neither side won a clear victory in this struggle.

Hibakusha: The Struggle for State Care

For the first decade after the atomic bombings, efforts to help the victims were limited in scale. In Hiroshima and Nagasaki, city officials and groups of physicians organized various relief efforts and a U.S. research group, the Atomic Bomb Casualty Commission (ABCC), provided minimal medical care. One of the largest of the several *hibakusha* self-help groups was the Atomic Bomb Victims Association (Genbaku Higaisha no Kai), founded in Hiroshima in 1952. This association claimed the United States owed them reparation for damages. It also encouraged exhibits and lectures as a means for promoting peace and called for state and municipal medical care, welfare, and job placement assistance for the destitute. These groups won little public aid beyond the minimal medical care that the cities of Hiroshima and Nagasaki were already providing.[12]

Hibakusha interest groups coalesced into a national organization only in 1956 when the Japan Council of Atomic and Hydrogen Bomb Victim Groups (Nihon Gensuibaku Higaisha Dantai Kyōgikai, or

Hidankyō) was formed as a subsidiary effort of the ban-the-bomb movement. Besides international cooperation in developing treatments for "atomic bomb syndrome" *(genbakushō)* and an international ban on nuclear weapons, Hidankyō called for the government to create and fund a system for guaranteeing *hibakusha* health and livelihood. From its inception the group sought "state compensation based on the special nature of atomic bomb damage."[13]

The national adoption of atomic victimhood in the middle 1950s popularized and legitimized *hibakusha* efforts. Since then bipartisan support for helping atomic bomb victims has always been strong, although the conservative government and Socialist-led opposition have consistently clashed over the extent and type of aid as well as its theoretical rationale. Socialist representatives have presented themselves as the champions of *hibakusha* medical care, linking such aid to the ban-the-bomb movement and insisting that the government has an obligation to provide more than simple medical care. In Diet discussions over the 1957 Medical Care Law, for example, Socialist Satake Shin'ichi (Hiroshima) portrayed the *hibakusha* plight as symbolic of the entire nation's situation. Although the main issue under debate was *hibakusha* medical care and welfare conditions, Satake began with a complaint that "the whole nation's wish for the bomb to be banned" was not being respected abroad:

> Experiments are being conducted at Bikini as well as within the Soviet Union, and it is our Japanese nation *(waga Nihon no minzoku)* that has fallen into the distressing and extraordinary fate of having to drench ourselves in this radioactive fallout. . . . In deliberating this bill, [we are discussing] not just the atomic bomb, which was dropped on Hiroshima and Nagasaki in 1945, but a bill of wide scope including the managed prevention of this unfortunate condition into which Shōwa Japan has been placed.

Accordingly, he said, the government ought to take care of the *hibakusha* precisely because they represented an essential reality of the Japanese nation: "The totally innocent and guiltless have had the atomic bomb thrown at them by America because of war and are facing this tragic fate. It is proper that the country should attend to them."[14] Such Socialist rhetoric was clearly intended to make *hibakusha* relief an ideological weapon against Japan's foreign policy alliance with the United States.

Despite their embrace of Hiroshima as a uniquely privileging Japanese national victim experience, the ruling conservative administrations limited the foreign policy and larger political impact of *hiba-kusha* aid by consistently defining such relief as simply a special kind of social welfare. From the very beginning of Diet action on *hiba-kusha* aid, LDP representatives stressed the special medical needs of the atomic bomb victims, whose radiation sickness caused recurring illness. Unfortunately for the *hibakusha,* this conservative desire to keep the issue in check tended to limit the amount of government aid. In December 1956, the Diet passed a bipartisan "Resolution on Medical Care for the A-Bomb Disabled" that called for the nation to "establish suitable measures for the care and health maintenance of these special victims." Recognizing that the bombings were "unprece-dented in our country's medical history" and that atomic bomb victims led "extremely uncertain lives," the resolution declared that "from a humanitarian standpoint [the situation] is unbearable, and as a nation we need to encourage extensive research in medical care for these special victims."[15]

The March 1957 Atomic Bomb Victim Medical Care Law (known as the Iryōhō, or Medical Care Law) provided medical care only for *hibakusha* who suffered from certain diseases considered directly and verifiably related to their exposure to bomb radiation.[16] The law fell far short of *hibakusha* and Socialist hopes for state guarantees of good health and livelihood. Socialist Kihara Tsuyoshi (Nagasaki) voiced a common complaint in the Lower House Social and Labor Affairs Committee when he protested there was not even an allow-ance for income lost while undergoing medical treatment. *Hiba-kusha* aid activists nicknamed the law the Zaru-hō (Sieve Law).[17]

In their attempt to amend the Medical Care Law in the Thirty-third Diet in November 1959, the Socialists carried to its logical con-sequence their assertion that the atomic bomb victims held special status as symbols of the nation. Besides adding a travel allowance and subsidies for food and family maintenance during treatment, the amendment would have granted *hibakusha* privileges comparable to those already given war veterans and bereaved families. If the amend-ment had passed, bereaved *hibakusha* families would have been given 30,000 yen in condolence money as well as 15,000-yen annual pensions for each family member lost. Eligibility for these grants would have been determined by the same criteria as designated by the 1952 Wounded Veteran and Bereaved Families Assistance Act, and anyone who already qualified for these veteran benefits would have been ineligible for the *hibakusha* grants. As Socialist Ohara Tōru (Hiroshima) argued in the Lower House Social and Labor Affairs Committee, since Japan was the only country to have been afflicted with the atomic bomb in war, the government should recognize its "responsibility for compensation, the country's responsibility to aid the *hibakusha*." Ohara even argued that since all Japanese were subjected to general mobilization, theoretically all those injured because of the war should be given the same pension and guarantees that repatriates and even "war criminals" were being given.[18] Ohara's intent seems to have been to mitigate the positive value that veteran privilege accorded military service, as well as to elevate innocent victimhood to similar privilege.

Socialist advocacy of aid for the *hibakusha* was part of a larger strategy to force the government into a stronger rejection of nuclear weapons. At one point in the Diet committee hearings, Ohara linked *hibakusha* aid with the ban-the-bomb movement, calling them "two sides of the same coin," and accused the conservative Kishi administration of negligence in carrying out the state's duty to denounce the bombings as violations of international law. The conservative government was wary of limiting its foreign policy options—and especially cautious about compromising its defense position within the American nuclear alliance. Ohara attempted to overcome this wariness when, in pressing Foreign Minister Fujiyama Ai'ichirō to admit the impropriety of the atomic bombings, he pointedly if disingenuously disavowed any intention of denouncing the United States. Fujiyama and his Foreign Ministry colleagues would only admit that it was against the spirit of international law and wrong "from a humanitarian point of view."[19] Although the proposal failed, a 1960 amendment added general medical expenses up to 2,000 yen for those *hibakusha* below a specified income level.[20]

In the early 1960s, the *hibakusha* aid movement became divided by factionalism in the antinuclear organization Gensuikyō,[21] but a ruling by the Tokyo District Court in December 1963 gave their cause a boost.[22] Although the court ruled that individual *hibakusha* had no legal right to sue their government for reparations, it did note that "the question of state compensation *(kokka hoshō)* naturally arises, based on [the government's] resultant responsibility *(kekka sekinin)* for war damages." The court deplored the inadequacy of government steps to address *hibakusha* suffering. Taking the government to task for neglecting its "resultant responsibility"—the idea that the atomic bombing of civilians was the end result of the government starting the war on its own authority—the court strongly recommended that government and Diet act to aid them.[23]

The time was right for resolving various loose ends left over from defeat and occupation, for repatriates and landlord compensation drives were beginning to see committee action in legislative chambers. During the Forty-sixth Diet in the spring of 1964, Socialist Representative Kawano Tadashi noted that *hibakusha* aid was one of several issues collectively called "bringing resolution to the postwar" *(sengo shori).* Kawano observed that the government ought to be able to afford sufficient relief measures now because of the ongoing economic growth, especially considering how other issues he deemed less deserving were being seriously discussed:

> Today, twenty years after the war's end, when we refer to compensation for farmland [sold under compulsion in the Occupation land reform] and [lost] overseas assets [repatriate compensation] as postwar resolution measures, we still feel deep regret that we have not yet effected sufficient policies for the atomic bomb victims whom, from a humanitarian standpoint, we cannot ignore.[24]

In introducing the Forty-sixth Diet's Resolution for Increasing Aid to the Atomic Bomb Victims, Fujino Shigeo (LDP: Nagasaki), himself a *hibakusha,* reflected that legislation for various groups of war victims was being enacted as the nation was recovering its economic strength. He added:

> Furthermore, in this Diet session, a special measures bill has been proposed for pensioned recipients of the old Order of the Golden Kite [the highest award for meritorious military service, which had been abolished in 1947]. Considering how these postwar resolution measures are being set up one after another, I think we should explore expanding measures for the atomic bomb *hibakusha* appropriate to their special health and emotional conditions.[25]

Legislators on both sides of the aisle agreed that unresolved issues should now be resolved. What they could not agree on was which issues remained unresolved and how *hibakusha* aid should be addressed.

In February 1964, the Socialists proposed a resolution on *hibakusha* aid that cited the Tokyo District Court decision, explicitly called for "compensation" from the government, and described aid as "the natural obligation of the only nation on earth to be atom-bombed." Hiroshima Socialist Councillor Fujita Susumu argued: "It is the natural obligation of the only atom-bombed nation in the world to establish various policies for compensatory relief *(hoshō kyūen)* for *hibakusha* and their families." Furthermore, their compensation should parallel that for "officials, namely former military or war criminals and repatriates."[26]

The Socialists were fighting a losing battle with such rhetoric. The conservative Diet majority would never pass a resolution that negated the special position given veterans or one that carried such a blatant political message against Japan's postwar conservative state and its security accommodation under the U.S. nuclear umbrella. The ruling LDP did, however, accept a consensus resolution that was considerably toned down. Although it included increased aid in the form of old age homes, other new facilities for *hibakusha* care, and special livelihood subsidies, it was silent on the question of nuclear policy.[27]

Acting on this resolution, the Welfare Ministry duly conducted a comprehensive study of *hibakusha* living conditions. The findings became the basis for the second major legislation for *hibakusha* relief: the Atomic Bomb Victim Special Measures Act *(Genshibakudan hibakusha ni tai suru tokubetsu sochi ni kan suru hōritsu)*, sponsored by the Satō cabinet and enacted in the spring of 1968. This law was also explicitly a "plan for improving the welfare of the *hibakusha*." Under it the Welfare Ministry designated some *hibakusha* for monthly allowances for support and medical maintenance, provided their incomes did not exceed a specified level.[28]

In interpellation on this legislation in the Diet, Socialist representative and *hibakusha* Yamada Hajime complained about the delay in acting to redress the inadequacies of the Medical Care Law, about the niggardly amount of condolence money compared to the compensation the United States gave the Lucky Dragon victims (5 million yen to Kuboyama's widow, 2 million yen to the others), and about the income restrictions on the special allowances. He also accused the government of caving in to special interests: "As for [the government's] basic attitude, it seems it was decided that aid for the atomic bomb patients does not carry enough political value to merit giving as much compensation as former landlords and overseas assets [repatriates] got."[29] Yamada was essentially correct. By 1968 both these groups had won nonwelfare payments that were intended to take the place of compensation.

It was not until a decade later that the Supreme Court ruled in March 1978 that government aid for *hibakusha* was fundamentally state compensation when it decided in favor of a Korean *hibakusha* whose application for benefits had been denied. Even with this court sanction, Welfare Minister Ozawa Tatsuo would only allow that such aid occupied a middle ground between social welfare and state compensation.[30] This insistence on honoring the principle of equity in social welfare was a strategy used by Socialists as well as LDP politicians to deny a particular grievance group's claim to state compensation. Just as conservatives insisted on framing *hibakusha* aid as welfare, progressives fought compensation for landlords and repatriates by insisting they prove a welfare need.

Compensation for Dispossessed Landlords

Land reform is counted among the U.S. occupation's major successes because it established the large yeoman class that became the foundation for Japan's postwar political stability and economic growth. Despite its apparent success, the reform created a major problem for post-Occupation governments. Because the reform was accomplished by forcing landlords to sell at prices so devalued by inflation as to be the equivalent of confiscation, it created a large and influential grievance group. During the occupation SCAP did not brook any effective landlord opposition. It simply dictated that landlord organizations be disbanded.[31] Former landlords' hopes were raised temporarily when Gen. Matthew Ridgway announced in May 1951 that he would allow a review of Occupation legislation. Although the first postindependence Diet reversed or modified many Occupation-era reforms that concerned labor and the economy, it decided to make land reform permanent in the form of the Basic Agriculture Law.

The government's reasons for standing firm on land reform were clear from the very beginning. The Ministry of Agriculture and Forestry announced: "The especially important problem . . . [from the viewpoint of the] entire society is that the majority of cultivators stabilize their positions as cultivators. . . . Even if this means forcing the smallest degree of sacrifice onto the owners of uncultivated land or on landowners [that is, dispossessed landlords] . . . such sacrifice should naturally be considered necessary for public welfare." In other words: the reform had established a medium-sized freeholding farmer class that would help create a stable society for the benefit of all, including those forced to sacrifice.[32] Landlords found they could no longer rely on the conservative politicians who had been their natural allies since the Meiji era. Although the powerful prewar conservative political culture had been deeply rooted in the rural landlord class, postwar politicians recognized that former tenants far outnumbered former landlords. As Finance Minister and future Prime Minister Ikeda Hayato argued persuasively to his Liberal Party colleagues in 1952, in creating a large owner-cultivator class the land reform "built the ideal *jiban* [constituency base] for a conservative party—and we've got to keep it."[33]

At first, landlord organizations were divided by conflict over whether simply to work for fair compensation or to pursue the more radical course of revising the land law so they could reclaim land-ownership.[34] Although it took several years for all landlord associations to resign themselves to it, eventually they were forced to admit that repossession was impossible—short of another revolution such as had occurred in the U.S. occupation. Former tenants, now property owners, held too central a position in the postwar polity. Efforts for judicial redress reached a dead end when the Supreme Court ruled in December 1953 that the reform had been conducted within the bounds of the law and landlords had received just compensation.[35] Nevertheless, landlord organizations continued to entertain the idea that better compensation might be possible. Optimists looked to the government's reversal of the Occupation-era abolition of military pensions earlier that year. As R. P. Dore notes in his landmark 1959 reform study, many landlords reasoned as follows: "If compensation could be paid to those who had suffered by military service in the war . . . why should it not also be paid to those who had suffered from the war by the loss of property at the hands of the occupation Army?"[36]

Some landlords had been allowed to retain ownership of small parcels they continued to rent at regulated rates, and tensions rose in late 1955 after the Land Rent Policy Commission raised rents less than expected. There were a few attempts at forcible repossession—most notably in Ishikawa prefecture in November 1955—and then, perhaps because of the rise in class consciousness due to these disturbances, landlord interests coalesced on a national scale for the first time in December with the organization of the National League for State Compensation of Liberated Farmland (Zenkoku Kaihō Nōchi Kokkahoshō Rengōkai). The league announced in its first convention in January 1956 that while it did not oppose the land reform or wish to exacerbate class conflict, it did insist on immediate state compensation as well as "resolute action on amending the Basic Agriculture Law" to return ownership of land the state had not yet redistributed.[37]

The league's unity was complicated not only by personal conflict among its national leadership but also by disagreement between advocates of compensation and diehards seeking repossession. This conflict led to the organization of two short-lived splinter groups in early 1957: the Japan League of Farmland Victims (Nihon Nōchi Giseisha Renmei) and the Japan League for State Compensation for Dispossessed Farmland (Nihon Hibaishūnōchi Kokka Hosei Rengo-kai).[38] In the spring of 1957 the three major national landlord organizations agreed to limit demands to better compensation, and compensation became the rallying cry of the reunited national organization, the National Farmland League (Zenkoku Nōchi Dōmei), formed in December 1957.[39]

In late 1956 and early 1957, landlord groups were encouraged by the progress repatriate organizations seemed to be making in their claims for government compensation for lost overseas assets. Still, government and LDP party leaders were adamant that the landlords would not benefit from the repatriates' success. Even after the Japan League of Farmland Victims managed to pressure the LDP into establishing a subcommittee on the "agriculture problem" in February 1957, the chair announced that he considered landlord compensation a question of welfare policy, not agricultural policy.[40] As the principle of social equity would apply, confining the issue to consideration as a welfare policy forestalled classwide compensation. Agriculture and Forestry Minister Ide Ichitarō told the Lower House Committee on Agriculture, Forestry, and Fisheries in February 1957 that there was no rational basis for landlord compensation so far as his ministry was concerned: "Landlord organizations have become active recently, but I advise them to give up as it is wasted effort."[41] In May he noted that the former landlords had had their property taken by the Japanese government, not by foreign states, and the landlords had already been legally compensated.[42] Prime Minister Kishi could not have made this attitude any clearer when he flatly told the Diet's Lower House budget committee in March 1957: "The government has no obligation for compensation." A few days later in the Upper House budget committee he said: "I have no particular intention of considering special social welfare because someone is a former landlord."[43]

The Socialists too opposed special treatment for the landlords—partly out of natural antipathy for what socialist dogma considered a parasitic class, but also out of a fear of trivializing war victim status. Although landlords considered themselves the "political victims of occupation policy excess,"[44] Socialists denied that dispossessed landlords were truly war victims. In the Thirty-first Diet in March 1959, for example, when the government first proposed a cabinet investigative committee, JSP Diet Representative Takada Tomiyuki complained: "It seems that some groups [hold] the opinion that, like repatriates, former landlords are war victims." The JSP was in favor of helping those few landlords who were destitute, but not dispossessed landlords as a class, victimized by the very reforms that created a democratic Japan. Here the Socialists and the government were in agreement. Individual cases of hardship could best be handled through a social welfare system that made no distinction between former landlords and tenants.[45]

As an early study of the politics of their campaign for compensation notes, the landlords would only succeed when they convinced "the government (and public opinion) . . . that the dispossessed landowners were actually in economic difficulties and deserved special 'political' consideration . . . out of public funds."[46] Their strategy was two-pronged. The first prong consisted of applying public pressure through mass rallies and petitions to individual party and government leaders. One point in their favor was the fact that ex-tenants were generally sympathetic toward the landlords, who had lost all their land and received a mere pittance for it. The league was not reticent when it came to playing for sympathy. Its second convention, held in Tokyo in December 1956, was the stage for a display of the landlords' sense of persecution. In an atmosphere redolent of wartime service, delegates sang songs to the tune of wartime marches with verses of unrequited victimhood such as:

> Father hanged himself and died.
> His rice fields stolen, he died.
> As the red sun sets, I see,
> The image of my father, rising before me.

Dore relates: "With loud-speaker vans playing records of war-songs, carrying banners and wearing tightly tied around their heads the narrow white bands which are a traditional symbol of 'militant heroics,' the delegates . . . marched to the Ministry of Agriculture. There, each section of the procession shouted at its indifferent windows 'Banzai for the Victims of the Land Reform' and quietly dispersed."[47]

Even the leftist journal *Sekai* admitted that many ex-landlords deserved sympathy. But most print media comment was hostile since, as contemporary impression suggested and later surveys verified, the vast majority of landlords were actually better off than their former tenants.[48] The *Asahi shinbun*'s "Tensei jingo" column for March 6, 1956, asked the perennial rhetorical question used to deny a group's claim to exceptional victim status: If landlords were war victims, then who was not? Mirroring the conventional wisdom of the time, the column argued that cases of individual hardship should be handled by improving the social security system.[49]

In the *Mainichi shinbun* in April 1957, columnist Abe Shinnosuke warned that awarding the landlords compensation would unnecessarily undo a previously resolved issue and threaten the postwar order:

> For good or ill, the land reform has been a dead issue for ten years now. We should not dig up graves and force dead spirits back into this world. I fear it would be the spark that explodes into a chain reaction which would plummet Japanese society into confusion beyond description. . . . If former landlords can be given compensation because they lost land, every war victim in Japan will clamor for compensation, crying me too, me too! And the government would have no justification for denying them.[50]

Three days later the *Mainichi shinbun* expressed its suspicions in an editorial:

> The landlords' demand is ostensibly only monetary compensation for liberated farmland, but it won't end with that. We must recognize above all else that by its nature it will next lead to revision of the current agricultural system. . . . We give the postwar agricultural land reform high praise as a historic measure that modernized the land system. Here too we cannot approve of the former landlords' compensation claims.[51]

The second prong in the landlord's strategy to overcome this monolithic opposition was simple and effective. They worked to commit rank-and-file LDP Diet members to their cause and bring pressure to bear from within the party. In May 1957, the governing board of the Japan League of Farmland Victims decided to attempt to "install a majority of Diet members as advisers" and by the end of the year had enlisted seventy-nine Diet members as advisers or board members.[52] Apparently to accommodate this movement from within, the party leadership decided to form a new special committee on the farmland issue in September. The chair of this enormous committee —it included seventy-one members from both houses of the Diet— was former Agriculture Minister Tago Ichimin, who promptly mediated the reunification of the landlord associations in late 1957.[53]

The LDP reorganized the committee in February 1958, including experts from outside the party in order to conduct a proper survey. The December report painted a picture of dissatisfaction among the dispossessed landlords. It recommended that a cabinet commission be established to develop policy measures and, in addition, suggested a title transfer tax for land being switched to nonagricultural use.[54] Despite a Ministry of Agriculture and Forestry report of October 1958 that former landlords were incomparably better off than most farm households,[55] the momentum within the party was such that the LDP introduced its first bill to establish the cabinet commission in the Thirty-first Diet in 1959. Socialists staunchly opposed this attempt and it died in Upper House committee.[56]

The LDP took advantage of turmoil in the Thirty-fourth Diet—known as the Anpo Diet because the conservatives bulldozed opposition to the new security treaty—to pass the bill for cabinet commission. The Kudō Commission, as it came to be known after its chair, banker Kudō Shōshirō, reported in May 1962 that the former landlords actually had a substantially higher standard of living than other farming households. In the tradition of equity in social welfare that hindered all claims for special war victim payments, the commission recommended special loans only for those who were destitute. Despite this report's recommendations, continuing pressure from the league had already persuaded the LDP leadership to push for government payments.[57]

Once the LDP committed to payments, the problem was how to justify them. Clearly there was no welfare justification for such payments. The findings of both bureaucratic and cabinet commissions showed that, as a class, former landlords were patently not in economic difficulties. Payments could not be justified as compensation for lost farmland, either, since the courts had ruled against it and the government had long denied any responsibility. The ultimate solution was found in turning the tables on the landlords' critics—and necessitated that the landlords embrace the very land reform they felt had victimized them.

The critics of the landlords' efforts suspected that the league's real aim was to undermine the land redistribution that had brought prosperity to former tenants and the nation. The *Mainichi shinbun* opposed monetary compensation to the landlords in April 1957, for example, because it doubted landlords' intentions toward the land reform, which it considered "the historic measure that modernized the land system." In 1959 the *Hokkaidō shinbun* went so far as to call the former landlords' campaign for "recompensation" contrary to "the spirit of democratization of agriculture" (*nōgyō minshuka no shisō ni han suru mono*).[58] In other words: the liberal national dailies had pigeonholed the National Farmland League as the enemy of the land reform that had established the basis for Japan's successful postwar economic and political reconstruction.

The impression that the landlords were antagonistic toward the land reform had to be eliminated. Demands for compensation implied such antagonism, however, especially if they were funded by a title transfer tax on farmland as the landlords proposed in late February 1957.[59] By the end of 1961, the LDP had decided to resolve the landlord problem through payments, not in the form of "compensation" (hoshō) for assets unfairly seized, but as "rewards" or "remuneration" (hōshō) for cooperating with the land reform.[60] In January 1962 the LDP's Farmland Problem Committee proposed a bill for "reward" payments (hōshōkin), and on April 25 the party decided to drop the controversial scheme to fund these honoraria with title transfer taxes, which released the former tenants from having to pay for them.[61]

From April to June 1964, representatives from the LDP and government ministries met to iron out a bill that both could accept. The main points of difference concerned the scope of the bill, mainly eligibility restrictions on types of landlords and lands. Even at this late point, the bureaucratic position excluded landlords above a certain income level. The bill that became law in the Forty-sixth Diet in 1965 allowed for a total of 145 billion yen in nonnegotiable bonds paying over ten years. There were no income restrictions on eligibility. As if to stress the appearance that this was money given to citizens who performed a service for their nation, foreign landowners were excluded from benefits even if they met all other qualifications.[62]

Usui Sōichi, director of general affairs in the Prime Minister's Office, introduced the bill to the Lower House of the Diet by praising the economic and democratic benefits of the land reform. He noted that a few landlords experienced drastic changes in economic conditions and lifestyle and considerable emotional shock because of it. Smoothly eliding the distinction between the land reform and landowners, Usui explained: "In appreciation of the contributions (kōken) of those who were forced to sell farmland in the land reform, and considering the psychological impact they received, [the government] thinks it appropriate to implement remuneration (hōshō) to these people."[63]

The Socialists and newspapers cried foul. But the LDP had the votes and the political will to pass the bill despite this opposition, which included the "cow-walk" filibuster, even extending the Diet nine days to do it.[64] JSP Diet member Yamauchi Hiroshi argued against "recompensation," saying that nobody was fooled by the attempt to "grant benefits by the verbal deception of calling compensation *(hoshō)* remuneration *(hōshō)*."[65] The *Asahi shinbun* would admit no justification for paying former landlords and lamented that democratic justice had been grievously harmed. The *Mainichi shinbun* complained that the power of special interests had prevailed. Why, it asked, did the LDP never feel it necessary to extend Diet deliberations for a more important issue such as housing policy or restraining rising land prices?[66]

The LDP's policy journal, *Seisaku geppō,* tried to show the law in a better light. The law was designed, insisted the journal, to resolve social tension left behind from the land redistribution. It must have been hard, the journal noted, to accept "being forced to release one's ancestors' land, which is irreplaceable in terms of emotional attachment and property." Considering the profits that some former tenants had reaped from the astronomical increase in the land's value due to the country's economic development, the journal argued that the bill was an acceptable means to reward the "contributions" *(kōken)* of those who were forced to sell cheap:

> The postwar land reform not only served an exceptionally important role in our country's democratization and economic development of agricultural villages, but without the farmland holders' cooperation —even recognizing that it was the irrefutable order of the Occupation administration—it could not have been achieved so smoothly.[67]

LDP Diet member and former landlord Sakata Michita explained his personal belief in the reward bill in 1966:

> I was a landowner myself and suffered from all the difficulties caused by the land reform. . . . It was thanks to this reform that Japan was saved from communism and I believe it is natural, even for that reason alone, that former landowners should be properly rewarded.[68]

With the help of LDP tacticians, the landlords succeeded in adopting the mantle of the land reform's service to the nation. By dropping the revanchist claim for repossession, they were able to turn to their own advantage the argument of the land reform's defenders—that it had established a basis for postwar Japan's economic growth and democratic processes. On paper and in their own minds at least, they attached heroic value to their own victim experience, transforming it from unmitigated victimization into meaningful sacrifice.

Compensation for Repatriates

Japan's defeat in 1945 stranded more than 3 million Japanese civilians overseas.[69] Once the privileged elite of the Greater East Asia Coprosperity Sphere, they suffered the opprobrium of the very peoples Japan's expansion was purported to help. Many had their persons violated; most had private assets seized without recompense. They had to abandon everything but what they could carry on their backs when they were forcibly repatriated. In Manchuria, facing near starvation and just a slim chance of survival on their trek back to Japan, thousands made the desperate decision to entrust their small children's lives to kindhearted Chinese families.

As they had no possessions, no homes, and no livelihoods, the repatriates' travails did not end on reaching Japan.[70] Even those who had connections of some sort might meet an unwelcome reception. In a passage censored from the *Hikiage dōhō*, a repatriate journal, one returnee complained: "It is a somber reality that many parents and children . . . have but one ball of rice and one cup of broth to share. Their journey back to the homeland began with heavy steps. . . . Because of the defeat, we had no choice but to return home, regardless of our own desires. And yet, there are those who look at us and turn a cold shoulder, only calling us nuisances who have appeared out of nowhere."[71]

Compared to atomic bomb victims and dispossessed landlords, the repatriates received substantial government help in rebuilding their lives in the immediate postwar years. On September 20, 1945, the Repatriation Civil Affairs Office (Hikiage Minjishō), forerunner of the Repatriates' Relief Bureau (Hikiage engokyoku; RRB) was set up to oversee repatriation in Japan.[72] The RRB saw them to their registered hometowns *(honseki),* and other government organizations provided welfare and job retraining services. In April 1946, the Ministry of Health and Welfare established special repatriate counseling centers in municipal offices across the country. These centers set up temporary housing and built new residences, helped returnees find jobs appropriate to their skills, and handed out free school supplies when needed. They distributed household necessities and clothing worth up to 500 yen in 1947, raised to 1,000 yen in 1948.[73] The Ministry of Agriculture and Forestry subsidized land purchases, provided five-year loans up to 15,000 yen, and assisted in resettling farmers.[74] Rural prefectures such as Ishikawa and Fukui, which escaped serious bomb damage during the war, were able to provide some relief in the form of cash grants, employment, and resettlement. Ishikawa prefecture was able to accommodate its nearly 18,000 returnees as of October 1947, building a new spinning mill and making land available for farming. Moreover, private associations formed for their benefit. In Fukui, for example, 15,000 families contributed an average of 5 yen each to help the local relief society care for its 58,000 returnees.[75]

In 1948 and 1949 the RRB subsidized a coalition of private welfare groups in a public relations effort—known as the Charity Movement (Ai no Undō)—for increasing public sympathy and help for reintegrating repatriates into domestic Japanese society. Two campaigns (held December 17–23, 1948, and April 20–30, 1949) honored repatriates in ceremonies and home visits and encouraged public-spirited help in finding them housing and employment. During these campaigns, department store windows featured special displays, philanthropic societies sponsored children's essays and drawings for exhibit, and the national radio station broadcast special "Charity Movement" programs popularizing the song "Furusato no tsuchi."[76]

Repatriates also organized self-help associations—typically along occupational and geographical lines. Those returning from the same overseas areas formed the largest organizations, which served political as well as social and economic purposes. The Relief Society of Compatriots Repatriated from Korea (Chōsen Hikiage Dōhō Sewa Kai; RSK) was extremely active in early efforts to gain compensation for seized overseas assets.[77] On August 7, 1946, representatives of repatriate organizations convened to discuss what RSK termed the most pressing concern of the returnees: compensation for lost overseas assets. In the opening remarks, RSK chair Hozumi Shinrokurō granted the plight of those who had lost so much in the firebombing at home but pleaded the special nature of the repatriates who had been deprived of all their resources. On August 10, in cooperation with most of the repatriate organizations, the RSK presented to the Diet and government ministries a petition claiming indemnification of lost overseas private assets since they could be credited toward war reparations.[78] Thus began the repatriates' twenty-year struggle for government compensation of their losses.

The campaign for compensation of lost overseas assets was broadly directed by the National Federation of Repatriate Groups (hereafter Zenren, the shortened form of the official name, Hikiagesha Dantai Zenkoku Rengokai).[79] Zenren was organized in June 1946 as a coalition to serve as a repatriate clearinghouse with monthly meetings of the various groups' leadership and to represent a united front for repatriate interests in dealing with the government. This organization also gathered information on repatriate conditions, provided counseling, assisted regional repatriate groups in participating in public works projects, and published a monthly magazine (*Shin kensetsu,* or "New Construction") with a circulation of 3,500.[80]

By the Diet election of April 1947, so many overseas Japanese had been repatriated and encountered resettlement problems that repatriation policy had become a campaign issue. No political party went further, however, than asserting in a general way that the government should assist repatriates in rebuilding their lives.[81] When RSK chair Hozumi, a newly elected member of the House of Councillors, challenged the Katayama administration on its plans concerning their seized assets, the government gave what became its standard response during the Occupation. It could not make any definitive policy plans until the Allied nations made their own position clear.[82]

The final disposition of overseas Japanese assets slowly became clear as negotiations for the peace treaty developed. In the fall of 1949, special U.S. State Department adviser John Foster Dulles announced that Allied countries might use the seized assets to meet their own citizens' demands for indemnification of losses under Japanese wartime rule. When Dulles visited Japan to expedite the peace treaty in January 1951, Zenren petitioned him to respect private property and return the seized assets. He replied that it would be impossible to return ownership of overseas assets. The Japanese government, he said, would have to take appropriate measures.[83]

Under the terms of the peace treaty of September 1951, Japan forfeited its right to sue treaty signatories for compensation for the seized assets of Japanese nationals. Zenren's most immediate response was symbolic. It flew the national flag at half mast. More pragmatically, a plenary session in October resolved to focus efforts on seeking compensation from the Japanese state. At what came to be called the "Constitution Protection Meeting" (*goken taikai*), Zenren decided to base its claims on Article 29, Section 3, which states: "Private property may be taken for public use upon just compensation therefor."[84]

Although repatriates would not receive any money for several years, they did get sympathetic if unencouraging responses from conservative government leaders. In the special Diet called to ratify the peace treaty, Prime Minister Yoshida went so far as to say: "I personally think the state ought to compensate, but we must also consider the state's finances." Attorney General Ōhashi Takeo testified somewhat enigmatically: "Overseas assets are outside the operation of the

Constitution, so it is not against Article 29 to waive such claims; however, one can consider assistance measures from the standpoint of respect for private property."[85]

Like the dispossessed landlords, repatriates were encouraged by the general trend toward government compensation for veterans and groups with a direct connection to the wartime government. Starting in 1952, the government began to make good on its overseas consular debts to Japanese private citizens, and in August 1953 it reinstated military pensions.[86] Expectations of regaining lost assets were raised when, starting in September 1953, tax officials began to return the old yen notes and bank deposit certificates the government had taken into custody at the time of repatriation.[87]

Repatriates put pressure on the government and political parties working from within and outside the normal governing process. In November 1952, repatriate groups formed the Alliance for the Achievement of Compensation for Overseas Assets (Zaigai Shisan Hoshō Kakutoku Kisei Dōmei, or Gaishidō), which focused on activist campaigning. In January 1953 and again in June 1955 they staged sit-ins at the prime minister's residence. In 1956 several repatriates gained attention when they held a hunger strike perched atop the Ministry of Finance's smokestack, and they often made their physical presence known in the hallways outside the offices of high officials.[88] After the 1955 sit-in, Prime Minister Hatoyama met with the repatriates but was reported to have said that "compensation for overseas assets is unthinkable in light of national finances." Nevertheless, soon afterwards both houses of the Diet passed resolutions calling for the government to move quickly to resolve the issue.

Zenren's political power was based on its purported influence on the votes of the 3.5 million repatriates.[89] It was this potential voting block that earned Zenren the influence in political backrooms to support its high-profile "direct lobbying tactics" on the doorsteps, hallways, and rooftops of government buildings. Conservative parties responded earliest with policy commitments. The Liberal Party committed itself to resolving the overseas assets issue in February 1953. Later the LDP made compensation part of its platform for the 1956 Upper House elections.[90] But the conservatives were not alone in responding to repatriate demands. In 1957 the Socialist Party proposed a bill with payments totaling 80 billion yen.[91]

Just as the landlords had done, Zenren came to rely on the conservative parties that could influence government policy formation more easily than others. As John Creighton Campbell notes in reference to Zenren's influence after 1955, this "conservative orientation and clear attachment to the LDP [or the dominant conservative parties before the formation of the LDP] meant that a threat to support a rival party would not be credible; therefore its leverage . . . rested on an ability to switch votes *among* LDP candidates in each district. Hence it was taken more seriously by individual rank-and-file Diet members than by the LDP's leadership." This characteristic of Zenren's influence helps explain why, despite reservations about the fiscal ramifications, the government eventually responded to repatriate demands.[92]

In November 1953, Yoshida's fifth cabinet established a board of inquiry exclusively for overseas assets.[93] On the advice of this board, the government passed the series of laws lifting restrictions on the conversion of the repatriates' old yen notes and establishing conversion rates for old military and overseas postal savings.[94] In July 1954 an Overseas Assets Advisory Council (Zaigai Zaisan Mondai Shingikai) was established in the Prime Minister's Office to determine whether or not the state was legally responsible for compensation of overseas private assets and, as well, to consider the political and social necessity of policies to address such compensation. It failed to come up with any definitive recommendations. In June 1955 both houses of the Diet passed resolutions urging the government to take the appropriate legal and financial measures necessary to resolve the issue. Immediately before the July 1956 House of Councillors' election, the government decided under Zenren pressure to restructure the council, substituting and increasing membership on the previously academic group from ten to twenty-three—adding nine Diet members, three repatriate representatives, and five bureaucrats to the previously academic membership. On June 4, 1956, Prime Minister Hatoyama Ichirō charged it with reexamining the issue with a mind toward making specific policy recommendations.[95]

This "second council," as it came to be known, conducted hearings on repatriate demands and investigated the actual extent of lost overseas assets.[96] Deliberations were marked by political pragmatism as well as a generally benign attitude toward repatriates. The council could not agree on whether the government was legally responsible for losses of assets seized by signatories of the San Francisco Peace Treaty, as the repatriate representatives argued, and determined that there could be no legal resolution of the issue with nonsignatories until diplomatic relations with them had been restored. Since in any case about 95 percent of all lost overseas assets were in China and Korea (nonsignatories), any legal decision on the government's actions in the peace treaty would make little difference concerning compensation payments. One suggestion was to specify payments as a special policy measure in consideration of the extraordinary suffering the repatriates experienced,[97] as a type of solatium *(mimaikin).* But it was only as a welfare measure—payments were distributed under the direction of the Ministry of Health and Welfare—that the council could reach a consensus in helping repatriates who had "lost the basis for their livelihoods." In December 1956 the council recommended that repatriates who had succeeded in rebuilding their livelihoods in the thirteen years since the end of the war should not be entitled to payments, since the policy would not be accepted by the public otherwise. It also recommended—with the proviso that due consideration be given to government finances and fairness to other war victims—that new business loans and assistance in employment and housing be extended to those who needed them.[98]

On the basis of the council's report, LDP General Secretary Tsukada and Welfare Minister Kanda began negotiations with repatriate group representatives in February. In early March they reached a settlement that was formalized and enacted in May.[99] The Repatriate Benefits Allowance Law *(Hikiagesha kyūfukin nado shikyū hō)* granted from 7,000 yen to those who were under eighteen at the end of the war up to 28,000 yen to those who were over fifty. Families of those who died while awaiting repatriation received comparable payments. Those who had yearly incomes more than 88,200 yen were excluded from the benefits, but an estimated 3.4 million people could expect to receive aid of some sort, and 50 billion yen was budgeted for the program.[100] Despite the welfare characteristics of the bill, the council's recommendations and resulting law were criticized in the liberal press as being motivated by political rather than welfare considerations. The *Asahi shinbun,* for example, credited Zenren chairman and Dietman Ōno Banboku (Liberal Party and then LDP faction leader from Gifu) with considerable political influence in achieving the payments bill and deplored the power of the special-interest group of 3.4 million voters.[101]

Demands for compensation fell off for the few years qualified repatriates were receiving payments in the late 1950s, but they picked up again in 1962 when the statute of limitation on debts threatened to nullify lost assets claims on the government. In April 1962, a few days before the tenth anniversary of the implementation of the peace treaty, Zenren delivered its claim to the Ministry of Justice. The repatriate organization reiterated its position that the government would be violating the constitutionally mandated respect for private property if it failed to make compensation.

Zenren also introduced at this time a new tone critical of the state's wartime policies. Akin to the long-standing Socialist rhetoric in support of *hibakusha* relief, this new campaign charged that the government was culpable for negligence in involving its citizens in such a disastrous war. In biting words the writ described how in the first place the government had led these citizens to emigrate to these overseas areas through its northern and southern advance policies, part of "our country's unique invention, the East Asia Coprosperity Sphere." The government leadership's policies resulted in international isolation and eventual defeat, in which Japanese citizens' overseas inroads were regarded as unjust.[102] The purport of this new claim was that the Japanese state was morally responsible for repatriate losses (and owed compensation of almost 1.1 trillion yen). Although the Prime Minister's Office maintained in March 1963 that the 1957 grant had discharged the government's responsibility to disadvantaged repatriates, pressure from the lower ranks in the LDP was so strong that a provisional office of inquiry was set up in the Prime Minister's Office within a month. On the occasion of a national repatriate convention in Tokyo in October 1963, a group of leading delegates pressured Prime Minister Ikeda at a press conference to promise the establishment of yet a third advisory council. Continued Zenren pressure through the LDP led to its establishment in 1964.[103]

After more than a year of deliberation, the third council recommended in November 1966 that while the Japanese government was not legally responsible for its citizens' losses, it should make some sort of payment to repatriates. The council pointed out that although the government in effect confiscated its citizens' property for public use when it signed a peace treaty that forfeited its right to represent claims for lost assets, it did so in a situation of unconditional surrender. Given these circumstances—and the fact that some 95 percent of the lost assets were in countries that did not sign the treaty—there really was no legal basis for making compensation. As a policy matter, however, lost assets could be considered a form of war damage and repatriates could rightly expect assistance to the extent that other war victims received it.[104] Even though repatriates had already received more government assistance than other victim groups, the assertion of inequity for the repatriates was one of the LDP rank-and-file's longstanding reasons for supporting repatriate compensation. In the June 1956 issue of *Seisaku geppō,* the LDP policy journal, the party argued that though the repatriates were the largest war victim group, they had not been given their proportionate share of government assistance. Here the comparison group was probably veterans, not *hibakusha,* and certainly not landlords at that date. In this respect, the repatriate efforts benefited from the success of the landlords in gaining special payments in 1965. If their losses could be considered special in some way—perhaps because they provided a service to the national recovery from war—they could receive payments beyond the strictures dictated by the principle of social welfare levels.

The council decided that the repatriates' losses were indeed exceptional in several ways. First, it noted that some of the Japanese citizens' assets actually served the needs of the state—at least in the sense that they lessened the burden of reparations. Although it made no reference to the 1965 Farmland Rewards Bill, the council seems to have adopted the reasoning behind landlord payments: that this victim group contributed significantly to postwar economic development. Unfortunately there was no way of determining, more than two decades after the end of the war, the relative contributions of the nearly 3.5 million individual repatriates. The council also observed rather boldly that repatriates were deserving of help because of the service they gave the wartime state—fundamentally an assertion that repatriates should be part of the favored group that included the veterans and others who were already being compensated for wartime service. Instead of suffering because of state policy, as the April 1962 Zenren court document asserted, the council determined that they suffered in service to state policy. The government might owe repatriates special consideration, then, because they had "made their living and worked in accordance with state policy on the front lines of state policy."

Second, the council distinguished repatriates' suffering in another way that implicitly associated them with a special class within that select group: the war widows. The report stated that repatriates had lost not only physical property but the nonmaterial "assets" which had been built on them, such as the community ties that gave them social standing and a sense of security. The loss of these "livelihood interests" *(seikatsu rieki)* made a special government measure appropriate. The report argued:

> The assets that repatriates lost were not merely property, but assets with special meaning and value. Regarding the loss of these assets of special meaning, [we] believe the state can resolve the final remaining

issue in the overseas assets problem, and put a period to this issue
as far as its responsibility is concerned, by recompensing these losses
with the special distribution of grants to repatriates.[105]

The "special meaning" reasoning was reflected in the council's guidelines for compensation. Because the proposed payments were compensation for past suffering, current income levels were not to be used
to disqualify recipients as they had been in the 1957 measure. Since
these livelihood interests were likely to depend on the person's age
and the length of time spent abroad, the report recommended that
these be used as criteria for determining the amount of grants. Despite
the statist basis of their arguments for repatriate payments, the council
also recognized that all Japanese had to some extent suffered in the
war and public opinion would have to be respected in making compensation to repatriates.[106]

Like the second council's report and the 1957 bill, the third
council's report gave rise to journalistic analysis and criticism of the
politics behind the compensation decision. The *Asahi shinbun,* for
example, made the same charges it had made in 1956. Just before the
bill was passed in late June, the paper complained that it was just
another example of the government giving in to special interests. It
also criticized the idea of according special treatment to repatriates
as war victims because almost all Japanese were to some extent war
victims. Finally, the paper lamented the political power that special
interests were gaining in general.[107] According to the *Asahi,* just as
the repatriates were encouraged by the 1965 landlord compensation
law, so too would other victim groups—survivors of the atomic bomb
and air raids, for example, and those who had lost their homes when
fire lines were constructed in the cities—take heart in their efforts for
government redress.[108]

The *Asahi* was not alone in its evaluation of the council's report
and the resulting law. In a panel discussion published in the January
1967 issue of the legal journal *Jurisuto,* several university professors
reviewed the council report. Tokyo University professor Satō Takeshi
attacked the notion that repatriates were the only ones to suffer the
special personal and community losses (livelihood interests). Several
groups could claim to have been war victims in this regard, he pointed
out, but the government only took "postwar resolution" measures
when those groups were sufficiently organized to present strong
political pressure. Other participants agreed with him that a second
grant to repatriates could only be justified as supplemental to the

1957 welfare disbursement: "It's just sentimentalism if all the government is doing is thanking and honoring them for having served our
nation well. If it's not a welfare measure, there is no basis for taking
policy action."[109]

In Diet questioning about the government's 192.5-billion-yen
proposal all these concerns were raised repeatedly.[110] When asked to
clarify how the current bill differed from its 1957 counterpart, the
director of the provisional office concerning overseas assets, Kuriyama Kempei, maintained that while the 1957 bill was a welfare measure, the 1967 bill was a "policy measure . . . in response to a past
blow." In a later comment, he testified that "the blow was extremely
serious. The state is making recompense for this blow not only for
property *(zaibutsu)*, but also for assets of a special meaning, and
with the idea of expressing appreciation for their troubles *(gokurō de
aru to iu imi de)*."[111] In other words: the government was trying to
present the bill in just the sentimental terms Professor Satō feared.

Government officials wanted to make this repatriate bill the final
"postwar resolution measure."[112] The problem was how to justify a
second round of repatriate payments without encouraging other victim
groups.[113] Justifying it as a welfare measure was difficult because an
inordinately long time had passed (twenty years) since the original
losses and the 1957 payment should have already corrected any ex-
cessive repatriate poverty. A welfare justification would also have
been problematic because the supporting rationale—that higher government revenues permitted larger repatriate payments—left open
the possibility of further repatriate claims should Japan become even
more affluent in the future. In any case, the repatriates were demanding compensation, not welfare aid. In fact, during the third council's
deliberations one of the arguments in favor of some kind of payment was that the 1957 law had left the main issue, compensation,
unaddressed.[114]

Because the 1966 council clearly ruled out any legal justification
for compensation, it created a policy obligation by sanctifying repatriate suffering as service to the state and redefining "lost assets" to
include extraordinary pain and suffering deserving of sympathy and,
in concrete terms, government compensation. In these recommendations it followed the solution to the demands for compensation by
the dispossessed landlords. Just as landlords switched from criticizing
the government's land reform policy to praising its successes, so did
the repatriates drop their open disparagement of the wartime government's continental expansion policy and put a positive spin on their

cooperation with that policy. This was a significant addition to the long-standing argument that lost assets helped cover reparation payments.[115] The government closed the door on future repatriate claims by admitting that although it was meeting demands for compensation for lost "livelihood interest" assets, the repatriates' case was special (acknowledging their service to the state and defining their lost assets in the special sense of "livelihood interest" assets).[116] Still, because of the widespread distrust of anything that might indicate approval of wartime activity, when it came to Diet interpellation the government could not be too explicit about arguing a moral obligation to repatriates for service to the wartime state.[117] Tsukahara Toshio, director general of the Prime Minister's Office, could only give an ambiguous answer in reply to a question about the state's responsibility for other war victims' losses. The only thing he was clear on was that the repatriates' losses were somehow "special."[118]

Repatriate campaigns for government compensation of lost assets did not draw many questions about their individual as opposed to state responsibility for Japanese actions in the overseas empire. In the dialogue about responsibility for the war debacle, overseas Japanese civilians were, after all, in an ambiguous position. On the one hand they were merely pawns in the militaristic leadership's strategies; on the other hand they benefited directly from the implementation of Japanese imperialism. Their livelihood interests were directly based on it. In its specific provisions the 1967 law did imply a vague degree of culpability for individual citizens who emigrated during wartime. Although the council had recommended only generally that compensation be based on the length of a person's stay abroad—on the assumption that older people had lost correspondingly greater livelihood interests—the final bill took account of this directive by awarding 10,000 yen more to those who had lived abroad for eight or more years. In selecting this threshold, the government was, even if only inadvertently, saying that those who went abroad during wartime were somehow less deserving. When questioned about the significance of paying more to those who had emigrated before the outbreak of hostilities in China in 1937, Director Kuriyama answered in the vague, evasive manner typical of the government's testimony on sensitive topics. There was "no special reason," he replied, "but those who went before the 'Japan-China Incident' were there in a period of peace and so seemed to have lived there longer."[119]

The liability of the Japanese government and not of the individual became the issue. In 1967, the government only indirectly suggested that individuals shared some responsibility. Even after recognizing that governments usually do not purposely alienate their citizenry, one might ask why. One reason, of course, was that individual responsibility for the nation's wartime activities was a politically sensitive topic, especially for conservative politicians. As we have seen, the ideology of war victimhood developed so that blame for the nation's wartime aggression was placed on militarist others. The repatriates' case is in fact a good example of how the war was remembered in a manner that obviated the issue of individual guilt. Clear victimization at the hands of Soviet soldiers and Asians no doubt muddied the location of responsibility and abetted the desire to avoid individual responsibility for national military and imperialist aggression. Despite the example of Gomikawa Junpei's *Human Condition* in fictional literature, most repatriate remembrances "were written from a victim's perspective, and there was hardly any sense of being the oppressor whose own country had invaded the various foreign countries as occupier."[120] The fight to overcome their government's reluctance to recompense private loss probably helped to divert responsibility from the individual repatriate. Complicity was not supposed to be the issue: government responsibility was.

Special inclusions in the bill show that the government was indeed shouldering responsibility. Although one full year of overseas residence was a prerequisite for eligibility, this requirement was waived for engineers and technicians the government had sent over to work on special projects and for agricultural emigrants who had gone to Manchuria under the government's auspices. In awarding exactly the same compensation to these groups for whose fates the wartime government was in effect contractually responsible, the postwar government was implicitly asserting its inheritance of the prewar state prerogatives of authority as well as obligation. Political progressives would welcome the state's claim of such obligation—provided it also acknowledged its obligation to all who suffered regardless of service to the state. But in line with the trends in elementary and junior high school textbooks, the government was building a connection between citizen and state that bridged defeat—the "great divide" in Shōwa history—with patriotic timber.[121]

If the repatriates' sacrifice of the fruits of living "in accordance with state policy on the front lines of state policy" was being honored, then by extension loyalty to either the wartime state or its expansionist policies must also have been esteemed. Yet if it was national loyalty that was indeed being honored, as it clearly must have been, then why appear to penalize those who emigrated with government approval after 1937 by letting that year determine greater or lesser payment? There is a clear conflict between this validation of the wartime loyalty to the government's policies and the discounting of the same loyalty in the 1967 compensation bill. What we have here is a dialectic in which the repatriates' demands for compensation were accommodated—their experience incorporated into the national heritage—in a manner reflecting the citizenry's contradictory feelings about the war and loyalty to the state.

Public compensation, justified in this manner, endorses a sacrifice as the community's own. The repatriate experience had to be seen as part of the nation's collective history and not just the story of one subgroup. Otherwise, how could the public accept repatriate payments taken from the national government's coffers? It is evident from the media's criticism of the political pressures behind the 1967 bill that many opinion makers still did not consider the repatriate experience to be exceptionally symbolic of the nation's experience. But if the repatriate experience had not been fully accepted as part of the nation's collective remembrance of the war by 1967—in other words, if the measure was purely a political expedient as the newspapers maintained—then one must recognize that the compensation bill certainly helped validate and legitimize repatriate belief that it indeed was national history.

In the early 1980s the repatriate experience was in fact relived as a national tragedy as thousands of abandoned orphans came to Japan from China to search for their relatives. National television news shows and newspapers broadcast tearjerking stories of separation in the confusion and fear immediately after defeat in Manchuria. Inevitably the cameras would zoom in on any unusual identifying birthmark or scar, photograph or document.[122] Despite resistance in the 1960s, the nation was eventually to adopt the repatriate experience as a shared national myth with an emphasis on their postwar travail as victim and relative neglect of wartime complicity. By sanctioning repatriate sacrifices, the government validated patriotism at the same time it made it easier for all Japanese to see themselves as victims of the war.

That repatriate group leaders desired recognition of their suffering as "sacrifice" is clear from the remarks of the editor of a 1974 compilation of repatriate memoirs. The editor, himself a repatriate, complained that peace and democracy advocates who branded overseas Japanese the tools of strategic imperialism failed to understand two very important things: the repatriates' love of country and their history of suffering "on the front lines of the Japanese nation's *(minzoku)* overseas development."[123] By connecting the two he was trying to assure the inclusion of the repatriate experience in the nation's historical construction of the war. He was also associating patriotism with victimization. The repatriates were merely the frontline victims of the war: the nation was a victim as well.

The Struggle to Assign Meaning

The Ikeda and Satō "consensus politics" is often regarded as a departure from the ideological struggles of the Kishi years. But the struggle over whose vision of a post-postwar Japan would prevail continued in the realm of policy formulation and in the rhetoric of legislation. "Postwar resolution measures" were in tune with the government's efforts to build a "respectable neonationalism" that promoted a popular identification with the imperial family and other measures mentioned at the beginning of this study.[124] The rising consciousness of Japan as an economic power meant that heroes could be made of those who contributed to the nation's economic success. War victims were honored, not only as symbols of Japan's identity as a pacifist nation, but also for their service to the new mercantilist nation. Through its position as leader of the government and the Diet, the LDP was able to legislate compensation for its clients. But it had to justify them in politically permissible language—that is, in ways that modified rather than destroyed the pacifist ideology of war victimhood. The key to legitimacy for landlords was their "sacrifice," which promoted the central postwar values of economic growth and democracy. The repatriates, it was argued, had contributed to postwar prosperity through automatic application of their losses toward war reparations. Their case, however, was complicated by the fact that they had served the policies of the wartime state. The attempt to ascribe honor to their prewar example of loyalty and service to the state simply made that honor ambiguous. In the 1960s conservatives tried to impute value to patriotism by making victims heroes. But the victims had to be situated, even if disingenuously, as contributors to a peace-loving and democratic as well as economically dynamic nation.

The question remains why the atomic bomb victims, who had become national icons of a sort in the middle 1950s, received government assistance only slowly and seemingly grudgingly. On the political level, the answer is simple: the repatriates and landlords had used the tangible leverage of sizable voting blocks; the *hibakusha* never had such leverage, though their municipal, prefectural, and national representatives did advocate their cause.[125] At a more basic level the problem lay in the flawed strategy of the Hidankyō's leadership and their Socialist backers. The Socialists used the *hibakusha* cause to push for a political agenda that probably exceeded national consensus and certainly antagonized the conservative government. Although the majority of Japanese opposed nuclear weapons, most generally favored or at least felt it was best to assent to the government's close relationship with the United States.[126] Yet it was this close relationship that the Socialists denounced in arguing for *hibakusha* aid.[127] Hidankyō general secretary and university professor Itō Takeshi illustrated the problem for *hibakusha* aid advocates in 1975:

> The Japanese government has cooperated closely with this American postwar strategy [of posing nuclear deterrence against the Soviet Union]. . . . It is precisely because of this that the Japanese government is extremely sensitive to the "nuclear issue." And might we not say that it is the subject on which it has been most vague with the people? It has not been the Japanese people who have had a "nuclear allergy" but postwar Japan's ruling class itself. And this "high-level political" treatment of the nuclear issue by the United States and the Japanese government has inevitably led them to ignore atomic bomb victims' various demands and build a political environment that discriminates in favor of the military and related persons.

Itō was right about the connection between the government's reluctance to embrace a total *hibakusha* aid policy and sensitivity to criticism of its reliance on the U.S. nuclear umbrella. But he neglected to mention the Socialists' own responsibility for alienating the conservative government from the *hibakusha* cause. In the passage just quoted, for example, he uses language that assumes a division between the "Japanese people" (and Socialists) on one side and the government "ruling class" on the other.[128] The irony of his analysis is that it was just as much the Socialists' highly politicized advocacy of the *hibakusha* that hindered the effort for sufficient assistance.[129]

Trying to accord *hibakusha* the same state benefits that veterans enjoyed belittled values of loyalty to the state that conservatives held dear—especially when Socialists took to calling such beneficiaries "war criminals." Conservative leaders naturally resisted statements that condemned wartime predecessors who were, after all, often their mentors.[130] And the more Socialists insisted that conservatives shoulder war responsibility, all the more tenaciously did conservative leaders resist. Conservative foot-dragging might also be attributed to sensitivity to charges that the emperor and the wartime government prolonged the war needlessly until the United States felt it had to use the bomb. *Hibakusha* could not be honored for service to the state without raising embarrassing and complicating questions about Japanese responsibility for the atomic attacks.[131]

Itō implies that the conservatives repressed *hibakusha* accounts. But it is closer to the truth to say they assigned them a safe meaning that countered the Socialists' imputations. For conservatives, the saga of Japanese *hibakusha* served to limit U.S. hegemony in Japan, not eliminate it. Atomic victimhood established Japan's bona fides as a pacifist nation that could speak its own moral mind on nuclear and war issues. But it also highlighted Japan's excuse for inaction in foreign military policy while it remained subservient to the U.S. line. Perhaps most important—and this need not have been conscious—it served to construct a history of the war that diverted opprobrium away from the Japanese and even gained them sympathy. Considering the conservative embrace of Ibuse Masuji's *Black Rain,* one wonders if ruling conservative forces might have done better by *hibakusha* with less Socialist antagonism.

This chapter has explored how politicians chose to promote the agendas of three victim groups in ways that validated their experiences as symbolic of the nation's history. The atomic bombings and the 1950s ban-the-bomb movement established Japan's special status as victim, and *hibakusha* received special medical aid in recognition of their status as national icons. As it turned out, this aid was inadequate. But Socialists and the associated Hidankyō *hibakusha* organization failed to obtain better government treatment until they moderated their rhetorical condemnation of the state. If they could not get privileges equal to those accorded veterans—a step that would have established their status as national symbols in a material way—they were at least able to obtain better treatment in the context of the success of other self-styled victim groups that were better politically positioned with the ruling conservative party. The campaigns for landlord and repatriate compensation and the official validation of their experiences, however challenged, signifies the centrality of war victimhood in the national psyche. Where the 1950s ban-the-bomb movement created a pacifist legacy from the *hibaku* victim experience and the political consensus for state aid, the rhetorical justification of repatriate and landlord remuneration and solatia asserted an eco-

nomic legacy of these groups' sacrifices in laying down the foundations for postwar growth. These groups reflect the evolving locus of
nationalist sentiment from the 1950s pacifism to the 1960s mercan-
tilism as much as the continuing centrality of war victimhood in defining the war experience. Ambiguities remained, to be sure, as is
clear from the limited conservative promotion of *hibakusha* well-
being and the widespread dissatisfaction with the repatriate and
landlord legislation. But the contest was not over denying victimization: it was about giving it meaning and asserting how it constituted
heroic sacrifice for the nation.

CHAPTER 7

Beyond the Postwar

T HIS book has traced the emergence of the ideology of Japanese war victimhood and shown how its iconography has served various interests in the first three decades since the Asia-Pacific War. As I began this study a decade ago, I thought to excavate the origins of an amnesia over Japanese war aggressions by revealing the emergence of victim consciousness as the major mechanism to that amnesia. At that time, I understood victim consciousness to have become hegemonic in public discourse by the middle 1960s, only to be superseded by a gradually emerging public awareness and then concern with national and personal war responsibility. While I still think this construction of the history of war victim consciousness is useful—and that it is important to reveal how victim consciousness became an accepted attitude toward the national past—I now have a greater appreciation that the amnesia was intermittent and often only partial. In fact, there have always been voices of conscience, just as there have always been incidences of inadvertent and willful neglect of Japan's aggressive past. Rather than dwell on this amnesia, one needs also to trace the selective and manipulated remembrance of those aggressions.

Before ending this study, I want to point out important components from the second act in the amnesia narrative of war responsibility—a tale of a gradually emerging democratic consciousness of the people's war responsibility up to the 1990s. In this reconstruction, it is usually asserted that the conscientious observations by Itami Mansaku, Ōkuma Nobuyuki, and others in the first decade were neglected in the rush to cast blame on the wartime leadership and recover from the war's material and psychological devastation. In the same period that the mid-1950s atomic bomb victim exceptionalism tended to divert attention from Japanese war responsibility, Yoshimoto Takaaki, Maruyama Masao, Tsurumi Shunsuke, and many others were addressing this very issue in general-interest journals of the day, especially with regard to the war responsiblity of the intelligentsia.[1]

I have already noted Beheiren's response in the 1960s to Japanese state support for the American war in Vietnam. Other examples of a rising awareness of a "postwar responsibility" to own up to past and present aggression and complicity can be seen in the Japanese United Church of Christ's 1967 admission of complicity in wartime Japan, Kaikō Takeshi's novels of disillusionment in Vietnam, and Honda Katsuichi's reportage on Japanese aggression in China.[2] News of Germany's "Generation of 1969" provided a model for the Japanese man on the street to reassess the war experience in terms of personal complicity. In the 1970s, in Kita Kyūshū, for example, the citizen's movement to memorialize that city's firebombing took pains to emphasize citizens' wartime support for the Japanese war effort.[3] Similarly, efforts were made to include Korean *hibakusha* in government aid programs, to gain pension benefits for former colonial members of the imperial armed services, and to bring attention to the plight of Koreans left in Sakhalin at the end of the war. The 1970s also saw a rise in academic interest in the situation of *zainichi* Koreans residing in Japan and in media revelations about such atrocities as Ishii Shirō's biological weapons experiments in the now infamous Unit 731. In the 1980s and 1990s, Japanese scholars such as Ōnuma Yasuaki, Okabe Makio, Yoshimi Yoshiaki, and Yoshida Yutaka began to publish perceptive histories of war responsibility including analyses of the people's role.[4] One scholar has suggested that the early 1980s marked a shift in *hibakusha* testimony that challenged the nationalist appropriation of their experience. Certainly there is evidence that by the 1990s at the latest the nationalist and guilt-diverting character of the ban-the-bomb movement was recognized within the Japanese scholarly community.[5] Moreover, Asian victims of Japanese war aggression began to argue their case in Japan, often bringing suit in Japanese courts to find redress. In the 1990s the plight of the mostly Korean "comfort women," who were forced to serve in brothels for Japanese servicemen, became an important diplomatic issue that also drew attention to the gendered dynamics of war victimization. Their cause was boosted by an *Asahi shinbun* forum, "The Women's Pacific War" (Onnatachi no Taiheiyō Sensō), in which everyday women were invited to write about their own wartime experiences for publication in this major newspaper. Although the early letters from Japanese women related sentimentalized victim narratives, soon non-

Japanese women were writing about their experiences, and eventually Japanese men as well as women were writing about their roles in victimizing these women.[6]

The horror of the atomic bombings, the terror of the firebombings, the oppressive regimentation at the home front under a government at total war, the loneliness of civilians and foot soldiers abandoned by their state on the open Manchurian plain or in the Philippine jungle, the brutalization of the common man at the hands of fanatical militarists in the armed services—such was the crucible from which postwar Japanese rose to become a peace-loving, democratic people. But the victim-hero's sentimental pacifism harbored hidden meanings and sustained several agendas.

Heroes are public commodities, and in a democratizing postwar Japan it was inevitable that competing political groups would struggle over control of the powerful ideological construct of the people as victim. The U.S. military and Occupation reformers set the early parameters for the victim mythology. But it was the progressives, themselves among the prime beneficiaries of the American reforms, who were the first to put the image of the people as victims of the state to work for them in opposing the postwar conservative government. With the development of a national sense of atomic victimhood, conservatives too recognized the importance of establishing a presence in the contest over the meanings assigned to war victimhood. Thus "the people as victim" became a trope whose import was contested for domestic as much as for international purposes.

Although it is essential to recognize that an amnesia about Japanese aggression against Asia accompanied and abetted this Japanese victim consciousness,[7] this study has shown that the ideology of Japanese war victimhood involved selective remembrance and reconstruction that often recognized the victimization of others. To be sure, neglect of Japanese responsibility is a key element of the Japanese discourse on victimhood, and it was a strong tendency in the ban-the-bomb movement. But it should be clear from the foregoing analysis that Asian suffering was a vital concern of both progressives and conservatives in many discursive fields, including war victimhood.

A central element of war responsibility and war victimhood in this regard was the desire to identify with Asian victimhood rather than deny it. This was certainly true of the progressives, who saw solidarity with Asian peoples as symbolic of the struggle against capitalist imperialism. The adoption of atomic victimhood as national heritage—and the emergence in the middle 1950s of independent states out of the former European colonies in Africa and Asia—made Asian solidarity a desirable goal again. Narratives that characterized these events as Asian and African ethnic national *(minzoku)* struggles against Western hegemony carried echoes of the wartime ideology that supported Japan's invasion of the Asian continent as a war of liberation. One widely influential postwar construction of that conflict is Takeuchi Yoshimi's notion that there had in fact been two wars: one involving a Japanese invasion of the Asian mainland, the other involving competition among imperialist states. Although contested by those such as Kuno Osamu who argue that such conceptions ignore the equally important conflict between the fascist and antifascist states, the dual construction of the war that seemed to grant a measure of legitimacy to Japanese aggression gained wide conservative acceptance even into the post-Hosokawa 1990s.[8] This is one reason why treatment of Asian suffering in primary and secondary textbooks increased steadily over the years—despite the popular impression that conservative government review procedures resulted in the opposite.

Japanese history textbooks, which since the late 1970s have been remarkably frank in their admission of wrongs done to other nationalities, have toyed with a nationalist parochialism in the preponderance of "sentimental" passages that seem to accord equal status to Japanese and Asian war victims. Despite textbook recognition of a Japanese record of aggression and the need to own up to this past, the victim mindset does tend to qualify the people's sense of complicity and hence responsibility for Japan's wartime acts. Textbook revisions that emphasize Japanese victimhood and thus mitigate Japanese aggressions violate Asian sensibilities because they discount Asian victimhood. On the international level—as was evident in Chinese protests over (erroneous) reports in 1982 that Ministry of Education textbook officers directed that the Japanese "invasion" be termed an "advance"—the main issue is control over one's own history. In this age of tenacious nationalism in the face of increasingly rapid and thorough global communication, self-serving constructions of history are unacceptable when they violate other nations' mythologies. This modern reality is particularly clear, of course, when conservative cabinet members fail to exercise discretion regarding a colonial past they do not regard as shameful. But a pacifism that recognizes Japan's past as victimizer while insisting on elevating Japanese victimhood to an equal or higher level than Asian victimhood is also self-serving and ultimately apologist.

As we have seen, the ideology of Japanese war victimhood contained a domestic struggle over defining who "the people" were—hence what the Japanese "nation" was—while negotiating some national understanding of the common war experience that affected responsibility toward domestic as well as foreign victims. Viewed this way, one can say that war victimhood helped privilege pacifism as a fundamental value of postwar Japan in the 1950s and was manipulated in the 1960s to support a neomercantilist national identity. Yet as observers from different perspectives such as Doi Takeo and Oda Makoto have noted, the *amae* ("indulgence") inherent in the victim psychology also disempowers because of its reliance on an other's exercise of power. As a hero figure, the victim lacks the subjectivity needed for full participation in a truly democratic process of self-government.

In a series of essays published in general-interest magazines in 1956 and 1957 that came to be called the Shōwa History debate, Kamei Katsuichirō argued that progressive historiography of the time had omitted the people as active agents. It was a "history without people" in the sense that they were portrayed merely as passive followers. In particular he criticized Tōyama Shigeki et al.'s *Shōwa-shi,* a book widely read by community "study circles," for attributing political agency only to the elite class of militarists, politicians, and industrialists on the one side and the communists and liberals on the other. Essentially, Kamei's concern was to regain a sense of subjectivity for the average person as a participating member of the Japanese nation.[9] And one result of these discussions was that Tōyama and his colleagues revised later editions to give the masses a greater historical presence.

In his Shōwa History essays, Kamei articulated an enduring conservative concern with reestablishing a national sense of self through recognition of historical subjectivity. In the summer of 1978, for example, the politically conservative journal *Shokun* brought together a widely respected member of the conservative banking establishment, Yoshida Mitsuru, and a leading progressive intellectual, Tsurumi Shunsuke, to discuss the issue "What the 'Postwar' Has Lost."[10] Yoshida, author of the Occupation-era memoir *Senkan Yamato no saigo* (Battleship Yamato) and self-conscious spokesman for the wartime generation *(senchū-ha),* had long been a frequent contributor to the general-interest magazines regarding reflection on war responsibility. In what was a conflation of his own generation's midlife crisis with an inadequate sense of national direction in the late 1970s, Yoshida argued that the root of the problem lay in a crisis of national identity. And this crisis, he contended, was the result of an inadequate public examination of the popular rejection of nationalist sentiment at the time of defeat. Very few people, Yoshida argued, publicly reflected on their shift in thinking at the end of the war and admitted exactly how their wartime beliefs had been flawed. This absence of public reflection over wartime actions, Yoshida argued, left contemporary Japan with an incomplete sense of national identity and consequently a weak grip on its own destiny.[11] Tsurumi agreed that there was a crisis and its origins lay in an inadequate examination of war responsibility. But he conceived of the problem in terms of a crisis in individual identity. While the moderate conservative perceived the problem to be one of the people's identity as a nation, the liberal progressive preferred to keep the focus on the individual. Representing conservative and liberal positions that first emerged in the late-nineteenth-century Meiji era, both desired a citizenry with more subjectivity. But where the conservative saw it in a renewed nationalism, the liberal saw it in universalistic terms. Oda Makoto expressed the division well in his 1966 essay quoted at the beginning of this study: people either "identify themselves with the state, and perceive in it the solvent of both individual and universal principles, or they recognize the inevitable discrepancy between state principles and their own experience, and seek to augment their own individuality and autonomy by adopting universal principles directly."[12]

The astonishing admissions in the 1990s of prewar Japanese aggression suggest a radical transformation in the ideology of war victimhood that has expanded the parameters of permissible debate. Yet much seems not to have changed at all. To cite just one example: while the conservative LDP temporarily lost its control of the government and several prime ministers apologized to Asian peoples for waging a war that caused such unbearable suffering, conservative cabinet members continued to make comments denying Japanese colonial excesses, resigning only after the offended nation protested.[13]

Japanese have been criticized so often for neglecting their past as aggressors in war that it has become a truism. But in ending this study of war victimhood, one must recognize again that many members of Japanese society have struggled with their obligations to remember their past with integrity and compassion for all who suffered during World War II in Asia and the Pacific. Furthermore, as I noted in Chapter 1, Japan is not the only nation to have sustained an ideology of war victimhood. In the 1990s Germans were still arguing over who had the right to commemorate the Nazi holocaust and decide on the proper venue.[14] The inability of the Smithsonian Air and Space Museum to display the *Enola Gay* in a manner that honored Japanese victim sentiments shows that the United States has its own groups contesting the Hiroshima bombings and the privilege of victimhood.[15] Victim mythologies have been constructed in the early stages of feminist discourse in the United States; and the idea that men practice violence and women are victims seems at one time to have underlaid feminist theory in the West German women's movement as well.[16]

We are all susceptible to the indulgent blindness engendered by sentimentalization of war victimhood. It may be the inevitable concomitant of compassion for the injured and downtrodden. And if that is so, it is part of what makes us human. As individuals might we not take solace in our common humanity as we use that very same awareness to resist the victim's "sentimental humanism"? Was this not, after all, professor/prisoner Wang's answer to "the meaningless limits on the human condition"?

Of course, we live within social groups that demand social identities. In postwar Japan, victim consciousness helped to create a pacifist people. Whether this people was a proletariat in an international struggle against militarism, a civic nation engaged in rebuilding from the ravages of war, or an ethnic nation at variance or in league with its state depended on one's ideological position. The question is: When Japan's long postwar ends—and with it, perhaps, the salience of war victimhood to the national psyche—what will the new icons be and what kind of nation will they define?

Appendix 1
The Stockholm Appeal

Appeal of the World Peace Committee

We demand the absolute banning of the atom weapon, arm of terror, and mass extermination of populations.

We demand the establishment of strict international control to ensure the implementation of this banning measure.

We consider that any government which would be first to use the atom weapon against any country whatsoever would be committing a crime against humanity and should be dealt with as a war criminal.

We call on all men of goodwill throughout the world to sign this appeal.

This appeal was signed by all the members of the World Peace Committee and thousands of signatures are already being received in every country all the world over.[1]

APPENDIX 2

Suginami Ward's Petition to Ban the Hydrogen Bomb

Cover Message

> Let all the people petition for banning hydrogen bombs;
> Let us call on all the governments and peoples of the world;
> Let us protect humankind's life and happiness.

Main Text

Through a national people's movement let us call on all the world to ban the hydrogen bomb.

After the tragedies of Hiroshima and Nagasaki, now we the Japanese people have received for the third time the egregious injury of atomic and hydrogen bombs. The fishermen who were exposed to the ash of death are suffering from the horrible atomic sickness, and many businessmen in the fishing trade are worried as their livelihoods are threatened. The average citizen, who depends on fish as an important source of nutrition, is deeply anxious.

This state of affairs is due simply to testing the hydrogen bomb, so the horror in case a nuclear war happens is more than one can imagine. Just four hydrogen bombs would turn all of Japan into scorched earth. Beginning with Dr. Einstein the world's scientists have warned that nuclear war would destroy mankind.

At this time of grave danger, resolutions to ban the hydrogen bomb have been passed in the Diet and similar resolutions have been passed in regional assemblies while petition movements to ban the bomb are progressing everywhere. These earnest petition movements will carry little weight, however, if they are conducted separately. We must combine all the people's petition movements.

In Suginami Ward the ward assembly, representing the people of the ward, passed a resolution for banning the hydrogen bomb on April 17. Then, based in Suginami Ward, we began a petition campaign for banning the hydrogen bomb. Let us develop this further into a national people's petition movement. Then, based on the resolution of all the people as clearly expressed in this petition, let us call on the world to ban hydrogen bombs and all production, use, and testing of nuclear weapons.

This petition is not the movement of a specific faction but a movement to join all the people of various positions. And those we are addressing in this petition are not any specific states but every state's government and people as well as the United Nations and other international organizations and assemblies.

We believe that when, through this petition movement by all the Japanese people, we earnestly call for banning the hydrogen bomb, our voice will sway the conscience of all the world's people and the first step toward protecting humankind's life and happiness will have been taken.

May 1954   Suginami Council for a Ban-the-H-Bomb Petition Movement
                Yasui Kaoru, Chairman[1]

Notes

Chapter 1: Victims, Victimizers, and Mythology

1. Sakamoto Yoshikazu, "Kenryoku seiji to heiwa undō," *Sekai* 191 (November 1961):20.

2. In translating terms (here Japanese into English), one always encounters difficulties communicating the nuance intended in their original expression. *"Minshū," "kokumin,"* and *"minzoku,"* for example, cannot be translated mechanically as proletarian "masses," "civic nation," and "ethnic nation," for their meanings depend on the linguistic and discursive context, reflecting slippage of meaning (ambiguity) as well as intentional difference in usage. Here I want to clarify the meanings of these terms and explain my strategies to communicate my understanding of the original discourse. As suggested in the discussions that follow, both the postwar Marxist and liberal terms for the national collective—respectively, *minzoku* (ethnic nationalism as a form of resistance to the postwar state) and *kokumin* (civic nation)—no doubt carried echoes from their wartime usage in ultranationalist rhetoric—with the general meanings, respectively, of *Volk* and loyal subjects. Ban-the-bomb leader Yasui Kaoru used the term "masses" *(minshū)* in ways that did not always connote the revolutionary import this term carries in English and used *"kokumin"* in ways that suggested an ethnicization of the civic nation. I recognize that *"kokumin"* is also used sometimes simply to designate the collectivity of those who have legal Japanese citizenship. With due recognition of the difficulties presented by such slippage of precision in meaning, one can discern important shared meanings. Progressive formulations of war victimhood tended to construct a vision of the Japanese people that distanced them—whether as an ethnic nation *(minzoku)* or somewhat paradoxically (as Rikki Kersten suggests, dysfunctionally) as a democratic citizenry or civic nation *(kokumin)*—from the postwar Japanese state. To communicate the ambiguities as well as the nuances of the original Japanese usage, in the pages that follow I use the English terms "people," "nation," "ethnic nation," "civic nation," "citizenry," "masses," and the like in ways that seem semantically and stylistically appropriate to the specific text. In cases where ambiguities in English may arise, I add bracketed English and sometimes the original Japanese enclosed in following parentheses. In this way I hope to communicate my interpretation in readable English without closing a window onto the texture of the original phrasing. On ethnicity formation see the classic essay by Fredrik Barth, "Introduction," in *Ethnic Groups and Boun-*

daries: The Social Organization of Culture Difference (London: Allen & Unwin, 1969), pp. 9–38. See also Kevin M. Doak, "What Is a Nation and Who Belongs? National Narratives and the Ethnic Imagination in Twentieth-Century Japan," *American Historical Review* 102(2) (April 1997):283–309; Rikki Kersten, *Democracy in Postwar Japan: Maruyama Masao and the Search for Autonomy* (London: Routledge, 1996).

3. Konaka Yōtarō, "Oda Makoto: Hanoi kara minami Taiheiyō e—'Nanshi' to 'kyōsei.' " In Nihon Ajia-Afurika Sakka Kaigi, *Sengo bungaku to Ajia* (Tokyo: Mainichi Shinbunsha, 1978), p. 105. Konaka was born in 1934, Oda in 1932.

4. Unless noted otherwise, all translations of Oda's essay "Heiwa no rinri to ronri" are from Koschmann's abridged translation, "The Ethics of Peace," in J. Victor Koschmann, ed., *Authority and the Individual in Japan: Citizen Protest in Historical Perspective* (Tokyo: University of Tokyo Press, 1978), pp. 154–170. This particular quote is from p. 166.

5. Oda, "Ethics of Peace," p. 168.

6. Ibid., p. 165.

7. For two recent treatments of the questions of political autonomy and subjectivity as they developed out of the "subjectivity" *(shutaisei)* debates early in the Occupation, see J. Victor Koschmann, *Revolution and Subjectivity in Postwar Japan* (Chicago: University of Chicago Press, 1996), and Kersten, *Democracy in Postwar Japan*.

8. Shimizu Ikutarō, "Kore made no jūnen kore kara no jūnen—Zenmenkōwaronsha no tachiba kara," *Sekai* 162 (June 1959):49–51; emphasis in the original. Shimizu knew whereof he spoke. As a central member of the Peace Problems Study Group, the group of intellectuals brought together by *Sekai* magazine in the late 1940s to consider such issues, he participated in the formation of Japan's first indigenous peace movement. See, for example, the records of the December 1948 meeting of this group published in *Sekai* (July 1985):256–314, especially pp. 305–312, for a discussion of how the peace movement should construct the people's subjectivity in war.

9. Oda shares this reaction with the *minshūshi* historians of the same generation, who according to Gluck "experienced not guilt, but betrayal." See Carol Gluck, "The People in History," *Journal of Asian Studies* 38(1) (November 1978):25–50.

10. Oda tells of his revelation while viewing a film of the American invasion of Okinawa. He was taking in the grisly battle scenes with equanimity until he realized that they were Japanese, not Chinese, who were being burned by flamethrowers. See Oda, "Ethics of Peace," p. 160.

11. See Kano Masanao's analysis in *"Torijima" wa haitte iru ka: Rekishi ishiki no genzai to rekishigaku* (Tokyo: Iwanami Shoten, 1988): "When in cross-examining the war as it relates to one's self the victim's perspective is revealed, the seal to inner emotions is broken, and one begins to relate not just what one suffered but also what one inflicted. Usually before this happens there are repeated second thoughts and anxiety. But as a result of this repeated self-examination, pretty much from the 1970s on, albeit sporadically, more and more previously taciturn people have crossed the Rubicon and talked" (p. 96).

12. One of the most celebrated of such confessions was Nagasaki Mayor Motoshima's statement that the emperor should accept responsibility, as Motoshima did for his own small part.

13. *Asahi shinbun* editor Mori Kyōzō, himself a veteran of the wartime naval press corps in Southeast Asia, commented in the January 3, 1973, *Asahi shinbun* that

"the Japanese people became conscious of their own responsibility for aggression in the Pacific War with the bombing of North Vietnam. It was an awareness that the Japanese military had once prosecuted evil of the same character as the American military"; quoted by Ubukata Naokichi in "Tōkyō saiban o meguru shoronten: 'Jindō ni tai suru tsumi' to jikō," *Shisō* 719 (May 1984):106. I take this as corroboration that the anti–Vietnam War movement in Japan raised such awareness, but that it was far slower to reach the full light of day than Mori suggests. It certainly had this immediate effect on many peace activists. If it truly affected the masses, then one can only surmise that it did so only in restricted contexts and they could forget again in other contexts after the Vietnam War ended.

14. See Oda Makoto, " 'Nanshi' no shisō," *Tenbō* (January 1965), reprinted in *"Nanshi" no shisō* (Tokyo: Iwanami Shoten, 1991), pp. 3–40; translated as "The Meaning of Meaningless Death," *Journal of Social and Political Ideas in Japan* 4(2) (August 1966):75–85.

15. For a useful overview of the war responsibility literature see Okabe Makio, "Sensō sekinin to kokumin bunka," *Sekai* (August 1990):32–41; see also *Rekishi hyōron* 460 (August 1988), a special issue devoted to war responsibility. The most thorough student of the legal and moral repercussions of the Tokyo Trials is Ōnuma Yasuaki. See his "Tōkyō saiban-sensō sekinin-sengo sekinin," *Shisō* 719 (May 1984):70–100. This particular issue of *Shisō* carries a number of articles on the Tokyo Trials. Also useful are Sumitani Takeshi's "Sensō hanzai saiban ron," *Shisō* 719 (May 1984):123–131, and Ubukata Naokichi's numerous articles on the trials.

16. Auschwitz and Hiroshima have been mutually appropriated and denied by their respective victims. See Robert Jay Lifton's many studies that link the nuclear and Nazi holocausts. See also David Goodman and Masanori Miyazawa, *Jews in the Japanese Mind: The History and Uses of a Cultural Stereotype* (New York: Free Press, 1995), especially chap. 6, "Identification and Denial: The Uses of the Jews in the Postwar Period," pp. 135–182.

17. Robert G. Moeller, "War Stories: The Search for a Usable Past in the Federal Republic of Germany," *American Historical Review* 101(4) (October 1996):1008–1048.

18. See Shimizu Masayoshi et al., "Nishi-Doitsu ni okeru 'Nachizumu-go' no seiji to rekishi ishiki," in Fujiwara Akira and Arai Shin'ichi, eds., *Gendaishi ni okeru sensō sekinin* (Tokyo: Aoki Shoten, 1990), as well as the other essays in this volume.

19. Doi Takeo, *The Anatomy of Dependence,* 3rd ed., trans. John Bester (Tokyo: Kodansha International, 1981), especially pp. 23–27 and 158–162. Doi (p. 20) likens *amae* to Balint's description of "passive object love" in Michael Balint, *Primary Love and Psychoanalytic Technique* (New York: Liveright, 1965).

Chapter 2: Leaders and Victims

1. This new image was necessary if the emperor were to survive the trials and the purge. As is well known, SCAP relied on the emperor's prestige to assure compliance to its reform program, and the Japanese government wished to retain what until recently had been considered (and for many still was) the "national essence."

2. See especially Arai Shin'ichi, "Sensō sekinin to sengo shori," in Fujiwara Akira and Arai Shin'ichi, eds., *Gendaishi ni okeru sensō sekinin* (Tokyo: Aoki Shoten, 1990), pp. 24–53. This characterization of the war crimes trials, which included conventional B-class and C-class trials conducted throughout East Asia, is problematic. Even at the

A-class trials in Tokyo, for example, Gen. Matsui Iwane, commander-in-chief of Japanese forces in Central China during the Rape of Nanjing, was executed for his negligence in permitting atrocities in China. See Richard Minear, *Victor's Justice: The Tokyo War Crimes Trial* (Princeton: Princeton University Press, 1971).

3. Ōnuma Yasuaki, one of the most thorough students of war responsibility, connects this relative Asian "amnesia" with the *datsu-A nyū-O* ("escape Asia, join Europe") ideology that informs so much of modern Japanese history. See Ōnuma Yasuaki, "Tōkyō saiban-sensō sekinin-sengo sekinin," *Shisō* 719 (May 1984):70–100.

4. U.S. Army Forces in the Pacific, Psychological Warfare Branch, "Implementation of the Basic Military Plan for Psychological Warfare Against Japan," *Report on Psychological Warfare Against Japan in the Southwest Pacific Area, 1944–1945*, Annex 6, app. A, p. 8; in Hoover Archives, U.S. Army Forces in the Pacific, Psychological Warfare Branch, Box 1. This report was presented under Brig. Gen. G. S. C. Bonner F. Fellers' signature to a conference for coordinating propaganda efforts in Manila in early May.

5. Ibid., pp. 9, 12–13.

6. U.S. Office of War Information, Bureau of Overseas Intelligence, Foreign Morale Analysis Division, "Special Report No. V: Current Psychological and Social Tensions in Japan" (June 1, 1945), p. 32; in Hoover Archives, U.S. Office of War Information, Box 3, Folder "Foreign Morale Analysis Division."

7. Leaflet 106-J-1. U.S. Army, Forces in the Pacific, Psychological Warfare Branch, "Scrapbook"; in Hoover Archives, Accession xx400-8m.38., in Psychological Warfare Branch, "Scrapbook." Propaganda from 1945, which tended to absolve the average Japanese from war guilt while attempting to discredit military leadership, included a leaflet (112-J-1) carrying President Truman's May 8 statement (assuring the Japanese people his goal was not the extermination of the Japanese race) with the bold headline "The Defeat of the Militarists Is Victory for the Japanese People" *(Gunbu no kōfuku wa zenkokumin no shōri)*. A leaflet titled "Words and Deeds" (123-J-1), intended for Japanese civilians, used the Ninomiya Sontoku dictum that the good government considers what it can give to the people and the bad government considers what it can take away. The leaflet ended with a query: "How does this compare with the actions of the militarists?" Leaflet 147-J-1 depicted the traditional setting for ritual suicide with the comment that the central military leadership should take responsibility for Japan's crushing losses instead of trying to shift blame onto the people. The next leaflet in the series, labeled "Desire for Peace Crushed," recounted the war's history from Pearl Harbor and declared that the militarists had ignored the people's true desires from the beginning. All leaflets are in the Psychological Warfare Branch "Scrapbook."

8. The Article 4 text: "The time has come for Japan to decide whether she will continue to be controlled by those self-willed militaristic advisers whose unintelligent calculations have brought the Empire of Japan to the threshold of annihilation, or whether she will follow the path of reason."

9. Foreign Morale Analysis Division, "Special Report No. V," p. 36.

10. Leaflet 122-J-1, Psychological Warfare Branch, "Scrapbook."

11. Supreme Commander for the Allied Powers (SCAP), Government Section, *Political Reorientation of Japan (PRJ)* (1949), p. 737.

12. *PRJ*, p. 756.

13. *PRJ*, p. 745. As a basis for that democracy, MacArthur envisioned a more assertive citizenry. In his 1947 New Year's statement to the Japanese people he said he had tried to "destroy entrenched totalitarian controls and raise the individual Japanese citi-

zen to exert a dominant influence over his own destiny. For once the citizen has acquired the power of self-determination, limited only by rational convention and individual conscience, he may be counted upon firmly to preserve that power and to apply it fearlessly and intelligently, both for his own benefit and the common benefit of all." See *PRJ,* p. 761.

14. Douglas MacArthur, *Reminiscences* (London: Heinemann, 1965), p. 288, as quoted in Stephen Large, *Emperor Hirohito and Shōwa Japan: A Political Biography* (London: Routledge, 1992), p. 135.

15. Between September 11 and December 6, 1945, more than one hundred Japanese were arrested for A-class war crimes. The list of twenty-eight defendants for the first trial was announced on the emperor's birthday, April 29, 1946, and the Tokyo trials began on May 3. They lasted until April 16, 1948; the verdicts were handed down on November 12. Twenty-five of the defendants were found guilty, and Okawa Shūmei was determined unfit for trial. Matsuoka Yōsuke and Nagano Osami died during the trial. After Tōjō and six others were hanged on December 23, the remaining untried were released on Christmas Eve. See Sumitani Takeshi et al., eds., *Tōkyō saiban handobukku* (Tokyo: Aoki Shoten, 1989), pp. 4–5.

16. Government and business later conducted a Red Purge in the course of "reconstruction."

17. By the end of the Shōwa era, the idea of individual responsibility for national crimes was applied in public discourse to all citizens, making every Japanese in some sense individually responsible for the nation's aggressions; but in the early years, it worked to exempt the majority of Japanese.

18. Ōnuma, "Tōkyō saiban-sensō sekinin-sengo sekinin," p. 74. Ōnuma does not present any specific evidence as his whole approach is legalistic—mainly concerned with the theoretical issue of what the war responsibility debates logically signified as texts in and of themselves.

19. Kazuo Kawai attributes the "little sense of personal identification" with the war crimes defendants to cultural characteristics such as situational ethics or "Buddhist fatalism." He says it was not "an attempt to run away from a sub-conscious sense of guilt." In this respect, Kawai offers an alternative cultural explanation to Ōnuma's legalistic analysis based on the logic of individual responsibility. See Kazuo Kawai, *Japan's American Interlude* (Chicago: University of Chicago Press, 1960), p. 23–24. Kawai was editor of the main English-language daily in Japan during the Occupation.

20. The original Japanese of this poem, composed by one Gamō Seitarō, is: *"Tōkyō saiban hanketsu no sokubō kogarashi ni hatameku o hito kaerimiru nashi."* See Yoshimi Yoshiaki, "Senryōki no Nihon no minshū ishiki—Sensō sekinin o megutte," *Shisō* 811 (January 1992):81, 84.

21. Perhaps the best known of these purge lists was Odagiri Hideo's list of twenty-five writers and critics with the heaviest responsibility for the reactionary social structure or for praising the war of aggression. See Odagiri Hideo, "Bungaku ni okeru sensō sekinin no tsuikyū," *Shin Nihon bungaku* (June 1946), reprinted in Usui Yoshimi, ed., *Sengo bungaku ronsō,* vol. 1 (Tokyo: Bancho Shobō, 1972), pp. 115–117. Note that the leftists were addressing responsibility for the war of aggression rather than defeat, in addition to responsibility for the wartime domestic system of thought control.

22. For example, in a panel discussion of the central group of young writers who formed the New Japan Literary Club (Shin Nihon Bungakkai) and its journal, *Kindai bungaku,* Honda Shūgo warned: "When we make statements on the issue of war re-

sponsibility in the literary world, we shouldn't think of ourselves as standing separate [from the issue]. We mustn't forget that we too have been permeated physically and chemically [sic] and that war responsibility is our own problem too." See Ara Masato et al., "Bungakusha no sekimu," *Ningen* (April 1946), reprinted in Usui, *Sengo bungaku ronsō*, I:56.

23. Jiyū Eigajin Shudan, "Eiga sensō sekininsha no kaimei," *Eiga seisaku* (July 1946), reprinted in Ogawa Tōru, ed., *Gendai Nihon eigaron taikei*, vol. 1: *Sengo eiga no shuppatsu* (Tokyo: Fuyukisha, 1971), p. 103. The Democratic Scientists Association (Minshushugi Kagakusha Kyōkai) met at the beginning of June 1946 to purge their ranks. See Ōkuma Nobuyuki, "Kono eigajin o miyo: Itami Mansaku to sono sensō sekininron in tsuite," *Eiga shunjū* (November 1947), reprinted in *Sengo eiga no shuppatsu*, p. 129. "People's Assemblies to Purge War Criminals," organized by Communists, were held in six major cities on December 8, 1945.

24. Itami Mansaku, "Sensō sekininsha no mondai," *Eiga shunjū* (August 1946), in Ogawa Tōru, ed., *Sengo eiga no shuppatsu* (Tokyo: Tojusha, 1971), p. 114.

25. Ōkuma Nobuyuki, "Hansei naki no minzoku," *Bungei shunjū* 25(9) (September 1947):11. Matsumoto Sannosuke's analysis of Okuma's postwar thinking on the interrelationship among the individual, ethnic nation, and state suggests that Okuma later came to assign war responsibility mainly to the state. See Matsumoto, "Ōkuma Nobuyuki ni okeru kokka no mondai—'Kokka kagaku' kara 'Kokka aku' made," *Shisō* 837 (March 1994):4–39.

26. See, for example, Tsurumi Shunsuke, "Heiwa no shisō," introduction to *Sengo Nihon shisō taikei*, vol. 4: *Heiwa no shisō* (Tokyo: Chikuma Shobō, 1968), p. 5.

27. Between 1956 and 1957 numerous intellectuals such as Kamei Katsuichirō and Maruyama Masao wrote essays that shared Itami's insights about political and moral war responsibility and the problem of allowing oneself to be deceived. See Kamei Katsuichirō's series of essays in *Bungei shunjū* and *Chūō kōron* in 1956, and see Maruyama Masao, "Sensō sekinin ron no mōten," *Shisō* (March 1956).

28. "Chūgokujin no kōsen ishiki to Nihonjin no dōtoku ishiki," *Chisei* (May 1949), reprinted in Tsurumi, *Heiwa no shisō*, p. 129. See also Takeuchi Yoshimi, "Chūgoku no kindai to Nihon no kindai," in Takeuchi et al., *Tōyōteki shakai rinriteki seikaku* (Tokyo: Hakujitsu Shoin, 1948), pp. 3–60; Ōnuma Yasuaki places Takeuchi along with Tsurumi Shunsuke and Honda Katsuichi in the vanguard of writers who helped discredit victim consciousness over the course of the postwar era. See Ōnuma, "Tokyo saiban-sensō sekinin-sengo sekinin," pp. 85–86.

29. *Asahi shinbun*, July 8, 1946.

30. Yoshimi, "Senryōki no Nihon no minshū ishiki," pp. 73–99. Yoshimi used the Prange Collection as his primary source for this rich and insightful study of popular understanding of war responsibility during the Occupation. Despite all the examples to the contrary, he stops short of challenging the scholarly consensus that such views were rare and ultimately inconsequential.

31. R Fukuinsei [Former Soldier R], "Fukuinsha no kotoba," *Shintetsu bunka* (June 1947), quoted in Yoshimi, "Senryōki no Nihon no minshū ishiki," pp. 85–86. Another Niigata worker complained of the average worker's consciousness: "Just like bamboo shoots after a rain, there sprout those who emphasize their righteousness by abusing the oppressive Tōjō government. It makes you want to ask them, if they knew it was so bad why didn't they cry out against it then at the top of their lungs" (p. 85). In

early 1948, on the other hand, there was a small wave of popular sympathy for Tōjō when he asserted that he was morally and politically justified in starting the war. See "Tensei jingo," *Asahi shinbun*, January 8, 1948.

32. Yoshida Mitsuru and Tsurumi Shunsuke, "Sengo ga ushinatta mono," *Shokun* 10(8) (August 1978):55–56.

33. Yoshida Mitsuru, "Sensō kyōryoku no sekinin wa doko ni aru ka—*Senkan Yamato* ni taisuru hihan no bunseki," *Shisō no kagaku* 20 (August 1960):63.

34. Nanbara Shigeru, "Heiwa ka sensō ka," pp. 107, 122–123. For a discussion of Nanbara's thinking on individual morality within the context of ethnic community and state see Andrew Barshay, *State and Intellectual in Imperial Japan: The Public Man in Crisis* (Berkeley: University of California Press, 1988).

35. Some 73.9 percent of the men respondents felt more or less that leaders should take some sort of responsibility (17.5 percent did not see any need; 29.1 percent of the women said they did not know what to think). Some 45 percent of the men and 64 percent of the women remained uncritical *(muhihanteki)* of the decision to start the war. Some 53 percent of the women and 57 percent of the men with an opinion felt most of those purged had not been leaders in the war effort. See Japan, Prime Minister's Office, National Public Opinion Survey Institute, "Kōshoku tsuihō ni tsuite no seron chōsa kekka hōkokusho," 5, 21–26, in Hoover Archives, John D. Montgomery Collection, Box 8, folder 3.

36. Kawai, *Japan's American Interlude*, pp. 82–83.

37. There was some question as to whether the emperor could save the imperial institution by taking personal responsibility through abdication. His chief adviser, Kidō Kōichi, persuaded him to forgo this solution as he feared it might backfire by introducing debate over turning Japan into a republic. SCAP opposed abdication as late as 1948 when the emperor was considering such a move during the late stages of the Tokyo Trials. See, for example, Stephen Large's discussion on this topic in *Emperor Hirohito and Shōwa Japan*, pp. 132–147.

38. Nihon, Shūgiin, Sangiin, *Gikaiseido 70-nen shi* 3 (1962):1021–1022.

39. *Gikaiseido 70-nen shi* 3:1028.

40. *Asahi shinbun*, September 21, 1945.

41. *Asahi shinbun*, November 11, 1945.

42. Ibid.

43. *Asahi shinbun*, April 30, 1946. See also Takeda Kiyoko, *Dual Image of the Japanese Emperor* (New York: New York University Press, 1988), p. 139.

44. Quoted in Fujiwara Akira et al., eds., *Tennō no shōwa-shi* (Tokyo: Shin Nihon Shuppansha, 1984), p. 138.

45. Some 65 percent felt no need for abdication; 17.6 percent thought he should abdicate at the proper time; 9.3 percent insisted he abdicate immediately. Interestingly, the younger and better-educated were more likely to favor abdication: 34.6 percent of those under thirty and 49.7 percent with higher education favored abdication. The poll was conducted by the Osaka Yoron Chōsa Kenkyū-jo (711 respondents); data are taken from Yoshimi, "Senryōki Nihon no minshu ishiki," p. 91. A poll conducted after the emperor's death in 1989 found that the ratio of Japanese who felt the emperor bore responsibility for the war remained relatively unchanged: 25 percent said he bore responsibility, 31 percent said he did not, and 38 percent did not know. See *Asahi shinbun*, February 8, 1989, as cited in Gluck, "The Idea of Showa," p. 16.

46. Yasumitsu Ryōzen, "Tōjōra hanketsu no kansō (Ge no ni)," *Sekai bukkyō* (April 1949); cited in Yoshimi, "Senryōki Nihon no minshu ishiki," p. 92. Yasumitsu was chief priest of the Sōenji temple.

47. See Large, *Emperor Hirohito and Shōwa Japan,* p. 140f.

48. *Asahi shinbun,* December 24, 1948; quoted in Iritani Toshio, *Group Psychology of the Japanese in Wartime* (London: Kegan Paul International, 1991), p. 227.

49. As quoted in Takeda, *Dual Image,* p. 141. Keenan's statement was reported in the *Asahi shinbun,* November 21, 1948.

50. *Asahi shinbun,* December 24, 1948. In his "Tensei jingo" column, Aragaki Hideo also accepted this image of the emperor. The November 21, 1946, column, for example, criticized his close advisers for caring too much for their personal safety and not confronting the militarists. As for the emperor, Aragaki maintained that even though he wanted peace he could not rein in the militarists because, "under the emperor system of the Meiji Constitution, sovereignty really already rested in the militarist clique."

51. As quoted in Takeda, *Dual Image,* p. 141; *Asahi shinbun,* November 21, 1948.

52. *Asahi shinbun,* May 3, 1952. The *Asahi* headline read: "An End to the Abdication Theory" *(Tai-i-setsu ni shushi fuda).* The day before, the emperor had attended a government-sponsored memorial service for the war dead. He offered a few simple words of condolence but no expression of personal responsibility.

53. David Titus, "The Making of the 'Symbol Emperor System' in Postwar Japan," *Modern Asian Studies* 14(4) (1980):558–559.

54. Ibid., p. 560. The weekly magazine was *Shūkan myōjo* 33 (August 11, 1963).

55. Quoted in Shinobu Seizaburō, *Sengo Nihon seijishi* I (1965):171; translation from James William Morley, "The First Seven Weeks," *Japan Interpreter* 6(2) (Summer 1970):159.

56. After the Tokyo Trials the emperor sent President Truman a message thanking him for his considerate treatment and promising "to work as hard as I can in my position as emperor to foster among the Japanese people the development of democracy just like America's." See Fujiwara et al., *Tennō no shōwa-shi,* p. 138.

57. Ueyama Shunpei described four models that structured historical understanding of the war: the *Daitō-A sensō* (Greater East Asia War) perspective; *Taiheiyō sensō* (Pacific War) perspective; *Teikokushugi sensō* (Imperialist War) perspective; and *Kōnichi sensō* (Anti-Japanese War) perspective. Except for the *Kōnichi sensō* perspective, which represents the native Chinese view of the war as a struggle for liberation against Japan as a colonial power, all these constructs posit a central conflict between Japan and the United States and its allies. See Ueyama Shunpei, "Daitō-A sensō no shisōshi-teki igi," in *Daitō-A sensō no imi—Gendaishi bunseki no shiten* (Tokyo: Chūō Kōronsha, 1964), pp. 4–6.

58. See "Nihon kindaika no higeki," *Chūō kōron* (August 1958), reprinted in *Kamei Katsuichirō zenshū* 16 (Tokyo: Kodansha, 1972), p. 227. Others reported they were relieved that they were finally fighting the "real enemy," a view presented in wartime films such as *Kaigun.*

59. Although difficult to prove, the American presence probably operated in more subtle ways as well. Daily contact with American troops made it easy to remember the war as an American-Japanese conflict. No doubt many Japanese experienced anxiety over the possible ill humor of U.S. soldiers on dates of American significance such as December 8. Dates such as July 7, the date of the Marco Polo Bridge Incident, or Sep-

tember 18, the date of the Mukden Incident, were not so significant for the Americans, and consequently Japanese were not forced to remember them every year. Memory of Pearl Harbor remained strong enough in popular consciousness that thirty-nine years later the author's Japanese junior high school students wanted to talk about it in class on December 8.

60. See, for example, Tōyama Shigeki et al., *Shōwa-shi* (Tokyo: Iwanami Shoten, 1955).

61. Ienaga Saburō, perhaps the most famous proponent of the "Fifteen-Year War" construct, admits in the introduction to his *Taiheiyō sensō* that the term had "not yet been accepted by the Japanese public." For the English translation see Ienaga Saburō, *The Pacific War, 1931–1945: A Critical Perspective on Japan's Role in World War II* (New York: Pantheon, 1978), p. xiii. In the 1990s, the term "Asia-Pacific War" gained acceptance as it recognized the Asian theater with little ideological baggage.

62. Oda Makoto, "Takeuchi Yoshimi no Ajia-ron ni tsuite," in Nihon Ajia-Afurika Sakka Kaigi, ed., *Sengo bungaku to Ajia* (Tokyo: Mainichi Shinbunsha, 1978), p. 222. Asia did not disappear from accounts of the war; it simply was not remembered as the enemy. As Kamei Katsuichirō put it: "In the course of World War II, the major enemy was China, the battle opponent over the ten years from the Manchurian Incident to the Pacific War. It was a characteristic of the defeat that we forgot that for a while." See Kamei, "Sengo Nihon ni tsuite no oboegaki," *Gendaishi no kadai* (Tokyo: Chūō Kōronsha, 1957).

63. Kamei, "Sengo Nihon ni tsuite no oboegaki," p. 268. Kamei does not seem to have thought the Philippines a colony.

64. Maruyama Masao argued in a similar vein a decade later. See his "Shisō no kotoba," *Shisō* 381 (March 1956):322–325. See also Rikki Kersten's analysis of the interrelated individual and associative aspects of the postwar Japanese discourse on political subjectivity—as she terms them, "personal autonomy" and "social autonomy"—in her *Democracy in Postwar Japan*. And see J. Victor Koshmann's analysis of Marxist themes in this discourse in his *Revolution and Subjectivity in Postwar Japan*.

65. The contending types of democratic understanding differentiated by Yoshino Sakuzō in the two terms *"minshushugi"* and *"minponshugi"* can be imputed to two distinct postwar personalities. The Niigata railway worker would exemplify the successful *minshushugi* type who, since citizens should be assertive and involved in their governance, felt that both he and the emperor should accept some responsibility for the wartime state's actions. The second *minponshugi* type seems to have become the majority. This personality was more amenable to victimhood since the democratic government would not require the person's active participation, only that his best interests be honored.

66. This ideology was the basis for Prime Minister Higashikuni's appeal for *sōzange,* which was rejected because spreading blame to everyone meant that those with relatively more responsibility escaped their fair share. This appeal could only succeed for those who either had no need to assign relative guilt or did not think there was really much to blame in the first place.

67. Yoshino believed that popular participation was probably advisable and inevitable but by no means completely necessary. He considered the emperor's will and the people's will to be naturally identical. See Yoshino Sakuzō, *Minpon shugi ron,* as abridged and translated in Ryusaku Tsunoda et al., eds., *Sources of Japanese Tradition,* vol. 2 (New York: Columbia University Press, 1958), pp. 217–239.

68. See W. Theodore de Bary's discussion of Chinese, Korean, and Japanese versions of dynastic institutions in his *East Asian Civilizations: A Dialogue in Five Stages* (Cambridge, Mass.: Harvard University Press, 1988), especially pp. 27–35.

69. The author of a patriotic pamphlet widely distributed to demobilized servicemen spoke from this tradition when he declared that defeat had brought two great blessings to Japan: SCAP had eliminated the evil powers from the country and removed the wall between the emperor and the people. See Soda Gen'yo, *Atarashiki inochi e*, as summarized in GHQ, SCAP, Civil Information and Education Section, Analysis and Research Division, "The Re-education of Japanese Ex-Servicemen" (July 25, 1946), Hoover Archives, Joseph C. Trainor Collection, Box 12. At least 50,000 copies of Soda's pamphlet were sold to the Second Demobilization Center, which was in charge of demobilizing and repatriating naval personnel.

Chapter 3: Hiroshima and *Yuiitsu no hibakukoku*

1. By the end of the decade, *Kuroi ame* was considered among the top three literary treatments of the Hiroshima bombing, along with Ōta Yōko's *Shikabane no machi* (City of Corpses; a highly censored version published in 1948) and Hara Tamiki's *Natsu no hana* (Flower of Summer, 1947). See *Shinchō Nihon bungaku shōjiten* (Tokyo: Shinchōsha, 1968). See also the analysis in Chapter 5.

2. See the frequent references to Japan's nonnuclear policies in the official prize announcement, presentation speech, and Satō's own acceptance speech in Irwin Abrams, ed, *Peace: Nobel Lectures in Peace, 1971–1980* (Singapore: World Scientific, 1997), pp. 59–82. See also Aase Lionaes' prize presentation speech in the archives at the Nobel Prize website, http://www.nobel.se/enm-index.html. Although his two predecessors made similar statements, Satō was the first to formalize as part of the ruling Liberal Democratic Party's plank the pledge not to possess, produce, or permit entry of nuclear weapons into Japan. He declared these principles in January 1968, ironically, even as his government continued to rely implicitly on the U.S. nuclear umbrella under the U.S.–Japan Security Treaty.

3. *Asahi shinbun*, Tokyo evening ed., March 14, 1955. See also "Tensei jingo," *Asahi shinbun*, March 15, 1955. The front page of the March 18 *Asahi* carried a political cartoon showing Hatoyama reclining on a bed of letters in the shape of a mushroom cloud. The caption made reference to a popular *manga* character and, loosely translated, read: "Hey, lazy Daddy, a whole lot of letters came protesting your 'A-bomb storage' slip" (*"Nonki na tōsan— 'genbaku chozō' hantai no tosho ga zuibun kita yo"*).

4. Kishi continually restated his nonnuclear position in response to Japan Socialist Party (JSP) questioning in the Diet. He included his opposition to entry of nuclear weapons in his 1958 New Year's statement. And in an interview with *Mainichi shinbun* on January 28, he said: "I entirely agree that weapon research should be undertaken so as to strengthen Japan's defense. But I believe that atomic energy should never be used for weapons—although the great powers are doing so. . . . Just as treaties prohibit use of poison gas and bacterial warfare, atomic weapons should be prohibited. In any case, I will neither allow the SDF to be equipped with nuclear weapons nor allow such weapons to be introduced to Japan" (translation from U.S. Forces Japan, Office of Information Services, "Japanese Press Translations"). On February 11, 1958, he was forced to admit to the Lower House Committee on the Budget that he could not prevent U.S. patrol planes stationed in Okinawa from carrying nuclear arms in Japanese air space (*Asahi shinbun*, February 12, 1958). For a discussion of Kishi's nuclear posi-

tion by an antinuclear activist see Imahori Seiji, *Gensuibaku kinshi undō* (Tokyo: Ushio Shuppansha, 1974), p. 85ff.

5. Hiroshima Mayor Hiraoka Takashi moved to address this lapse in his August 1991 Peace Statement. See *Chūgoku shinbun*, evening ed., August 6, 1991.

6. As translated in Robert J. C. Butow, *Japan's Decision to Surrender* (Stanford: Stanford University Press, 1954), p. 248. See also Herbert P. Bix, "The Shōwa Emperor's 'Monologue' and the Problem of War Responsibility," *Journal of Japanese Studies* 18(2) (Summer 1992):301.

7. On September 15, for example, only one month after the bombings, the Tokyo *Asahi shinbun* published former Education Minister Hatoyama Ichirō's comment that "the atomic bombing is more against international law than the use of poison gas and is a war crime." SCAP stopped the paper's presses for two days for publishing an item it considered detrimental to American authority (and to the forthcoming war crimes trials). The Osaka *Asahi* published the same quote but escaped reprimand because Allied troops had not yet occupied the Kansai area. The Osaka *Asahi* continued to report on the Hiroshima bomb damage, describing the nature of human casualties in the month before the Occupation started on September 25. The paper first published four photographs of Hiroshima and the atomic bomb victims on September 4, eventually printing a total of twenty-one photographs accounting for one-third of all photo space in that month's editions. SCAP censorship put an end to this reportage after September. See Osaka *Asahi shinbun*, August 18, 1992. Occupation censorship guidelines prohibited texts that could be construed as critical of the United States or its allies. See the censorship guidelines in the Gordon C. Prange Collection, University of Maryland.

8. See John Dower's elucidation of this ironic development in "The Bombed: Hiroshimas and Nagasakis in Japanese Memory," in Michael J. Hogan, ed., *Hiroshima in History and Memory* (Cambridge: Cambridge University Press, 1996), pp. 116–142 (especially pp. 121–124), originally published in *Diplomatic History* 19(2) (Spring 1995):275–295. The original guiding policies of the U.S. Occupation were demilitarization and democratization—goals that were transmuted into Japanese parlance in the shibboleth of rebuilding Japan into a "peaceful and cultural nation." Occupation censorship regarding Hiroshima tended to encourage the association of the bomb with scientific achievement just as surely as censored presentations of "smart bomb" technology in the Gulf War. Both suggest American morality in war. In his widely read column in the national daily *Asahi shinbun*, Aragaki Hideo reflected a common approach to Hiroshima when he characterized nuclear energy as a dangerous animal that could either be tamed or let run wild: a force that could shatter modern civilization as in Hiroshima or help unite the world in peace. See Aragaki Hideo, "Tensei jingo," *Asahi shinbun*, June 17, 1946.

9. I am indebted to John Treat for this insight. For an incisive discussion of the marginalization of atomic bomb literature see his *Writing Ground Zero: Japanese Literature and the Atomic Bomb* (Chicago: University of Chicago Press, 1995), pp. 83–120. See pp. 52–56 for his discussion of Hersey's *Hiroshima*.

10. This number, issued on the first anniversary of the atomic bombings after Japan's independence, was completely devoted to photographs of the aftermath.

11. Peace and culture were linked in the early postwar rhetoric for national reconstruction. The 1947 "Fundamental Law on Education," for example, set as education's goal the building of a peaceful and cultural nation. See Chapter 4. See also Walter

Edwards, "Buried Discourse: The Toro Archaeological Site and Japanese National Identity in the Early Postwar Period," *Journal of Japanese Studies* 17(1) (1991):1–23.

12. Kuno Osamu, "Heiwa no ronri, sensō no ronri," *Sekai* (November 1949), reprinted in Kuno Osamu, *Heiwa no ronri, sensō no ronri* (Tokyo: Iwanami Shoten, 1972), p. 6. Kuno was a graduate of the Philosophy Faculty of Kyoto University who spent two years in jail for violation of the Peace Protection Law. After the war, he was active in various peace movements including the Beheiren. He was also a member of the Peace Issues Discussion Group (Heiwa Mondai Danwakai), which was formed by Iwanami Bunko to unite progressive intellectuals in campaigning for a peace treaty embodying the Four Peace Principles (comprehensive peace treaty; no foreign military bases on Japanese soil; neutrality; and no remilitarization).

13. See Tanimoto's afterword, "Atogaki," in John Hersey, *Hiroshima*, trans. Tanimoto and Ishikawa Kin'ichi (Tokyo: Hōsei Daigaku Shuppankyoku, 1949), pp. 146–159.

14. *Asahi shinbun*, September 26, 1945, p. 1. Although in the days between defeat and occupation, members of the conservative elite considered condemning U.S. use of atomic bombs as a means of defending themselves from like charges of war crimes, once the Occupation began conservatives who escaped arrest or the purge of wartime leadership adopted a more conciliatory line. See Dower, "The Bombed," pp. 116–117.

15. The screenwriter Sawamura Ben, whose wartime films included *Shanghai rikusentai* and other militarist films, became known for writing passionate anti-Soviet and pro–Self Defense Force scripts in the postwar era. See Satō Tadao, "Gensuibaku to eiga," *Bungaku* 28(8) (August 1960):30–31. Elsewhere Satō notes that the president of the production company, Nagata Masaichi, had close ties to conservative politicians, especially later LDP kingpin Kōno Ichirō, and was well known for his behind-the-scenes maneuvering in conservative party circles. See Satō's entry on Nagata in Asahi Shinbunsha, ed., *Gendai Nihon Asahi jinbutsu jiten* (Tokyo: Asahi Shinbunsha, 1990), pp. 1154–1155.

16. *Nagasaki no uta wa wasureji* (Daiei, 1952); Satō, "Gensuibaku to eiga," pp. 30–31. Another narrative of reconciliation, Nagai Takashi's *Nagasaki no kane,* recounts disturbing human suffering caused by the Nagasaki bombing, but the net effect is non-condemnatory and rather benign for U.S.-Japanese relations. Nagai was mainly interested in rescuing spiritual meaning from the disaster—or at least affirmation of his faith in his Catholic religion and scientific progress. Occupation authorities also insisted that his book be published (in 1949) with an appendix outlining Japanese atrocities in the Philippines, probably with the idea that the atomic bombings were just retribution but also suggesting a quid-pro-quo. See William Johnston's introduction to his English translation of Nagai's book, *Bells of Nagasaki* (Tokyo: Kodansha International, 1984), pp. vi–vii. Also see Treat, *Writing Ground Zero*, pp. 310–315.

17. Pressure from Occupation and Japanese government authorities kept moderate socialist and other labor organizations wary of joining in such communist initiatives as the Stockholm Appeal, an early petition movement calling for a ban on nuclear weapons and labeling their first use a crime against humanity. See Imahori, *Gensuibaku kinshi undō*, p. 8. Yoshida's resistance to rearmament was founded on pragmatic diplomatic reasons rather than a commitment to peace, despite his tactical manipulation of socialist pacifist protest in order to convince John Foster Dulles of the threat that significant remilitarization posed to the Japanese social fabric. Moreover, Yoshida gave Dulles other reasons against rapid rearmament: Japan could not afford it, the militarists

might attempt to regain power, and it would hinder Japan's international rehabilitation by breeding antipathy among other countries in the region. See Dower, *Empire and Aftermath;* and see Igarashi Takeshi, "Peace-Making and Party Politics: The Formation of the Domestic Foreign-Policy System in Postwar Japan," *Journal of Japanese Studies* 11(2) (Summer 1985):323–356.

18. Kuno Osamu, socialist intellectual activist, was typical in his understanding that the laboring classes had to aggressively resist the state's infringements on their liberties during peacetime, for in doing so they developed the ability to resist the state's claims on them to fight wars. See Kuno Osamu, "Heiwa no ronri, sensō no ronri," *Sekai* (November 1949); also in Kuno, *Heiwa no ronri, sensō no ronri,* pp. 1–24. Kuno argued in a 1951 essay that the peaceful potential of nuclear energy was being "torn asunder by the reality of rivalry among states *(kokka tairitsu)*." See Kuno Osamu, "Futatsu no heiwa wa sekai heiwa ni tsunagaru ka," *Sekai* (November 1951); reprinted in Kuno, *Heiwa no ronri, sensō no ronri,* pp. 25–44.

19. Satō, "Gensuibaku to eiga," p. 32. Yagi Yasutarō was a well-known leftist screenwriter who chaired the early postwar communist Nihon Eiga Engeki Rōdōkumiai (Motion Picture and Drama Employees Union). See also Joseph L. Anderson and Donald Richie, *The Japanese Film: Art and Industry* (Rutland: Tuttle, 1959), pp. 218–219, and David Desser, "Japan: An Ambivalent Nation, an Ambivalent Cinema," *Swords and Ploughshares* 9(3–4) (Spring–Summer 1995).

20. *Genbaku no ko,* Kindai Eiga Kyōkai/Gekidan Mingei, 1952; Anderson and Richie, *Japanese Film,* pp. 218–219.

21. "Tensei jingo," *Asahi shinbun,* August 24, 1952. The film's producer/director was Yoshimura Kōsaburō. The idea that the Hiroshima and Nagasaki bombings were a special Japanese experience appeared again in the June 21, 1953, column on Ethel and Julius Rosenberg's execution. In this essay on McCarthyism and declining civil liberties in the United States, Aragaki associates by juxtaposition the Rosenbergs' victimhood with Japanese victimhood. The essay begins: "The Rosenbergs, atomic bomb spies, were executed by electric chair at Singsing prison just recently on the night of the nineteenth. Over three hundred thousand Japanese of Hiroshima and Nagasaki died directly from the atomic bomb, but here two lives were burned out by electricity for the sin of selling American atomic bomb secrets to the Soviet Union." See Aragaki Hideo, *Tensei jingo* II (Tokyo: Asahi Shinbunsha, 1981), pp. 226–227. The Rosenbergs' own book in translation, *Ai wa shi o koete,* ranked second on the Shuppan Nyūsusha bestseller list for 1954.

22. "Through atomic energy, humankind is on the threshold of attaining the surest means for realizing his long-held dreams. But instead at this very moment, atomic energy is being torn asunder by the reality of opposing states *(kokka tairitsu),* ending all dreams, and turning into a tool of complete self-destruction pulling all mankind into the grave." See Kuno Osamu, "Futatsu no heiwa," *Sekai* (November 1951); reprinted in Kuno, *Heiwa no ronri, sensō no ronri,* p. 26.

23. Kuno, "Futatsu no heiwa," pp. 27–29. Kuno argued that the Japanese had significant status as the first (rather than only) atomic victims since future use of atomic bombs seemed all too likely. As a future nuclear exchange became increasingly unlikely, the uniqueness of Japanese atomic victimhood made Hiroshima and Nagasaki that much more important as symbols in Japanese pacifist nationalism.

24. In a panel discussion among left-wing intellectuals organized by the progressive journal *Kaizō* in early 1954, there was a general lament over the inability to rally

many people to the peace movement. Economist Toyoda Shirō, for example, expressed his frustration in failing to attract many people to a Shinjuku Peace Meeting with a reduced-price admission to the film *Hiroshima*. See Kuno Osamu et al., "Nihon minzoku no enerugii, II," *Kaizō* (February 1954):84–96.

25. Kumakura Hiroyasu, *Gensuibaku kinshi undō 30 nen* (Tokyo: Rōdōkyōiku Sentaa, 1978), p. 34ff. Kumakura discusses ambiguity about the mission of the early peace organizations, which led to confusion and disagreement over priorities. This confusion was exacerbated by internal Japan Communist Party (JCP) divisiveness caused by Cominform criticism of party leader Nozaka Sanzō's parliamentary tactics.

26. Kumakura, *Gensuibaku kinshi undō 30 nen*, pp. 16–21. SCAP pressure—or fear of it (that is, self-censorship)—may account for the failure to mention atomic bombing or nuclear weapons. Regardless of the cause, the Japanese public was not exposed to negative news about the Hiroshima and Nagasaki bombings through the peace movement until later.

27. This predecessor to the World Peace Council was formed in April 1945 in Paris but was forced to relocate its headquarters to Prague. Its first world convention was also scheduled to be held only in Paris, but a simultaneous convention was quickly organized in Prague to allow participation by the communist-bloc delegates who were denied entry by the French government. See Hiroshima Heiwa Bunka Sentaa, ed., *Heiwa jiten* (Tokyo: Keiso Shobō, 1991), p. 61.

28. For the Tokyo meeting's public declaration, the eight-point "Outline for Peace" *(Heiwa kōryō)*, see Kumakura, *Gensuibaku kinshi undō 30 nen*, pp. 21–22.

29. The official name in April 1949 was the "Heiwa o Mamoru Kai Junbikai," a temporary committee formed to organize a Japanese association to maintain peace. JAMP was formally established in February 1950. See *Heiwa jiten*, p. 65.

30. See Kumakura, *Gensuibaku kinshi undō 30 nen*, pp. 22–24. The communist backing of this appeal is evident in the geographic distribution of signatures: 3 million in the United States, 15 million in France, and an impressive 115 million in the USSR. JCMP was a subsidiary organ of JAMP. The Stockholm Appeal was the product of the March 1950 meeting of the executive committee of the World Peace Council. For an international perspective on the early antinuclear movement see Lawrence S. Wittner, *One World or None: A History of the World Nuclear Disarmament Movement Through 1953* (Stanford: Stanford University Press, 1993); see p. 182ff. for the Stockholm Appeal and the World Peace Council.

31. Imahori, *Gensuibaku kinshi undō*, p. 8. The efficacy of the Red Purge in suppressing the more radical opposition should not be discounted. After the start of fighting on the Korean peninsula in 1950, even the peace ceremonies in Hiroshima were prohibited.

32. For a discussion of the influential Peace Issues Discussion Group (Heiwa Mondai Danwakai) and the politics of peace at the end of the Occupation see Igarashi, "Peace-Making and Party Politics."

33. Interestingly, he complains in passing that the peace movement in Japan is discounted as merely a movement of the left. See Ōyama Ikuo, "Nihon wa heiwa no kichi tare—Molotov, Kim Il-sung, Chou Enlai kaiken kara," *Kaizō* (February 1954):2–11.

34. In September 1951, Abe Yoshishige and the *Bunkajin* Council for Promoting a Comprehensive Peace Treaty included protection of the Constitution in a declaration for a comprehensive peace treaty and neutrality. See Kumakura, *Gensuibaku kinshi undō 30 nen*, p. 40.

35. Kuno et al., "Nihon minzoku no enerugii, II," pp. 84–96; for Tsurumi's quote see p. 95.

36. See Dower, *Empire and Aftermath*, p. 450.

37. Imahori Seiji, *Gensuibaku jidai*, vol. 2 (Tokyo: San'ichi Shobō, 1959–1960), p. 128.

38. After this incident many who had entered Hiroshima within a month of the bombing began to attribute minor health problems to radiation exposure—so many, in fact, that their concern came to be called "Hiroshima neurosis." See Fujishima Udai, Maruyama Kunio, and Murakami Hyōe, "Hiroshima—sono go 13 nen," *Chūō kōron* 842 (August 1958):249. The central character in Ibuse's *Black Rain* was a victim of such radioactive fallout. The novel affirmed this sense of "connectedness" that all Japanese were atomic victims. (See Chapter 5.) Godzilla, having been roused from his deep-sea slumber by the Bikini test, made his first appearance in movie theaters in October 1954. Breathing radioactive fire, Godzilla terrorizes Tokyoites in ways impervious to conventional defense measures, yet the film encourages viewers to relive vicariously their own war memories and reconstruct them in the context of a nuclear victimhood. In one particularly suggestive scene, for example, young trolley-car commuters wonder if they will have to evacuate the city again as they presumably did as children during the war.

39. Interestingly, its resolution was worded in a manner that mirrored the dichotomous approach to nuclear energy seen in the April 1954 *Kaizō*. The resolution demanded two things: "a ban on the use of nuclear energy for nuclear weapons; and the peaceful use of nuclear energy." See Imahori, *Gensuibaku jidai*, 2:128. The Diet resolution called for international control of nuclear energy, including testing.

40. Yasui later wrote that he thought the best way to reflect the will of hundreds of thousands of people was through a petition campaign. See Yasui Kaoru, *Minshū to heiwa: Mirai o tsukuru mono* (Tokyo: Otsuki Shoten, 1955), p. 55.

41. See Yasui Kaoru, "Shizukanaru shomei undō," *Kaizō* (August 1954):134–138, for his contemporary account of the movement's progress.

42. Although the parallel is not generally recognized, two things about the National Council as a popular movement make it a forerunner of the anti–Vietnam War Beheiren movement of the 1960s, which was noted for its innovative organization. First, efforts were made to choose representatives who had not been linked to peace movements beforehand—a big factor in Beheiren's choice of the writer Oda Makoto. Second, care was taken to guarantee that the National Council would perform only a communications role. Yasui wrote that these safeguards were necessary to prevent the national organization from being drawn into a factional or party fracas. This was a real concern since not all the local movements had the grassroots beginnings of Suginami. Some were organized by town or ward chiefs and hence were tinged with political considerations. In any case, the National Council remained above these entanglements and the local movements retained their autonomy. See Yasui, *Minshū to heiwa*, p. 76ff. For Beheiren see Thomas Havens, *Fire Across the Sea* (Princeton: Princeton University Press, 1987).

43. Yasui, *Minshū to heiwa*, pp. 64–67. Imahori describes the background behind these activities in *Gensuibaku jidai*, 2:137ff.

44. On the growth of Gensuikyō see Imahori, *Gensuibaku kinshi undō*, and Kumakura, *Gensuibaku kinshi undō 30 nen*. The cabinet sponsored the first rudimentary *hibakusha* aid bill, which became law in the Twenty-sixth Diet in 1957. For com-

plaints over local conservative politicians' use of Gensuikyō affiliates for political gains see Arase Yutaka, "Jihyō: Gensuibaku kinshi undō no chokumen suru kadai," *Shisō* 406 (April 1958):107. Conversely, the ruling conservative Liberal Democratic Party leadership complained at times about local LDP time and money going to Gensuikyō activities. See George O. Totten and Tamio Kawakami, "Gensuikyō and the Peace Movement in Japan," *Asian Survey* 4(5) (May 1964):840.

45. Yasui, *Minshū to heiwa*, p. 16ff. For an analysis of Yasui's civic activism as it relates to his intellectual development see my "Yasui Kaoru: Citizen-Scholar in War and Peace," *Japan Forum* 12 (2000):1–14. On the politics behind Yasui's purge see Hata Ikuhiko, "Shōwashi no nazo o tou, Dai-30-kai. Kyōshoku tsuihō—Yasui Kaoru no baai," *Seiron* 230 (October 1991):350–363. Yasui was only one of many progressive intellectuals who found themselves working for grassroots democratic development. Leslie Pincus has shown how Nakai Masakazu also worked for a "revolution of consciousness" *(ishiki kakumei)* for the laborers and smallholders in Onomichi in late 1945 through 1947. See "Nakai Masakazu and the Postwar Hiroshima Culture Movement," paper presented at the Association for Asian Studies annual meeting, Chicago, 1997. See also Yasui's farewell letter at the time of his purge: Yasui Kaoru, "Gakumon to ryōshin no jiyū," *Tōkyō daigaku shinbun* (March 18, 1948), reprinted in *Michi — Yasui Kaoru Inochi no kiseki* (Tokyo: Hōsei Daigaku Shuppankyoku, 1983), pp. 44–47.

46. See E. H. Carr, *The New Society* (London: Macmillan, 1951), especially pp. 74–75, for a revealing assessment of the emotional appeal required for a successful mass movement.

47. Yasui, *Minshū to heiwa*, pp. 54–56.

48. Ibid., p. 90. On the question of democratic subjectivity in postwar Japan see Rikki Kersten, *Democracy in Postwar Japan: Maruyama Masao and the Search for Autonomy* (London: Routledge, 1996); and J. Victor Koschmann, *Revolution and Subjectivity in Postwar Japan* (Chicago: University of Chicago Press, 1997). Carr had emphasized in *New Society*, as did many others of the day, the emergence of former colonial peoples of Asia and Africa as driving forces in postwar international society; Carr, *New Society*, pp. 80–99.

49. Yasui, "Shizukanaru shomei undō," pp. 135–137; Yasui, *Minshū to heiwa*, pp. 59–61. The three slogans that preceded the Suginami Appeal showed the council's concern to avoid factional infighting and maintain unity of purpose by keeping the movement focused on the simple rejection of nuclear weapons. The first slogan declared the need for "all the Japanese people" *(zenkokumin)*, regardless of faction or class, to be united in rejecting hydrogen bombs. The second slogan represented their global ambitions for the movement as well as their wariness of the divisive political problems of the U.S. relationship. In the third slogan, they tried to keep the movement humane and protect it from turning into a violent political movement. See Appendix 2.

50. Yasui, *Minshū to heiwa*, pp. 12–13. This juxtaposition of reason with emotion suggests the influence of E. H. Carr. In his chapter "From Individualism to Mass Democracy," Carr outlines his ideas on the role of reason in earlier democracies, which had been controlled essentially by an elite class, and the role of fear and other emotions in the new mass democracies. Carr placed his hopes in the power of reason, via the education of the masses, to bring the different social classes together peacefully, but he recognized that rational argument alone was not enough to persuade masses of people. See Carr, *New Society*, pp. 61–79.

51. See Gensuibaku Kinshi Sekaitaikai Nihon Junbikai (Japan Committee for the

World Conference Against Atomic and Hydrogen Bombs), ed., *Genbaku yurusumaji: Gensuibaku kinshi sekaitaikai no kiroku* (Tokyo, 1955); for the Shiga representative's comments see pp. 34 and 109; for Yasui's summation see pp. 112–115. Despite the inherently universal appeal of a ban on nuclear weapons—indeed, despite Yasui's eventual goal of a global movement against nuclear weapons—Japanese parochial appropriation of nuclear victimhood is evident in mainstream (that is, politically moderate) discussions. After Kuboyama Aikichi died in September 1954, for example, columnist Aragaki Hideo wrote about nuclear fallout as if it affected only Japan: "From the North and from the South, from both the USSR and the U.S., we cannot just sit still while the Japanese archipelago is put in the dark valley of hydrogen bomb testing. . . . Bomb testing and production must cease lest humanity sink into hopeless hell." Aragaki prefaced this statement with the observation that the Japanese became the first "ethnic nation" *(minzoku)* to have lives taken by atomic and hydrogen bombs. See "Tensei jingo," *Asahi shinbun,* September 25, 1954.

52. A record of all speeches made at the 1955 convention was published in book form and sold by the labor federation Sōhyō. See *Genbaku yurusumaji,* p. 114. In a passage from *New Society* that must have assuaged Yasui's regret over his naive wartime collaboration, and which Yasui often cited, E. H. Carr unequivocally recognizes that the militarist Japanese state's action in World War II "brought the colonial revolution to a head." Carr contends that the "peoples of Asia, though divided among themselves by as many differences and mutual antagonisms as the peoples of Europe, are at present united in their desire to be rid of European political or military interference. Whatever acts of aggression may be committed in Asia . . . from the Asiatic standpoint, any white armies fighting against Asiatic armies on the soil of Asia are *ipso facto* the aggressors." At heart a patriot, Yasui seems to have accepted what in some Marxist contexts would be condemned as bourgeois nationalist tendencies in the ban-the-bomb movement. See Carr, *New Society,* pp. 92–93.

53. Kevin M. Doak, "What Is a Nation and Who Belongs? National Narratives and the Ethnic Imagination in Twentieth-Century Japan," *American Historical Review* 102(2) (April 1997):283–309, especially p. 302ff. Yasui's linkage here of the civic and ethnic terms for the Japanese nation suggests both his suppport for the civic foundations of the postwar political order as well as his conception of a fundamentally ethnic basis for that sovereign people.

54. Kano Masanao and Nishikawa Masao reflect on the relatively recent realization that the ban-the-bomb movement was a nationalist endeavor; see "Dō toraeru ka— 'Kindai' to kindaishi kenkyū," *Rekishi hyōron* 562 (February 1997):17–18.

55. Noma Hiroshi, "Genbaku ni tsuite," *Bungakkai* (March 1953); reprinted in Kaku-sensō no kiken o uttaeru bungakusha, ed., *Nihon genbaku bungaku,* vol. 15: *Hyōron/essei* (Tokyo: Horupu Shuppan, 1983), pp. 145–148.

56. See, for example, Robert Jay Lifton and Greg Mitchell, *Hiroshima in America: Fifty Years of Denial* (New York: Putnam, 1995), and Robert Jay Lifton and Eric Markusen, *The Genocidal Mentality: Nazi Holocaust and Nuclear Threat* (New York: Basic Books, 1990). See also Lifton's pathbreaking and still essential psychological study of Hiroshima *hibakusha: Death in Life: Survivors of Hiroshima* (New York: Random House, 1967), reprinted by University of North Carolina Press, 1991.

57. In coded praise of the Soviet socialist system and condemnation of the U.S. intention to "use the hydrogen bomb as a weapon to subjugate the world," Noma juxtaposes the U.S. bomb tests with the Soviet construction of a nuclear power generation plant:

It's the same nuclear energy, but on the one hand it leads to the destruction of humankind, on the other to humankind's unlimited development. . . . Facing the danger of the annihilation of humankind, we have found a way to join the strength of all humankind, and therein we can see for the first time the path toward humankind's unlimited development and happiness. It is precisely by joining together all our strength to ban the hydrogen bomb that threatens humankind's destruction that for the first time we overcome the contradiction between these two aspects of nuclear energy—the destruction of humankind versus unlimited happiness—and grasp in an immediate sense the position to move forward toward the unlimited happiness of humankind. We can sense with our own bodies, our own five senses, that [unlimited happiness] lies with the Soviets. This really cannot be hidden *(ōikakusu koto no dekinai koto de aru)* from us who are every day forced to drink tea and eat vegetables that have radioactivity in them.

See Noma Hiroshi, "Suibaku to ningen—Atarashii ningen no musubitsuki," *Bungaku no tomo* (September 1954); reprinted in *Nihon genbaku bungaku*, 15:149–153. See also Noma Hiroshi, "Jinrui ishiki no hassei," *Bungei* (December 1954), reprinted in *Nihon genbaku bungaku*, 15:154–157; "Jinrui no tachiba," *Sekai* (January 1955), reprinted in *Nihon genbaku bungaku*, 15:158–166. Noma avoided the potential conflict between national consciousness and human consciousness by simply commenting that global peace movements necessarily assure the sovereignty of ethnic nations *(minzoku jishu-ken no kakuritsu)* and the independence of ethnic nations *(minzoku no dokuritsu)*.

58. Yasui later wrote that he advocated inserting this guarantee in the final drafts of the prospectus; Yasui, *Minshū to heiwa*, pp. 64–65.

59. Ibid., p. 68. For a concise analysis of communist-led antinuclear movements in this era see Lawrence S. Wittner, *Resisting the Bomb: A History of the World Nuclear Disarmament Movement* (Stanford: Stanford University Press, 1997), pp. 86–92.

60. Yasui, *Minshū to heiwa*, p. 85.

61. For a discussion of the early state construction of Japanese feminine ideal see Sharon H. Nolte and Sally Ann Hastings, "The Meiji State's Policy Toward Women, 1890–1910," in Gail Lee Bernstein, ed., *Recreating Japanese Women, 1600–1945* (Berkeley: University of California Press, 1991), pp. 151–174. Joanne Izbicki has shown how in early postwar Japanese films women were often portrayed to be the natural leaders toward a more progressive future: "Heading for the Hills: Marriage and Democracy in Japanese Cinema," paper presented at the 112th annual meeting of the American Historical Association, 1998. Regarding the Freudian association of masculinity with war in Japanese film see also Marie Thorsten Morimoto, "The 'Peace Dividend' in Japanese Cinema: Metaphors of a Demilitarized Nation," in Wimal Dissanayake, ed., *Colonialism and Nationalism in Asian Cinema* (Bloomington: Indiana University Press, 1994), pp. 11–29. In *Japanese Film*, Anderson and Richie write acerbically about the *"hahamono"* genre of film in which sympathy for the suffering of mothers seems to dissolve questions of sons' war responsibility. These films "showed how mother still loved and waited for her imprisoned boy, no matter how many people he had tortured, and which sought to prove that imprisoning mothers' sons was very immoral since their captivity caused mothers so much anguish" (p. 221). There is of course a large body of literature on the gendered construction of war as a masculine endeavor contrasted to peace as a feminine enterprise. For two suggestive discussions of women as symbolic war victims in national narratives of postwar Germany see Petra Goedde,

"From Villains to Victims: Fraternization and the Feminization of Germany, 1945–1947," *Diplomatic History* 23(1) (Winter 1999):1–20; and Elizabeth Heinemann, "The Hour of the Woman: Memories of Germany's 'Crisis Years' and West German National Identity," *American Historical Review* 101(2) (April 1996):354–395.

62. Dower, "The Bombed," p. 134. Such iconography has a long history in Japan, appearing for example in a description of the social and natural dislocation attending famine in the middle ages. See A. L. Sadler's translation of "Hōjōki" in Kamo Chōmei, *Ten Foot Square Hut and Tales of the Heike* (Tokyo: Tuttle, 1972), p. 8. I am indebted to Erik Lofgren for this reference.

63. It is a measure of the special honor given motherhood in Japan that Japanese Catholics are known for their special reverence for the Mother Mary. The Nagasaki bomb damage was centered in the city's Catholic neighborhoods.

64. *Genbaku yurusumaji*, pp. 20–22.

65. Kamei Katsuichirō, "Nihon no tachiba kara gensuibaku ni tsuite," in *Kamei Katsuichirō zenshu*, vol. 19 (Tokyo: Kodansha, 1973), pp. 222–226, originally published as part of the column "Shakai jihyō" in *Kasutomusu* in 1956–1957.

66. Lisa Yoneyama, *Hiroshima Traces: Time, Space, and the Dialectics of Memory* (Berkeley: University of California Press, 1999), pp. 187–210. Gensuikin was a socialist-sponsored ban-the-bomb organization formed in the early 1960s. Honda Ishirō's original *Gojira* of 1954 includes a scene in which concerned middle-aged women Diet members righteously challenge conservative male majority members who seek to keep confidential the news that Godzilla was unleashed by an American hydrogen bomb test. Otherwise there is no American presence in this film. See *Gojira* (Tōhō, 1954).

67. Treat, *Writing Ground Zero*, pp. 364–368.

68. Yasui, *Minshū to heiwa*, pp. 13–15. In loose translation, the complete quotation is: "I who have survived / more than anything want to be human / more than anything else as a mother / red-cheeked infant / and the blue sky which lies over our many futures / one day suddenly is rent apart / when our many futures are about to be extinguished / the tears I shed over the dead bodies / I will pour over the living / more than anything I oppose war. / A mother rejects her child's death / even if that is punished under some name / that day's hell is burned onto my retinas / I will not flee, I will not hide . . . as a surviving witness of Hiroshima I will / go anywhere and testify / and sing with all my life / 'let us renounce war.' "

69. Yoneyama, *Hiroshima Traces*, p. 208.

70. Ibid., p. 202. The Hiroshima Maidens program was lead by Norman Cousins in the United States and by Rev. Tanimoto Kiyoshi in Japan. For U.S. government anxiety and ultimate satisfaction with this program see Wittner, *Resisting the Bomb*, pp. 157–159. Sonya O. Rose has written suggestively of the power of a masculinized reason and community-inspired moral self-discipline in constructions of proper women's citizenship in wartime Great Britain; see "Sex, Citizenship, and the Nation in World War II Britain," *American Historical Review* 103(4) (October 1998):1147–1176. In postwar Japanese discourse on peace, mothers and wives were portrayed as the virtuous women whose plight symbolized the nation's nuclear victimhood—though the source of their virtue lay more in their emotional commitment to their families' well-being rather than their rational commitment to community welfare. In regard to Rose's discussion of the association of reason with European men and the body with women and racialized men, it is interesting to note that U.S. Secretary of State John Foster Dulles understood the Japanese discomfort with nuclear weapons to be "more emotional than reasonable.

The American people perhaps reason about this, while the Japanese see the problem emotionally." See U.S. Department of State, "Memorandum of a Conversation, Secretary Dulles' Office, Department of State, Washington, September 23, 1957," *Foreign Relations of the United States, 1955–1957, Volume XXIII* (Washington: Department of State, 1991), pp. 497–498.

71. During the student protests in the late 1960s, otherwise radical male student activists at Kyoto University still expected their female peers to perform such womanly supporting roles as making sandwiches and serving tea (personal interview, Ms. Tomoko Nakajima, May 1992). See also the discussion in Chapter 5 of Ibuse Masuji's *Black Rain* for another important work that domesticated Hiroshima within a conservative social framework.

72. Imahori thinks this was intentional—that the leaders purposely avoided pushing for aid to *hibakusha*—and as evidence he suggests they directed the petition against "hydrogen bombs" *(suibaku)* instead of atomic and hydrogen bombs *(gensuibaku)*. It is perplexing that the petition published in August 1954 called for banning the hydrogen bomb, but by August 1955, with the publication of Yasui's *Minshū to heiwa* on the occasion of the first World Convention in Hiroshima, all published texts, including Imahori's own *Gensuibaku jidai* II (1960), printed "atomic and hydrogen bombs." Neither Imahori nor Yasui even mention the switch. See Appendix 2.

73. Imahori, *Gensuibaku kinshi undō*, pp. 9–11.

74. Yasui, *Minshū to heiwa*, p. 68.

75. Ibid., p. 79.

76. See the Democratic Party's founding charter; Nihon Minshutō, Jimukyoku, *Nihon minshutō* (1954–1956).

77. Yasui, *Minshū to heiwa*, p. 67.

78. The speech was made on January 22, 1955, in the 21st Diet; quote taken from Japan Democratic Party publication, *Dai 21 Kokkai ni okeru Hatoyama naikaku shiseihōshin enzetsushū*, 1955.

79. Martin E. Weinstein, *Japan's Postwar Defense Policy, 1947–1968* (New York: Columbia University Press, 1971), p. 80ff.

80. Hatoyama did not plan to be quite so blunt. When asked a direct question by one of the foreign journalists, instead of merely sidestepping the question he answered: "I don't expect the condition of 'peace based on strength' will last long. But if you admit the reasonableness of 'peace based on strength,' then I'd have to allow it." See *Asahi shinbun*, Tokyo evening ed., March 14, 1955. Hatoyama clarified what he meant two days later: it was a hypothetical answer to a hypothetical question, he emphasized, and said that there had not been any such request. He said storing nuclear weapons was thinkable only if you granted that a world peace based on strength was justified. If nuclear weapons threatened world peace, they should not exist. Although Hatoyama implied that he felt "peace based on strength" was untenable in the long run, he was committed to its epitome: the U.S. nuclear umbrella.

81. On July 28, the U.S. Army announced it would equip its forces in Japan with "Honest John" missiles, which were designed to be nuclear-tipped. Appearing before the Foreign Affairs Committee of the House of Councilors, Hatoyama assured Socialist Diet members that the missiles were not nuclear-tipped. In May, he continued, the foreign minister had reached an agreement with U.S. Ambassador Allison that the United States would consult the Japanese government before bringing nuclear weapons into Japan. Hatoyama then made the statement on resorting to nuclear weapons in an emergency. See Weinstein, *Japan's Postwar Defense Policy*, p. 80ff.

82. The three-day convention was held in Hiroshima starting on August 6; supporting conventions were held in various Japanese cities and abroad.

83. See *Heiwa jiten*, p. 68; all of Imahori Seiji's treatments; and Tōyama Shigeki, "Sōgō bukai hōkoku: Sengo heiwa undō no rekishi," *Rekishigaku kenkyū* 297 (February 1965):47–51.

84. "The power of public opinion that arose in this petition movement based on humanism moved the Japanese government. The Yoshida cabinet, which took the attitude of cooperation with atomic bomb experiments, fell and the Hatoyama cabinet was established." Yasui could not point to any specific measure Hatoyama's administration had taken. See *Genbaku yurusumaji*, p. 6.

85. His greeting was followed by former Prime Minister (1945) Higashikuni Naruhiko's short description of atomic bombs as shameful and a plea to remember the souls of its victims. After resigning the premiership, Higashikuni formed a new religion in 1948 and was active in religious affairs until his death in 1990 at the age of 102.

86. The people in his prefecture were "against colonies, for complete independence, and against unfair treaties," but they could not support a mass movement that was too explicit in its goals. See *Genbaku yurusumaji*, p. 62.

87. Ibid., p. 114.

88. The reference was to the Vienna Appeal, which was the main petition abroad. It did not get as many signatures in Japan, however, because Yasui opposed it on the strategic rationale mentioned earlier: it might have diffused the movement's momentum with complex and divisive issues.

89. It is clear from the context and language that the declaration is referring to the struggle against U.S. military base expansions in Japan. The words used for nuclear weapon stockpiling actually mean "storage of nuclear weapons" *(genshi heiki no chozō)* —the issue that Hatoyama fumbled in March 1955—and the antibase movement in Japan took off when Uchinada and Sunakawa bases were expanded.

90. Opposition to nuclear weapons and aid for *hibakusha* were called the two wheels for the movement in the late 1950s. Nonpartisan support resulted in a cabinet-sponsored bill that became law in the Twenty-sixth Diet in 1957.

91. Lifton, *Death in Life*, p. 246, credits a Christian "day-laborer" activist with the intitiative in mobilizing support for the children's monument.

92. See Chapter 4 for an analysis of postwar textbook treatments. In 1985, some 161,000 elementary, 156,000 middle, and 257,000 high school students visited Hiroshima's peace museum as part of official school groups, accounting respectively for 11 percent, 11 percent, and 18 percent (rounded numbers) of the total 1.442 million visitors. Some 57 percent of the high school visitors were from the Kantō region. See Hiroshima Heiwa Kinen Shiryokan, ed., *30-nen no ayumi* (n.d.). Until it was revamped in the early 1990s, this museum presented a victim narrative silent on Japanese predations during the war that preceded the bombings and silent, too, regarding Hiroshima's prebomb status as a military headquarters for continental operations ever since the Emperor Meiji's days there during the first Sino-Japanese War in 1894. Meeting halls and convention facilities accommodate numerous peace symposia, and memorial ceremonies on August 6 are always reported in the national media.

93. Fujishima et al., "Hiroshima—Sono go 13 nen," *Chūō kōron* 842 (August 1958):264; the warning is on pp. 267–268.

94. For an informed and discerning discussion of defeat as a new beginning for the Japanese see Carol Gluck, "The Idea of Showa," *Daedalus* 119(3) (Summer 1990): 1–26.

95. See E. J. Hobsbawm, *Nations and Nationalism Since 1780: Program, Myth, and Reality* (Cambridge: Cambridge University Press, 1990).

96. Sakamoto actually termed the Japanese preoccupation with their victimization at the hands of militarism the "psychology of victimhood" *(higaisha shinri)*. See "Heiwa undō ni okeru shinri to ronri," *Sekai* (August 1962), reprinted in Sakamoto Yoshikazu, *Shinpan Kakujidai no kokusai seiji* (Tokyo: Iwanami Shoten, 1982), p. 130: "For example, leaving aside *for the moment* considerations for Japan's external security, the opposition to rearmament which was one base of the total peace treaty movement relied *in actuality* on the people's strong psychology of victimhood toward militarism; and when this victim psychology weakens, remilitarization will be recognized *in actuality* [without thoroughly addressing] the question of its international impact."

97. Sakamoto Yoshikazu, "Kenryoku seiji to heiwa undō," *Sekai* 191 (November 1961):20. Where Sakamoto is generally favorably disposed toward atomic victim consciousness, Shimizu Ikutarō was becoming vaguely suspicious of it. See Shimizu Ikutarō, "Kore made no jūnen kore kara no jūnen—Zenmen kōwaronsha no tachiba kara," *Sekai* 162 (June 1959):42–51, especially pp. 49–50.

98. Shimizu Ikutarō, the leading progressive sociologist who later became an avid promoter of conservative and traditional Japan, noted that victim consciousness *(higaisha ishiki)* tended to weaken "victimizer consciousness" *(kagaisha ishiki)* as early as June 1959. See Shimizu, "Kore made no jūnen," p. 49; see also the quotation in Chapter 1.

99. This sense of irresponsibility was precisely Itami Mansaku's point of concern (Chapter 2).

100. Yasui, *Minshū to heiwa,* pp. 90–91.

101. Fukuda had just returned from a year's stay in the United States on a Fulbright scholarship. He faulted the activists—in protests against military base expansion, for example—for essentially trying to establish this link even in local issues that were more easily solved in isolation from national issues. He wrote that the movement was ineffective for two reasons. The obvious reason was that they were ideologically absolutist—phrasing the issues as "peace or not" or "communism versus capitalism." While claiming to be for peaceful coexistence between the socialist and capitalist worlds, in reality they credit only the socialist world with sincerity and condemn the capitalist world for its militarism (p. 27). The second reason is more subtle: in trying to gather the largest numbers to their cause, they connected anything and everything to peace and in the process neglected the best resolution to the local problem. See Fukuda Tsuneari, "Heiwa-ron no susumekata ni tsuite no gimon: Dō kakugo o kimetara ii ka," *Chūō kōron* (December 1954):18–30.

102. Fukuda, "Heiwa-ron," p. 26.

103. The *Asahi shinbun* editorial for August 15, 1964, dealt with the weakness of Japanese sense of nationhood—a subject of extensive debate in the general interest journals in the early 1960s. After stating that the "Japanese are the only nation to have been atom bombed" *(yuiitsu no hibakukokumin),* the editorial described the contemporary conditions on the extremes of the ideological spectrum: "There are some among the conservatives who intend to take advantage of nationalism to revive the old order, and the progressives lean toward opposing everything in delusions of victimhood." Seki Yoshihiko expressed this same sentiment in his introduction to the inaugural issue of the *Journal of Social and Political Ideas in Japan* 1(1) (April 1963):5: "Pro-

gressive intellectuals here place all their faith in the Japanese peace movement, which calls for the abolition of armaments, especially atomic arms. They take this rather general position for the attainment of peace instead of trying to eliminate the causes of conflict one by one."

104. The Hatoyama government, which was trying to establish a foreign policy independent of the United States and had pledged cooperation with the ban-the-bomb movement, was wary about acting in the real world on its espoused theoretical ideals. The government took no action to protest the United States' continued hydrogen bomb testing after the Diet's February resolution calling for an end to nuclear bomb testing, for example, as it was committed to the U.S. alliance for Japan's security. In a literal interpretation of the resolution's wording, the Foreign Ministry's Chief of Euro-American Affairs Bureau told the Lower House that the ministry did not protest because the resolution called for a cessation of nuclear testing *through an international agreement,* not that the current testing be stopped. See Imahori, *Gensuibaku jidai,* 2:142. Miyazawa Ki'ichi related a particularly amusing anecdote about the language of obfuscation conservatives and government representatives resorted to in dealing with military issues (reported in the *New York Times,* October 19, 1953). During the negotiations that resulted in the Ikeda-Robertson Agreements, a reporter asked Ikeda Hayato to explain how an "increase in defense capabilities" *(bōeiryoku no zōkyō)* could be constitutional but "remilitarization" *(saigunbi)* not. To the Western mind, the reporter said, this distinction is indecipherable as remilitarization automatically translates into strengthening defense capabilities. In an answer greeted with appreciative laughter, Ikeda explained that the Eastern mind is much more subtle, so this distinction is quite plain to the Japanese. See Miyazawa Ki'ichi, *Tōkyō-Washinton no mitsudan* (Tokyo: Jitsugyō no Nihonsha, 1956), pp. 255–256. Americans were equally capable of perceiving such subtle distinctions, of course. The Truman administration had, after all, changed the Department of War into the Department of Defense.

105. See *Asahi shinbun,* July 26, 1957.

106. See Arase Yutaka, "Jihyō: Gensuibaku kinshi undō," pp. 104–108.

107. Ibid., pp. 107–108. What was needed in 1958, according to the New Year's edition of Gensuikyō's newsletter, *Gensuibaku kinshi nyūsu,* was a sense of responsibility as a people for their own government—a responsibility that would bridge their consciousness as individuals and as humans. According to Arase, only when the Japanese relation to the state *(kokka)* was mended would this failing be resolved.

108. The "Tensei jingo" essay for August 6, 1959, for example, caps a discussion of the death of a "second Kuboyama" with a milquetoast plea to the leaders of the nuclear powers to end the nuclear danger. Aragaki made similar pleas to other governments, and none to his own, in several other essays such as that written for the tenth anniversary of the end of the Occupation (April 28, 1962), which he concluded by asking the United States and the Soviet Union to "please take care of the world and humanity." The *Asahi's* editorials shared this tone. On the anniversaries of the Hiroshima bombing in 1960 and 1961, the editorials credit public opinion for persuading the nuclear powers to temporarily forgo testing but sums up by calling on them to end the nuclear threat. The sense of special Japanese victimhood, of course, remained strong. Aragaki's "Tensei jingo" column for the 1961 anniversary began: "Today . . . is a day Japanese can never forget. . . . Even if you try you cannot forget that ill-fated day of Hiroshima's bombing, when Japanese were the first of humanity to be hit by the atomic bomb."

109. When the UNESCO selection committee chose to add the atomic dome to the list of World Heritage sites, the Chinese government protested for precisely this reason: "During the Second World War, it was the other Asian countries and peoples who suffered the greatest loss in life and property. But today there are still few people [*sic*] trying to deny this fact of history. As such being the case, if Hiroshima nomination is approved to be included on the World Heritage List, even though on an exceptional basis, it may be utilized for harmful purpose by these few people [*sic*]. This will, of course, not be conducive to the safeguarding of world peace and security. For this reason China has reservations on the approval of this nomination." The United States objected to a war-related site being included in the list. See UNESCO's World Heritage website, http://www.unesco.org/whc/archive/repcom96.htm#775, or see UNESCO World Heritage Committee, "Report of the Twentieth Session, Merida, Mexico, 1996." All the other Japanese sites on the list are either natural wonders (such as Yakushima Island) or premodern Japanese cultural or religious sites of a more conventional sort (such as Hōryūji Buddhist temple).

110. John Dower, "Triumphal and Tragic Narratives of the War in Asia," in Laura Hein and Mark Selden, eds., *Living with the Bomb: American and Japanese Cultural Conflicts in the Nuclear Age* (Armonk, N.Y.: M. E. Sharpe, 1997), pp. 37–51 (quote on p. 44). Although there were voices reflecting this complex perception throughout the postwar era, it does seem that such awareness became more widely and publicly expressed in the 1970s and 1980s.

Chapter 4: Educating a Peace-Loving People

1. *Kuni no ayumi* was the one official history textbook used during the Occupation in upper elementary and junior high schools. *Minshushugi,* sometimes called the "Primer for Democracy," was the text used in tenth grade and adult education classes. Both texts were written by Japanese specialists under the close supervision of SCAP's Civil Information and Education (CIE) Section. Translations are adapted from those made for CIE officers, available in the Trainor Collection, Hoover Archives. Original texts were reproduced by the Ministry of Education in *Shakaika kyōkasho* (1981).

2. See Seki Yoshihiko's comments on this equation of democracy with Article 9 of the Constitution in his "Introduction," *Journal of Social and Political Ideas in Japan* 1(1) (April 1963):7.

3. For an example of extreme conservative revanchism see the views of Amano Teiyū, Yoshida's minister of education, as expressed in his late 1951 "Outline of Ethical Practice for the Japanese People." In language startlingly similar to the Confucianist, corporate statist arguments of the preeminent late-Meiji civil law scholar Hozumi Yatsuka, arguments that helped establish the emperor-centered family state ideology, Amano asserted the primacy of the state as the "parent body of the individual; without the State there would be no individuals"; quoted in John Dower, *Empire and Aftermath: Yoshida Shigeru and the Japanese Experience, 1878–1954* (Cambridge, Mass.: Harvard Council on East Asian Studies, 1979), pp. 353–356. For an informed contemporary report on the early debate on morals and patriotism in education see R. P. Dore, "The Ethics of the New Japan," *Pacific Affairs* 25(2) (June 1952):147–159.

4. I use the term "conservative" to indicate not just the ruling conservative parties but also those who wished to reestablish a close identification between Japanese and their state, even if they called themselves liberal nationalists. One noteworthy recent effort along these lines was the two groups founded by Tokyo University professor

of education Fujioka Nobukatsu: the Liberal View of History Study Group (Jiyūshugi Shikan Kenkyūkai) and the Japanese Society for History Textbook Reform (Atarashii Rekishi Kyōkashō o Tsukuru Kai), founded respectively in 1995 and 1996. There is a large body of literature that deconstructs the efforts of these groups in rewriting history textbooks as the promotion of a less problematic patriotic identification with a mono-ethnic Japanese nation. In English see "Textbook Nationalism, Citizenship, and War: Comparative Perspectives," a special issue of *Bulletin of Concerned Asian Scholars* 30(2) (April–June 1998), ed. Laura Hein and Mark Selden. For the revisionist perspective see "Restoration of a National History," a pamphlet published by the Japanese Society for History Textbook Reform (Tokyo, 1998).

5. In the February general election, the Democratic Party platform included a plan for improving the quality of education and lowering costs by standardizing textbooks; in July the party raised the issue of education policy in the Twenty-second Diet's Administrative Oversight Committee. *Ureubeki kyōkasho,* a fifty-page pamphlet distributed by the party in August 1955, criticized textbooks written by members of the Japan Teachers Union (Nikkyōso) on four counts: they praised the Soviet and Chinese communists and disparaged Japan; the texts were unconditionally favorable to the Teachers Union and its political activism; they promoted a radical and destructive labor movement; and they attempted to instill Marxist/Leninist thought in the minds of the children. The striking example of these tendencies, the pamphlet asserted, was Chūkyō's sixth-grade social studies text, *Akarui shakai,* written by a group of union-affiliated academics under Hidaka Rokurō. The slighted authors tried to refute these accusations with their own pamphlet, *Nihon Minshutō no "Ureubeki kyōkasho no mondai" wa dono yō ni machigatte iru ka.* The Democratic Party's pamphlet and related documents are reprinted in Sengo Nihon Kyōiku Shiryō Shūsei Iinkai, ed., *55-nen taisei shita no kyōiku* (Tokyo: San'ichi Shobō, 1982), p. 236ff. See also Ōtsuki Takeshi, ed., *Kyōkasho kokusho* (Tokyo: Rōdō Junpō, 1969), p. 228.

6. For a short review of changes in textbook certification procedures from the Meiji era to the 1960s see Satō Nobuo, "Kyōkasho kentei ni okeru Monbushō gawa no taido," *Rekishigaku kenkyū* 306 (November 1965):23–26; or Matsumoto Shigeo, "Kyōkasho seido ni tsuite," in Ienaga Soshō Shien Shimin no Kai, ed., *Taiheiyō sensō to kyōkasho,* pp. 228–234; or in English, Lawrence Ward Beer, *Freedom of Expression in Japan* (Tokyo: Kodansha, 1984), pp. 254–264. For progressive academics' approach to government influence on textbooks see contemporary essays in *Rekishigaku kenkyū* 245 (September 1960) or Tokutake Toshio, *Kyōkasho no sengoshi* (Tokyo: Shin Nihon Shuppansha, 1995).

7. Ienaga brought suits against the ministry in 1965, in 1967, and again in 1984. The final Supreme Court ruling was handed down on August 29, 1997. For a useful analysis of the first two suits see Beer, *Freedom of Expression in Japan,* pp. 264–270.

8. Ibid., p. 255. See also R. P. Dore, "Textbook Censorship in Japan: The Ienaga Case," *Pacific Affairs* 43 (1970–1971):549. Dore cites an *Asahi shinbun* article of July 14, 1970, that suggests such countervailing ideological pressures. Beginning in 1957 the league of publishing unions, Nihon Shuppan Rōdō Kumiai Kyōgikai, began publishing the annual "Textbook Report" *(Kyōkasho repōto)* under the editorship of the Shuppan Rōren Kyōkasho Taisaku Iinkai. The reports shed light on the dealings between Ministry of Education textbook officers and publishers/authors.

9. Personal discussion with Nakamura Masanori, professor of modern Japanese history at Hitotsubashi University, June 10, 1997.

10. The Ministry of Education's *Chūgakkō shakai shidōsho,* a guide for teaching junior high school social studies, recommended in 1959 that the connection between Japan's continental advance and China's ethnic national movements for sovereignty and independence be made clear (1959, p. 133). By the 1970s the ministry directed that the full picture be presented. With the 1970 reissue, the guide suggested a Japanese inspiration for Asian liberation movements, stressing that the Russo-Japanese War raised Asian people's ethnic national consciousness *(Ajiajin no minzokuteki jikaku).* But it also stressed that antiwar feeling existed among the Japanese people during this war and that the Japanese ethnic national consciousness eventually turned into a "great nation consciousness" *(taikoku ishiki)* and a superiority complex toward Asian ethnic nationalities (1970, pp. 190–192).

11. See, for example, U.S. Office of War Information, Bureau of Overseas Intelligence, Foreign Morale Analysis Division, "Special Report No. V: Current Psychological and Social Tensions in Japan" (June 1, 1945), p. 32; in Hoover Archives, U.S. Office of War Information, Box 3, Folder "Foreign Morale Analysis Division." See the discussion in Chapter 2.

12. SCAP's reeducation policy was firm, not vindictive. For example, Lt. Col. D. R. Nugent, chief of the CIE Section of GHQ for much of the Occupation, welcomed new personnel with this note of caution and encouragement: "Patience and persistence, in addition to enthusiasm and understanding, are indispensable to those who would make a real contribution to the long-term program of reorientation and rehabilitation of the Japanese people." See Nugent's introductory letter to SCAP, GHQ, CIE Section, "Orientation Pamphlet," February 22, 1947, revised January 15, 1948, in the Joseph C. Trainor Collection, Box 7, "SCAP GHQ CIE Orientation Pamphlet Feb. 1947" folder, Hoover Archives. CIE was the section responsible for SCAP objectives in the fields of information, education, religion, culture, and sociology, maintaining liaison and guidance to Japanese planning agencies in these fields.

13. SCAP Directive AG 350 (October 22, 1945) CIE, "Administration of the Educational System of Japan"; copy in the Trainor Collection, Box 54, "Textbook Revision" folder. This was the first of the four main directives that established policy on textbook revision. The other three were AG 000.3 (December 15, 1945) CIE, which prohibited Shinto doctrine from education; AG 000.8 (December 31, 1945) CIE, which suspended classes in morals, geography, and history; and AG 35 (January 17, 1946) CIE, which commanded the Ministry of Education to submit to SCAP all textbooks along with English translations for review and approval. A handwritten editing note on a CIE draft of its own 1950 report on "Development of Education Policy" comments that the Education Section was guided more by the SCAP directive of October 22, 1945, than by the Far Eastern Commission directive. See " 'Development of Education Policy' Chapter XXI" folder, Trainor Collection, Box 20.

14. Hidaka Daishirō to SCAP, "On Education," in Trainor Collection, Box 3, Ministry of Education, Miscellaneous, 1946–1952 folder. After a stint as vice-minister of education, Hidaka became a professor at International Christian University in Tokyo and president of Gakushūin Women's Junior College.

15. Japan, Ministry of Education, "Guide to New Education in Japan, Volume One: Fundamental Problems of the Establishment of New Japan" (1946), p. 3; English typescript in Trainor Collection, Box 2. The guide begins with a rejection of war as a means for solving disagreements because it leads to "trying to solve international problems by war, committing outrages on civilian population, and maltreating prisoners of war."

16. Ibid., p. 9.

17. Ibid., p. 20.

18. Ibid., p. 58. "True will" seemed really to mean "best interests." The guide notes earlier, for example, that "ultranationalism is an attitude of loving one's country too much, which causes the sacrifice of individual welfare under the pretext of serving the country"; p. 14. It is also a rhetorical echo of imperial and popular exemption from responsibility in the face of ministerial abuse of power. See the discussion of emperor and people as innocent victims in Chapter 2.

19. Monbushō, *Kuni no ayumi* II (1946), reprinted in 1981 in Monbushō, *Shakaika kyōkasho* 2:48ff.; quote is on p. 51. For an English translation see Trainor Collection, Box 2, Ministry of Education, "Elementary School History Courses" folder.

20. *Minshushugi* (1949), p. 255. See the SCAP translation, *Democracy*, p. 10, in Trainor Collection. According to CIE files, this text aroused more general interest than any other textbook published in the first five years after the war. The text was designed for tenth-graders, and 3.5 million copies of its first volume were distributed. Some 300,000 copies of a condensed version were distributed to repatriated Japanese in 1949. See "Monthly Summary, 15 May 1951," in Trainor Collection, Box 7 [2].

21. Mark T. Orr, chief of CIE's Education Division, received a memorandum to this effect on December 20, 1947, from K. M. Harkness, textbook and curriculum officer. See Trainor Collection, Box 54, "Textbook Authorization (1945–1951)" folder. Although the American Education Commission that visited Japan in March 1946 recommended that the preparation and publication of textbooks be left to open competition, paper shortages and SCAP concern over keeping educational materials free of militarist and ultranationalist influence made this course impractical in the early years of the Occupation. By July 1950, SCAP was no longer reviewing textbooks. Although the focus of this chapter is textbook treatment of war, one ongoing premise should be noted briefly. All the privately produced social studies textbooks continued to take the Occupation-era Ministry of Education textbook position that Japan could most properly contribute to world peace in the arena of culture—broadly conceived to include science, economic development, the arts, and sports—and that the only way to contribute was to cooperate with other nations in various international organizations such as the Red Cross, the United Nations, UNESCO, and the Olympics. The cultural emphasis was especially pervasive in the elementary school texts: all devoted long sections to peace education. Switzerland was usually advanced as the ideal pacifist country. Nihon Shoseki's *Sekai o tsunagu mono* (*shōsha* 606) (1950), for example, devoted ten pages to the "Land of Peace," followed by a long discussion by children about how to build a peaceful world. These model students decided that Japan could contribute by manufacturing products for export, building sewer systems and social welfare facilities such as hospitals, and working hard in science and farming. Everyone could help by improving their country's economic, technical, and social welfare. Kyō-iku Shuppan's *Nihon to sekai* (*shōsha* 631) (1952) called the desire to raise Japan's cultural level a kind of patriotism: "We want Japan to contribute to promoting world culture. To become a country that better expresses the human principles of freedom and equality. And finally, to fulfill the role of stopping a world war. We must each strive to make Japan that kind of country. Therein is our patriotism. That kind of patriotism is connected to love for all of humankind." Other countries were portrayed as sharing this sentiment, and the idea was to work in concert with them to maintain peace. The text was explicit that Japan could use science and technology to serve the Asian countries it had harmed during the war. See Kyōiku Shuppan, *Nihon to sekai*

(*shōsha* 631) (1952), pp. 123 and 131. In the early 1950s there seems to have been an implicit consensus in these textbooks' conception of culture that mirrored the government's emphasis on national economic reconstruction.

22. Unless noted otherwise, the information on textbooks was gathered through a reading of primary (sixth grade) and junior high school (seventh and eighth grade) social studies and history books in the collections at the Textbook Research Center (Kyōkasho Kenkyū Sentaa), the Tōkyō Shoseki Publisher's Collection (Tōshobunko), and the Osaka National University of Education (Osaka Kokuritsu Kyōiku Daigaku). Beginning with those texts authorized by the Ministry of Education in 1950, publishers of sixth-grade textbooks include Gakkō Tosho, Nihon Shoseki, Tōkyō Shoseki, Futaba, Osaka Shoseki, Chūkyō Shuppan, Fuji Kyōkasho, Shūei, Kyōiku Shuppan, Jitsugyō no Nipponsha, Dai-Nihon Tosho, and Teikoku Shoin. The complete series of junior high texts published by Tōkyō Shoseki, Nihon Shoseki, Kyōiku Shuppan, and Chūkyō Shuppan were surveyed, as well as many of the texts from Osaka Shoseki and Gakkō Tosho. Textbooks are identified by year of authorization—usually one year prior to the first year of use—and by the Ministry of Education identification number when available. The Ministry code indicates the level and school subject. For example, *"shōsha"* is an abbreviation for *"shōgaku shakaika,"* or elementary school social studies. The first digit in the number indicates the grade level, the last digits the text itself. Significantly revised editions of the same title were given new identifying numbers.

23. *Kyōkasho no hensan: Hakkō nado kyōkasho seido no henreki ni kansuru chōsa kenkyū,* compiled by Nakamura Kikuji (Tokyo: Kyōkasho Kenkyū Sentaa, 1997), pp. 95 and 105. See also Ienaga Soshō Shien Shimin no Kai, ed., *Taiheiyō sensō to kyōkasho* (Tokyo: Shisō no Kagaku-sha, 1970), pp. 14–15.

24. At Kyōiku Shuppan, the authors included Tokyo University education professor Munakata Seiya, JTU activist and supporter of Ienaga in his suits against the Ministry of Education, and Kanazawa Kaichi, an elementary school teacher and principal known for his strong dedication to "never repeat the mistake" of sending students off to war again. See Kanazawa's *Aru shōgakkōchō no kaisō* (Tokyo: Iwanami Shoten, 1967). Chūkyō Shuppan employed JTU activist Tokutake Toshio as an editor. See Tokutake Toshio, *Kyōkasho no sengo shi* (Tokyo: Shin Nihon Shuppansha, 1995), pp. 72–73.

25. Kyōiku Shuppan, *Nihon to sekai* (*shōsha* 631) (1952), pp. 83–84, 89–101, 119–123. The precursor volume to this text, *Seikatsu to seiji* (*shōsha* 630) (1952), quite clearly constructed the people as a *kokumin* in the civic sense of having political authority via their representation in the Diet. In *Nihon to sekai,* the implication is that this political nation *(kokumin)* was also ethnically constructed. In addition to the admonition against condescension toward other (ethnic) nations, the passage on the war ends with the comment that while other *minzoku* earned their democracy through internal struggle, Japan (Nihon) was given it by losing a war against foreign countries (pp. 100–102).

26. Chūkyō Shuppan, *Akarui shakai* (*shōsha* 647) (1953), pp. 129–131, 133. This text was written by a group of scholars affiliated with the Rekikyōkyō, a JTU-connected organization concerned with history education.

27. Ibid., pp. 129–130. The Japanese people were victims of the same state power that threatened the peoples of Asia. For example, this connection is implicit in the following passage, which makes the narrative transition from the Japanese army's occupation of Manchuria to its murderous seizure of the Japanese government and suppression of domestic dissent. A Chinese poem begins the transition:

Beautiful mountains, nostalgic rivers,
We've been chased, driven away
On an endless journey
I meet waves of companions on the road [or: Tears are our companion]
But none has found good fortune [or: We find no happiness]
Neither inside, nor outside, our land.

Chinese people *(hitobito)* who had been driven off by the Japanese army sang this song as they wandered the wide plains aimlessly. At that time in Japan, one after another bloody incidents occurred, reckless soldiers killing statesmen and the like who didn't fall in line with their thinking, and the Diet became one in name only.... The government suppressed antiwar voices by rounding up scholars, intellectuals, and artists. [Ibid., pp. 126–127; also carried in Ienaga Soshō Shien Shimin no Kai, *Taiheiyō sensō to kyōkasho*, pp. 18–19.]

28. Chūkyō Shuppan, *Akarui shakai* (1953), pp. 131–133.

29. Teikoku Shoin, *Sekai to musubu Nihon (shōsha* 662) (1954), pp. 80–128. Nihon Shoseki's 1954 *Nihon to sekai* (vol. 1, *shōsha* 659; vol. 2, *shōsha* 660) was the most direct in its cultural focus, its message that war victimizes, and its matter-of-fact treatment of the Hiroshima bombing. The text for the first half of the year gave a simple, factual version of World War II. The second half-year's text highlighted its peace theme with the frontispiece title, "Plea for Peace" *(Heiwa e no negai)* printed in bold type, and with two photographs: one of the Red Cross's International Headquarters in Geneva and the other of the Matterhorn captioned "Switzerland, Land of Peace." The title page depicted a dove with olive branch positioned over a globe so that Japan was under its wing. The long thirty-five-page section on peace began with a description of Japanese losses in the Pacific War and an explanation that modern war involved civilian casualties. Students were told that the problem of the day was that science, the source of progress, could also be used to take life as in the atomic bombing of Hiroshima. The way to do away with war was for people to respect each other, and the pragmatic means to do this was to cooperate in international organizations such as the Red Cross, the United Nations, and UNESCO.

30. Tōkyō Shoseki, *Atarashii shakaika: Chūgaku 3-nen* (919) (1951), pp. 225–226. It appears that the idea that some wars might be justifiable—as in this text and Chūkyō Shuppan's *Akarui shakai* (647) (1953), p. 129; rev. ed. 674 (1954), p. 113—was dropped when Japanese pacifism redefined itself in terms of antinuclearism.

31. Tōkyō Shoseki, *Atarashii Nihonshi (chūsha* 788) (1953), pp. 186–193.

32. Nihon Shoseki, *Chūgakusei no shakai: Jidai to seikatsu-ge (rekishiteki naiyō o shu to suru mono) (chūsha* 7-721) (1954), pp. 221 and 230.

33. Chūkyō Shuppan, *Kindai no sekai to Nihon (chūsha* 7-765) (1954), pp. 198–199. Befitting the progressive position of its authors, this text gingerly suggested that the military alliance with the United States be reconsidered; see p. 181.

34. Left-wing intellectuals looked on the nonaligned countries as champions of neutralism. Seki Yoshihiko explains how progressive intellectuals feared Japan would become the "orphan of Asia"—a term that future Hatoyama administration foreign minister Shigemitsu used to denounce Yoshida diplomacy. See Seki Yoshihiko, "Introduction," *Journal of Social and Political Ideas in Japan* 1(1) (April 1963):9. Enthusiasm for Hatoyama Ichirō's "independent" foreign policy from late 1954 through 1956 suggests a general desire to participate in this movement. Japanese interest in indepen-

dence through a closer identification with Asia is also suggested by special issues of the general-interest magazines in October 1954: *Sekai*'s "Rising Asia and Japanese Independence" and *Chūō kōron*'s "Asia for Asians."

35. See Carol Gluck, "The 'People' in Japanese Historiography," *Journal of Asian Studies* 38(1) (November 1978):25–50. See also Kamei Katsuichirō's series of essays critical of progressive histories—especially Tōyama Shigeki et al.'s *Shōwa-shi,* which sparked the intellectual exchanges known as the "Shōwa History Debates" in the general-interest magazines *Chūō kōron* and *Bungei shunjū* in 1955 and 1956.

36. See, for example, Chūkyō Shuppan's *Akarui shakai* I (*shōsha* 647) (1953), p. 133, and *Akarui Shakai* II (*shōsha* 648), pp. 144–147.

37. Kyōiku Shuppan, *Nihon to sekai* (1952), pp. 104–108.

38. Nihon Shoseki's text expanded its section on world peace, which noted that modern warfare involves civilians, and focused on the enormous extent of Japanese death and destruction in the Pacific War. Before describing the usual international peace organizations, the text noted that science was now sometimes used to take life, as in the atomic bomb. See Nihon Shoseki, *Nihon to sekai* (1954).

39. The editorial board took special care in its development, reviewing midstream compilations from August 1953 to April 1954. See Tōkyō Shoseki Kabushikikaisha, Shashi-hen Iinkai, ed., *Kindai kyōkasho no henreki: Tōkyō Shoseki 70-nen shi* (Tokyo: Tōkyō Shoseki, 1980), pp. 486–489.

40. The sole recommended assignment topic for this section was to investigate how difficult people's lives were during the war. The "bells of peace" is an oblique reference to Nagai Takashi's best-selling *Bells of Nagasaki.* See Tōkyō Shoseki, *Atarashii shakai* (*shōsha* 664) (1954), pp. 109–110; (*shōsha* 681) (1955), p. 102. The 1955 text (*shōsha* 680 and 681) was slightly revised from the 1954 version (*shōsha* 663 and 664). Although the 1954 edition did not introduce much information about Asian national liberation struggles, in succeeding years the text gradually added such passages. The issue of increasing treatment of Asian national liberation movements will be discussed shortly. For the moment the reader may wish to know that in Tōkyō Shoseki's sixth-grade text these movements were presented mainly within the context of European imperialism—one exception was the 1960 text, which merely noted the existence of Chinese boycotts on Japanese goods after Japan forced "unfavorable" treaties (*shōsha* 6008, pp. 117–118). The 1973 text carried the joint statement on resumption of diplomatic relations in the early 1970s that "Japan brought great harm to the Chinese people *(Chūgoku kokumin)* in war" (*shōsha* 6071, p. 165). The major change came with a new editorial group formed for the 1976 text.

41. Tōkyō Shoseki, *Atarashii shakai* (1955), pp. 113–114 and 122–123. The 1951 text had ended with a vague mention of the "Japanese responsibility to the people of the world" to work for peace, but it did not clarify why; *Atarashii shakaika* (*shōsha* 633) (1952). The 1957 text (*shōsha* 664) made it even more clear than the 1954 text that wartime suffering legitimated Japan's postwar pacifist stance: "This resolve [based on the atomic victim experience] to pursue peace, no matter how far it is required, is recognized everywhere in the world"; Tōkyō Shoseki, *Atarashii shakai* (*shōsha* 6-603) (1957), pp. 118–119. In later texts, the sense of Japanese victimhood must have been strengthened by what appears to have been an unfortunate misreading of statistics in the *World Almanac* for World War II deaths and casualties. The 1957 version introduced a bar graph of deaths and casualties showing a combined figure of 6 million for Japanese versus 3 million for Chinese. Peak Japanese strength of arms was taken for the

Japanese total casualty figure, while the Chinese figure seems to have been the number of Chinese government battle deaths; see *Atarashii shakai* (1957), p. 112. In the 1964 edition this graph was amended to indicate only military deaths, but it still showed more Japanese deaths than Chinese—contrary to the cited source; *Atarashii shakai* (*shōsha* 6021) (1964), p. 89. See *World Almanac and Book of Facts* (New York: New York World Telegram and Sun, 1962), p. 736. This graph lasted until the 1970 edition, when it showed slightly more Chinese deaths than Japanese—though it still indicated about a million fewer Chinese deaths than listed in the *World Almanac; Atarashii Shakai* (*shōsha* 6022) (1970), p. 83.

42. Kyōiku Shuppan, *Hyōjun shōgaku shakai kaiteihan* (*shōsha* 686) (1955), pp. 101–111. The passage added to the Russo-Japanese War account was: "But during this war many people *(ōku no hitobito)* opposed the war because they were saddened that so many precious lives were being lost" (p. 101).

43. Ibid.

44. Ibid., pp. 118–119. The 1956 version (*shōsha* 698) connected atomic victim pacifism more explicitly to cooperation with other peoples, changing the end of this sentence to read: "Especially we, who . . . learned how horrible future war will be, should join hands with people around the world to work for peace so that war will absolutely never happen again." See Kyōiku Shuppan, *Hyōjun shōgaku shakai kaiteihan* (*shōsha* 698) (1956), p. 119. The Japanese phrase used for "people around the world" is *sekaijū no hitotachi*. This edition adds the atomic bombings on Hiroshima and Nagasaki and the Bikini hydrogen bomb testing to world events on its foldout timeline, as well as a discussion of the Bandung Conference and Asian and African national liberation movements *(minzoku dokuritsu no undō)*.

45. The 1955 text added the observation that the Hiroshima bombing was the first in history. See Tōkyō Shoseki, *Atarashii shakai, 4* (*chūsha* 7-758) (September 30, 1954), pp. 173–174; (*chūsha* 7-759) (September 30, 1954), p. 113; Tōkyō Shoseki, *Shinpen Atarashii shakai 4: Sekai no hatten, gendai no ugoki* (*chūsha* A-779) (1955), pp. 132 and 150–153. The 1958 edition made no changes in the text regarding the atomic bombings. Kyōiku Shuppan's junior high texts also merely note that Japan was the first nation to be A-bombed at Hiroshima and Nagasaki. See Kyōiku Shuppan, *Hyōjun chūgaku shakai: Rekishi no nagare, ge* (*chūsha* 7-797) (1954), p. 113; *Rekishi no nagare, ge* (*chūsha* B-723) (1956), pp. 103–104.

46. Tōkyō Shoseki, *Shinpen Atarashii shakai (4) sekai no hatten, gendai no ugoki* (*chūsha* A-779) (1955), p. 126.

47. Ibid., p. 123.

48. Ibid., pp. 131–132. This was the same phrasing used in the 1953 text (p. 193).

49. In its final pages the text also highlighted the Bandung Conference of Asian and African countries. See Nihon Shoseki, *Shinpan chūgakusei no shakai: Jidai to seikatsu* (*chūsha* B-714) (1956), pp. 100–102, 122–123, 144–145.

50. The section titled "What Is the New Japan Aiming For?" began: "The Pacific War ended in our country's defeat. While it is important to consider why it ended in defeat, what is more important for us is the path postwar Japan should pursue. Under occupation by a foreign army we have for the moment come up with an answer to this great question; but we don't know yet whether or not it is the correct answer. We have become an independent country. Let's use our own heads to solve our problems. To do this, let's reconsider, one by one, our steps after the war." The 1954 version used the *Children of Hiroshima* photograph to show that children in cities across the

country had to find unusual places to play. See Chūkyō Shuppan, *Chūgakusei no shakaika: Nihon no ayumi to sekai (rekishiteki naiyō o shu to suru mono)* (*chūsha* 7-765) (1954), pp. 179 and 181.

51. Chūkyō Shuppan, *Chūgakusei no shakaika: Nihon no ayumi to sekai (rekishiteki naiyō o shu to suru mono) kaiteihan* (*chūsha* B-703) (1956), p. 114. The book's final section on nuclear energy and peace began with this atomic exceptionalist statement: "Mankind is soon entering the era of nuclear energy, and we Japanese are the only people *(minzoku)* to have personally experienced the horrible destructive power of nuclear energy. How shall we address this new age?" See *Kindai no sekai to Nihon* (1956), p. 142ff.

52. Ibid., p. 115.

53. Takayama's objections included the comments that it was an error to include Yosano Akiko among those who opposed the [Russo-Japanese] war, that it was not good to raise antiwar thought with Matsui Noboru's painting, "A Soldier's Bereaved Family" [Gunjin no Izoku], and "regarding the Pacific War, don't write so badly of Japan —for example, even if it's the truth, express it romantically" (Taiheiyō sensō ni tsuite wa, Nihon no waruguchi wa amari kakanaide, tatoe sore ga jijitsu de atte mo, roman-chikku ni hyōgen se yo). Since Chūkyō's junior and senior high texts were among those rejected, the publisher tried to secure approval on second submission by adding a colleague of Takayama's to the editorial board, Kimura Yoshisuke, whose addition led members of the original board such as Hidaka Rokurō to resign. See Beer, *Freedom of Expression*, p. 260; Ōtsuki, *Kyōkasho kokusho*, p. 516; Tokutake, *Kyōkasho no sengo shi*, pp. 92–94. For an insider's account at Chūkyō Shuppan see Tokutake Toshio, *Atarashii rekishi kyōkasho e no michi* (Tokyo: Hato no Mori Shobō, 1973), pp. 67–125.

54. Some 30 percent of social studies texts failed in this round. Some 85.5 percent of texts were rejected in 1950, the year screening was instituted. See Beer, *Freedom of Expression*, pp. 260–264; Tokutake, *Kyōkasho no sengo shi*, pp. 100–105. Tokutake suggests that the textbook examiners were rather arbitrary in their decisions this round, noting that politically middle-of-the-road and conservative authors' books were failed as well. See also Satō Kōmei, *Kyōkasho kentei no genba kara: 17-nenkan no insaido repōto* (Tokyo: Waseda Daigaku Shuppan, 1987), pp. 27–70, for a useful account of the review procedures from an Education Ministry officer's perspective.

55. For a detailed account of *Akarui shakai*'s fate see the memoir of one of its editors, Tokutake, *Atarashii rekishi kyōkasho*, pp. 106–125.

56. Kyōiku Shuppan, *Hyōjun shakai* (*shakai* 6010) (1960). The following passage from pp. 101–102 conveys the tone of this text: "The Meiji government frequently sent missions abroad to negotiate repeal of these treaties but as national strength was weak it just could not achieve this national goal. But with the establishment of constitutional government and civilization and enlightenment *(bunmei kaika)*, victory in the Sino and Russo-Japanese wars, and the annexation of Korea, Japan's strength was recognized by the world's countries, and through the people's *(kokumin no)* efforts and the government's unflagging efforts at negotiation, it succeeded in gaining repeal in 1911."

57. Kyōiku Shuppan, *Shakai* (*shakai* 6006) (1960), pp. 134, 142, 144, 146; (*shakai* 6007), p. 123. See also Tokutake, *Atarashii rekishi kyōkasho*, p. 122.

58. Kyōiku Shuppan, *Hyōjun shakai* (*shakai* 6016) (1964), p. 87.

59. Kyōiku Shuppan, *Hyōjun shakai* (*shakai* 6017) (1964), pp. 110–111.

60. Kyōiku Shuppan, *Hyōjun shakai* (*shakai* 6034) (1967), pp. 97–98. With the 1970 addition of a paragraph on students having to work in factories and the 1973

addition of a sidebar on the typical wartime diet, the 1970 and 1973 texts added to the sense of the people suffering under the prewar political parties and during the war.

61. Tōkyō Shoseki, *Shinpen Atarashii Shakai* (*shōsha* 6-603) (1957), pp. 97–98; (*shakai* 6008) (1960), pp. 109–122. The 1964 text does not change in any significant way except that the map of "all nations' advances into Asia" (p. 109) is relabeled "European nations' advances into Asia," and Japan's territories are then omitted from the map showing imperialist influence in Asia. See *Shakai* 6020 (1964), p. 121.

62. Waseda Daigaku Kyōikugakubu Rekishigaku Kenkyūkai, "Sengo rekishi kyō-kasho wa dō kawatte iru ka (3)," *Rekishi hyōron* 182 (October 1965):10–25; see pp. 24–25 for the quoted passages. The 1956 version was not appreciably different from the 1954 version, except that it is the Japanese military that attacked Hawai'i and began the Pacific War. See Nihon Shoseki, *Shinpan chūgakusei no shakai: Jidai to seikatsu* (*chūsha* B-7614) (1956), pp. 125–127; Nihon Shoseki, *Chūgaku shakai: Rekishiteki bunya, 2-nen* (*shakai* 8006) (1961), pp. 267–268. The Waseda article also indicated subtler changes—as in the Shimizu publisher's text that softened the fact of surrender by dropping the term itself. The new edition simply noted that "Japan accepted the Potsdam Declaration and on August 15 the emperor notified the people by radio that the war had ended." For an extremely progressive critique of the conservative impact of the Education Ministry's certification process see Ōtsuki, *Kyōkasho kokusho,* a "black paper" on education.

63. Waseda Daigaku Kyōikugakubu Rekishigaku Kenkyūkai, "Sengo rekishi kyō-kasho," p. 19. The "newer" version was probably the 1961 edition.

64. Ibid., p. 23.

65. Ibid., p. 25.

66. The text does not challenge the idea that Japan eventually followed along with this imperialist course. The 1961 text characterizes the 1921 Washington naval limitation treaty as "prejudicial" (*sabetsuteki*) to Japan where previous editions noted that such treaties lessened the economic burden on the people (*kokumin*). In 1961, moreover, the previous characterization of the Japanese military's "invasion of northern China" (*shinryaku*) after the Manchurian Incident is changed to the less condemning "advance" (*shinshutsu*). See Tōkyō Shoseki, *Shinpen atarashii shakai* (*chūsha* B-780) (1958), pp. 108–109, 126–127, 129; Tōkyō Shoseki, *Atarashii shakai* (*shakai* 8004) (1961), pp. 274 and 291–292.

67. Nihon Shoseki, *Shinpan chūgakusei no shakai: Jidai to seikatsu* (*chusha* B-714) (1956), pp. 105, 117–121, 129; *Chūgaku shakai: Rekishiteki bunya 2-nen* (*shakai* 8006) (1961), pp. 262–264 and 271 (Japanese government ignoring Potsdam Declaration); *Chūgaku shakai: Rekishiteki bunya 2-nen* (*shakai* 8022) (1965), pp. 264, 266, 279–284. The passage is: "The Japanese government ignored [the Potsdam Declaration] and de-cided to continue fighting. But America dropped an atom bomb on August 6 . . ." The connection is made more explicit in the 1971 text: "When the Japanese govern-ment . . . , America dropped an atom bomb . . ." (*rekishi* 704), p. 316. Chūkyō Shup-pan's junior high text also introduces this idea in 1961 with more explicit causality: "But our country ignored [the Potsdam Declaration], so America dropped atomic bombs on Hiroshima and Nagasaki in August" (Chūkyō Shuppan, *Nihon no ayumi to sekai* (*shakai* 8002), pp. 292–293). This passage remains the same until "the Japanese government" replaces "our country" in the 1971 text (*rekishi* 705), p. 283.

68. In the 1960s the government was valorizing the wartime suffering of several victim groups as worthy service to the state. See Chapter 6.

69. Tōkyō Shoseki, *Atarashii shakai 2* (*shakai* 8004) (1961), pp. 290, 296, 319–

320. This text mentioned the Lucky Dragon Incident, but without expressing any Japanese nuclear exceptionalism it praised Japan's efforts at nuclear research to improve the people's livelihood. Contrition and a sense of responsibility in the closing pages were less evident in later Tōkyō Shoseki texts, which indulged in atomic exceptionalism. The 1983 Tōkyō Shoseki text (rekishi 720)—which shared with other publishers' texts of the early 1980s extensive sections on Chinese and Korean people's liberation movements against Japan—also emphasized Japan's special status as atomic-bomb victim. The text ended with the preamble of the Constitution introduced with this statement: "Japan, which has become one of the world's influential states, is expected to fulfill its role in international society and to contribute to world peace. The people (kokumin) of Japan, the only country (kuni) on earth to have suffered the affliction of atomic bombing, feel acutely how very important peace is" (p. 319).

70. Beginning in 1968, for example, this publisher's texts noted that many people supported the military's intervention in the 1930s because it helped the economy recover. See Tōkyō Shoseki, Atarashii shakai (1968), p. 295. The sense of the people's qualified complicity in militant foreign policies was eventually reflected in Nihon Shoseki's junior high texts as well. Beginning with the 1961 edition, texts dropped the lengthy 1956 explanation about the people being propagandized into supporting the war, only noting that speech against (the militarist-dominated) government policy was strictly suppressed. Future texts related that those who retained doubts about the war were encouraged by early victories in the Pacific War and worked hard on the home front to increase military production. By 1983 the text described how some people actually supported "advancing onto the continent" (tairiku ni shinshutsu) as a means of stabilizing their livelihoods. It must be admitted, though, that these passages appear in the context of police pressure on freedom of speech—and from 1965, texts added the comment that the government did not tell the people the truth about losses later in the Pacific War. The Japanese people's failings are understandable because they were overly influenced by the militarists among them. See Nihon Shoseki, Chūgaku shakai: Rekishiteki bunya 2-nen (shakai 8022) (1961), pp. 264–265 and 269–270; 1983 text (rekishi 719), p. 255.

71. Tōkyō Shoseki's texts carried this comment from 1965 at least but discontinued it in the 1974 edition. The text referred to Japan's victory as the first instance of a colored race (yūshoku jinshu) defeating a white race (hakushoku jinshu). See Atarashii shakai shakai 8021 (1965), p. 249; Shintei atarashii shakai rekishi 711 (1974), p. 251. Chūkyō Shuppan introduced this favorable comment on Japanese imperialism in its 1961 edition but dropped it from the 1971 edition. It added the comment again to the 1977 edition, though by then it was greatly expanding exposition on indigenous Korean opposition to Japanese colonization policies. See Nihon no ayumi to sekai shakai 8002 (1961), p. 231; Nihon no ayumi to sekai rekishi 705 (1971), p. 228; Nihon no ayumi to sekai rekishi 721 (1977), pp. 243–244.

72. Tōkyō Shoseki, Kindai kyōkasho no hensen: Tōkyō Shoseki 70-nenshi (1980), p. 524.

73. Tōkyō Shoseki, Atarashii shakai (chūsha B 780) (1958), p. 131; (shakai 8004) (1961), p. 296; (shakai 8021) (1965), pp. 250, 273, 295.

74. Nihon Shoseki, Shinpan chūgakusei no shakai: Jidai to seikatsu (1956), pp. 100–102, 125, 128; Chūgaku shakai: Rekishiteki bunya 2-nen (1961), pp. 267–271; Chūgaku shakai: Rekishiteki bunya 2-nen (1965), pp. 255, 262–264, 267, 284, 289.

75. There were no depictions of Japan as atomic exceptionalist victim. The 1968

text contained a significant oversight in its special section on Asian national liberation struggles. In the text, such efforts in Persia, Burma, Indonesia, and even Korea were mentioned but none in Japanese-held territory. Until this oversight was corrected in the 1980 text, only those people's movements in various Western colonies were indicated, and these were labeled with the first letter of the names of the Western colonizers, as in war maps emphasizing Japan's "encirclement": in the Philippines (A); India, Burma, and the Middle East (B); Indonesia (D); and Indochina (F). See Chūkyō Shuppan, *Nihon no ayumi to sekai* (*shakai* 8002) (1961), pp. 254ff. and 285 ("military movements"); (*shakai* 8028) (1968), pp. 221–223, 241ff., 250 (for chained China map), 270 (photograph), 285 ("invasion").

76. Tōkyō Shoseki, *Atarashii shakai* (*rekishi* 711) (1974), pp. 246–247, 267, 280, 282, 288.

77. Ibid., pp. 271 and 290–291.

78. Tōkyō Shoseki, *Atarashii shakai* (*rekishi* 717) (1977), pp. 261, 272, 282.

79. Tōkyō Shoseki, *Atarashii shakai* (*rekishi* 728) (1986), pp. 275–277; see also *Atarashii shakai* (*rekishi* 720) (1983), pp. 274–276.

80. Chūkyō Shuppan, *Nihon no ayumi to sekai* (*rekishi* 705) (1971), pp. 253–254, 259, 276, 285; see also *Shinpan Nihon no ayumi to sekai* (*shakai* 8028) (1968), pp. 250, 255, 273, 280, 284.

81. In Tōkyō Shoseki's sixth-grade texts, the trend toward apologist history shifted in 1967 as the military began to be criticized for Japanese aggression in the 1930s and the people were depicted as suffering under their oppression. Students read in 1967 that the military "forced" (*oshisusumeta*) militarist thought instead of simply strengthening it, and began hostilities with the Chinese army in the Manchurian Incident (which in previous texts simply "happened"). Now students learned that it was Japan's advance into Southeast Asia that worsened relations with the United States. The 1970 text presented a more balanced treatment of Chinese and Japanese competition for influence in Korea in the 1890s and explained for the first time that the Japanese navy began the Pacific War with the attack on Pearl Harbor. From the 1976 text on students learned that the Japanese army blew up the rail tracks as provocation in the Manchurian Incident. See Tōkyō Shoseki, *Shinpen Atarashii shakai* (*shakai* 6020) (1964), p. 135ff.; *Shintei Atarashii shakai* (*shakai* 6032) (1967), pp. 134–137; *Atarashii shakai* (*shakai* 6021) (1970), pp. 134 and 151; *Shinpen Atarashii shakai* (*shakai* 6162) (1976), pp. 150–151.

82. Tōkyō Shoseki, *Shinpen Atarashii shakai* (*shakai* 6162) (1976), p. 134ff.; *Atarashii shakai* (*shakai* 603) (1979), pp. 29 and 36f.

83. *Atarashii shakai* (*shakai* 628) (1985), p. 30.

84. Kyōiku Shuppan, *Shinpan Shakai* (*shakai* 6141) (1976), pp. 106–124. In keeping with the generally progressive aspect, this text noted that it was following Washington's advice that Japan established the Police Reserve Forces in the early 1950s (p. 128).

85. Kyōiku Shuppan, *Shōgaku shakai* (*shakai* 611) (1979), p. 101ff.; (*shakai* 612) (1979), pp. 65–66. This general tone is maintained in later editions.

86. JTU activism was originally based on a firm awareness of teachers' war responsibility and accompanying resolve never again to make the mistake of teaching students to support war. The earnestness of this dedication is apparent in the following poem by Takeda Junji published in the Kōchi Prefecture Teachers Union newsletter and recited by the Japanese delegate to the first world conference on education held in Vienna in July 1953:

"Students I've Sent to Die in War"

You students who have died, never to come back,
My hands are smeared in blood.
I was holding the end of that rope that strangled you, alas.
What good is the excuse that "we were both fooled"?
What kind of compensation is it, even adding together shame,
    remorse, and repentance?
You who have died won't return.
Even now, I cleanse my corrupt hands as I wipe my tears and swear
    to your grave post,
"Never again will I let it happen, never."

See Tokutake, *Kyōkasho no sengo shi,* pp. 73–74; originally published in the Kōchi Prefecture Teachers Union newsletter, *Runesansu,* January 30, 1952.

87. Atomic exceptionalism energized Japanese pacifism on the basis of nationally experienced victimhood and an absolute rejection of war that did not require reference to conventional sins. Kyōiku Shuppan's sixth-grade text and Chūkyō Shuppan's junior high text both exhibited this tendency in years of heightened interest in Japan's nuclear victim heritage.

88. It was in this era of apologist textbooks that Oda Makoto came forward with his warnings about the dangers of myopic victim consciousness. Oda himself worked in *juku* cram schools and therefore had contact with the younger generation. With regard to the tendency toward alienation from the state in progressive texts, one is reminded of the phrase *"sensō o shiranai"* from the popular 1971 protest song that carries the added sense of refusing to have anything to do with the establishment as well as with war. The lyrics of this song, written and sung by folk artist and later psychiatrist/critic Kitayama Osamu, claimed for the postwar generation an uncorrupted moral position explicitly distinct from the establishment. The first two stanzas and refrain are: "We were born after the war ended / We grew up without knowing war / Becoming adults we begin to walk / singing a song of peace. (*Refrain:* We want you to remember our name / We're the children who never knew war.) If you won't let us because we're too young / If you won't let us because our hair is long / The only thing left for me to do now / is to hold back my tears and just sing. (*Refrain.*)" Kitayama's group "Jirōzu" released the song on the Toshiba-EMI label in February 1971; lyrics from *Shōgakukan CD Bukku "Shōwa no uta"* (Tokyo: Shōgakukan, 1991), p. 296.

Chapter 5: "Sentimental Humanism": The Victim in Novels and Film

1. Beside novels and film, popular media of this era include newspapers, magazines, *manga* (narrative comics), plays, and, increasingly, television. I am focusing on film and novels because of their accessibility and their enduring presence in the popular mind.

2. Quoted in Satō Tadao, *Currents in Japanese Cinema: Essays by Tadao Sato,* trans. Gregory Barrett (Tokyo: Kodansha International, 1982), p. 113.

3. Tsuboi originally published her book in serialized form from February to November 1952 in *New Age,* a journal for Christian households. It was first published by Kōbunsha in December 1952 and then reissued as the first Kappa Book in late

1954. See Odagiri Hideo, "Kaisetsu," in Tsuboi Sakae, *Tsuboi Sakae zenshū,* vol. 6 (Tokyo: Chikuma Shobō, 1968), p. 285; Satō Tadao, "Tsuboi Sakae 'Nijūshi no hitomi' —Anshin shite nakeru kyoyō shōsetsu," *Asahi jaanaru* 8(19) (May 8, 1966):35. Kinoshita's film was ranked the best film in *Kinema jumpo*'s list for 1954 and earned the Mainichi Shinbun Film Council prize and the sports newspaper association's Blue Ribbon.

4. The first segment of the film version won the Venice Film Festival's San Georgio Prize and was ranked fifth on *Kinema jumpo*'s 1959 list of best films. Besides the work's compelling exploration of personal war responsibility, its popularity lay in the fact that the last Japanese POWs were returned from Siberian labor camps in 1957 and 1958. Most of the letters sent to Gomikawa were from wives, daughters, and mothers of men who never returned. According to Gomikawa, they generally wondered whether the novel presented the conditions under which their loved ones died. See Gomikawa Junpei and Aratama Michiyo, "Taidan: Katsumoku shite machimashō," *Chūō kōron* 74(6) (May 1959):158.

5. *Human Condition* is perhaps less broadly known than the other two, but it is popular among university students and is reputed to continue to draw audiences to all-night showings of the nine-hour film. All three books are available in *bunko* (publisher's library) versions, and in the early 1990s the films were usually available in neighborhood video rental stores.

6. There are several potential candidates: Ōoka Shōhei's *Nobi* (1954), translated by Ivan Morris as *Fires on the Plain* (Tokyo: Tuttle, 1957), film by Ichikawa Kon (Daiei, 1959); Takeyama Michio's *Biruma no tategoto* (1947), translated by Howard Hibbett as *Harp of Burma* (Tokyo: Tuttle, 1966), film versions by Ichikawa Kon (Nikkatsu, 1956; Fuji et al., 1985); Ishino Keichirō's *Himeyuri no tō* (1950)/*Himeyuri butai* (1952), film version by Imai Tadashi, *Himeyuri no tō* (Tōei, 1953); Noma Hiroshi's *Shinkūjitai* (1952), film by Yamamoto Satsuo (Shinsei, 1952); Shindō Kaneto's *Genbaku no ko* (Kindai Eiga Kyōkai, 1952); and even Honda Ishirō's *Gojira* series beginning in 1954.

7. I have benefited from the theoretical writings in John E. O'Connor, ed., *Image as Artifact: The Historical Analysis of Film and Television* (Malabar, Fla.: Krieger, 1990) —especially O'Connor's introductory essays (pp. 1–42 and 108–118) and Robert Sklar's essay, "Moving Image Media in Culture and Society: Paradigms for Historical Interpretation" (pp. 119–135).

8. Odagiri, "Kaisetsu," pp. 279–280.

9. Satō, *Currents,* p. 109.

10. Kinoshita follows suit in the film *Nijūshi no hitomi* (Tōhō, 1954). For stylistic reasons I will refer only to the novel rather than both the novel and the film. Most of the analysis applies to the film as well as the novel, however, since Kinoshita follows Tsuboi's lead in most respects; regardless of whether Kinoshita omits a particular passage he remains faithful to the tone of the book.

11. "Cape children" refers to the village's location at the tip of a cape. Page references are to the Kadokawa *bunko* edition—Tsuboi Sakae, *Nijūshi no hitomi* (hereafter *NJ*) (Tokyo: Kadokawa Shoten, 1971), p. 86—and to Akira Miura's English translation, *Twenty-Four Eyes* (hereafter *TFE*) (Rutland: Tuttle, 1983), p. 97. Translations are both my own and Miura's (modified where appropriate).

12. The lyrics of "Tebiki no Iwa" (Huge Rocks): "Huge rocks are not so heavy / As our duty toward our country. / On that day that counts, that day we meet the

enemy, we must brave through / All the arrows and the bullets; / We must rush forward for our nation / Realizing our purity of heart and fulfilling our duty as men" *(Tebiki no iwa wa omokarazu / kokka ni tsukusu gi wa omoshi / koto aru sono hi, teki aru sono hi / furikuru yadama no tada naka wo / okashite susumite kuni no tame / tsukuse ya danji no honbun wo, sekishin wo); NJ,* p. 49. This translation is a modification of Akira Miura's *(TFE,* p. 55). The old man used the *hi-fu-mi-yo-i-mu-na-hi* scale while the children were used to the *do-re-mi* scale. Kinoshita incorporates the essence of this passage in the film. As Miss Ōishi leaves the village for what seems to be the last time, the children spontaneously sing a favorite "silly" song when the man teacher tells them to sing "Tebiki no Iwa."

13. *NJ,* pp. 137–139; *TFE,* pp. 156–158.

14. *NJ,* pp. 138–139; *TFE,* p. 158.

15. Readers and viewers know of this only through the teachers' timorous gossip and Ōishi's talk with the principal.

16. In the 1930s a number of young teachers in rural primary schools used Inagawa's technique of having students write about their lives. This practice, known as the "Life Composition Movement" *(Seikatsu tsuzurikata undō),* was suppressed by the government because they considered it leftist. It is likely that Tsuboi was also protesting Japan's postwar Red Purge with this story.

17. *NJ,* p. 114; *TFE,* pp. 128–129.

18. "Aikoku chūshin de ikō" is the phrase used in the film. The phrase in the novel was more descriptive, at least in the original Japanese. See *NJ,* p. 116; *TFE,* p. 130.

19. *NJ,* p. 115; *TFE,* p. 130.

20. *NJ,* p. 21; *TFE,* p. 22.

21. In the film Kinoshita intersperses scenes of the Red paranoia at school with scenes of the girl Matchan's orphaning because of her mother's death in childbirth, suggesting that Ōishi shared with Matchan an inability to change her situation.

22. *NJ,* p. 151; *TFE,* pp. 171–172.

23. From this old man we learn that Ōishi comes from a family with a progressive tradition. Her father organized a strike among his fellow elementary students when a teacher mistreated him, and he managed to evade the draft by becoming a sailor. See *NJ,* pp. 71–72 and 156; *TFE,* pp. 80 and 177.

24. *NJ,* p. 154; *TFE,* p. 175.

25. *NJ,* p. 174; *TFE,* p. 200.

26. *NJ,* p. 199; *TFE,* p. 231.

27. One exception to this is the noodle shop owner to whom the orphaned student Matchan is indentured. She is a nameless person and appears as simply a character type, certainly not someone with whom most readers and viewers would identify.

28. Satō, *Currents,* p. 112. Ōishi repeatedly tells her students that they are not at fault for their problems. Even at the grave of one of her boys who died as a soldier in the war, she mumbles to herself, "He was a guiltless child" *(Tsumi no nai ko deshita).*

29. Keiko McDonald, "Kinoshita and the Gift of Tears: *Twenty-Four Eyes,*" in her *Cinema East: A Critical Study of Major Japanese Films* (Rutherford, N.J.: Fairleigh Dickinson University Press, 1983), pp. 250–251.

30. Satō places this film in the same category as Italian director Vittorio De Sica's *The Bicycle Thief* (1948) because it presents "Japanese as on the whole nothing more than the good-willed victims of war." See Satō Tadao, *Eiga o dō miru ka* (Tokyo: Kodansha, 1976), pp. 22–23.

31. "Dō shite mo nogareru koto no dekinai otoko no tadoru michi." See *NJ*, pp. 157–159; *TFE*, p. 179.

32. Satō, *Currents*, p. 113.

33. William B. Hauser, "Women and War: The Japanese Film Image," in Gail Lee Bernstein, ed., *Recreating Japanese Women: 1600–1945* (Berkeley: University of California Press, 1991), pp. 307–313; quote is on p. 312. Regarding the Freudian association of masculinity with war in Japanese film see also Marie Thorsten Morimoto, "The 'Peace Dividend' in Japanese Cinema: Metaphors of a Demilitarized Nation," in Wimal Dissanayake, ed., *Colonialism and Nationalism in Asian Cinema* (Bloomington: Indiana University Press, 1994), pp. 11–29.

34. Her stated purpose in writing this children's story reminds one of Yasui Kaoru's statements on the goal of the antinuclear movement three years later. In the afterword to the first edition in 1952, she wrote: "I simply had to emphasize that war only brings unhappiness to mankind." See *Nijūshi no hitomi* (Tokyo: Kōbunsha, 1952), as quoted in *NJ*, p. 216.

35. These comments are from a 1954 article in *Shūkan Asahi* as quoted in Odagiri Hideo, "Kaisetsu," p. 288. Audie Bock notes that *Twenty-Four Eyes* marked a shift in Kinoshita's films: "Evil becomes more anonymous, less possible to pinpoint and attack." Bock implies that Kinoshita concluded "it was useless to try to say anything meaningful to" the Japanese people since they did not take him seriously. See Audi Bock, *Japanese Film Directors* (Tokyo: Kodansha International, 1978), p. 205.

36. Gomikawa Junpei, *Ningen no jōken* (Tokyo: Bungei Shunjū, 1979), originally published in 1956–1958. Since there are several editions of this novel, and this *bunko* edition has six volumes, book and chapter are included with pagination.

37. Kobayashi's film version makes this last issue even clearer in the opening scene, which has Kaji running away from a marching squad of soldiers, followed by Michiko's challenge that he is running away.

38. This attitude was shared by many leftist intellectuals in the early postwar era. See, especially, Ara Masato's comments in a panel discussion carried in the journal with the possibly noncoincidental title *Ningen*: Ara Masato et al., "Bungakusha no sekimu," *Ningen* (April 1946), reprinted in Usui Yoshimi, ed., *Sengo bungakuronsō* 1 (1972):55–71. The idea that one must maintain a rigorously uncompromising humanism—to go to jail or even die if necessary—was actually articulated in this panel discussion. Novelist Haniya Yutaka, who had been jailed in the early 1930s for his own communism, argued that one of the lessons of the war was that one had to stand firm on one's humanity *(ningen o ningen to shite)*. See p. 70.

39. Gomikawa, *Ningen*, bk. 1, chap. 5.

40. A slightly older, considerably more experienced, and perhaps wiser colleague, Okishima encourages Kaji to be honest about his self-deceptions regarding his own integrity in the face of overwhelming pressures. Okishima is fond of Kaji, for like Kaji he is at heart an earnest man who wants to maintain his own and others' self-respect. Kaji is blessed with many such friends who serve as foils for his conscience: Kageyama at the company headquarters and for a short time in the army; Shinjo, who eventually deserts the army; and Tange in the military hospital.

41. Gomikawa, *Ningen*, bk. 1, chap. 12, p. 72.

42. Kaji is as horrified by this act as Gao, but as labor supervisor he automatically becomes the one in charge of procuring bordello services for the prisoners. It was the mine manager who insisted that the best way to get the men to work hard is to reward their basest instincts. See Gomikawa, *Ningen*, bk. 1, chaps. 32 and 34.

43. "Just as the company has, in order to get Kaji the watchdog to round up the worker sheep, thrown him the bait of a draft exemption and gotten him married to the bitch Michiko, so would Kaji, in order to pacify the special laborers [POWs], use Yang's male partner [Gao] by throwing him the bait of a home outside the barbed-wire fence, and having him marry her." See Gomikawa, *Ningen,* bk. 1, chap. 47, p. 269. Kaji and Michiko eventually end up in the same situation: Kaji dying as an escaped POW, Michiko helplessly waiting for him in the city.

44. *Kyoto gakuen shinbun* (September 24, 1956), as cited in Ogiya Shōzō, "Sengo besutoseraa monogatari 46: Gomikawa Junpei—Ningen no jōken: gendaiteki 'kyūdō' no sho," *Asahi jaanaru* 8(37) (September 4, 1966):38.

45. "Guinea pig" is a common term used to express anger over U.S. interest in the medical effects of atomic bomb radiation. Gomikawa's decision to include Unit 703 medical experiments in this fashion fits his general message that the Japanese people suffered because, among other reasons, they had caused similar suffering to other peoples.

46. Gomikawa, *Ningen,* bk. 2, chap. 2, p. 21. Wang's letter (pp. 14–26) is not included in Kobayashi's film version, but the message is equally clear.

47. See Gomikawa, *Ningen,* bk. 2, chap. 2, pp. 27–28.

48. Taken from Kobayashi Masaki, "Ningen no jōken," pt. 1. See also Gomikawa, *Ningen,* bk. 2, chap. 36. In the book Wang adds: "Kaji, you have succumbed to a defeatism in which human beings are isolated and debilitated under the rule of violence, more so than you realize. . . . You have less faith in human beings than you think."

49. In the book Kaji's discussion with Wang occurs on the morning of the execution day after a night of anguish. See Gomikawa, *Ningen,* bk. 2, chaps. 35–36.

50. See Gomikawa, *Ningen,* bk. 2, chap. 34, p. 194.

51. William Hauser notes that in both wartime and postwar movies the "protection of the family and the community is what should concern women: leave political discourse to the men." See Hauser, "Women and War," pp. 312–313.

52. The sergeant tells the police adjutant that one should pour water over the blade beforehand. It helps the blade cut through more smoothly because it prevents flesh and blood from sticking. *("Tōshin ni mizu o tsukeru to yoku kireru. Abura ga tsukanai kara da.")* Here is a good example of Gomikawa's use of detail to convey the Japanese military's brutality. See Gomikawa, *Ningen,* bk. 2, chap. 38, p. 212.

53. In the book Kaji tells himself that he is a brute—a beast wearing the skin of a human being; Gomikawa, *Ningen,* bk. 2, chap. 38, pp. 216–217. In the film, Kobayashi puts words to the same effect into Gao's mouth as he is being brutally slashed.

54. Gomikawa Junpei, "Maegaki," in Gomikawa, *Ningen,* bk. 1, p. 3.

55. *Tokyo shinbun,* September 17, 1956, quoted in Ogiya, "Sengo besutoseraa monogatari 46," p. 38.

56. *Kyoto gakuen shinbun,* September 24, 1956, quoted in Ogiya, "Sengo besutoseraa monogatari 46," p. 38.

57. *Akahata,* October 26, 1957, quoted in Ogiya, "Sengo besutoseraa monogatari 46," p. 38.

58. Gomikawa, *Ningen,* bk. 2, chap. 39, p. 226.

59. Gomikawa, *Ningen,* bk. 2, chap. 2, p. 26.

60. Each of the six volumes of the novel *Ningen no jōken* sold well, apparently among this university-age group, until the last volume was published in February 1958.

That month it jumped to the top of the bestseller lists and remained there into the summer after the weekly magazine *Shūkan Asahi* devoted several articles and a cover to what it called a "hidden bestseller" *(kakureta besutosera)*. See *Shūkan Asahi*, February 16, 1958, noted in Ogiya, "Sengo besutoseraa monogatari 46," pp. 35–36.

61. See Ogiya, "Sengo besutoseraa monogatari 46," p. 38; and "Wadai no nenmatsu chōsei," *Mainichi shinbun*, December 17, 1958, cited in same.

62. Psychologist Erik Erikson describes this period of ego development in early adulthood as a struggle between mutually incompatible potentialities he labels "identity consolidation" and "identity confusion" followed by a similar struggle between "intimacy" and "aloneness." See Erik H. Erikson, "Identity and the Life Cycle," *Psychological Issues* 1 (1959):1–171. Daniel J. Levinson, developing Erikson's insights in clinical studies, describes the two potentially contradictory major tasks of early adulthood: exploring the possibilities of adult living (while keeping options open) and creating a stable life structure. See Daniel J. Levinson et al., *The Seasons of a Man's Life* (New York: Ballantine, 1977).

63. "Gendai no atarashii eiyū," as noted in Hori Hidehiko, "Seibugeki 'Ningen no jōken,' " *Shinchō* 55(7) (July 1958):67.

64. See, for example, Gomikawa, *Ningen*, bk. 1, chap. 15, pp. 99–100.

65. Gomikawa, *Ningen*, bk. 1, chaps. 30–31.

66. Gomikawa, *Ningen*, bk. 1, chap. 35, p. 198.

67. Gomikawa, *Ningen*, bk. 2, chap. 38, p. 214.

68. In his first army unit his commanding officer recognizes that recalcitrant men *(otoko)* like Kaji often make the best soldiers because of their will to survive and ability to command their fellow soldiers' respect. In the Soviet POW camp, the Japanese commanding officer recognizes the threat *otoko* like Kaji pose to reestablishing the old order.

69. See Morimoto, " 'Peace Dividend' in Japanese Cinema," pp. 19–20.

70. Satō, *Currents*, pp. 16–17 and 35.

71. Hori, "Seibugeki," pp. 66–69.

72. Ivan Morris' assertion of a Japanese penchant for this type of hero may be truer for the postwar era than for the rest of Japanese history. See Ivan Morris, *The Nobility of Failure: Tragic Heroes in the History of Japan* (New York: Holt, 1975).

73. Kobayashi Masaki, "Eiga 'Ningen no jōken' no omoide," *Bungei shunjū* (May 1995):310–311.

74. See Ibuse Masuji, *Kuroi ame*, rev. ed. (Tokyo: Shinchōsha, 1985), pp. 6–8. Translated by John Bester as *Black Rain* (Tokyo: Kodansha International, 1969), pp. 11–13. During the war, Shigematsu and his niece Yasuko work in a clothing factory that, although important to the war effort, is relatively benign in its contribution. (I use Bester's translation for the most part, with minor alterations where appropriate.)

75. Ibuse, *Kuroi ame*, pp. 205–206; *Black Rain*, p. 193.

76. Ibuse, *Kuroi ame*, pp. 66–67; *Black Rain*, pp. 65–66.

77. The man complains that officials were lax in reporting to divisional headquarters after the attack, but Ibuse inserts a special author's note, complete with citation of his source, to the effect that the officials tried their best to fulfill their duties but were stymied when they found that the divisional office no longer existed. This note not only adds a touch of verisimilitude: it exonerates the civilian bureaucracy in this context and distinguishes it from the clearly culpable military.

78. Ibuse, *Kuroi ame*, pp. 127–129; *Black Rain*, pp. 121–122.

79. Ibuse is thus expressing the same faith that the 1950s antibomb movement had—that witnessing the horror of the atomic bombing is the most effective way to turn people against war and for peace. See Chapter 3.

80. Ibuse, *Kuroi ame,* p. 170; *Black Rain,* p. 161. This attitude, of course, is similar to that underlying the phrase "Better Red than Dead." Part of *Black Rain*'s success outside Japan can be traced to this shared fear of nuclear destruction.

81. *"Washira wa, kokka no nai kuni ni umaretakatta noo."* Ibuse, *Kuroi ame,* pp. 171–172; *Black Rain,* p. 162.

82. Ibuse, *Kuroi ame,* pp. 300–302; *Black Rain,* pp. 282–283.

83. Ibuse, *Kuroi ame,* p. 305; *Black Rain,* p. 287.

84. Etō Jun, "Bungei jihyō," *Asahi shinbun,* evening ed., August 25, 1966; reprinted in *Bungei nenkan* (1967):60–61.

85. Yamamoto Kenkichi, "Chi ni tsuita heijōshin," *Asahi shinbun,* evening ed., October 24, 1966; quoted in John Whittier Treat, "Ibuse Masuji: Nature, Nostalgia, Memory," in Treat, *Writing Ground Zero: Japanese Literature and the Atomic Bomb* (Chicago: University of Chicago Press, 1995), p. 265. Ibuse's *Black Rain* is universally accorded prominence in the troika of "exemplary" *(daihyōteki)* works of atomic bomb literature, which includes Ohta Yōko's *Shikabane no machi* (1947), translated by Richard Minear as *City of Corpses* in his edited collection *Hiroshima: Three Witnesses* (Princeton: Princeton University Press, 1990), and Hara Tamiki's *Natsu no hana* (1947), translated by Minear as *Summer Flowers* in same. Besides the items mentioned in the preceding paragraphs, *Kuroi ame* contains many expressions of antiwar sentiment that contradict Yamamoto. Shigeko ends her short account of wartime diet with the abrupt statement that "war is a sadistic killer of young and old, men and women, alike." See Ibuse, *Kuroi ame,* p. 73; *Black Rain,* p. 71. And Yasuko's short entry for August 7 achieves the astounding feat of turning the actual atomic-bomb victim experience immediately into a form of antiwar protest: "Hiroshima is a burnt-out city, a city of ashes, a city of death, a city of destruction, the heaps of corpses a mute protest against war." See Ibuse, *Kuroi ame,* pp. 13–14; *Black Rain,* p. 18.

86. In his testimony of the bombing, Dr. Iwatake attributes his knowledge that flames tend to sweep over the surface of rivers—which helped him survive the Hiroshima firestorm—to his experience in the Tokyo firebombing. See Ibuse, *Kuroi ame,* p. 260; *Black Rain,* p. 244. The firebombing of nearby Fukuyama City is described by another survivor. See Ibuse, *Kuroi ame,* pp. 195–197; *Black Rain,* pp. 184–185.

87. John Treat notes that conservative readers appreciated the fact that *Black Rain* does not "exploit the moral indignation of Hiroshima and Nagasaki to score anti-Western, pro-communist points." See Treat, *Writing Ground Zero,* p. 266. Treat ably describes the conservative ideological nature of *Black Rain* with an emphasis on literary theory. My own understanding of the conservative ideological affinities for the novel benefited from Treat's treatise and from a contemporary panel discussion by critics in the literary journal *Nihon bungaku.* See Aihara Kazuo et al., "Ibuse Masuji 'Kuroi ame,' " *Nihon bungaku* 16(4) (April 1967):244–255.

88. Etō Jun, "Bungei jihyō," *Asahi shinbun,* evening ed., August 25, 1996. See also Treat, *Writing Ground Zero,* pp. 266–268.

89. See Carol Gluck's comments on Yasumaru Yoshio's appreciation of the "homely collection of village values—diligence, frugality, humility, filiality—though not revolutionary or concerned with the transformation of objective social and political traditions, was nonetheless of inestimable importance in giving the people a sense of par-

ticipation in their own destiny. . . . One could do something about one's lot and in the process hold the family and the village together." See Gluck, "The People in History," *Journal of Asian Studies* 38(1) (November 1978):39.

90. Isogai thinks Ibuse's "logic of the common man" *(shomin ronri)* is the most effective antidote to Mishima Yukio's "aristocratic aesthetic" *(kizokuteki bigaku).* See Aihara et al., "Ibuse Masuji 'Kuroi ame,' " pp. 250–251 and 255.

91. Aihara et al., "Ibuse Masuji 'Kuroi ame,' " p. 250. Aihara is suspicious of the book precisely because of this *nōhonshugi* type of appeal: "One wonders if criticism [of the bomb and war] based on such principles can succeed in clearly warning about the atomic bomb, war, and especially the capitalist system which brought them about."

92. Ibuse, *Kuroi ame,* pp. 316–317; *Black Rain,* pp. 296–298. Note the convenient ambiguity in which the bully could symbolize both the Japanese militarists and the American enemy. There is also, of course, an Oedipal image at work here: a subliminal fulfillment of the desire to achieve union with the peaceful and secure mother and cast off the militarist figure of manhood. If only in a camouflaged and incomplete way, then, *Black Rain* shares with *Human Condition* the message that the old militarist conception of manhood must be replaced with a more humane image. In the same section, the imagery of eels swimming upstream suggests a new opportunity in a rebirth for the nation.

93. See former Education Minister and future Prime Minister Hatoyama Ichirō's September 15, 1945, comments in the Tokyo *Asahi shinbun* that "the atomic bombing is more against international law than the use of poison gas and is a war crime."

94. Satō Tadao, *Eiga o dō miru ka* (Tokyo: Kodansha, 1976), pp. 8–14. As examples of this "narcissistic national mythmaking" he notes Roberto Rossellini's *Roma, Citta Aperta* (Open City, 1945) and *On the Edge of Battle* (1946), and French filmmaker René Clement's *La Bataille du rail* (Battle of the Rails, 1945). See Michel Foucault's comments on French cinema's cynical rejection of this Gaullist myth in the middle 1970s in "Film and Popular Memory: An Interview with Michel Foucault," *Radical Philosophy* 11 (1975):24–29.

95. Satō likens *Twenty-Four Eyes* to Vittorio De Sica's *Ladri di biciclette* (The Bicycle Thief, 1948) because it portrays the hopelessness of the average person in the face of an impersonal system; Satō, *Eiga o dō miru ka,* pp. 22–24.

96. John Dower has succinctly expressed this depiction of pure victimhood as a legacy of the wartime propaganda films: "The overriding image . . . is of the Japanese as an innocent, suffering, self-sacrificing people. It is the image, in the end, of the Japanese as eternal victims—victims of war, of fate, of noble commitments, of vague enemies, of misguided antagonists, of whatever one might choose to imagine." See John Dower, "Japanese Cinema Goes to War," *Japan Society Newsletter* (July 1987):9.

97. See Edmund Leach, "Myth as a Justification for Faction and Social Change," in Robert A. Georges, ed., *Studies on Mythology* (Homewood, Ill.: Irwin, 1968), p. 198, as quoted by Lawrence Levine, "The Folklore of Industrial Society: Popular Culture and Its Audiences," *American Historical Review* 97(5) (December 1992):1399. In his study of American popular black culture, Levine found no single overarching thematic matrix.

98. John Treat notes that the destruction of city hall as depicted in *Black Rain* was historically accurate and symbolic of the bomb's destruction of the Japanese state, the coercive organization that had brought about such desolation. See Treat, *Writing Ground Zero,* pp. 275–276. He might equally have noted the irony that the only

buildings still standing in the downtown area were a department store and the Chamber of Commerce building—symbolic perhaps of postwar Japan's rise as a mercantilist nation.

Chapter 6: Compensating Victims

1. The other two memorials were held on the occasion of independence in May 1952 and completion of the war dead cemetery in Tokyo in 1959.

2. Kano Masanao, *"Torijima" wa haitte iru ka* (Tokyo: Iwanami Shoten, 1988), pp. 221–227. The six Hakone volumes included such standard texts such as Marius B. Jansen, ed., *Changing Japanese Attitudes Toward Modernization* (Princeton: Princeton University Press, 1965), and Donald H. Shiveley, ed., *Tradition and Modernization in Japanese Culture* (Princeton: Princeton University Press, 1971).

3. See George R. Packard's description of the renewed interest in nationalism among progressive intellectuals in *Protest in Tokyo* (Princeton: Princeton University Press, 1966), pp. 328–330 and 334–338, especially p. 337; and see various essays in the special issue of *Shisō* 444 (June 1961), especially Kyōgoku Jun'ichi's " 'Demokurashii' to 'nashonarizumu'—Gendai Nihon ni okeru ishiki to kōdō."

4. *Asahi shinbun,* August 15, 1963. See also the *Asahi* editorial for August 15, 1964, as well as the discussions in the general-interest magazine *Chūō kōron* in the early 1960s, especially the October 1962 essays on "Considering Japan" *(Nihon o kangaeru).*

5. *Asahi shinbun,* August 14, 1963. See also "Seizonsha jokun seido no fukkatsu," *Sekai* 215 (November 1963):139–142.

6. *Asahi shinbun,* evening ed., August 14, 1963.

7. SCAP implemented its reforms through the civilian bureaucracy, and of course civil service pensions were not included in this reform.

8. Shimodaira Hiromi explores the policy consequences of the social equity thesis for *hibakusha* relief in "Genbaku hibakusha ni tai suru 'kokka hoshō' o kangaeru," *Kikan rōdō hō* 123 (March 1982):122–130. According to Shimodaira, in the early 1950s stalwart defenders of social equity could equivocate that veterans' benefits could be classified as compensation owed as a contractual obligation by the state as their former employers.

9. Interestingly, Nishimura recognized that everyone more or less made sacrifices in the war; but the state could not cover all losses. He admitted that the question of general war victims was an enormous problem, but these people would just have to find help in the social welfare system. It could only help them as the nation's economic conditions permitted: "As far as the state is concerned . . . broadly speaking everyone has to a greater or lesser extent sustained war losses *(sensō no gisei);* but as for the state trying to cover these losses, we have given as much aid as the nation's economic condition, and the country's general conditions, permit. Accordingly, first we have aid for the war wounded and their families, and aid for those who have been repatriated from abroad. . . . " See Nihon, Kokkai, *Dai 43 Shūgiin Shakai rōdō iinkaigiroku* 23 (March 26, 1963).

10. Muramatsu Michio, "Bringing Politics Back into Japan," *Daedalus* 119(3) (Summer 1990):141–155.

11. Prime Minister Nakasone Yasuhiro's "political resolution to the postwar" *(seijiteki sōgō kessan)* of the mid-1980s involved the same kind of struggle.

12. SCAP censorship in the Occupation years hindered early efforts. In 1948, for

example, SCAP prevented the Labor Ministry from publishing victims' demands for aid at one of its sponsored meetings, the Injured Women's Cooperative Meeting (Shōi Fujin Kyōryoku Taikai). These demands included state-funded medical research, a systematic program of medical examinations, and religious and vocational education as a means for promoting economic and emotional security. Another well-known self-help society was the Hiroshima Atomic Bomb Injured Welfare Society (Hiroshima Genbaku Shōgaisha Kōseikai) organized by Yoshikawa Kiyoshi in August 1951 after he had recuperated enough to leave the hospital. Tanimoto Kiyoshi and Norman Cousins recruited their "atomic bomb maidens" *(genbaku otome)* from this group. See Itō Takeshi, *Hibakusha engohō no tame ni hibaku no shisō to undō* (hereafter *Hibaku no shisō to undō*) (Tokyo: Shinhyōron, 1975), pp. 187–188.

13. Hidankyō was formed in Nagasaki during the second World Convention Against Atomic and Hydrogen Bombs. Its founding declaration credited the first World Convention of 1955 for enabling its formation. See Itō, *Hibaku no shisō to undō*, p. 190.

14. Comments made in the Lower House Social and Labor Affairs Committee on March 25, 1957. See Nihon, Kokkai, *Dai 26 Kokkai shūgiin kaigiroku—Shakai rōdō iinkaigiroku* 29 (March 25, 1957).

15. For the resolution *(Genbaku shōgaisha no chiryō ni kansuru ketsugi an)* and Lower House speeches see Nihon, Kokkai, *Shūgiin kaigiroku* 17, from *Kampō (gogai)* (December 12, 1956):12–14.

16. The 1957 Medical Care Bill provided for annual examinations and medical consultations, as well as medical care necessary to treat illness originating in exposure to bomb radiation, at clinics designated by the minister of welfare. The bill provided for a special commission of experts to investigate the medical care needed. See Nihon, Shūgiin/Sangiin, *Gikaiseidō 70-nen shi,* 12 vols. (1962), 5:523.

17. Itō, *Hibaku no shisō to undō*, p. 190.

18. Nihon, Kokkai, *Dai 33 Kokkai shūgiin kaigiroku—Shakai rōdō iinkaigiroku* (November 28, 1959). Despite his implication that repatriates had been given veteran-style treatment, repatriate payments of the 1950s were justified on a social equity rationale.

19. See Foreign Ministry Treaty Section Chief Takashi Michitoshi's responses to Ohara in Nihon, Kokkai, *Dai 33 Kokkai shūgiin kaigiroku—Shakai rōdō iinkaigiroku* (November 19, 1959).

20. Income caps were standard on social welfare subsidies such as livelihood protection, so their elimination is a convenient indicator that a group had succeeded in getting legislative validation of their claim to special treatment. This is why Welfare Minister Nishimura insisted in the Diet in March 1963 that war widow payments should be considered distinct from income requirements since they were an attempt at consolation for nonmaterial loss. See Nihon, Kokkai, *Dai 43 Shūgiin shakai rōdō iinkaigiroku* 23 (March 26, 1963).

21. In August 1962, Hidankyō's general meeting was rent by debate over whether or not to join Gensuikyō's rival, the Kinkaku Kaigi, because that organization had decided to shift its aim to amending the Medical Care Law. A new Relief Law had been Hidankyō's stated goal since August 1961. Although in the interest of unity it was decided not to change affiliation on the national level, the Oita prefectural Hidankyō association decided to join the rival All Japan Association of Hibakusha (Zen Nihon Hibakusha Kyōgikai), an alternative group formed by a large number of Hiroshima and Nagasaki *hibakusha* in May 1962. As a result of confusion caused by too close an

affiliation with the Gensuikyō—Hidankyō's chair, Moritaki Ichirō, was also on the Gensuikyō board until he was ousted in June 1964—the Hidankyō board of directors eventually decided to sever ties in February 1965. See Itō, *Hibaku no shisō to undō,* p. 193.

22. In January 1954, Okamoto Kōichi, an Osaka lawyer, began a long judicial process to force the government to provide help. He organized the League for Atomic Bomb Damage Compensation (Genbakusongai Kyūshō Dōmei) in order to sue the national government for state reparation. See Itō, *Hibaku no shisō to undō,* p. 188. The Tokyo District Court's decision was the judicial outcome of Okamoto's April 1955 suit against the Japanese government for reparations *(songai baishō).* See *Heiwa jiten* (1991), p. 429.

23. The court ruled that the bombings had violated international law, but the mitigating factors of war, occupation, and the peace treaty prevented individuals from suing the state. For a transcript of the ruling and commentary see *Jurisuto* (January 1964).

24. Nihon, Kokkai, *Dai 46 Kokkai shūgiin kaigiroku* 21 (April 3, 1964).

25. This reference to special health and emotional conditions indicates that Fujino was discussing *hibakusha* aid as a postwar resolution measure without departing from the mainstream LDP/government position that such aid was essentially social welfare, not state compensation. See Nihon, Kokkai, *Dai 46 Kokkai sangiin kaigiroku* 13 (March 27, 1964).

26. Ibid.

27. The opposition resolution was proposed on February 14, 1964. Socialist policy toward *hibakusha* relief hardly changed over the next quarter century. In the Fifty-first Diet in 1966, the JSP proposed basically the same amendments as the 1959 proposal, as well as changing the measure's name to the Atomic Bomb Victim Assistance Act *(Genshibakudan hibakusha engohō)* and abolishing income limitations on aid eligibility. See Nihon, Kokkai, *Dai 51 Kokkai shakairōdō iinkaigiroku* 48 (June 21, 1966). The JSP proposed an amendment in the Sixty-fifth Diet in 1971 to clarify that atomic bomb victim aid should be conducted in the spirit of state compensation. See Nihon, Kokkai, *Dai 65 Kokkai shakairōdōiin kaigiroku* 7 (February 25, 1971). Starting in 1974, the Socialists periodically introduced bills that would establish *hibakusha* pensions and improve aid based on the principle of state compensation. In the 114th Diet in 1989, the JSP advocate complained specifically about the unfairly unbalanced treatment of *hibakusha* compared to victims given aid under the wounded veterans' legislation. See Nihon, Kokkai, *Dai 114 Kokkai shakairōdō iinkaigiroku* (May 25, 1989).

28. Designated *hibakusha* received 10,000-yen monthly allowances plus 3,000 yen as a health subsidy. The government also shouldered 80 percent of nursing costs for those in need of such care. In 1969 funeral expenses were added; insurance subsidies were added in 1974.

29. Nihon, Kokkai, *Dai 58 Kokkai shūgiin kaigiroku* 19 (May 2, 1968).

30. Comments in the Social and Labor Affairs Committee, April 27, 1978. See Nihon, Kokkai, *Dai 84-kai Kokkai shūgiin kaigiroku* 28 (April 28, 1978). Welfare Minister Saitō Noboru had made this same concession in the Sixty-first Diet in 1969. See Moritake Ichirō, *Hankaku 30-nen* (Tokyo: Nihon Hyōronsha, 1976), p. 146.

31. SCAP's military authority quelled landlord obstruction of the reform. See SCAPIN 1855 (February 4, 1948) in Supreme Commander for the Allied Powers (SCAP), Government Section, *Political Reorientation of Japan, September 1945 to September 1948* (hereafter *PRJ)* (Washington, D.C.: GPO, 1949), p. 577.

32. Policy published in Nihon, Nōrinshō, Nōchika, *Shōwa 27, 28-nen nōchi nempō,* 220, as quoted in Waseda Minoru, "Nōchi hōshōhō to kyūjinushi dantai," *Hōritsu jihō* 37(9) (August 1965):36.

33. Ikeda played an important role in institutionalizing the land reform soon after independence. See R. P. Dore, *Land Reform in Japan* (London: Oxford University Press, 1959), p. 422.

34. Waseda Minoru categorizes landlord organizations into two types: the large landholders with financial connections, mainly from the Tōhoku region, who spearheaded legal efforts to get the land reform declared unconstitutional, and the small to medium landholders, typically from the Kansai and Kyūshū regions, who tried to revise the specifics of the land reform to allow landlords to divide ownership of tenanted land among family members and decide for themselves which land would be sold. All landlords wanted to get sale prices adjusted upward for the lands they were forced to sell. See Waseda, "Nōchi hōshōhō to kyūjinushi dantai," pp. 35–36.

35. The dispossessed landowners appealed to the same constitutional guarantee of private property as the repatriates. Section 3 of the Constitution, Article 29, stipulated that "private property may be taken for public use upon just compensation therefor."

36. Dore, *Land Reform,* p. 434.

37. The state served as an intermediary in transferring title under the land reform, buying parcels from the landlords to sell to the tenants, often with financing. Apparently the state still retained title to some land in 1956. See Waseda, "Nōchi hōshōhō to kyūjinushi dantai," p. 36.

38. Dore, *Land Reform,* p. 439; Haruhiro Fukui, *Party in Power: The Japanese Liberal-Democrats and Policy-Making* (Berkeley: University of California Press, 1970), p. 176. Fukui's chapter "Compensating Former Landlords" is the standard English-language analysis of the political machinations behind landlord compensation.

39. *Nihon nōgyō nenkan* (1958), pp. 79–81. Dore notes that the slogans at the December rally were considerably muted. There was no sign for compensation, just "Aid for the Victims of Land Reform." See Dore, *Land Reform,* p. 441.

40. *Nihon nōgyō shinbun,* February 25, 1957, as cited in Dore, *Land Reform,* p. 440. This was the Farmland Policy Subcommittee (Nōchi Seisaku Koiinkai) headed by Matsuura Motosuke. In April and May, this subcommittee interviewed Tokyo and Kyoto University professors Ōtsuki Masao, Wagatsuma Sakae, Miyazawa Toshiyoshi, and Hashimoto Densaemon, former Vice-Minister of Agriculture and Forestry Tōbata Shirō, and *Asahi shinbun* editor Danno Nobuo on landlord compensation. Only Professor Hashimoto favored it. See *Nihon nōgyō nenkan* (1959), p. 70.

41. Comments of February 19, 1957; *Nihon nōgyō nenkan* (1958), pp. 81–82.

42. As paraphrased by Dore, *Land Reform,* p. 440.

43. Comments of March 8 and 14, 1957; *Nihon nōgyō nenkan* (1958), p. 82.

44. The National Farmland League's slogan was "Nōchi kaihōsha wa senryō seisaku yukisugi ni yoru seiji giseisha" (Dispossessed farmers are the political victims of Occupation policy excess). See Nihon, Kokkai, *Dai 34 kokkai shūgiin kaigiroku* 20 (April 5, 1960):20.

45. Takada dismissed the landlords' claims because, after all, the feudal land system was doomed to extinction in any case. See Nihon, Kokkai, *Dai 31 shūgiin kaigiroku* 21(1) (March 12, 1959):3–8. In the Thirty-fourth Diet, DSP member Nakamura Tokio rejected their claim to war victimhood because more or less it would mean that most Japanese had been war victims. Nakamura mentioned others who would have

an equal claim on victim status: those who lost their homes and possessions because of the war; mobilized students; and forced evacuees. See Nihon, Kokkai, *Dai 34 kokkai shūgiin kaigiroku* 20 (April 5, 1960):15–22. Socialist rhetoricians would use this argument often to belittle landlord and repatriate status as war victims. In the context of *hibakusha* relief, they adopted the opposite strategy—arguing that all Japanese were truly war victims—in order to stress the *hibakusha* status as victim symbol, to demote the special status accorded veterans, and perhaps to push for a better social security system. See Ohara Tōru's remarks in the Thirty-third Diet, November 1959, mentioned earlier.

46. Fukui, *Party in Power,* pp. 177–178. See pp. 185–186 for Fukui's description of the two-pronged strategy. The welfare minister seems not to have been petitioned, as this would not be consistent with the eventual "reward" rationale for the payments.

47. Dore, *Land Reform,* p. 436; the translation is Dore's.

48. See the Ministry of Agriculture and Forestry report of October 1958 and see Dore, *Land Reform,* p. 438. Dore surveyed 628 household heads and oldest sons in six villages throughout Japan and found that 75 percent felt sorry for the landlords.

49. Dore agrees that this was the general tone of newspaper comment on landlord compensation efforts; Dore, *Land Reform,* p. 439.

50. *Mainichi shinbun,* April 20, 1957, as quoted in *Nihon nōgyō nenkan* (1958), p. 82.

51. *Mainichi shinbun,* April 23, 1957, as quoted in *Nihon nōgyō nenkan* (1958), p. 82. As we shall see, advocates for the landlords eventually turned this logic to their advantage in the 1960s.

52. From the first day of its inaugural convention, this organization openly planned to get compensation by forcing the LDP to back its demands. On the day after Minister Ide's advice that the landlords give up their efforts, the League of Land Reform Victims resolved that the minister of agriculture and forestry should follow the LDP's party platform on this issue and not be allowed to discreetly ignore the league and its claims. After their first meeting they staged a sit-in at the Ministry of Agriculture and Forestry until 9 P.M. The convention proclaimed the following three statements:

- We expect respect for individual property rights and the speedy realization of state compensation for the farmland victims of [land] liberation.
- We expect the rehabilitation of farm villages based on love, peace, and principles of justice and fairness.
- We expect that the total united strength of 3 million victims [alone] cannot become the backbone for the nation's reconstruction.

See *Nihon nōgyō nenkan* (1958), p. 80. It is easy to see how the second of these statements seems to express the prewar *kyōdōtai* ideology that denied the existence of class strife. For the landlords, of course, it merely expressed their desire to return to the halcyon days when they ran village life.

53. This was the Nōchi Mondai Chōsa Tokubetsu Iinkai. See *Nihon nōgyō nenkan* (1959), p. 70. Neither Dore nor Fukui offers adequate explanation for the LDP's initiative in bringing the landlords together into one organization, except perhaps as an effort to gain their electoral support. Dore does suggest that some probably felt that bringing all landlords into one organization would facilitate a small compensation settlement which would end landlord agitation for good. See Dore, *Land Reform,* pp. 441–442, and Fukui, *Party in Power,* p. 176. In late January 1958, the *Asahi shinbun* noted

that reunification under the guidance of the LDP raised landlord hopes and warned the party leadership to squelch their momentum among the rank-and-file. See *Asahi shinbun,* January 29, 1958, as quoted in *Nihon nōgyō nenkan* (1959), p. 70.

54. One of the landlords' grievances was that farmland near urban areas was being resold at vastly higher prices for commercial and residential use—contravening the original intent of land reform. Although the title transfer tax was intended to tap such windfall profits directly, it proved politically detrimental since it threatened the interests of the new rural conservative constituency.

55. The ministry report was based on a 1955 study of agricultural conditions. Analysis showed that former landlords held on average over one hundred times the amount of land held by the typical household (1,006 hectares compared to 75 are), sold more of their yields (45.2 percent compared to 27.7 percent), and held nonfarming jobs of higher status and income (village chief, local official, and salaryman) when they were part-time farmers. The ministry announced its report on October 27, 1958. See *Nihon nōgyō nenkan* (1960), pp. 89–90.

56. Nihon, Shūgiin/Sangiin, *Gikaiseido 70-nen shi,* 12 vols. (1962), 12:394.

57. According to Fukui, the LDP executive council had decided to make "reward" payments in April 1962; see Fukui, *Party in Power,* p. 182. For a convenient summary of the commission report in Japanese see *Nihon nōgyō nenkan* (1963), p. 72.

58. The paper criticized the LDP's first bill to set up the cabinet commission as merely a ploy for votes and money. See *Hokkaidō shinbun,* March 16, 1959, as quoted in *Nihon nōgyō nenkan* (1960), p. 90.

59. *Nihon nōgyō shinbun,* March 1, 1957, as cited in Dore, *Land Reform,* p. 440.

60. Waseda, "Nōchi hōshōhō to kyūjinushi dantai," p. 35. "Rewards" is Fukui's translation for *hōshō.* In Japanese *"hōshō"* is commonly used to mean compensation in the sense of making amends; the less common *"hōshō,"* using the same Chinese character as the colloquial phrase *"mukui to shite,"* here indicates compensation in the sense of remuneration for good deeds or service.

61. *Nihon nōgyō nenkan* (1963), p. 72.

62. Landlords would be paid for lost land beginning with 20,000 yen per *tan* (equivalent to about one-quarter of an acre) up to 1 *chō* (10 *tan*), gradually less for remaining land up to a maximum total "reward" of 1 million yen. See *Jurisuto* 312 (December 15, 1964):55–56; *Nihon nōgyō nenkan* (1966), pp. 113–114. The Prime Minister's Office estimated that 1.67 million former landlords would be eligible; *Asahi nenkan* (1966), p. 300.

63. Nihon, Kokkai, *Dai 48 shūgiin kaigiroku* 21 (March 23, 1965):22–26. The comments on the emotional anguish echoed conservative justification for war widows' condolence payments in 1963 and were repeated as partial justification for the repatriate payments as well.

64. *Asahi nenkan* (1966), p. 270. The "cow-walk" *(gyūho)* filibuster strategy, employed by other political parties as well, involves walking exceedingly slowly toward the podium, especially while voting by ballot.

65. Nihon, Kokkai, *Dai 48 shūgiin kaigiroku* 21 (March 23, 1965):23. In the Upper House Finance Committee, Councillors Kimura and Kameda questioned why remuneration was not the same for everyone, how it related to the repatriates' lost overseas assets problem, and why the government maintained that these payments would not constitute a war resolution measure. See Nihon, Kokkai, Shūgiin Hōseikyoku, *Dai 48-kai Kokkai seiteihō shingi yōroku,* pp. 303–304. I have been unable to access the full

Diet records for this interpellation. The question about differentiated remuneration was probably meant to assert that payments were a form of compensation that the government had rejected long ago. One of the main concerns for all was that land-lord compensation would not spark new and extended claims by other victim groups. This concern probably lay behind the questions about the connection with overseas assets and about the government's insistence that this bill was not a war resolution measure. Given the nature of the bill—it was a reward for service to the nation—it seems odd that the government denied that it was a war resolution measure. In any case, it seems such denial was an aberration: the *Asahi nenkan* for 1966 relates that the LDP actually called landlord compensation one of the three laws which signaled the "completion of war resolution measures" (p. 216).

66. *Asahi shinbun,* May 30, 1965; *Mainichi shinbun,* May 30, 1965, as quoted in Waseda, "Nōchi hoshōhō to kyūjinushi dantai," p. 33.

67. *Seisaku geppō* 113 (June 1965):25–28.

68. Quoted by Fukui, *Party in Power,* p. 182.

69. Civilians were repatriated mainly from Manchuria (1,003,767 with an additional 215,045 from Dairen), the Korean peninsula (South Korea 414,897; North Korea 297,167), mainland China (484,814), Taiwan (322,107), and Sakhalin (276,606). Numbers represent those repatriated by 1953. See Nihon, Sōrifu, Tōkeikyoku, *Nihon tōkei nenkan* (1954), pp. 45–46.

70. The majority had to face a loss in social as well as economic status. Irene Taeuber notes: "All were adjusted to life in the upper classes of highly stratified societies. The men were trained for professional, executive, or managerial positions, not for labor. The women were trained for the life appropriate to the family status, not for the toil of the fields, the shops, or the factories." Agricultural colonists, of course, were quite familiar with physical labor, but they also lost their superior position as land-owners. See Irene Taeuber, *Population of Japan* (Princeton: Princeton University Press, 1958), pp. 346–347.

71. See "Censored Periodicals, 1945–1949," Prange Collection, microfilm reel 54, compiled and edited by Eizaburō Okuizumi.

72. In 1948 in Maizuru, the point of reentry for most repatriates, civilians were limited to 1,000 yen in currency they could exchange for new yen notes. Officials took custody of currency over this limit. (It was eventually returned starting in 1953.) The destitute were assured of RRB allowances of 250 up to 1,000 yen depending on the number of family members. An extra 100 yen was given to those responsible for babies. All were given identification cards that permitted them to travel within Japan. Nihon Kōtsūkōsha issued train tickets to the repatriates as they were put on special trains in groups organized by home prefecture. See Toyama-ken, Kōsei-bu, Shakaifukushi-ka, *Toyama-ken shusen shorishi* (Toyama, 1975), pp. 413–418. See also Nihon, Hikiage En-gochō, *Hikiage engo no kiroku* (1950), p. 63ff. Once home they had one month to register evidence of their lost assets with the Ministry of Finance; *Hikiage engo no kiroku,* p. 89.

73. *Hikiage engo no kiroku,* document 37, pp. 99–105.

74. Ibid., pp. 89–94 and 104–105. This last program was used by Manchurian agricultural colonies such as Nagano's well-publicized Ohinata-mura and Kumamoto's Tōyō-mura; but the program had only a limited impact. In Ibaraki, for example, the resettlement program only legitimized returning farmers who had already squatted on old military bases. See Ibaraki-ken Kaitaku Jūnenshi Henshū Iinkai, *Ibaraki-ken kaitaku*

jūnenshi (1955), pp. 6–9. By March 1950, some 73,411 agricultural colonist families had been repatriated. By the same date, some 27,028 families had been settled under the government resettlement program; as the Ibaraki case suggests, not all of these were repatriate households; *Hikiage engo no kiroku,* p. 103. For an anthropological study of Tōyō-mura's experience in resettlement see Araragi Shinzō, "Manshū kaitakudan o botai to suru kaitaku shuraku ni okeru 'kyōdōsei'—Kumamoto-ken Tōyō-mura," *Soshioroji* 33(1) (May 1988):115–117. The government loaned 1 billion yen in 1946, 816 million yen in 1947, 500 million yen in 1948, and 700 million yen in 1949. See *Hikiage engo no kiroku,* p. 120.

75. From the precensored October 1947 *Hikiage dōhō,* in "Censored Periodicals, 1945–1949," Prange Collection, microfilm reel 54. The southwestern prefectures of Oita, Kumamoto, and Yamaguchi received the highest percentage of repatriates relative to their populations. See *Hikiage engo no kiroku,* front charts.

76. The bureau allotted over 3 million yen for this campaign. See *Hikiage engo no kiroku,* p. 90; document 45, pp. 106–108. The text of "Furusato no tsuchi" (p. 92) is:

Furusato no yama wa natsukashi / furusato no kawa wa natsukashi / tsukaretaru kokoro idakite / ashi omoku kaerikureba / furusato ni yama wa arikeri / furusato ni kawa wa arikeri. ¶Chichi nomi no chichi wa natsukashi / tarachine no haha wa natsukashi / osanago no kokoro ni narite / mi mo kataku mon o kugureba / sukoyaka ni chichi wa mashikeri / nagoyaka ni haha wa mashikeri. ¶Furusato no tomo wa natsukashi / furusato no tsuchi wa natsukashi / komiaguru namida nomikomi / tomo no te o tsuchi o nigereba / atatakaku tomo wa arikeri / yawarakaku tsuchi wa arikeri.

A loose translation of "The Soil of My Village Home":

How I long for the mountains of my village home / how I long for the rivers of my village home / With wearied spirit / if I get back with heavy steps / In my village home there were mountains / In my village home there were rivers. ¶How I long for Father / how I long for Mother / Regaining the heart of a child / if I knock on the gate with hardened body / Father was healthy / Mother was gentle. ¶How I long for the friends of my village home / how I long for the soil of my village home / swallowing overflowing tears / if I grasp my friend's hand, grasp the soil / my friend was kind / the soil was yielding.

77. It published *Hikiage dōhō,* a monthly magazine with a circulation of two thousand starting in early 1946. Besides serving as a clearinghouse for repatriate conditions in the prefectures, the magazine was a forum for ideas on how to improve repatriates' chances for rebuilding their lives.

78. The other main repatriate groups who submitted the petition were colonialist groups from Sakhalin, Taiwan, China's Kwantgung province, and the mandated South Sea Islands. SCAP suppressed this petition's publication because it was deemed potentially critical of Allied nations. See the censor's comments in Prange Collection, October 1949 issue of *Hikiage dōhō.*

79. This is the same organization whose name R. P. Dore translated as the "National Federation of Returned Overseas Emigrants"; see Dore, *Land Reform,* p. 439. RSK Chairman Hozumi was one of its organizers.

80. Zenren actually did not acquire its name until November 1946; *Hikiage engo no kiroku,* pp. 101–102.

81. The Japan Communist Party went the furthest in advocating government-funded living subsidies; *Gikaiseido 70-nen shi,* p. 722. Interestingly, the JCP was the only party to oppose compensation in the 1967 bill. See John Creighton Campbell, "Compensation for Repatriates: A Case Study of Interest-Group Politics and Party-Government Negotiations in Japan," in T. J. Pempel, ed., *Policymaking in Contemporary Japan* (Ithaca: Cornell University Press, 1977), p. 128. Campbell's article is the standard English-language study of the repatriate political effort for compensation.

82. *Gikaiseido 70-nen shi,* p. 931. Both the legislative and executive branches of the government took provisional steps to investigate future policy options. Both houses of the Diet established deliberative committees in July 1947 to address general issues of concern to the repatriates: financial problems (mostly the loss of overseas assets); employment and livelihood; housing; and aid for families of detained soldiers. In August 1948 the Prime Minister's Office followed suit with the Repatriate Policy Advisory Council (Hikiage Dōhō Taisaku Shingikai). See Nihon, Sōrifu, *Zaigai zaisan mondai no shori kiroku* (1975), p. 5.

83. He did not explain exactly what measures would be appropriate. See *Zaigai zaisan mondai,* documents, p. 6.

84. *Zaigai zaisan mondai,* p. 6.

85. In late September 1946, Prime Minister Yoshida suggested in a cabinet meeting that the government might indemnify the repatriates' lost overseas assets to the extent government revenues allowed—if the payments were pooled in a financial institution that could invest in industrial ventures. Yoshida remarked that repatriate destitution was becoming one of the main causes of the worsening social unrest and required various relief measures. In October, Finance Minister Ishibashi Tanzan proposed that the issue of overseas assets be shelved for the time being and each repatriate household be granted 15,000 yen worth of emergency relief. Chief Cabinet Secretary Hayashi Jōji secretly informed repatriate group representatives of the cabinet's thinking, and on November 3 it was announced to the press. Late the next month, however, a group of impatient repatriates staged a sit-in at the Lower House of the Diet, demanding resolution of the overseas assets question. Prime Minister Yoshida met with the protesters, and at a special meeting on December 6 the cabinet decided to grant each family 15,000 yen. Unfortunately for the repatriates, SCAP vetoed the plan, perhaps for monetary reasons. See *Zaigai zaisan mondai,* documents, p. 4.

86. Ibid., p. 9.

87. Ibid., p. 11.

88. Ibid., p. 5; Campbell, "Compensation," p. 133.

89. Zenren rather exaggerated its claims to control as many as 5 million votes; Campbell estimates the number was probably closer to five or six hundred thousand. See Campbell, "Compensation," p. 129.

90. *Asahi shinbun,* March 6, 1957.

91. Both Socialist and LDP Diet members seem to have been sensitive to repatriate retribution at the polls. See Campbell, "Compensation," pp. 119–120.

92. Campbell, "Compensation," p. 105. Fukui makes a similar case for the landlords. Campbell's analysis suggests it was the perceived rather than actual electoral influence that gave Zenren leaders and closely connected LDP Diet members leverage within the LDP.

93. *Hikiage engo no kiroku,* p. 11.

94. 1954 laws 66, 105, 106, 107, and 108, as described in *Zaigai zaisan mondai,* pp. 11–12.

95. *Zaigai zaisan mondai*, p. 13; Campbell, "Compensation," p. 106.

96. This was Ministry of Health and Welfare 1956 Directive 13. See *Zaigai zaisan mondai*, p. 13.

97. Shakaihoken hōki kenkyūkai, *Nihon shakai hoshō daihyakka* III (Tokyo, 1966), p. 87.

98. *Zaigai zaisan mondai*, pp. 13–14.

99. *Asahi shinbun*, March 6, 1957. Kanda was an important member of the faction led by Ōno Banboku, who played a major role in getting the eventual bill passed. See Campbell, "Compensation," p. 107, n. 7.

100. *Gikaiseido 70-nen shi*, 5:524–525. Although these grants were disbursed over several years, the size of the commitment is evident from the fact that this sum would account for 1.5 percent of the total national government budget in 1957.

101. *Asahi shinbun*, March 6, 1957.

102. *Zaigai zaisan mondai*, pp. 15–16.

103. Campbell, "Compensation," p. 109; *Zaigai zaisan mondai*, pp. 16–21.

104. See pp. 192–195. For LDP stances on the 1967 bill see *Seisaku geppō* (November 1966):98ff.; and *Seisaku geppō* (January 1967):52–70.

105. See Taeuber's comments on this point of "livelihood interests" in note 70. A 1968 government publication presented the repatriates' special position in a curious play on words as it described the 1967 compensation proposal. It was "not an assistance measure like the 1957 payments but must be seen from the personal angle *(jinteki sokumen ni chakumoku sezaru o enai)*, and in contrast to other war victims it shows the existence of a special need of the repatriates." See Shakaihoken hōki kenkyūkai, *Nihon shakai hoshō daihyakka*, 3:87.

106. The council did not specify how much should be distributed, but it did remark that the government should consider national finances when deciding the amount. The text of the commission's report is reprinted in the documents section of *Zaigai zaisan mondai*, pp. 12–30; the quotes are on p. 23. The report was printed in several journals as well. See, for example, *Jurisuto* 362 (January 15, 1967):48–55.

107. Zenren was so widely considered the exemplar of interest groups that a compendium of postwar history—Tsuji Kiyoaki, ed., *Shiryo: Sengo nijunenshi*, 1: *Seiji* (Tokyo: Nihon Hyōronsha, 1966)—cited it in its entry on pressure groups *(atsuryoku dantai)*. A *Yomiuri shinbun* article of December 1, 1965, described how, at an early meeting of the LDP Diet members association for addressing the overseas assets problem, non-LDP politicians demanded to be allowed to join, and some first-time participants insisted on being made officers of the group. The political muscle of Zenren was evident in its over 3 million membership; the largest concentrations were in Fukuoka and Hokkaido (40,000 households each) and Nagano (20,000). The national group's annual budget at that time was about 30 million yen; see pp. 497–498. Campbell evaluates the reality behind the perceived political power of Zenren; see Campbell, "Compensation," p. 124 ff.

108. *Asahi shinbun*, June 28, 1967. Except for the *hibakusha*, these groups did not get any compensation—probably because they were not as well organized, possibly because there were simply too many of them. Compensating the whole population would have been nonsensical, as Diet speakers often implied when they wished to deny payments to an opposition-affiliated victim group.

109. *Jurisuto* 362 (January 15, 1967):25–47; Satō's comments are on p. 46.

110. The final bill included payments of 19.5 billion yen per year, totaling 192.5 billion yen over the years, from a national sinking fund. Those aged fifty or over at

the end of the war received 160,000 yen; those younger received progressively less; those under twenty but at least one year old got 20,000 yen. Those who had lived abroad at least eight years—that is, those who had moved abroad before the outbreak of hostilities in 1937—received a 10,000-yen bonus. See *Zaigai zaisan mondai*, pp. 41 and 60; the full text of the law is on pp. 40–48 of the documents section. Although opposition parties queried government officials on the reasoning behind the bill, only the Communists opposed it in the end. Zenren had used the same techniques with Socialist and Clean Government party Diet members as they had with LDP Diet members to enlist their support. See Campbell, "Compensation," pp. 127–128.

111. *Zaigai zaisan mondai*, p. 55. Yet when asked directly if this was an assets compensation measure, he replied that it was not (p. 50). He could not say that it was because the commission report had said there could be no fair compensation for lost assets.

112. The director general of the Prime Minister's Office, Tsukahara Toshio, made this clear in the Diet questioning on July 14, 1967; *Zaigai zaisan mondai*, p. 50.

113. One council member quipped: "Although the basic conclusions of the council had long since been settled, working out the pretexts had been hard work." See Campbell, "Compensation," p. 112.

114. The Prime Minister's Office had long considered the issue resolved—as one suspects many of the recipients of the 1950s payments assumed, as well, considering that they stopped pressuring the government for a few years.

115. In hindsight this switch may not be surprising since these victim groups' advocates were the same LDP party politicians. The repatriates could still maintain that the wartime government had erred and misled them. That was its crime and the source of its obligation to the repatriates who had properly and loyally followed the government's lead. The *hibakusha*'s consistently antagonistic position toward contemporary government policy, as asserted by the Socialists, made their success that more difficult and limited.

116. Kuriyama: "It's a matter of one kind of war victim that, compared to others, has a special characteristic." See *Zaigai zaisan mondai*, p. 64. As is clear from Professor Satō's comments, this line of argument was by no means accepted by everyone.

117. These are, of course, the "taboos" that former Prime Minister Nakasone spoke out against in the 1980s. For a sensitive discussion of the difficulties patriotic Japanese had in discovering their individual roles and responsibilities during and after the war see Yoshida Mitsuru's essays in *Senchūha no shiseikan* (Tokyo: Bungei shunjū, 1980).

118. *Zaigai zaisan mondai*, p. 53.

119. July 14, 1967, hearings; *Zaigai zaisan mondai*, pp. 49–50.

120. Shisō no Kagaku Kenkyūkai, *(Kyōdō kenkyū) Nihon senryō kenkyū jiten* (Tokyo: Iwanami Shoten, 1976), p. 119. Repatriate memories that blunted the everyday cruelty of Japanese colonialism tended to lead to a denial of the crueler aspects of Japanese state policy. We can add the repatriate case to the early 1960s textbook trend toward viewing prewar Japanese aggression as benign.

121. This kind of justification for honoring repatriates can be seen as a precursor to the efforts of conservative journalists in the 1970s. As Carol Gluck describes in her essay "The Idea of Shōwa," *Daedalus* 119(3) (Summer 1990):6, these writers "countered both the separateness and the sanctity of the idea of the postwar by examining the prewar parts of Showa and relating them to postwar developments in a direct positive sense. They were more favorably disposed than their opponents both to the

way things had turned out in post-high-growth Japan and to the parts of the past that they thought had contributed to it. Their assertion of Showa entire was part historical revisionism and part political attack on the progressives who had held the public floor for so long."

122. The "abandoned orphans" *(zanryū koji)*, oddly foreign-looking in their mainland Chinese clothes, came to Japan with Foreign Ministry support to find their lost relatives. They were "repatriates" in more ways than one, as those who found relatives and decided to stay in Japan had to learn Japanese language and custom. The theme of abandonment evident in the early tales of woe were repeated in rumors that actual relatives sometimes refrained from identifying themselves for the shame of having once abandoned helpless children.

123. Horiguchi Takuzō, ed., *Shōwa shi no senretsu na danmen: Saitama ken hikiagesha no shūki* (Tokyo: Saitama Hikiagesha Rengokai, 1974), p. 4.

124. The phrase is from Stephen Large, *Emperor Hirohito and Shōwa Japan: A Political Biography* (London: Routledge, 1992), p. 170.

125. Moritake Ichirō, *Hankaku 30-nen*, p. 141ff. A veteran Gensuikyō and Hidankyō leader, Moritake writes that it was the Hiroshima and Nagasaki prefectural and city government leaders who made the difference in persuading the national government to improve *hibakusha* aid in 1967.

126. Opinion polls show that most Japanese favored the U.S. Security Treaty system until the Anpō renewal crisis in 1960, when more than twice as many opposed it as favored it (46 percent versus 20 percent). Since then, polls show that most people have been unsure; but of those with an opinion, those approving the security relationship exceeded those opposed by a few percentage points in most years. In the late 1960s and early 1970s, most recognized its value to Japan despite feelings that the treaty benefited the United States more than Japan. Even at the height of the Vietnam conflict in late 1968, more than half agreed that Japan's economic development was attributable to U.S. military protection (55 percent versus 26 percent who disagreed). In 1969, two separate polls showed that despite the danger of involvement in wars because of the treaty, more than half thought it was helping to maintain Japan's peace and security. See NHK Hōsō Seron Chōsajo, *Zusetsu sengo seron shi* (Tokyo, 1975), pp. 168–171. Polls conducted by the Prime Minister's Office show that the proportion of people favoring the security treaty steadily increased from 40.9 percent in 1969 to a peak of 69.2 percent in 1984, dropping slightly to 67.4 percent in 1988. See *Seron chōsa* (August 1988):13.

127. The reader will recall that Yasui Kaoru, father of the ban-the-bomb petition movement, warned of vitiating the movement by including too many causes in the agenda, such as opposition to the security treaty.

128. Itō, *Hibaku no shisō to undō*, p. 305: "Kaku arerugii wa, Nihon kokumin no kawa ni atta no de naku, mushiro sengo Nihon no shihai kaikyū jishin ni koso atta no de aru."

129. It certainly did not help such conservative fears that the *hibakusha* movement was occasionally bankrolled by foreign communist organizations. The Soviet Union's Peace Committee and Chinese organizations each gave Gensuikyō the equivalent of 7.2 million yen in condolence money in 1955. In 1967, the Bolshoi Ballet Company contributed all profits from its Japan tour to Hidankyō, which was in financial straits at the time. The contribution enabled Hidankyō to present its case in the "Crane Pamphlet" *(Tsuru panfu)* and to conduct marches and convocations in its most activist

year. See Moritake, *Hankaku 30-nen,* pp. 134 and 140. I have read that Lucky Dragon survivors were embittered by callous use of their situation by antinuclear activists.

130. Prime Minister Kishi, a commerce and industry minister in General Tojo Hideki's wartime cabinet, was of course only the most prominent of these leaders.

131. I thank Peter Duus for suggesting this idea.

Chapter 7: Beyond the Postwar

1. Tsurumi Shunsuke, "Chishikijin to sensō sekinin," *Chūō kōron* (January 1956); Maruyama Masao, "Shisō no kotoba," *Shisō* 381 (March 1956):322–325, also reprinted as "Sensō sekininron no mōten," in Maruyama, *Senchū to sengo no aida* (Tokyo, 1976), pp. 596–602; Yoshimoto Takaaki, "Zen sedai no shijintachi—Tsuboi, Okamoto no hyōka ni tsuite," *Shigaku* (November 1955), as reprinted in Yoshimoto, *Bungakusha no sensō sekinin* (1956), pp. 49–70.

2. Kaikō Takeshi, *Kagayakeru yami* (1968), *Natsu no yami* (1973); Honda Katsuichi is prolific, but the reader may be referred to *Korosareru gawa no ronri* (1982) and *Korosu gawa no ronri* (1984); Yamazaki Ryūmei, "Sensekiron no fūka no naka de," *Sekai* 345 (August 1974):266–268.

3. Imamura Osamu, "Kakusho: 'Kengo' no sensōsekinin—Kūshū taiken kiroku undō no naka de," *Shisō no kagaku* 10 (November 1972):101–105.

4. See, for example, Akazawa Shirō, "Sensō sekininron no tenbo," *Rekishi hyōron* 460 (August 1988):16–25; Ōnuma Yasuaki, "Tōkyō saiban-sensō sekinin-sengo sekinin," *Shisō* 719 (May 1984):70–100; Sumitani Takeshi, "Sensō hanzai saibanron, sensō sekininron no dōkō," *Shisō* 719 (May 1984):123–131; Ubukata Naokichi, "Tōkyō saiban o meguru shoronten: 'Jindō ni tai suru tsumi' to jikō," *Shisō* 719 (May 1984):101–112. For other scholarly analyses around the time of the Shōwa emperor's death see Arai Shin'ichi, "Sensō sekinin to sengo shori," and Fujiwara Akira, "Nihon ni okeru sensō sekininron no shosō," in Arai Shin'ichi and Fujiwara Akira, eds., *Gendaishi ni okeru sensō sekinin* (Tokyo: Aoki Shoten, 1990), pp. 24–53 and 121–138; Okabe Makio, "Sensō sekinin to kokumin bunka," *Sekai* (August 1990):32–41; Yoshimi Yoshiaki, "Senryoki Nihon no minshū ishiki—Sensō sekininron o megutte," *Shisō* 811 (January 1992): 73–99; Yoshida Yutaka, "Nihonjin to jugo-nen sensōkan to sensō sekinin mondai," *Rekishi Hyōron* 460 (August 1988):2–14; and Yoshida Yutaka, "Senryoki ni okeru sensō sekininron," *Hitotsubashi ronso* 105(2) (February 1991):121–138.

5. See Yoneyama, *Hiroshima Traces;* Kano Masanao and Nishikawa Masao, "Dou toraeru ka—'Kindai' to kindaishi kenkyū," *Rekishi Hyōron* 562 (February 1997):3–32.

6. I owe thanks to Nakajima Tomoko for bringing this trend to my attention. Letters from this forum were collected in a three-volume edition, *Onnatachi no taiheiyō sensō* (Tokyo: Asahi Shinbunsha, 1991–1993).

7. This understanding underlies Norma Field's sensitive and compelling *In the Realm of a Dying Emperor* (New York: Pantheon, 1991), p. 66: "In the present day, in Okinawa and in the rest of Japan, to adopt the narrative of victimization, of Okinawans to Japanese and Japanese to Americans, is to forget the history of Japanese aggression in Asia." For Japanese examples see Arai Shin'ichi's comments on how the "absence of Asia" *(Ajia fuzai)* in the war crimes trials helps explain why Japanese war responsibility is still an issue in Asia. See Arai, "Sensō sekinin to sengo shori," pp. 40–41. See also Ōnuma Yasuaki's connection of this "amnesia" with *datsu-A nyū-O* tendencies ("Escape from Asia, join Europe") that has a genealogy at least as far back

as Fukuzawa Yukichi's alienation from Asia in the 1880s. See especially Ōnuma, "Tōkyō saiban-sensō sekinin-sengo sekinin," p. 92 ff.

8. See Takeuchi Yoshimi, "Chūgokujin no kōsen ishiki to Nihonjin no dōtoku ishiki," *Chisei* (May 1949), reprinted in Tsurumi Shunsuke, ed., *Sengo Nihon shisō taikei*, vol. 4: *Heiwa no shisō* (Tokyo: Chikuma Shobō, 1968), pp. 110–129. For a lucid, stream-lined discussion of these issues see Nakamura Masanori's Iwanami booklet, "Kingen-daishi o dou miru ka—Shiba shikan o tou," (Iwanami Booklet 427) (Tokyo: Iwanami, 1997), pp. 44–52.

9. In the first essay in this series, Kamei stated his belief that the study of history is an important means to confirm one's sense of origins as a Japanese and to discover a reaffirmation of ethics through an encounter with historical personages. See Kamei Katsuichirō, "Gendaishika e no gimon," *Bungei shunjū* (March 1956):58–68.

10. Yoshida Mitsuru, "Sengo ga ushinatta mono," *Shokun* 10(8) (August 1978): 48–62.

11. Ibid., pp. 55–56. In another essay, Yoshida expressed it this way: "Our failure immediately after World War II to recognize the importance of a sense of identity as Japanese that would bridge the wartime and postwar periods was the underlying cause of our confusion today, and . . . we must establish such an identity if we wish truly to stand on our own in the international community." See Yoshida Mitsuru, "Proxies for the War Dead," *Japan Echo* 7(2) (1980):75–80.

12. Oda Makoto, "Heiwa no rinri to ronri," as translated by J. Victor Koschmann, "The Ethics of Peace," in J. Victor Koschmann, ed., *Authority and the Individual in Japan: Citizen Protest in Historical Perspective* (Tokyo: University of Tokyo Press, 1978), p. 170. For a masterful analysis of the emergence of Meiji-era liberalism and conser-vatism see Kenneth B. Pyle, "Meiji Conservatism," *Cambridge History of Japan*, vol. 5: *The Nineteenth Century* (Cambridge: Cambridge University Press, 1989), pp. 674–720.

13. For example, Prime Minister Murayama apologized to the South Korean gov-ernment over cabinet minister Eto Takami's off-the-record comment that the Japanese occupation benefited Korea greatly in infrastructural development. Murayama's letter of apology noted that the "imperial-era" annexation "did not allow national self-deter-mination and dignity." See *Asahi Evening News* (e-mail ed.), November 17, 1995.

14. See, for example, Robert G. Moeller, "War Stories: The Search for a Usable Past in the Federal Republic of Germany," *American Historical Review* 101(4) (October 1996):1008–1048; Elizabeth Heineman, "The Hour of the Woman: Memories of Ger-many's 'Crisis Years' and West German National Identity," *American Historical Review* 101(2) (April 1996):354–395.

15. Several scholars have written sensitive analyses of these contests over the place of the atomic bombings in America's history. See, for example, Barton J. Bern-stein, "Seizing the Contested Terrain of Early Nuclear History: Stimson, Conant, and Their Allies Explain the Decision to Use the Atomic Bomb," *Diplomatic History* 17(1) (Winter 1993):35–72, for a treatment of early efforts at historical construction. See also Paul Boyer, "Exotic Resonances: Hiroshima in American Memory," *Diplomatic History* 19(2) (Spring 1995):297–318; Richard Minear, "Atomic Holocaust, Nazi Holocaust: Some Reflections," *Diplomatic History* 19(2) (Spring 1995):347–365; Edward T. Linenthal's short essay, "American Public Memory on the Washington Mall," *Tikkun* 10(3) (May–June 1995):20–21; and Robert J. Lifton and Greg Mitchell, *Hiroshima in America: Fifty Years of Denial* (New York: Putnam, 1995).

16. "Men practice violence; women are the victims. . . . By assuming the role of victim, one finds a way of legitimately rejecting an awareness of one's own unjust acts, as well as an awareness of the injustices committed by one's own society. In other words, the others are worse than we are." See Christina Thürmer-Rohr, "White Women and Racism" (1993), quoted in Ulrike Helwerth and Gislinde Schwarz, "Germany: The Walls That Have Yet to Fall," *Ms.* 3(6) (May–June 1993):19. Thürmer-Rohr is a prolific writer on gender in Germany.

Appendix 1: The Stockholm Appeal

1. Nihon Heiwa Iinkai, ed., *Heiwa undō 20-nen shiryōshu* (Tokyo, 1969), p. 8. The Japanese version of the appeal used the term *"jinrui"* or "mankind" rather than "populations" and *"hitobito"* or "people" rather than "men."

Appendix 2: Suginami Ward's Petition

1. Text printed in Yasui, "Shizuka naru shōmei undō," *Kaizō* (August 1954):136–137. The text published in Yasui's *Minshū to heiwa* (1955) substituted *"gensuibaku"* (atomic and hydrogen bombs) for *"suibaku"* (hydrogen bombs).

Bibliography

I have used archival sources from the following collections located in the Hoover Institution Archives, Stanford, California: Hubert C. Armstrong; Clarence E. Larson; John D. Montgomery; Joseph C. Trainor; U.S. Army Forces in the Pacific; and U.S. Office of War Information. I have also used the "Censored Periodicals, 1945–1949" microfilm, reel 54, compiled and edited by Eizaburō Okuizumi, from the Gordon W. Prange Collection of the University of Maryland. For Diet deliberations and interpolations I have relied on the Japanese National Diet committee records series *(Kokkai kaigiroku)*.

Japanese-Language Sources

Aihara Kazuo, Isogai H., Uesugi H., Teraō T., Hamamoto J., Makibayashi K., and Matsunaga N. "Ibuse Masuji 'Kuroi ame'" [Ibuse Masuji's *Black Rain*]. *Nihon bungaku* 16(4) (April 1967):244–255.

Akazawa Shiro. "Sensō sekininron no tenbo" [Prospects for the war responsibility debate]. *Rekishi hyōron* 460 (August 1988):16–25.

Ara Masato, Odagiri H., Sasaki K., Haniya Y., Hirano K., and Honda S. "Bungakusha no sekimu" [Obligations of the literati]. *Ningen* (April 1946). Reprinted in Usui Yoshimi, ed., *Sengo bungakuronsō* 1 (1972):55–71.

Arai Shin'ichi. "Sensō sekinin to sengo shori" [War responsibility and postwar resolution]. In Fujiwara Akira and Arai Shin'ichi, eds., *Gendaishi ni okeru sensō sekinin* [War responsibility in modern history]. Tokyo: Aoki Shoten, 1990.

Araragi Shinzō. "Manshū kaitakudan o botai to suru kaitaku shuraku ni okeru 'kyōdō-sei'—Kumamoto-ken Tōyō-mura" [Tōyō village, Kumamoto prefecture—'Community' in a settlement colony formed around a Manchurian pioneer group]. *Soshioroji* 33(1) (May 1988):115–117.

Arase Yutaka. "Jihyō: Gensuibaku kinshi undō no chokumen suru kadai" [Editorial notes: Issues facing the ban-the-bomb movement]. *Shisō* 406 (April 1958):104–108.

———. "Nihonjin no kokka ishiki" [Japanese people's state consciousness]. *Shisō* 434 (August 1960):41–49.

Asahi Shinbunsha, ed. *Onnatachi no taiheiyō sensō* [The women's Pacific War]. Tokyo: Asahi Shinbunsha, 1991–1993.

Edamatsu Shigenobu. "Heiwateki riyōhō no butai ura: Genshiryoku hō kaisei no haikei to mondaiten" [Behind the scenes of the law for peaceful use (of nuclear energy): Background and problems with revisions to the atomic energy law]. *Kaizō* (April 1954):116–119.

Etō Jun. "Bungei jihyō" [Literary notes]. *Asahi shinbun*, evening ed., August 25, 1966. Reprinted in *Bungei nenkan* (1967):60–61.

Fujishima Udai, Maruyama Kunio, and Murakami Hyōe. "Hiroshima—Sono go 13 nen" [Hiroshima—Thirteen years after]. *Chūō kōron* 842 (August 1958):248–270.

Fujiwara Akira. "Nihon ni okeru sensō sekininron no shosō" [Various aspects of the war responsibility debate in Japan]. In Fujiwara Akira and Arai Shin'ichi, eds., *Gendaishi ni okeru sensō sekinin* [War responsibility in modern history]. Tokyo: Aoki Shoten, 1990.

Fujiwara Akira, Yoshida Y., Itō S., and Kunugi T., eds. *Tennō no shōwa-shi* [The emperor's Shōwa history]. Tokyo: Shin Nihon Shuppansha, 1984.

Fukuda Tsuneari. "Heiwa-ron no susumekata ni tsuite no gimon: Dō kakugo o kimetara ii ka" [Doubts about peace advocacy: How should we resolve it?]. *Chūō kōron* (December 1954):18–30.

Fushimi Kōji. "Yume to genjitsu: Genshiryoku to heiwa" [Dream and reality: Atomic energy and peace]. *Kaizō* (April 1954):109–115.

Gensuibaku Kinshi Sekaitaikai Nihon Junbikai, ed. *Genbaku yurusumaji: Gensuibaku kinshi sekaitaikai no kiroku* [Reject the atom bomb: Record of the world conference to ban atomic and hydrogen bombs]. Tokyo, 1955.

Gomikawa Junpei. *Ningen no jōken* [The human condition]. Bunshun Library. 6 vols. Tokyo: Bungei Shunjū, 1979.

Gomikawa Junpei and Aratama Michiyo. "Taidan: Katsumoku shite machimashō" [Dialogue: Let's watch and wait]. *Chūō kōron* 74(6) (May 1959):156–163.

Hara Keigo. "Sengo kūhakuki no kaisō: Chōsen dōran made no go-nenkan" [Memoir of the postwar interregnum: Five years until the Korean disturbance]. *Jiyū* 8(8) (August 1966):152–157.

Hata Ikuhiko. "Shōwashi no nazo o tou, Dai-30-kai. Kyōshoku tsuihō—Yasui Kaoru no baai" [Interrogating the puzzles of Shōwa history, number 30. Faculty purges: The case of Yasui Kaoru]. *Seiron* 230 (October 1991):350–363

Hiroshima Heiwa Bunka Sentaa, ed. *Heiwa jiten* [Peace dictionary]. Tokyo: Keiso Shobō, 1991.

Hiroshima Heiwa Kinen Shiryokan, ed. *30-nen no ayumi* [Thirty years of history]. N.p., n.d.

Hori Hidehiko. "Seibugeki 'Ningen no jōken'" [The human condition, a western]. *Shinchō* 55(7) (July 1958):66–69.

Horigome Yōzō. *Rekishi to ningen* [History and people]. Tokyo: Nihon Hōsō Shuppan Kyōkai, 1965.

Horiguchi Takuzō, ed. *Shōwa shi no senretsu na danmen: Saitama ken hikiagesha no shūki* [Showa history's vivid profile: Notes of Saitama prefecture's repatriates]. Tokyo: Saitama Hikiagesha Rengokai, 1974.

Ibaraki-ken Kaitaku Jūnenshi Henshū Iinkai. *Ibaraki-ken kaitaku jūnenshi* [Ten-year history of Ibaraki prefecture's settlement]. 1955.

Ibuse Masuji. *Kuroi ame* [Black rain]. Rev. ed. Tokyo: Shinchōsha, 1985. Translated by John Bester as *Black Rain*. Tokyo: Kodansha International, 1969.

Ienaga Soshō Shien Shimin no Kai, ed. *Taiheiyō sensō to kyōkasho* [The Pacific War and textbooks]. Tokyo: Shisō no Kagaku-sha, 1970.

Imahori Seiji. *Gensuibaku jidai* [Era of atomic and hydrogen bombs]. 2 vols. Tokyo: San'ichi Shobō, 1959–1960.

————. *Gensuibaku kinshi undō* [Movement to ban atomic and hydrogen bombs]. Tokyo: Ushio Shuppansha, 1974.

————. "Gensuibaku kinshi undō no yakuwari to tenbō" [Role and prospects for the movement to ban atomic and hydrogen bombs]. In YMCA Kokusai Heiwa Kenkyūjō, ed., *Heiwa o tsukuru* [To build peace]. Tokyo: Keiso Shobō, 1985.

Imamura Osamu. "Kakusho: 'Kengo' no sensōsekinin—Kūshū taiken kiroku undō no naka de" [War responsibility "behind the lines"—Inside the movement to record the firebombing experience]. *Shisō no kagaku* 10 (November 1972):101–105.

Itami Mansaku. "Sensō sekininsha no mondai" [The issue of who is responsible for the war]. *Eiga shunjū* (August 1946). Reprinted in Ogawa Tōru, ed., *Gendai Nihon eigaron taikei* [Outline of modern Japanese film], vol. 1: *Sengo eiga no shuppatsu* [Departure for postwar film]. Tokyo: Fuyukisha, 1971.

Itō Takeshi. *Hibakusha engobō no tame ni hibaku no shisō to undō* [The thought and activities of the atomic bomb (survivors), in favor of an assistance law for them]. Tokyo: Shinhyōron, 1975.

Jiyū Eigajin Shudan. "Eiga sensō sekininsha no kaimei" [Clarification of war responsibility among filmmakers]. *Eiga seisaku* (July 1946). Reprinted in Ogawa Tōru, ed., *Gendai Nihon eigaron taikei* [Outline of modern Japanese film critique], vol. 1: *Sengo eiga no shuppatsu* [Departure for postwar film]. Tokyo: Fuyukisha, 1971.

Kamei Katsuichirō. "Gendaishika e no gimon" [Doubts over modern historians]. *Bungei shunjū* (March 1956):58–68.

————. "Giji shūkyō kokka" [A false state religion]. *Chūō kōron* (September 1956). Reprinted in *Kamei Katsuichirō zenshū* [Complete works of Kamei Katsuichirō] 16: 229–246. Tokyo: Kodansha, 1972.

————. "Nihon kindaika no higeki" [The tragedy of Japan's modernization]. *Chūō kōron* (August 1956). Reprinted in *Kamei Katsuichirō zenshū* [Complete works of Kamei Katsuichirō] 16:212–228. Tokyo: Kodansha, 1972.

————. "Nihon no tachiba kara gensuibaku ni tsuite" [The nuclear bomb from Japan's standpoint]. Reprinted in *Kamei Katsuichirō zenshu* [Complete works of Kamei Katsuichirō] 19:222–226. Tokyo: Kodansha, 1973. Originally published as part of the column "Shakai jihyō" [Social commentary] in *Kasutomusu,* 1956–1957.

————. "Rekishika no shutaisei ni tsuite" [On the historian's subjectivity] *Chūō kōron* (July 1956). Reprinted in *Kamei Katsuichirō zenshū* [Complete works of Kamei Katsuichirō] 16:200–211. Tokyo: Kodansha, 1972.

————. "Sengo Nihon ni tsuite no oboegaki" [Memorandum on postwar Japan]. In Kamei Katsuichirō, *Gendaishi no kadai* [Topics for modern history]. Tokyo: Chūō Kōronsha, [1957]. Reprinted in *Kamei Katsuichirō zenshū* [Complete works of Kamei Katsuichirō] 16:266–281. Tokyo: Kodansha, 1972.

Kamiyama Shigeo. "Nihon no heiwa undō to sekai" [Japan's peace movement and the world]. *Chūō kōron* 901 (November 1962):136–144.

Kanazawa Kaichi. *Aru shōgakkōchō no kaisō* [Reflections of an elementary school principal]. Tokyo: Iwanami Shoten, 1967.

Kano Masanao. *"Torijima" wa haitte iru ka: Rekishi ishiki no genzai to rekishigaku* [Is "Torijima" included? Contemporary history consciousness and history]. Tokyo: Iwanami Shoten, 1988.

Kano Masanao and Nishikawa Masao. "Dō toraeru ka: 'Kindai' to kindaishi kenkyū" [Researching the 'modern' and modern history: How to come to grips with it]. *Rekishi hyōron* 562 (February 1997):3–32.

Kobayashi Masaki. "Eiga 'Ningen no jōken' no omoide" [Memories of the film *Human Condition*]. *Bungei shunjū* (May 1995):306–311.

Konaka Yōtarō. "Oda Makoto: Hanoi kara minami Taiheiyō e—'nanshi' to 'kyōsei' " [Oda Makoto: From Hanoi to the South Pacific—"Meaningless death" and symbiosis]. In Nihon Ajia-Afurika Sakka Kaigi, ed., *Sengo bungaku to Ajia* [Postwar literature and Asia]. Tokyo: Mainichi Shinbunsha, 1978.

Kubokawa Tsurujirō. "Kaisetsu" [Commentary]. In Tsuboi Sakae, *Nijūshi no hitomi* [Twenty-four eyes]. Tokyo: Kadokawa Shoten, 1961.

Kumakura Hiroyasu. *Gensuibaku kinshi undō 30 nen* [Thirty years with the movement to ban atomic and hydrogen bombs]. Tokyo: Rōdōkyōiku Sentaa, 1978.

Kuno Osamu. "Futatsu no heiwa wa sekai heiwa ni tsunagaru ka" [Are the two peaces connected to world peace?]. *Sekai* (November 1951). Reprinted in Kuno Osamu, *Heiwa no ronri, sensō no ronri* [The logic of peace, the logic of war]. Tokyo: Iwanami Shoten, 1972.

———. "Heiwa no ronri, sensō no ronri" [The logic of peace, the logic of war]. *Sekai* (November 1949). Reprinted in Kuno Osamu, *Heiwa no ronri, sensō no ronri* [The logic of peace, the logic of war]. Tokyo: Iwanami Shoten, 1972.

Kuno Osamu, Toyoda S., Hamada I., Matsumoto T., Yamashita H., and Tsurumi K. "Nihon minzoku no enerugii, II" [The energy of the Japanese people, II]. *Kaizō* (February 1954):84–96.

Kyōgoku Jun'ichi. " 'Demokurashii' to 'nashonarizumu'—Gendai Nihon ni okeru ishiki to kōdō" ["Democracy" and "nationalism"—Awareness and action in modern Japan]. *Shisō* 444 (June 1961):69–83.

Maruyama Masao. "Shisō no kotoba" [Words for thought]. *Shisō* 381 (March 1956): 322–325. Reprinted as "Sensō sekinin ron no mōten" [Blind spots in the debate over war responsibility] in Maruyama Masao, *Senchū to sengo no aida, 1936–1957* [Between war and postwar, 1936–1957]. Tokyo: Misuzu Shobō, 1976.

Matsumoto Sannosuke. "Ōkuma Nobuyuki ni okeru kokka no mondai—'Kokka kagaku' kara 'Kokka aku' made" [Ōkuma Nobuyuki and the problem of the state: From "state science" to "state evil"]. *Shisō* 837 (March 1994):4–39.

Matsumoto Shigeo. "Kyōkasho seido ni tsuite" [Regarding the textbook system]. In Ienaga Soshō Shien Shimin no Kai, ed., *Taiheiyō sensō to kyōkasho* [The Pacific War and textbooks]. Tokyo: Shisō no Kagaku-sha, 1970.

Minshushugi Kenkyūkai. "Sengo Nihon no aikokushin o meguru shomondai" [Various issues concerning postwar Japanese patriotism]. N.p., March 1962. In the Hoover Institution East Asia Library.

Miyazawa Ki'ichi. *Tōkyō-Washinton no mitsudan* [Secret talks between Tokyo and Washington]. Tokyo: Jitsugyō no Nihonsha, 1956.

Moritake Ichirō. *Hankaku 30-nen* [Thirty years against nuclear weapons]. Tokyo: Nihon Hyōronsha, 1976.

Nakamura Kikuji. *Kyōkasho no hensan: Hakkō nado kyōkasho seido no henreki ni kansuru chōsa kenkyū* [Textbook compilation: Investigative research relating to changes in the textbook system such as publishing]. Tokyo: Kyōkasho Kenkyū Sentaa, 1997.

Nakamura Masanori. "Kingendaishi o dou miru ka—Shiba shikan o tou" [How to regard early modern and modern history: Interrogating the Shiba historical view]. Iwanami Booklet 427. Tokyo: Iwanami, 1997.

Nanbara Shigeru. "Heiwa ka sensō ka—Nihon saiken no seishinteki konran" [Peace or war?—Spiritual confusion in Japan's reconstruction]. In Nanbara Shigeru, *Heiwa no senden* [A call for peace]. Tokyo: Tokyo Daigaku Shuppanbu, 1951.

NHK Hōsō Seron Chōsajo. *Zusetsu sengo seron shi* [History of postwar opinion in diagrams]. Tokyo: Nihon Hōsōkyoku, 1975.

Nihon. Hikiage Engochō. *Hikiage engo no kiroku* [Record of repatriate relief]. 1950.

Nihon. Monbushō. *Chūgakkō shakai shidōsho* [Junior high school social studies (teacher's) guide]. 1959.

———. *Shakaika kyōkasho* [Social studies texts]. 1981.

Nihon. Shūgiin/Sangiin. *Gikaiseido 70-nen shi* [Seventy-year history of the Diet system]. 12 vols. 1960–1963.

Nihon. Sōrifu. Tōkeikyoku. *Nihon tōkei nenkan* [Japan statistical yearbook]. 1954.

———. *Zaigai zaisan mondai no shori kiroku* [Record of resolution of the overseas assets issue]. 1975.

Nihon Heiwa Iinkai, ed. *Heiwa undō 20-nen shiryōshū* [Twenty years of documents for the peace movement]. Tokyo, 1969.

Nihon Minshutō. *Dai 21 Kokkai ni okeru Hatoyama naikaku shiseihōshin enzetsu shū* [Collection of policy speeches of the Hatoyama cabinet in the 21st Diet]. January 1955.

———. *Nihon Minshutō seisaku yōkō: Senkyo taisaku shiryō dai 1 shū* [Japan Democratic Party policy prospectus: Campaign documents, first group]. January 1955.

———. *Shinseisaku kaisetsu enzetsushū: Senkyo taisaku shiryō, dai 3 shū* [Collection of speeches explicating new policy: Campaign documents, third group]. January 1955.

Nihon Minshutō. Jimukyoku. *Nihon minshutō* [Japan Democratic Party (party charter)]. [1954–1956].

Noma Hiroshi. "Genbaku ni tsuite" [On the atomic bomb]. *Bungakkai* (March 1953). Reprinted in Kaku-sensō no kiken o uttaeru bungakusha, ed., *Nihon genbaku bungaku*, vol. 15: *Hyōron/essei* (Tokyo: Horupu Shuppan, 1983).

———. "Jinrui ishiki no hassei" [The birth of a consciousness of humankind]. *Bungei* (December 1954). Reprinted in *Nihon genbaku bungaku*, vol. 15.

———. "Jinrui no tachiba" [The standpoint of humanity]. *Sekai* (January 1955). Reprinted in *Nihon genbaku bungaku*, vol. 15.

———. "Suibaku to ningen—Atarashii ningen no musubitsuki" [The hydrogen bomb and human beings—A new connecting thread for human beings]. *Bungaku no tomo* (September 1954). Reprinted in *Nihon genbaku bungaku*, vol. 15.

Oda Makoto. "Heiwa no rinri to ronri" [The ethics and logic of peace]. *Tenbō* (August 1966). Reprinted in Oda, *"Nanshi" no shisō*. Tokyo: Iwanami Shoten, 1991. Also translated into English and abridged by J. Victor Koschmann as "The Ethics of Peace," in Koschmann, ed., *Authority and the Individual in Japan: Citizen Protest in Historical Perspective*. Tokyo: University of Tokyo Press, 1978.

———. "'Nanshi' no shisō" [The ideology of "meaningless death"]. *Tenbō* (January 1965). Reprinted in Oda, *"Nanshi" no shisō*. Tokyo: Iwanami Shoten, 1991. Also translated as "The Meaning of Meaningless Death," *Journal of Social and Political Ideas in Japan* 4(2) (August 1966):75–85.

———. *"Nanshi" no shisō* [The ideology of "meaningless death"]. Tokyo: Iwanami Shoten, 1991.

———. "Sandaime no nashonarizumu" [Third-generation nationalism]. *Chūō kōron* 900 (October 1962):162–172.

248   BIBLIOGRAPHY

————. "Takeuchi Yoshimi no Ajia-ron ni tsuite" [On Takeuchi Yoshimi's Asia theories]. In Nihon Ajia-Afurika Sakka Kaigi, ed., *Sengo bungaku to Ajia* [Postwar literature and Asia]. Tokyo: Mainichi Shinbunsha, 1978.

Odagiri Hideo. "Bungaku ni okeru sensō sekinin no tsuikyū" [Pursuing war responsibility in literature]. *Shin Nihon bungaku* (June 1946). Reprinted in Usui Yoshimi, ed., *Sengo bungaku ronsō* [Postwar literary debates], vol. 1. Tokyo: Bancho Shobō, 1972.

————. "Kaisetsu" [Commentary]. In Tsuboi Sakae, *Tsuboi Sakae zenshū* [Complete works of Tsuboi Sakae], vol. 6. Tokyo: Chikuma Shobō, 1968.

Ogiya Shōzō. "Sengo besutoseraa monogatari 46: Gomikawa Junpei—Ningen no jōken: gendaiteki 'kyūdō' no sho" [Tales of postwar bestsellers, 46: Gomikawa Junpei—*Human Condition:* Book of a modern search for truth]. *Asahi jaanaru* 8(37) (September 4, 1966):34–39.

Okabe Makio. "Sensō sekinin to kokumin bunka" [War responsibility and national culture]. *Sekai* (August 1990):32–41.

Ōkuma Nobuyuki. "Hansei naki no minzoku" [An unreflective people]. *Bungei shunjū* 25(9) (September 1947):10–17.

————. "Kono eigajin o miyo: Itami Mansaku to sono sensō sekininron in tsuite" [Look at this filmmaker: On Itami Mansaku and that war responsibility debate]. *Eiga shunjū* (November 1947). Reprinted in Ogawa Tōru, ed., *Gendai Nihon eigaron taikei* [Outline of modern Japanese film critique], vol. 1: *Sengo eiga no shuppatsu* [Departure for postwar film]. Tokyo: Fuyukisha, 1971.

Ōnuma Yasuaki. "Tōkyō saiban-sensō sekinin-sengo sekinin" [Tokyo trials, war responsibility, postwar responsibility]. *Shisō* 719 (May 1984):70–100.

Ōtsuki Takeshi, ed. *Kyōkasho kokusho* [Textbook black paper]. Tokyo: Rōdō Junpō, 1969.

Ōyama Ikuo. "Nihon wa heiwa no kichi tare—Molotov, Kim Il-sung, Chou Enlai kaiken kara" [Japan, become a base for peace—Molotov, Kim Il-sung, Chou Enlai]. *Kaizō* (February 1954):2–11.

Sakamoto Yoshikazu. "Heiwa undō ni okeru shinri to ronri" [Ethics and logic in the peace movement]. *Sekai* (August 1962). Reprinted in Sakamoto, *Shinpan Kakujidai no kokusai seiji* [International politics in the nuclear age, new edition]. Tokyo: Iwanami Shoten, 1982.

————. "Kenryoku seiji to heiwa undō." [The politics of power and the peace movement]. *Sekai* 191 (November 1961):11–23.

————. "Nihon gaikō no shisōteki tenkan—Nikkan teikei ni okeru Bei-Chū taiketsu" [Ideological conversion of Japan's foreign policy—American and Chinese confrontation in Japan-Korea cooperation]. *Sekai* (January 1966). Reprinted in Sakamoto, *Shinpan Kakujidai no kokusai seiji.*

————. "Nihon ni okeru kokusai reisen to kokunai reisen" [The cold war in Japan and the domestic cold war] [1963]. Reprinted in Sakamoto, *Shinpan Kakujidai no kokusai seiji.*

Satō Kōmei. *Kyōkasho kentei no genba kara: 17-nenkan no insaido repōto* [On the scene of textbook certification: Inside report on 17 years]. Tokyo: Waseda Daigaku Shuppan, 1987.

Satō Nobuo. "Kyōkasho kentei ni okeru Monbushō gawa no taido" [The attitude of the Ministry of Education in textbook certification]. *Rekishigaku kenkyū* 306 (November 1965):23–26.

Satō Tadao. *Eiga o dō miru ka* [How to view movies]. Tokyo: Kodansha, 1976.

————. "Gensuibaku to eiga" [Nuclear bombs and film]. *Bungaku* 28(8) (August 1960).

————. "Tsuboi Sakae 'Nijūshi no hitomi'—Anshin shite nakeru kyoyō shosetsu" [Tsuboi Sakae's *Twenty-Four Eyes*—An edifying novel one can safely cry over]. *Asahi jaanaru* 8(19) (May 8, 1966):35–40.

"Seizonsha jokun seido no fukkatsu" [Revival of the system of decorations for survivors]. *Sekai* 215 (November 1963):139–142.

"Sengo ni okeru aikokushinrongi no tenbō" [Prospects for a postwar discussion of patriotism]. *Chōsa geppō* 85 (January 1963):17–30.

Sengo Nihon Kyōiku Shiryo Shusei Iinkai, ed. *Sengo Nihon kyōiku shiryo shusei* [Compilation of Japan's postwar education documents]. 13 vols. Vol. 5: *55-nen taisei shita no kyōiku* [Education under the 1955 system]. Tokyo: San'ichi Shobō, 1982–1984.

Shakaihoken Hōki Kenkyūkai. *Nihon shakai hoshō daihyakka* [Encyclopedia of Japan's social security]. Tokyo, 1966.

Shimizu Ikutarō. "Heiwa undō no kokuseki" [The peace movement's nationality]. *Chūō kōron* 900 (October 1962):90–104.

————. "Kore made no jūnen kore kara no jūnen—Zenmenkōwaronsha no tachiba kara" [Ten years past, ten years ahead—The view of an advocate for a total peace treaty]. *Sekai* 162 (June 1959):42–51.

Shimizu Masayoshi et al. "Nishi-Doitsu ni okeru 'Nachizumu-go' no seiji to rekishi ishiki" [Post-Nazi political and historical consciousness in West Germany]. In Fujiwara Akira and Arai Shin'ichi, eds., *Gendaishi ni okeru sensō sekinin* [War responsibility in modern history]. Tokyo: Aoki Shoten, 1990.

Shimodaira Hiromi. "Genbaku hibakusha ni tai suru 'kokka hoshō' o kangaeru" [Thinking about "state compensation" for atomic bomb survivors]. *Kikan rōdō hō* 123 (March 1982):122–130.

Shinobu Seizaburō. *Sengo Nihon seijishi* [Postwar Japan's political history]. Tokyo: Keiso Shobō, 1965.

Shisō no Kagaku Kenkyūkai. *(Kyōdō kenkyū) Nihon senryō kenkyū jiten* [Dictionary of research on Japan's occupation]. Tokyo: Iwanami Shoten, 1976.

Shōgakukan, ed. *Shōgakukan CD Bukku "Shōwa no uta"* [Shōgakukan's CD book "Songs of Shōwa"]. Tokyo: Shōgakukan, 1991.

Sumitani Takeshi. "Sensō hanzai saibanron, sensō sekininron no dōkō" [War crimes trial theory: Trends in war responsibility theory]. *Shisō* 719 (May 1984):123–131.

Tada Michitarō. "Sengo besutoseraa monogatari 71: Ibuse Masuji, *Kuroi ame*, Furusato ni ochita genbaku" [Tales of postwar bestsellers, 71: Ibuse Masuji's *Black Rain*, A-bomb fell on the hometown]. *Asahi jaanaru* 9(10) (March 5, 1967):35–40.

Takane Masaaki. "Heiwa undō no kabe" [The peace movement's barrier]. *Chūō kōron* 843 (September 1958):154–161.

Takeuchi Yoshimi. "Chūgoku no kindai to Nihon no kindai" [China's modern age and Japan's modern age]. In Takeuchi Yoshimi, Yoshikawa K., Nohara S., and Niida N., *Tōyō-teki shakai rinri-teki seikaku* [The nature of ethics in the oriental type of society]. Tokyo: Hakujitsu Shoin, 1948.

————. "Chūgokujin no kōsen ishiki to Nihonjin no dōtoku ishiki" [Chinese war consciousness and Japanese moral consciousness]. *Chisei* (May 1949). Reprinted in Tsurumi Shunsuke, ed., *Heiwa no shisō* [Peace ideology]. Tokyo: Chikuma Shobō, 1968.

Takeya Mitsuo. "Genshiryoku no heiwateki riyō to sekai" [Peaceful uses of nuclear energy and the world]. *Kaizō* (April 1954):93–101.

Tanimoto Kiyoshi. "Atogaki" [Afterword]. In John Hersey, *Hiroshima*, translated by Tanimoto Kiyoshi and Ishikawa Kin'ichi. Tokyo: Hōsei Daigaku Shuppankyoku, 1949.

Tokutake Toshio. *Atarashii rekishi kyōkasho e no michi* [The path toward new history textbooks]. Tokyo: Hato no Mori Shobō, 1973.

―――. *Kyōkasho no sengo shi* [Postwar history of textbooks]. Tokyo: Shin Nihon Shuppansha, 1995.

Tōkyō Saiban Handobukku Henshu Iinkai [Sumitani Takeshi et al.], ed. *Tōkyō saiban handobukku* [Tokyo trials handbook]. Tokyo: Aoki Shoten, 1989.

Tōkyō Shoseki Kabushikikaisha. Shashi-hen Iinkai [Social Studies and History Editorial Committee], ed. *Kindai kyōkasho no henreki: Tōkyō Shoseki 70-nen shi* [History of the modern textbook: Tōkyō Shoseki's 70 years]. Tokyo: Tōkyō Shoseki, 1980.

Tōyama Shigeki. "Sōgō bukai hōkoku: Sengo heiwa undō no rekishi" [Report from all quarters: A history of the postwar peace movement]. *Rekishigaku kenkyū* 297 (February 1965):47–51.

Tōyama Shigeki, Imai Sei'ichi, and Fujiwara Akira. *Shōwa-shi* [Shōwa history]. Tokyo: Iwanami Shoten, 1955.

Toyama-ken. Kōsei-bu. Shakaifukushi-ka. *Toyama-ken shusen shorishi* [History of the war's end in Toyama prefecture]. Toyama, 1975.

Tsuboi Sakae. *Nijūshi no hitomi* [Twenty-four eyes]. Tokyo: Kadokawa Shoten, 1971. Also translated by Akira Miura as *Twenty-Four Eyes*. Rutland: Tuttle, 1983.

Tsuji Kiyoaki, ed. *Shiryo: Sengo nijūnenshi* [Documents: Twenty years of postwar history]. Vol. 1: *Seiji* [Politics]. Tokyo: Nihon Hyōronsha, 1966.

Tsurumi Shunsuke. "Chishikijin no sensō sekinin" [War responsibility of the intelligentsia]. *Chūō kōron* 71(1) (January 1956):57–63.

―――. "Senryō to Nihon" [Occupation and Japan]. *Sekai* 244 (August 1964):60–68.

―――, ed. *Heiwa no shisō* [Peace ideology]. Tokyo: Chikuma Shobō, 1968.

Ubukata Naokichi. "Tōkyō saiban o meguru shoronten: 'Jindō ni tai suru tsumi' to jikō" [Various points of debate concerning the Tokyo trials: "Crimes against humanity" and the statute of limitations]. *Shisō* 719 (May 1984):101–112.

Ueyama Shunpei. "Shisōshiteki igi" [The meaning of the Greater East Asia War in intellectual history]. *Chūō kōron* (January 1961). Reprinted in Ueyama Shunpei, *Daitō-A sensō no imi—Gendaishi bunseki no shiten* [The meaning of the Greater East Asia War—Analytical perspective of modern history]. Tokyo: Chūō Kōronsha, 1964.

Waseda Daigaku Kyōikugakubu Rekishigaku Kenkyūkai. "Sengo rekishi kyōkasho wa dō kawatte iru ka (3): Chūgaku rekishi kyōkasho no bunseki" [How postwar history textbooks have changed (3): Analysis of junior high school history textbooks]. *Rekishi hyōron* 182 (October 1965):10–25.

Waseda Minoru. "Nōchi hōshōhō to kyūjinushi dantai" [Farmland rewards bill and the former landlord associations]. *Hōritsu jihō* 37(9) (August 1965):33–38.

Yamazaki Ryūmei. "Sensekiron no fūka no naka de" [In the midst of the waning debate on war responsibility]. *Sekai* 345 (August 1974):266–268.

Yasui Kaoru. "Gakumon to ryōshin no jiyū [Academic freedom and freedom of conscience]. *Tokyo daigaku shinbun* (March 18, 1948). Reprinted in *Michi—Yasui Kaoru inochi no kiseki*. Tokyo: Hōsei Daigaku Shuppankyoku, 1983.

————. "Hansei to kibō" [Reflection and hopes]. *Kaizō* (August 1954):139.

————. *Minshū to heiwa: Mirai o tsukuru mono* [The masses and peace: Making the future]. Tokyo: Otsuki Shoten, 1955.

————. "Shizukanaru shomei undō" [The quiet petition movement]. *Kaizō* (August 1954):134–138.

Yoshida Mitsuru. *Senchūha no shiseikan* [The wartime generation's view of life and death]. Tokyo: Bungei Shunjū, 1980.

————. "Sensō kyōryoku no sekinin wa doko ni aru ka—*Senkan Yamato* ni taisuru hihan no bunseki" [Where lies responsibility for war cooperation?—Analysis of criticism of *Senkan Yamato*]. *Shisō no kagaku* 20 (August 1960):59–68.

————. "Wakamono to sensō" [Youth and war]. *Chūō kōron* (September 1963):309–310.

Yoshida Mitsuru and Tsurumi Shunsuke. "Sengo ga ushinatta mono" [What the postwar has lost]. *Shokun* 10(8) (August 1978):48–62.

Yoshida Yutaka. "Nihonjin to jūgo-nen sensōkan to sensō sekinin mondai" [Japanese, the Fifteen-Year War, and the problem of war responsibility]. *Rekishi Hyōron* 460 (August 1988):2–14.

————. "Senryoki ni okeru sensō sekininron" [War responsibility debates during the Occupation]. *Hitotsubashi ronso* 105(2) (February 1991):121–138.

Yoshimi Yoshiaki. "Senryōki no Nihon no minshū ishiki—Sensō sekininron o megutte" [Japanese mass consciousness during the Occupation—Concerning the war responsibility debates]. *Shisō* 811 (January 1992):73–99.

Yoshimoto Takaaki. "Zen sedai no shijintachi—Tsuboi, Okamoto no hyōka ni tsuite" [Poets of the previous generation—Critique of Tsuboi and Okamoto]. *Shigaku* (November 1955). Reprinted in Yoshimoto Takaaki, *Bungakusha no sensō sekinin* [War responsibility of the literati]. Tokyo: Awaji Shobō, 1956.

Yoshino Sakuzō. *Minpon shugi ron* [People as base-ism *(sic)*]. Abridged and translated in Ryusaku Tsunoda, W. Theodore de Bary, and Donald Keene, eds., *Sources of Japanese Tradition,* vol. 2. New York: Columbia University Press, 1958.

Japanese Periodicals

Asahi jaanaru
Asahi nenkan
Asahi shinbun
Bungei nenkan
Bungei shunjū
Chisei
Chōsa geppō
Chūō kōron
Eiga seisaku
Eiga shunjū
Hōritsu jihō
Jiyū
Jurisuto
Kaizō
Kikan rōdō hō
Mainichi shinbun
Nihon bungaku

Nihon nōgyō nenkan
Nihon tōkei nenkan
Rekishi hyōron
Rekishigaku kenkyū
Seisaku geppō
Sekai
Seron chōsa
Shin Nihon bungaku
Shinchō
Shisō
Shisō no kagaku
Shokun
Socioroji
Tenbō
Yomiuri shinbun

Japanese Films

Genbaku no ko [Children of Hiroshima]. Directed by Shindō Kaneto. Kindai Eiga Kyōkai/Gekidan Mingei, 1952.

Gojira [Godzilla]. Directed by Honda Ishirō. Tōhō, 1954.

Hiroshima [Hiroshima]. Screenplay by Yagi Yasutarō. 1952.

Nagasaki no uta wa wasureji [Never forget the song of Nagasaki]. Directed by Tasaka Tomotaka. Daiei (Tokyo), 1952.

Nijūshi no hitomi [Twenty-four eyes]. Directed by Kinoshita Keisuke. Shōchiku (Ofuna), 1954.

Ningen no jōken [The human condition]. Directed by Kobayashi Masaki. Parts 1 and 2: Ninjin Kurabu/Kabukiza Eiga, 1959. Parts 3 and 4: Ningen Puro, 1959. Parts 5 and 6: Shōchiku (Ofuna)/Bungei Puro Ninjin Kurabu, 1961.

English-Language Sources

Abrams, Irwin, ed. *Peace: Nobel Lectures in Peace: 1971–1980*. Singapore: World Scientific, 1997.

Anderson, Joseph L., and Donald Richie. *The Japanese Film: Art and Industry*. Rutland: Tuttle, 1959.

Asada Sadao. "The Mushroom Cloud and National Psyches: Japanese and American Perceptions of the A-Bomb Decision, 1945–1995." *Journal of American–East Asian Relations* 4(2) (Summer 1995):95–116.

Barshay, Andrew. *State and Intellectual in Imperial Japan: The Public Man in Crisis*. Berkeley: University of California Press, 1988.

Barth, Fredrik. "Introduction." In Fredrik Barth, ed., *Ethnic Groups and Boundaries: The Social Organization of Culture Difference*. London: Allen & Unwin, 1969.

Beer, Lawrence Ward. *Freedom of Expression in Japan*. Tokyo: Kodansha, 1984.

Bernstein, Barton J. "Seizing the Contested Terrain of Early Nuclear History: Stimson, Conant, and Their Allies Explain the Decision to Use the Atomic Bomb." *Diplomatic History* 17(1) (Winter 1993):35–72.

Bix, Herbert P. "The Shōwa Emperor's 'Monologue' and the Problem of War Responsibility." *Journal of Japanese Studies* 18(2) (Summer 1992):295–363.

Bock, Audi. *Japanese Film Directors*. Tokyo: Kodansha International, 1978.

Boyer, Paul. "Exotic Resonances: Hiroshima in American Memory." *Diplomatic History* 19(2) (Spring 1995):297–318.

Butow, Robert J. C. *Japan's Decision to Surrender.* Stanford: Stanford University Press, 1954.

Campbell, John Creighton. "Compensation for Repatriates: A Case Study of Interest-Group Politics and Party-Government Negotiations in Japan." In T. J. Pempel, ed., *Policymaking in Contemporary Japan.* Ithaca: Cornell University Press, 1977.

———. *Contemporary Japanese Budget Politics.* Berkeley: University of California Press, 1977.

Campbell, Joseph. *The Hero with a Thousand Faces.* 2nd ed. Bollingen Series, no. 17. Princeton: Princeton University Press, 1968.

Carr, E. H. *The New Society.* London: Macmillan, 1951.

de Bary, W. Theodore. *East Asian Civilizations: A Dialogue in Five Stages.* Cambridge, Mass.: Harvard University Press, 1988.

Desser, David. "Japan: An Ambivalent Nation, an Ambivalent Cinema." *Swords and Ploughshares* 9(3–4) (Spring–Summer 1995).

Doak, Kevin M. "What Is a Nation and Who Belongs? National Narratives and the Ethnic Imagination in Twentieth-Century Japan." *American Historical Review* 102(2) (April 1997):283–309.

Doi Takeo. *The Anatomy of Dependence.* Translated by John Bester. 3rd ed. Tokyo: Kodansha International, 1981.

Dore, R. P. *Land Reform in Japan.* London: Oxford University Press, 1959.

———. "Textbook Censorship in Japan: The Ienaga Case." *Pacific Affairs* 43(4) (Winter 1970–1971):548–556.

———. "The Ethics of the New Japan." *Pacific Affairs* 25(2) (June 1952):147–159.

Dower, John. *Embracing Defeat: Japan in the Wake of World War II.* New York: Norton/New Press, 1999.

———. *Empire and Aftermath: Yoshida Shigeru and the Japanese Experience, 1878–1954.* Cambridge, Mass.: Harvard Council on East Asian Studies, 1979.

———. "Japanese Cinema Goes to War." *Japan Society Newsletter* (July 1987):2–9.

———. "The Bombed: Hiroshimas and Nagasakis in Japanese Memory." In Michael J. Hogan, ed., *Hiroshima in History and Memory.* Cambridge: Cambridge University Press, 1996.

———. "Triumphal and Tragic Narratives of the War in Asia." In Laura Hein and Mark Selden, eds., *Living with the Bomb: American and Japanese Cultural Conflicts in the Nuclear Age.* Armonk, N.Y.: M. E. Sharpe, 1997.

Duara, Prasenjit. "Provincial Narratives of the Nation: Centralism and Federalism in Republican China." In Harumi Befu, ed., *Cultural Nationalism in East Asia.* Berkeley: University of California Press, 1993.

Duus, Peter. "Nagai Ryūtarō and the 'White Peril,' 1905–1944." *Journal of Asian Studies* 31(1) (November 1971):41–48.

Edwards, Walter. "Buried Discourse: The Toro Archaeological Site and Japanese National Identity in the Early Postwar Period." *Journal of Japanese Studies* 17(1) (1991):1–23.

Erikson, Erik H. "Identity and the Life Cycle." *Psychological Issues* 1 (1959):1–171.

Field, Norma. *In the Realm of a Dying Emperor.* New York: Pantheon, 1991.

Foucault, Michel. "Film and Popular Memory: An Interview with Michel Foucault." *Radical Philosophy* 11 (1975):24–29.

Fritzsche, Peter. "Machine Dreams: Airmindedness and the Reinvention of Germany." *American Historical Review* 98(3) (June 1993):685–709.

Fukui, Haruhiro. *Party in Power: The Japanese Liberal-Democrats and Policy-Making.* Berkeley: University of California Press, 1970.

Gluck, Carol. "The Idea of Showa." *Daedalus* 119(3) (Summer 1990):1–26.

———. "The People in History: Recent Trends in Japanese Historiography." *Journal of Asian Studies* 38(1) (November 1978):25–50.

Goedde, Petra. "From Villains to Victims: Fraternization and the Feminization of Germany, 1945–1947." *Diplomatic History* 23(1) (Winter 1999):1–20.

Goodman, David, and Masanori Miyazawa. *Jews in the Japanese Mind: The History and Uses of a Cultural Stereotype.* New York: Free Press, 1995.

Hauser, William B. "Women and War: The Japanese Film Image." In Gail Lee Bernstein, ed., *Recreating Japanese Women: 1600–1945.* Berkeley: University of California Press, 1991.

Havens, Thomas. *Fire Across the Sea.* Princeton: Princeton University Press, 1987.

Hein, Laura, and Mark Selden, guest eds. "Textbook Nationalism, Citizenship, and War: Comparative Perspectives." *Bulletin of Concerned Asian Scholars* 30(2) (April–June 1998).

Heineman, Elizabeth. "The Hour of the Woman: Memories of Germany's 'Crisis Years' and West German National Identity." *American Historical Review* 101(2) (April 1996):354–395.

Helwerth, Ulrike, and Gislinde Schwarz. "Germany: The Walls That Have Yet to Fall." *Ms.* 3(6) (May–June 1993):18–21.

Hersey, John. *Hiroshima.* New York: Knopf, 1946.

Hobsbawm, E. J. *Nations and Nationalism Since 1780: Program, Myth, and Reality.* Cambridge: Cambridge University Press, 1990.

Ibuse Masuji. *Black Rain.* Translated by John Bester. Tokyo: Kodansha International, 1969.

Ienaga Saburō. *The Pacific War, 1931–1945: A Critical Perspective on Japan's Role in World War II.* New York: Pantheon, 1978.

Igarashi Takeshi. "Peace-Making and Party Politics: The Formation of the Domestic Foreign-Policy System in Postwar Japan." *Journal of Japanese Studies* 11(2) (Summer 1985):323–356.

Iritani Toshio. *Group Psychology of the Japanese in Wartime.* London: Kegan Paul International, 1991.

Izbicki, Joanne. "Heading for the Hills: Marriage and Democracy in Japanese Cinema." Paper presented at the American Historical Association meeting, Seattle, 1998.

Japanese Society for History Textbook Reform. "Restoration of a National History." Tokyo, 1998.

Kamō Chōmei. "Hōjōki." In *Ten Foot Square Hut and Tales of the Heike.* Translated by A. L. Sadler. Tokyo: Tuttle, 1972.

Kawai, Kazuo. *Japan's American Interlude.* Chicago: University of Chicago Press, 1960.

Kersten, Rikki. *Democracy in Postwar Japan: Maruyama Masao and the Search for Autonomy.* London: Routledge, 1996.

Koschmann, J. Victor. *Revolution and Subjectivity in Postwar Japan.* Chicago: University of Chicago Press, 1996.

———. "The Debate on Subjectivity in Postwar Japan: Foundations of Modernism as a Political Critique." *Pacific Affairs* 54(4) (Winter 1981–1982):609–631.

Large, Stephen. *Emperor Hirohito and Shōwa Japan: A Political Biography*. London: Routledge, 1992.

Levine, Lawrence W. "The Folklore of Industrial Society: Popular Culture and Its Audiences." *American Historical Review* 97(5) (December 1992):1369–1399.

Levinson, Daniel J., C. N. Darrow, E. B. Klein, M. H. Levinson, and B. McKee. *The Seasons of a Man's Life*. New York: Ballantine, 1977.

Lifton, Robert Jay. *Death in Life: Survivors of Hiroshima*. New York: Random House, 1967.

Lifton, Robert Jay, and Eric Markusen. *The Genocidal Mentality: Nazi Holocaust and Nuclear Threat*. New York: Basic Books, 1990.

Lifton, Robert Jay, and Greg Mitchell. *Hiroshima in America: Fifty Years of Denial*. New York: Putnam, 1995.

Linenthal, Edward T. "American Public Memory on the Washington Mall." *Tikkun* 10 (3) (May–June 1995):20–21.

McDonald, Keiko. "Kinoshita and the Gift of Tears: *Twenty-Four Eyes*." In Keiko McDonald, *Cinema East: A Critical Study of Major Japanese Films*. Rutherford, N.J.: Fairleigh Dickinson University Press, 1983.

Minear, Richard. "Atomic Holocaust, Nazi Holocaust: Some Reflections." *Diplomatic History* 19(2) (Spring 1995):347–365.

———. *Victor's Justice: The Tokyo War Crimes Trial*. Princeton: Princeton University Press, 1971.

Moeller, Robert G. "War Stories: The Search for a Usable Past in the Federal Republic of Germany." *American Historical Review* 101(4) (October 1996):1008–1048.

Morimoto, Marie Thorsten. "The 'Peace Dividend' in Japanese Cinema: Metaphors of a Demilitarized Nation." In Wimal Dissanayake, ed., *Colonialism and Nationalism in Asian Cinema*. Bloomington: Indiana University Press, 1994.

Morley, James William. "The First Seven Weeks." *Japan Interpreter* 6(2) (Summer 1970): 151–164.

Morris, Ivan. *The Nobility of Failure: Tragic Heroes in the History of Japan*. New York: Holt, 1975.

Muramatsu Michio. "Bringing Politics Back into Japan." *Daedalus* 119(3) (Summer 1990):141–155.

Nagahara Keiji. "Reflections on Recent Trends in Japanese Historiography." *Journal of Japanese Studies* 10(1) (Winter 1984):180–181.

Nagai Takashi. *Bells of Nagasaki*. Translated by William Johnston. Tokyo: Kodansha International, 1984.

Nolte, Sharon H., and Sally Ann Hastings. "The Meiji State's Policy Toward Women, 1890–1910." In Gail Lee Bernstein, ed., *Recreating Japanese Women, 1600–1945*. Berkeley: University of California Press, 1991.

O'Connor, John E., ed. *Image as Artifact: The Historical Analysis of Film and Television*. Malabar, Fla.: Krieger, 1990.

Orr, James J. "Yasui Kaoru: Citizen-Scholar in War and Peace." *Japan Forum* 12 (2000):1–14.

Packard, George R. *Protest in Tokyo: The Security Treaty Crisis of 1960*. Princeton: Princeton University Press, 1966.

Pincus, Leslie. "The Postwar Culture Movement in Hiroshima." Paper delivered at the Association for Asian Studies annual meeting, Chicago, 1997.

Pyle, Kenneth B. "Meiji Conservatism." In *Cambridge History of Japan*, vol. 5: *The Nine-*

teenth Century, ed. Marius B. Jansen. Cambridge: Cambridge University Press, 1989.

Rose, Sonyo O. "Sex, Citizenship, and the Nation in World War II Britain." *American Historical Review* 103(4) (October 1998):1147–1176.

Satō Tadao. *Currents in Japanese Cinema: Essays by Tadao Sato.* Tokyo: Kodansha International, 1982. Translation by Gregory Barrett of *Nihon eiga shisōshi* (Philosophical History of Japanese Film, 1970).

Seki Yoshihiko. "Introduction." *Journal of Social and Political Ideas in Japan* 1(1) (April 1963):2–10.

Sklar, Robert. "Moving Image Media in Culture and Society: Paradigms for Historical Interpretation." In John E. O'Connor, ed., *Image as Artifact: The Historical Analysis of Film and Television.* Malabar, Fla.: Krieger, 1990.

Supreme Commander for the Allied Powers. Government Section. *Political Reorientation of Japan, September 1945 to September 1948.* Washington, D.C.: GPO, 1949.

Takeda Kiyoko. *Dual Image of the Japanese Emperor.* New York: New York University Press, 1988.

Taeuber, Irene. *Population of Japan.* Princeton: Princeton University Press, 1958.

Titus, David. "The Making of the 'Symbol Emperor System' in Postwar Japan." *Modern Asian Studies* 14(4) (1980):529–578.

Totten, George O., and Tamio Kawakami. "Gensuikyō and the Peace Movement in Japan." *Asian Survey* 4(5) (May 1964):833–841.

Treat, John Whittier. *Writing Ground Zero: Japanese Literature and the Atomic Bomb.* Chicago: University of Chicago Press, 1995.

Tsuboi Sakae. *Twenty-Four Eyes.* Translated by Akira Miura. Rutland: Tuttle, 1983.

UNESCO World Heritage Committee. "Report of the Twentieth Session, Merida, Mexico, 1996." Also available at http://www.unesco.org/whc/archive/repcom96.htm#775.

United States. Department of State. *Foreign Relations of the United States, 1955–1957.* Vol. 23. Washington, D.C.: Department of State, 1991.

Weinstein, Martin E. *Japan's Postwar Defense Policy, 1947–1968.* New York: Columbia University Press, 1971.

Whiting, Allen S. "The War as Historical Heritage." In Allen S. Whiting, *China Eyes Japan.* Berkeley: University of California Press, 1989.

Wittner, Lawrence S. *One World or None: A History of the World Nuclear Disarmament Movement Through 1953.* Stanford: Stanford University Press, 1993.

———. *Resisting the Bomb: A History of the World Nuclear Disarmament Movement.* Stanford: Stanford University Press, 1997.

Yoneyama, Lisa. *Hiroshima Traces: Time, Space, and the Dialectics of Memory.* Berkeley: University of California Press, 1999.

Yoshida Mitsuru. "Proxies for the War Dead." *Japan Echo* 7(2) (1980):75–80.

Index

ABCC. *See* Atomic Bomb Casualty
    Commission
Abe Shinnosuke, 152
academia, purge in war responsibility
    debate, 20–21, 189n. 21
aggression, Japanese, in World War II:
    amnesia about, 173, 175; attitudes
    of postwar generation, 6, 32; contri-
    tion of individuals, 14–15, 16; histo-
    ries of, 174; ignored by ban-the-
    bomb movement, 44, 69–70; text-
    book discussions, 74–75, 80. *See
    also* Asia, Japanese aggression in;
    victimizers; war responsibility
agriculture. *See* land reform
Agriculture and Forestry, Ministry of, 148,
    151, 153, 156, 232n. 52, 234n. 74
Aihara Kazuo, 133
Ai no Undō. *See* Charity Movement
Akahata, 124
Alliance for the Achievement of Com-
    pensation for Overseas Assets. *See*
    Gaishidō
Allied powers. *See* Occupation; United
    States
amae (self-indulgence), 12–13, 69, 177
Amano Teiyū, 208n. 3
antinuclear movement. *See* ban-the-
    bomb movement
Aragaki Hideo, 22, 39–40, 42–43, 65,
    197n. 21, 200n. 51, 207n. 108
Arase Yutaka, 68–69
Asahi gurafu, 40, 42
Asahi shinbun, 26–27, 28–29, 68, 69,
    155, 161, 164; editorials, 138; polls,
    68; "Tensei jingo" columns, 22, 39–

40, 42–43, 69, 151–152; "Women's
    Pacific War" forum, 174–175
Ashida Hitoshi, 26
Asia, Japanese aggression in: apologies
    for, 178, 241n. 13; de-emphasized
    by Occupation, 31; denials of guilt,
    178, 241n. 13; excesses not acknowl-
    edged, 11; histories of, 32; libera-
    tion ideology justification, 67, 97,
    176; not recognized by peace
    movement, 66; postwar generation
    not conscious of, 32; teaching guide-
    lines, 210n. 10; textbook discussions,
    73–75, 87, 88, 92–93, 95–96, 97–103.
    See also aggression, Japanese, in
    World War II; Asian victims of war;
    China; Korea; Manchuria
Asia, Japanese residents. *See* repatriates
Asian national independence move-
    ments: solidarity with, 176; teach-
    ing guidelines, 210n. 10; textbook
    discussions (1950s), 73, 83, 85,
    214n. 40; textbook discussions
    (1960s), 87, 91, 97, 98, 104–105,
    218n. 75; textbook discussions
    (1970s), 97, 99, 100, 101; textbook
    discussions (1980s and 1990s),
    73–74
Asian victims of war: casualty statistics,
    214n. 41; lack of attention in war
    crimes trials, 15–16; lawsuits and
    testimony of experiences, 174–175;
    textbook discussions, 9, 74–75, 87,
    98, 100, 101, 176
Atomic Bomb Casualty Commission
    (ABCC), 142

About the Author

James J. Orr, who received his doctorate in history from Stanford University in 1996, teaches in
the Department of East Asian Studies at Bucknell
University. He is the author, among other publications, of "Yasui Kaoru: Citizen-Scholar in War
and Peace," *Japan Forum* (2000). *The Victim as
Hero* is his first book.